INSPIRE / PLAN / DISCOVER / EXPERIENCE

THAILAND

THAILAND

CONTENTS

DISCOVER THAILAND 6

EXPERIENCE BANGKOK 74

EXPERIENCE THAILAND 160

NEED TO KNOW 358

Left: Vibrant paper umbrellas in Thailand
Previous page: A fisherman throwing a net in Krabi
Front cover: Sun setting over rice fields at Chiang Mai

DISCOVER

Dense tropical forest on Krabi's coast

WELCOME TO THAILAND

Home to serene Buddhist temples, legendarily wild nightlife, pristine ancient rainforest, bustling markets, and one of Southeast Asia's biggest metropolises, Thailand is as diverse as it is fascinating. Whatever your dream trip to the country entails, this DK Eyewitness Travel Guide will prove the perfect companion.

1 Elephants enjoying one of Thailand's many rivers.

2 Boat perched on the coastline of Krabi Town.

3 Thai street food from a traditional market at dusk.

4 Buddha statues at Nakhon Si Thammarat.

Located at the beating heart of Southeast Asia, Thailand is known worldwide for its lush islands and delectable cuisine. The capital city, Bangkok, is a multisensory feast which teems with people, sounds, color, and life. This is the place to eat the world's best street food at sizzling Chinatown stalls, and discover Thailand's thriving contemporary culture.

Heading north, and worlds away from buzzing Bangkok, Buddhism continues to thrive in the peaceful countryside of Chiang Mai, with its host of awe-inspiring temples. Crumbling ancient cities at Ayutthaya and Sukhothai, meanwhile, echo with the region's rich cultural history, while hill tribes continue to practice a unique and vibrant culture in the isolation of the northern mountains.

Thailand's coastline is blessed with some of the most gorgeous beaches in the world, while its 1,000-plus offshore islands range from party paradises to renowned scuba diving hotspots. Nature lovers can explore the rainforests of Khao Sok, said to be the oldest on the planet, or spot elephants roaming the jungles of Khao Yai. However you choose to experience Thailand's natural beauty, it will not disappoint.

The sheer diversity of Thailand can be overwhelming, but this guidebook breaks the country down into easily navigable chapters, full of expert knowledge and insider tips. We've created detailed itineraries and colorful maps to help you plan the perfect trip, whether you're on a flying visit or an exciting extended adventure. Enjoy the book, and enjoy Thailand.

REASONS TO LOVE
THAILAND

With the pristine wilds of its countryside, the rich culture and history of its cities, and an abundance of delicious cuisine, there are endless reasons to love Thailand. Here, we pick some of our favorites.

1 PARADISE ISLANDS

Whether you want to scuba dive, party, or simply relax, Thailand has over 1,000 islands – most of them tropical gems smothered in jungle and skirted by fine white sand.

BUZZING BANGKOK 2

Ancient and contemporary Thai culture vibrantly blend in the capital *(p74)*, a center of endless markets, nightlife both raucous and refined, and some of the greatest monuments.

3 CRUISING ON THE MEKONG

The lifeblood of much of Southeast Asia, the mighty Mekong is best enjoyed on a long-tail boat trip from Chiang Khan *(p278)*, winding past wooden riverfront houses.

PEACEFUL CHIANG MAI 4

The "Rose of the North" *(p208)* is Thailand's second city, but it's a far cry from noisy Bangkok. Stroll down the temple-lined streets or embark on a cycling tour of the countryside.

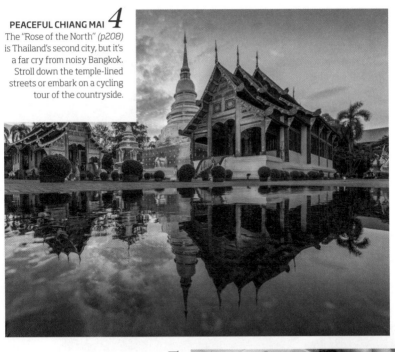

EXQUISITE FOOD 5

Striking the perfect balance between sweet, savory, spicy, and aromatic, Thai food is in a class of its own. Be sure to try the national dish, pad thai.

THE ANCIENT CAPITALS 6

Nowhere evokes the rich history of Thailand like the crumbling ruins of Ayutthaya *(p166)* and Sukhothai *(p188)*, brimming with Buddha statues and preserved *chedis*.

VIBRANT FESTIVALS 7

Whether it's seeing in the Thai New Year, Songkran *(p50)*, with a big water fight or enjoying the colorful Bo Sang Umbrella Fair *(p222)*, Thailand's festivals are bursting with joy and energy.

SERENE TEMPLES 8

Buddhism has exerted a powerful influence here for two millennia, and Thailand's beautiful temples remain soothing sanctuaries that give a feel for spiritual life.

9 WELLNESS AND HEALING

Thailand's ancient wellness traditions are tonics for the body and soul. Learn the art of Thai massage at Wat Pho *(p102)*, or join a meditation retreat in Chaiya *(p318)*.

10 TREKKING THE JUNGLES

Many spectacular hikes across northern Thailand afford breathtaking views *(p58)*, whether walking over the slopes of the highest mountain or visiting hill tribe villages.

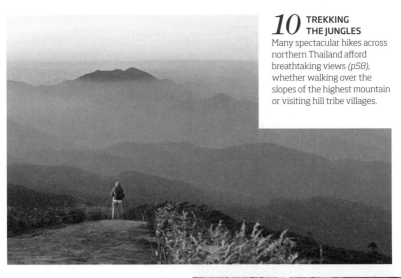

MARKET SHOPPING 11

A riot of color and sound characterizes Thai markets. Pick up Lao handicrafts in Nong Khai *(p270)* or try street food classics from one of Bangkok's floating markets.

REMOTE BEACHES 12

Beyond the iconic beaches are countless others undiscovered by crowds. Ko Pha Ngan *(p302)* is packed with untouched paradises, and Ao Kiu promises solitude on Ko Samet *(p288)*.

EXPLORE
THAILAND

This guide divides Thailand into eleven colour-coded sightseeing areas, as shown on this map. Find out more about each area on the following pages.

MYANMAR

Bago

Yangon

*Andaman
Sea*

SOUTHEAST ASIA

CHINA

JAPAN

BHUTAN
NEPAL
BANGLADESH
MYANMAR
INDIA
LAOS
THAILAND
VIETNAM
CAMBODIA
SRI LANKA
MALAYSIA
SINGAPORE
INDONESIA

*Pacific
Ocean*

*Indian
Ocean*

GETTING TO KNOW
THAILAND

Set within a lush, tropical landscape, Thailand is a riot of cultural and sensual vibrancy, comprising golden beaches on remote islands, ancient cities with crumbling temples, quaint towns with diverse peoples, and gorgeous national parks home to majestic mountains.

PAGE 74

BANGKOK

The capital of Thailand and one of Southeast Asia's great cities is a vast megalopolis which straddles the banks of the great Chao Phraya River. Bangkok is a banquet of delectable street food, elegant temples, and bewildering markets. The country's grandest palaces and best museums lie in this buzzing city, not to mention the finest arts scene in Thailand, both contemporary and classical. When the sun goes down, Bangkok's nightlife is as wild or sophisticated as you want it to be, with backpacker bars or classy rooftop restaurants to choose from.

Best for
Markets, street food, and legendary nightlife

Home to
Grand Palace, Wat Pho, National Museum, Jim Thompson House, Wat Arun

Experience
Delicious and unusual delicacies in the street food capital of the world, Chinatown

SOUTH CENTRAL PLAINS

Thailand's rice basket, and the historic heartland of the Tai people, this is the country's wealthiest and most densely populated region. Prosperous towns are surrounded by fields of sugarcane and rice, broken up by areas of pristine wilderness. This is where the evocative ruins at Ayutthaya tell of mighty kingdoms past and the enduring influence of Buddhism. The chief attraction, though, is Khao Yai, Thailand's original – and best – national park and a gorgeous tract of forests.

Best for
Ruined cities, history, and nature

Home to
Ayutthaya, Khao Yai National Park

Experience
Trekking through the jungles of Khao Yai, finishing with a dip in a spectacular waterfall

$\rightarrow$

PAGE 184

NORTH CENTRAL PLAINS

Going deeper into Thailand's agricultural heartland, the North Central Plains have a distinctly rural atmosphere, with less development and fewer large cities than the south plains. Instead, large areas of rice fields, hemmed in by mountains, are dotted with lovely towns, villages, and magnificent ruins. Sukhothai is the prime attraction, but Si Satchanalai-Chalieng is just as impressive in its ancient history. The influence of Myanmar, just across the border, is keenly felt in the western towns.

Best for
Peaceful countryside and ancient ruins

Home to
Sukhothai Historical Park, Si Satchanalai-Chalieng Historical Park

Experience
A performance of traditional Thai music and dance as the sun goes down over the ruins of Sukhothai

PAGE 200

NORTHWEST HEARTLAND

Centered on Thailand's second city, the laid-back temple town of Chiang Mai, the Northwest Heartland is the home of the Lanna people. Their rich culture and beautiful handicrafts are easy to find in the city, while the mountain villages in the countryside proudly uphold a traditional hill-tribe culture. Chiang Mai is tiny compared to the capital, but home to almost as many temples, including the mountaintop Wat Phra That Doi Suthep. Forested mountains, valleys, and waterfalls make up the picturesque countryside here.

Best for
Peaceful temples and Lanna culture

Home to
Wat Phra That Lampang Luang, Doi Suthep, Chiang Mai, Doi Inthanon National Park

Experience
A three-day trek from Chiang Mai, taking in hill-tribe villages and river rafting

PAGE 228

FAR NORTH

At the point where Thailand, Myanmar, and Laos meet, the so-called "Golden Triangle" of the Far North feels full of the promise of adventure. Characterized by photogenic mountains and sleepy towns strung along the Mekong, this remote region seems a long way from anywhere, even in its biggest city, the ancient Chiang Rai. Home to some beautiful old temples, the city is also a base for trekking to hill-tribe villages and learning about their culture. The Far North also offers one of the most remarkable temple-meets-art exhibits, Chiang Rai's Wat Rong Khun, which is unlike anything else here.

Best for
Mountain landscapes, temples, and trekking

Home to
Chiang Rai, Wat Phumin

Experience
A driving tour through the mountain villages of the Golden Triangle

→

PAGE 250

KHORAT PLATEAU

A region of dry shrubland elevated by mountain ranges, the Khorat Plateau retains a distinct identity. Though the land is barren and home to the poorest people in the nation, the plateau is alive with rich Isan culture, and Khorat is the major city in northeast Thailand. The Lao-speaking Isan people are responsible for some of Thailand's most eye-catching cultural displays, in particular the Yasothon Rocket Festival. Isan food is distinctive, too, with spicy *larb* and zingy *som tam* sure to linger long on the tongues of visitors.

Best for
Khmer temples and Isan culture

Home to
Prasat Hin Phimai, Prasat Hin Khao Phnom Rung

Experience
Visiting master potters at work in the ceramics factories of Dan Kwian

PAGE 264

MEKONG RIVER VALLEY

The life-giving waters of one of the world's greatest rivers give the Mekong River Valley its fertile land and agricultural flavor. The gilded temples of Vientiane are just across the border in Laos, while Nong Khai is the major Thai city in a region mostly populated by sleepy riverside villages. Like much of northern Thailand, the valley is largely unspoiled and features some beautiful national parks that are home to an array of wildlife that exists nowhere else in Thailand.

Best for
Pristine wilderness, Lao culture and Mekong villages

Home to
Phu Kradung National Park, Nong Khai, Vientiane, Wat Phra That Phanom

Experience
A long-tail riverboat cruise along the Mekong River

EASTERN SEABOARD

A diverse region encompassing beach resorts, gem-mining towns, and accessible island getaways, the Eastern Seaboard offers something for all tastes. The tourist hub is the party town of Pattaya, while those seeking a more languid beach escape can find it on the shores of the Eastern Seaboard's islands. The most interesting town is Chanthaburi, where gem traders gather among old Vietnamese shop-houses to trade precious stones. Ko Chang and Ko Samet offer a decent balance between development and seclusion, while Ko Kut and Ko Kradat still promise desert island escape.

Best for
Quiet islands, beach resorts, and jungle adventures

Home to
Ko Samet, Chanthaburi, Ko Chang

Experience
A boat trip around the tiny islands of the Ko Chang archipelago

$\rightarrow$

PAGE 298

WESTERN SEABOARD

Making up around half of Thailand's eastern coastline, the Western Seaboard is home to some of the country's most iconic islands, particularly those of the Ko Samui archipelago. Towns like Phetchaburi and Chumphon dot the coastline, and their temples and artwork reveal the area's rich history as a meeting point for different cultures. The most famous of the islands here have long been a mainstay on Thai travel itineraries. Ko Pha Ngan is famous both as a raucous party island and a boho wellness escape, while Ko Tao offers some of the world's best scuba diving.

Best for
Party islands, scuba diving, and Buddhist art

Home to
Ko Pha Ngan, Ko Tao, Ko Samui, and Phetchaburi

Experience
Joining a meditation retreat at a monastery in Chaiya

PAGE 320

UPPER ANDAMAN COAST

Stretching from the border with Myanmar to the beautiful limestone stacks of Phangnga Bay, the Upper Andaman Coast is perhaps Thailand's most picturesque region. The major hub is Phuket, the country's largest island, with popular and lively Ko Phi Phi and the quieter beaches of Ko Lanta across the bay to the east. The rainforests of Khao Sok, meanwhile, are among the oldest in the world, home to the bizarre, putrid-smelling flower *Rafflesia kerrii*.

Best for
Diving, coastal landscapes, and beachfront nightlife

Home to
Phuket, Phangnga Bay, Ko Phi Phi

Experience
Diving and snorkeling the colorful coral reefs of the Similan Islands

PAGE 344

DEEP SOUTH

The southern tip of Thailand is a region of great natural and cultural diversity. Nakhon Si Thammarat is the major hub and illustrates the region's long history as a cultural crossroads, with Hindu shrines jostling for space with Buddhist temples. From there, fertile lowlands stretch south, ending at the border with Malaysia and encompassing bird-rich wetlands, untouched offshore islands, and historic towns. Thailand's deep south has a unique atmosphere, thanks partly to its proximity to Malaysia and the influence of Islam, which many people practice here.

Best for
Seafood and Malay-influenced culture

Home to
Nakhon Si Thammarat, Tarutao National Marine Park

Experience
Spotting dugongs, gentle giants of the sea, in Trang's Andaman Islands

←

1 A golden Buddha at Wat Phra That Doi Suthep.

2 Admiring Wat Phra Kaeo.

3 A tempting *Khao soi* dish.

4 Buddha head at Wat Phra Mahathat in Ayutthaya.

Thailand brims with travel opportunities, from island hopping to grand odysseys of the entire region. These itineraries will help you to chart your own course through this vibrant country.

2 WEEKS
on a Grand Tour

Day 1

Start your journey in Chiang Mai (p208), the "Rose of the North". The mountaintop Wat Phra That Doi Suthep (p206) is the perfect first stop, affording stunning views over Thailand's second city. Make your way east to stop for a lunch of *Khao soi* at Huen Phen (p211) before exploring the lives of Northern Thailand's tribal people at the Lanna Folklife Museum (p211). Mannequins model traditional costumes, and dioramas depict dance and art. Soak up the vibrant atmosphere at Talat Pratu Night Market (p211) in the evening, and try Lanna delicacies.

Day 2

Begin the day with a peaceful visit to Chiang Mai's holiest temple, Wat Phra Singh (p208), built in 1345 to hold the ashes of King Kham Fu. Look out for the famous Phra Buddha Sihing statue here. After a calming morning, stop for a dim sum lunch at the classy Fujian (p211), then unwind on a six-hour direct bus journey to Sukhothai, once the seat of a great kingdom. Upon arrival, relax at the elegant Nham Khang Sukhothai (p188), enjoying classical music performances.

Day 3

Make your way to Sukhothai Historical Park (p188), one of Thailand's most atmospheric ancient cities, setting out early to avoid the midday heat. Rent a bike by the east gate and pay special attention to Wat Mahathat (p190), the former heart of the city. Escape from the afternoon heat with a late lunch at Junshine (p188) in Old Sukhothai. Spend the evening delighting in drinks in the many bars of Sukhothai's new city.

Day 4

Depart for Ayutthaya (p166), another of Thailand's great lost cities, on the five-and-a-half-hour bus ride from Sukhothai. Refresh after your journey at Coffee Old City (p169), then discover the ruins of Ayutthaya, beginning with the beautifully preserved Wat Phra Si Sanphet (p168). Move on to Wat Phra Mahathat (p167) and have your camera at the ready to photo-graph the eerie Buddha head engulfed by a tree. End your day on an atmospheric riverboat tour around Ayutthaya's main island, watching as the sun casts a gorgeous light on the ruins.

Day 5

Spend the morning expanding your knowledge on the history of Ayutthaya at the Chao Sam Phraya National Museum (p168), which exhibits gold, weapons, and jewelry from the city's heyday, and Ayutthaya Historical Study Center (p169). Stop for a classic Thai lunch at Malakor (p169), then catch a two-hour train to the bustling capital of Bangkok. Spend your first night in the city at the Bangkok Art and Culture Centre (p136), taking in one of the rotating art exhibitions.

Day 6

Start the day at Bangkok's famous Grand Palace (p94) and Wat Phra Kaeo (p98) complex, home to the stunning Emerald Buddha, considered the great palladium of Thailand. Have an afternoon rest at Sanam Luang (p109), a park just next door, while taking in the great views of the Grand Palace. Indulge in a spectacular dinner at the legendary Thipsamai (p105), which claims to be the original home of Thailand's national dish, pad thai.

→

Day 7

Rise early to get a bird's-eye view over Bangkok at the Golden Mount (p106), a sacred hill up some 300 steps. Descend and head to the river for a delicious Thai lunch at Eat Sight Story (p105) before jumping on the ferry to Wat Arun (p144), one of Thailand's most visually striking temples. Discover the heart of Bangkok's iconic backpacker scene in the evening, hopping between the bars and bustling street stalls of Khao San Road.

Day 8

Board an hour-long train from Hua Lamphong Station (p120) to Nakhon Pathom (p156). You'll want to admire the Phra Pathom Chedi, one of Thailand's most-visited pilgrimage sites, and can learn about the history of the area at the Phra Pathom Chedi National Museum (p156). Stop for a seafood lunch at Kung Ob Phu Kow Fai (p153) before catching another train for Ratchaburi (p152). Upon arrival, dine at Kuaytiew Khai (177/5 Khathathn Road, next to Phromphat Hospital), known for its noodle dishes.

Day 9

Start your day at Wat Mahathat, the town's most famous temple, with architecture modeled on Cambodia's Angkor Wat. The Ratchaburi National Museum is a great place to discover the area's past before heading down the road to Ramenmachi (Na Muang, Mueang Ratchaburi district) for Japanese food. Get a taxi to Khao Ngu (p152) and explore the caves that dot the sides of limestone mountains. Return to Bangkok and stroll along Bang Krachao (p156) to Lookjan (Soi Wat Rat Rangsan, Tambon Bang Kachao) for a Thai dinner.

Day 10

Begin your exploration of Thailand's islands at Ko Samui (p310), the third-largest and a one-hour flight from the capital. Once settled, check out one of Ko Samui's most stunning sights, the Big Buddha, which looms over Bangrak Beach (p311). After lunch at one of the restaurants lining the beach, head to the coast to relax. Finish your day with a walk to Fisherman's Village in Bophut (p311), an atmospheric area full of dinner options.

1 Phra Pathom Chedi.

2 Lush surroundings of Khao Ngu.

3 Ko Samui's famous Big Buddha.

4 The sunset over Ko Tao.

5 Chaweng Beach.

6 Scuba diving in Ko Tao.

Day 11

Head inland and follow the jungle hiking trails to the Namuang Waterfall *(p312)*, cooling off with a refreshing morning dip at the falls' natural swimming hole. It's a quick taxi ride from here to Chaweng Beach *(p312)*, Samui's most buzzing spot. Spend the afternoon sunbathing on the soft sand, and give windsurfing a try if you're feeling energetic. Chaweng's legendary nightlife will keep you entertained all evening; dive in to Thailand's blooming craft beer scene at Beer Masons *(p312)*, then dance the night away at Cha Cha Moon Beach Club *(p312)*.

Day 12

Board a boat to Ko Pha Ngan *(p302)*, an island famous for its iconic full moon parties. Discover its calmer side with a trek to the beautiful Nam Tok Phaeng waterfall and nearby Domsila Viewpoint *(p302)* for fantastic views. Take a taxi to Ao Thong Nai Pan *(p304)*, one of the most beautiful beaches here, and swim and snorkel in the calm waters. Soak up the evening atmosphere in the island's beach bars – or, if you're visiting at the time of the monthly full moon parties *(p305)*, revel in the wild side of Ko Pha Ngan.

Day 13

Continue your journey through the Gulf of Thailand's islands and hop on a boat to Ko Tao *(p306)*. It's one of the best places in the world to scuba dive, so head to one of its many dive shops and join a trip. Enjoy superb seafood at Barracuda *(p307)* before heading to the west coast to Hat Sai Ri *(p306)*, Ko Tao's busiest beach and the heart of its nightlife. Try P.Oy's Place *(p307)* for a home-style Thai dinner.

Day 14

Spend the final morning relaxing on Ao Leuk *(p308)*, home to one of the most beautiful beaches on Ko Tao. Head back to Hat Sai Ri for the best choice of lunch spots lining the beach, whether you're after authentic Thai cuisine or something international. End your day (and your trip) seeing out the sunset at one of Hat Sai Ri's beach bars, cocktail in hand.

←

1 Sunset at Ao Mae Hat.

2 Enjoying a drink over Ao Thong Nai Pan Noi.

3 The monumental Big Buddha statue at Bangrak.

4 Hat Rin's full moon party.

10 DAYS
of island-hopping

Day 1

Morning Prepare for your trip by getting in touch with your spiritual side at Bangkok's Wat Mahathat *(p104)*, where meditation classes are held in Thai and English. Once you're relaxed, board the hour-long flight to Ko Samui *(p310)*.

Afternoon Explore the waterfalls and jungles of the lush interior of the island, then catch some rays on Maenam *(p311)*, a beautiful beach on the north coast. Once you've had your fill of relaxation head east to Bangrak *(p311)* to take in the impressive Big Buddha statue.

Evening Nearby Bophut *(p311)* is the perfect spot for dinner, with street food stalls serving up a selection of delicious classic Thai dishes. Finish the evening at Chaweng Stadium *(166/16 Moo 2 Chaweng Beach Road)* taking in a performance of *muay thai*, Thailand's national martial art.

Day 2

Morning Check out the tiny offshore island of Ko Faan near Bangrak *(p311)*, loomed over by a giant Buddha statue, 38 ft (12 m) high. The island is connected to Ko Samui by a causeway.

Afternoon Head back to Bangrak for a seafood lunch at Bangrak Beach Club *(4171, Tambon Bo Put, Amphoe Ko Samui)*, then explore a quieter corner of the coast at the secluded cove of Thong Son *(p312)*.

Evening Continue down the east coast to Lamai Beach *(p310)*, the second longest on the island, and socialize at one of the many beach bars.

Day 3

Morning Spend a lazy morning swimming and relaxing on Lamai Beach, then make your way to Nathon *(p310)* on the north coast of the island to board a boat to Ko Pha Ngan *(p302)*. The short journey offers many spectacular photo opportunities of the coastline.

Afternoon Get a panoramic view over your new surroundings with lunch at the rooftop ThreeSixtyBar *(p303)*. Nearby Ao Mae Hat *(p303)* is a calming place to unwind on a beach swing before walking over to the tiny island of Ko Ma, connected by a sandbar to the mainland.

Evening Your relaxing day should give you the energy to spend the evening on Hat Rin *(p305)*, the legendary full moon party beach and home to daily fire shows, thumping beats, and booze buckets.

Day 4

Morning Ease yourself into the day with an exploration of Ao Thong Nai Pan Noi and Ao Thong Nai Pan Yai *(p304)*, two secluded coves in the northeast of Ko Pha Ngan, which rank among the island's most relaxing and photogenic spots.

Afternoon Ramp up the relaxation with a visit to Wat Pho in Baan Tai, a Buddhist temple home to a herbal sauna – perfect for detoxifying after a night in Hat Rin.

Evening Catch the sunset at Amsterdam Bar *(p303)*, where you can also get a good pad thai for dinner. See out the evening at Baan Tai Beach, lazing in a hammock with a beer from a beachside bar.

→

Day 5

Morning Pop in for breakfast and coffee at the trendy cafe The Fat Cat *(Walking Street Market, Thong Sala, Ko Pha Ngan)*, then walk to Thong Sala *(p302)* pier for a ferry to Ko Tao *(p306)*, the smaller sibling in the Samui archipelago.

Afternoon Wander around Ko Nang Yuan *(p307)*, a group of three tiny islands off the northwest tip of Ko Tao. A hilltop viewpoint over the islands is the perfect place to get a stunning photograph, while the waters here are rich in marine life, making them great for diving.

Evening Swap the busy bars of Hat Sai Ri for Banana Rock *(Sai Nuan Beach, Ban Ko Tao, Chumphon)*, a wooden bar built on stilts on the secluded Sai Nuan Beach.

Day 6

Morning Visit the stunning Ao Tanot *(p308)*, hemmed in by huge boulders. Head to one of the dive shops nearby to rent snorkeling equipment and spend the morning exploring the colorful corals teeming with fish.

Afternoon Continue exploring the underwater world of Ko Tao by making your way to Green Rock *(p309)*. It's ideal for any level of diver, and there are some awesome rock formations.

Evening After an eventful day, nestle into one of the beach bars on the island.

Day 7

Morning Sit back and take in splendid views on a two-hour ferry back to Ko Samui, then head to the airport to catch an onward flight to Phuket *(p324)*.

Afternoon Soak up the vibrant atmosphere at Hat Patong *(p324)*, the most developed beach on Phuket. Spend the afternoon parasailing and waterskiing, taking a break for lunch at La Gritta *(lagritta.com)*, a popular Italian.

Evening Immerse yourself in Hat Patong's lively nightlife scene, where you'll find some of Thailand's best beach bars. If you have the energy, head east to Music Matter *(Talat Yai, Mueang Phuket district)*, one of the few places in Phuket dedicated to live jazz.

1 The tiny islands at Ko Nang Yuan, connected by thin bars of sand.

2 Phuket's colorful town.

3 Whale shark in the waters of Ko Tao.

4 Palm trees swaying at Patong beach.

5 Ko Phi Phi's notorious alcohol buckets.

6 Boats on Phi Phi Leh.

Day 8

Morning Stroll along the historic streets of Phuket Town (p328), taking in the Sino-Portuguese architecture and the grand Chinese Mansions of Ranong Road. Pop into the Thavorn Hotel Lobby Exhibition (p328) to browse artifacts that tell the story of Phuket's history.

Afternoon Natural Restaurant (p327) is a fine spot for lunch, where world cuisine is served in a lovely garden. Continue exploring the Old Town, stopping at the Chinese Bang Niew Temple (p328) and the beautiful Wat Mongkol Nimit (p329).

Evening Make your way to Ko Sirey (p329), a small island connected to Phuket by bridge. Climb the hill to Wat Ko Sirey in time for sunset and appreciate the great views over the island and an impressive reclining Buddha statue.

Day 9

Morning It's back on the boat this morning for the two-hour journey to Ko Phi Phi Don (p334), one of Thailand's most beautiful islands. Begin your exploration at Hat Yao (p335), a gorgeous white-sand beach, perfect for a leisurely stroll.

Afternoon Grab some lunch at the swanky Phi Phi The Beach resort (phiphithebeach.com), then head inland to clamber up the island's two massifs, where you can enjoy sweeping views over Phi Phi and karst rocks along the coast.

Evening See out the evening at Ban Ton Sai (p334), Phi Phi's major hub, and enjoy an ocean-fresh dinner at Tonsai Seafood (Tonsai Village, Ko Phi Phi Don). Afterward, if you're feeling brave, sample Phi Phi's notorious alcohol buckets.

Day 10

Morning Spend the morning snorkeling among the vibrant coral gardens of Hin Pae, just off Hat Yao – a calming way to soothe sore heads from the night before.

Afternoon Embark on a boat trip to the sister island of Phi Phi Leh (p334), spotting rock paintings at Viking Cave.

Evening Return to Phi Phi Don and toast your island-hopping adventure with a cocktail in one of the many beach bars.

→

1 Bamboo rafts at Huai Krathing reservoir.

2 A *som tam* dish.

3 Walking through Indochina Market.

4 Sala Kaew Ku sculptures.

5 DAYS

in Northeast Thailand

Day 1

Morning Start by immersing yourself in the rich culture and history of Khorat (p260), the main hub of the Khorat Plateau. The best place to begin is at the Thao Suranari Monument at the western gate, built in honor of a woman who defended Khorat against a Lao invasion.

Afternoon To better understand the region's history, stop off at the Maha Weerawong National Museum and take in the religious artwork and ancient pottery on display. Afterward, enjoy a Japanese lunch at ANEGO (62/1 Jomsurang Road, Amphur Muang, Nakhon Ratchasima)

Evening Spend the evening leisurely exploring Khorat's Night Market, a good place to shop for local handicrafts and sample some street food.

Day 2

Morning Take the five-and-a-half-hour bus journey to Nong Khai (p270), a vibrant town on the Laotian border with beautiful traditional wooden shop-houses.

Afternoon Head to the Indochina Market to enjoy a traditional Lao lunch from one of the food stalls. Once satiated, check out the statue park of Sala Kaew Ku, full of impressive, and often scary, sculptures from Hindu and Buddhist mythology.

Evening Wind down with a delicious Thai dinner and a splendid view at Macky's Riverside Kitchen (960, Rim Khong Alley, Nai Mueang).

Day 3

Morning Embark on a two-hour drive to Than Thip Falls (p281), a spectacular three-tiered waterfall ending with a pool. After a refreshing dip, continue on a further two hours to Chiang Khan (p278).

Afternoon Indulge in a lunch of river fish overlooking the Mekong at Luk Phochana (304 Moo 1 Soi 9) before admiring Chiang Khan's most sacred temple, Wat Si Khun Muang, and its oldest, Wat Mahathat.

Evening Explore Chiang Khan's Walking Street, a night market full of food stalls where you can treat yourself to Lao delicacies for dinner.

Day 4

Morning Take an hour's drive to Loei (p277) and enjoy some hiking in Phu Ruea National Park (p277), home to bizarre rock formations shaped like mushrooms.

Afternoon Learn about Thailand's emerging wine-making scene at Chateau de Loei, within Phu Ruea. The climate here is not dissimilar to parts of southern France, and produces a great Chenin blanc – perfect for an afternoon treat.

Evening Close the day by tucking into *bun cha* (pork noodles) at Loei Da Nang (22/58 Soi P.R. House, Chum Sai Road), a well-regarded Vietnamese restaurant.

Day 5

Morning Rafting on the lake at Huai Krathing (p277), around an hour outside Loei, is a lovely way to pass the morning, before an early lunch in the middle of the reservoir. Restaurant boats serve a variety of food, with very tasty shrimp dishes.

Afternoon Hike the hills of Phu Bo Bit Forest Park, a 20-minute drive east of Loei, passing caves and shrines and finishing up with spectacular views over the mountainous countryside beyond.

Evening End your trip in the northeast tucking in to Isan cuisine at Baan Yai (Kut Pong, Mueang Loei district). Local delicacies include *som tam* (papaya salad).

←

 The monumental and unique Sanctuary of Truth.

2 Tropical Laem Yai beach.

3 A stunning hornbill.

4 Inspecting gem stones in Chanthaburi.

5 DAYS
on the Eastern Seaboard

Day 1

Morning Make the city of Pattaya (p295) your entry point for the Eastern Seaboard, starting at the remarkable Sanctuary of Truth temple (206/2 Moo 5, Soi Naklua 12, Pattaya-Naklua Road). Take your time to admire this structure and its ornate sculptures of figures from mythology.

Afternoon Head north for a traditional Thai lunch at the Pattaya Floating Market (p295), where food stalls, art exhibits, and cultural performances represent all four corners of Thailand. Afterward, take the ferry to Ko Larn (p295) for an afternoon wander across beautiful sandy beaches.

Evening Head back to the city to do some souvenir shopping on Pattaya Beach Road and watch the sunset.

Day 2

Morning A two-hour car and ferry journey brings you to Ko Samet (p288), where you can spend the morning relaxing on the secluded beach at Ao Nuan (p289).

Afternoon Head into the jungle interior of Ko Samet, following the hiking trails to spot hornbills, geckos, and various other creatures. Then, head to Ao Phai (p289) for swimming and sunbathing.

Evening Unwind at Hat Sai Kaeo (p288), Ko Samet's most popular beach, with a hearty seafood dinner at Ploy Talay (ploytalay.com) before finishing the night with a drink at Naga Bar (p289).

Day 3

Morning Enjoy a restorative breakfast at the laid-back Jump at Sea (p289), then stroll to the relaxed Laem Yai, a hilly cape on the eastern edge of Hat Sai Kaeo.

Afternoon Spend your final hours on Ko Samet relaxing before taking a ferry to Ban Phe to begin the 90-minute drive

to Chanthaburi (p290), a friendly and charming town with colonial houses and a choice of excellent restaurants.

Evening Savor Chanthaburi's famous blend of Thai and Chinese culinary influences at Chanthorn Phochana (p291).

Day 4

Morning Observe the bustle of hundreds of merchants gathering at Chanthaburi's weekend Gem Market (p290), where precious stones from Thailand, Myanmar, and Cambodia are traded. Wander through the atmospheric Vietnamese Quarter (p291), stopping to admire its latticed wooden shop fronts.

Afternoon A calming visit to the Cathedral of the Immaculate Conception (p290), the largest cathedral in Thailand, makes for a fantastic photo opportunity. Its striking exterior and stained-glass windows are particularly impressive.

Evening Finish your time in Chanthaburi with an evening meal at Tamajun (p291), an atmospheric riverside restaurant where you can enjoy regional dishes and listen to live music.

Day 5

Morning Make the 90-minute trip by road to Laem Ngop, then catch a ferry for the short journey to Ko Chang (p292). Follow a gentle 2-mile (3-km) hike to the photogenic Khlong Phlu waterfall (p293).

Afternoon Continue exploring crystal-clear waters with a snorkeling trip to the offshore island of Ko Kut, a kaleidoscopic underwater world off Ko Chang's coast.

Evening Treat yourself with a fresh dinner at Rim Had Seafood (rimhadseafood.com). Finish your Eastern Seaboard adventure at Ko Chang's busiest beach, Hat Sai Khao (p292), to see the sun sink over the horizon.

Hands-On Experience

There's no need to take a backseat all the time, as workshops around the country range from the ancient gold leaf painting technique to silver jewelry making. Craft connoisseurs will love Chiang Mai's Suranat Leather Studio *(suranatleather studio.com)* and its range of courses on creating a leather bag. Paintbar Bangkok *(paintbarbangkok.com)* takes a more relaxed approach as you enjoy a glass of wine while brushing up on your skills.

Mastering bag making at Suranat Leather Studio

THAILAND FOR
CRAFTS

Thailand's plethora of rich arts and crafts traditions is often the most visible expression of the country's myriad cultural groups. Whether you're browsing its colorful markets for traditional souvenirs or learning from the masters, Thailand's craft scene offers something for everyone.

Watch the Masters at Work

Thailand's artisans and craftspeople possess incredible artistic skill, and there are ample opportunities to appreciate this – particularly throughout Bangkok. In the suburb of Ban Bat *(p107)*, you can watch experts craft monks' alms bowls in the same way they have since the 1700s. At the Bangkok Doll Factory *(bangkokdolls.com)*, see a team of skilled artists create beautiful traditional dolls by hand, complete with ornate antique costumes.

Did You Know?

Thai silk production may even predate China's, which dates back to 2700 BC.

Shop For Souvenirs

Thailand's markets offer endless opportunities to pick up both unique and mass-produced Thai handicrafts. Purchase teak carvings and lacquerware in the Chiang Mai Night Bazaar *(p209)*, shop for silk and hill-tribe artifacts at Chatuchak Market *(p158)*, or browse precious stones in Chanthaburi's Gem Quarter *(p290)* for the best traditional crafts to take home with you.

↑ Browsing stalls in Chiang Mai and Chatuchak Market *(inset)*

TOP 5 THAI CRAFTS

Lanna Handicrafts
Intricate silverware, wood carving, and ceramics are sold in Chiang Mai *(p208)* and the surrounding villages.

Ceramics
Beautifully painted vases, plant pots, and wind chimes can be found at Dan Kwian pottery village *(p261)*.

Thai Silk-Weaving
Silk production in Thailand goes back thousands of years, and is still used in clothing and home decorations.

Gemstones
Deep blue sapphires and blood-red rubies are highly prized, and Chanthaburi *(p290)* is a huge gem center.

Hill-Tribe Artifacts
Akha coin headdresses, Lisu tunics, and Lahu blankets make for unique souvenirs.

↑ Craftswoman making traditional alms bowls to sell in Ban Bat

Picture Perfect

There's no need to feel temple fatigue in Thailand, with a host of unusual sights to jazz up your social media feed. Defying the golden temple norm is the gleaming white Wat Rong Khun (p234). Its ornately rendered scenes from Buddhist mythology make for a wacky and unique shot. Meanwhile, eco-friendly (and beer) aficionados can rejoice at the impressive Wat Pa Maha Chedi Kaew (Si, Khun Han district, Sisaket, 33150), which was built from 1.5 million recycled beer bottles.

→
Wat Rong Khun, one of Thailand's most photographed sights

THAILAND FOR
ASTOUNDING TEMPLES

Testament to the region's rich history and enduring spiritual traditions are the 40,000 temples in Thailand. From the iconic *wats* of Bangkok to remote island sanctuaries, you'll never run out of new ones to experience jaw-dropping moments of awe or the serenity temple life.

Taste of Temple Life

Visiting Thai temples is not limited to quiet observation, with great opportunities to uncover the inner workings of temple life and even meet the monks. Wat Mahathat (p104) in Bangkok holds three daily one-off meditation sessions in English, while Wat Chedi Luang (p208) is one of many Chiang Mai temples to hold "monk chat" sessions, where you can ask the monks about monastery life.

←
Buddhist monks performing an ancient ritual

Step Back in Time

While new, beautiful temples are showing up across the country fairly regularly, a large number of Thailand's temples have stood for centuries and offer a glimpse into the ancient past. Wat Pho (p102) is the oldest in Bangkok and will transport you back to the 1780s, but that's nothing compared to the Khmer complex at Prasat Hin Phimai (p254), thought to be around a thousand years old.

←

The ancient architecture of the historic Prasat Hin Phimai

THE WAT COMPLEX

A *wat* is a collection of buildings within an enclosure serving as a Buddhist monastery, temple, and community center. The layout of most *wats* follows set principles, as do the functions of its different buildings:

Bot (or ubosot)
The ordination hall reserved mainly for monks.

Wihan
An assembly hall that is very similar to, but usually larger than, a *bot*.

Chedi
A solid structure encasing a relic of the Buddha, such as a hair.

Prang
A tall tower-like spire that tends to be richly carved.

Mondop
A square-based structure topped with either a spire or a cruciform roof.

↑ Phra Pathom Chedi looming over Nakhon Pathom

Big Beauties

Thai temples tend not to do things by halves, and the country has a lot to boast about when it comes to size. Take a walk around the largest temple in the world, the otherworldly Wat Phra Dhammakaya *(23/2 Moo 7, Khlong Sam, Khlong Luang 12120)* outside Bangkok. Architect enthusiasts can admire the tallest Buddhist *stupa* in the world at Phra Pathom Chedi (p156).

THAI BUDDHISM

At least 90 percent of Thais practice Theravada Buddhism. This was first brought to the region from India around the 3rd century BC and is based on the ancient Pali canon of the Buddha's teachings (Tripitaka). However, Thai practice incorporates many Hindu, Tantric, and Mahayana Buddhist influences. The worship of Buddha images, for instance, is a Mahayana Buddhist practice. Animist beliefs in spirits and the magical and in astrology are also widespread. Thais believe that Buddhism is one of three forces that give their kingdom its strength, the other two being the monarchy and nationhood. Religious rituals color daily life, especially in the form of merit-making.

THE BASIC TENETS OF BUDDHISM

Buddhists believe each life is influenced by the actions of the previous one (perpetual reincarnation). This philosophy of cause and effect (karma) is symbolized by the "wheel of law." Enlightenment (nirvana) is the only state that will end the cycle of rebirth. To reach this, Buddhists try to develop morality, meditation, and wisdom (the "three pillars.")

↑ A Thai Buddhist monk worshipping the golden image of the Buddha

MERIT-MAKING

The act of merit-making is an essential part of religious life in Thailand. Practiced both by monks and lay people, it reflects an awareness that good deeds lead to good outcomes, either in this life or the next (as a more fortunate rebirth). Becoming a monk or sponsoring the ordination of a monk is the highest form of making merit.

MONKS IN THAILAND

Children are taught the moral codes of Buddhism from an early age. Most Thai males are ordained as monks at adolescence - a major rite of passage. They usually spend at least a few months as monks, earning merit for themselves and their families. Few women become nuns.

BUDDHIST RITUALS

The daily alms round - Bintabat takes place after dawn, when monks leave their temples to search for their daily meal. Giving food to monks is a popular way for lay people to earn merit. Monks are permitted to eat only food that has been offered to them.

Meditation - This purifies the mind and clears it of distractions. It is practiced by all monks and some lay people.

Visits to the *wat* - Many lay people in Thailand go to their local *wat* at least once a week. Typically they make offerings to an image of the Buddha, listen to the monks chanting and to a dharma talk, and receive blessings.

Gold leaf - Applying gold leaf to Buddha images is a popular act of merit-making.

[1] Buddhist monks collecting their alms from the local community.

[2] A monk practicing meditation.

[3] The interior of a *wat* in Thailand.

[4] A couple carefully applying thin leaves to a golden Buddha.

↑ Buddhist monks lighting stunning paper lanterns at a festival in Chiang Mai

The Must-Thai Classics

Pad thai, a stir-fried fusion of rice noodles, eggs, fish sauce, shrimp, and chopped peanuts, undoubtedly takes the title of Thailand's national dish. However, there are many more tasty dishes you should try. Rich massaman curries add to the rainbow of red, yellow, and green; sour *tom yam* soup will set your taste buds alight; and the intriguing papaya salad is often as sweet, sour, and savory as it is eye-wateringly spicy.

←

A tempting dish of beef pad thai and chicken satay

THAILAND FOR
LOCAL FLAVOR

Thai food is loved around the world for its delicate fusion of the sweet, sour, creamy, and spicy. Flagship dishes like pad thai may be available across the globe, but nothing compares to the diversity of Thai cuisine in its homeland, washed down with a refreshing Thailand-produced tipple.

Vegetarian Vibes

Thailand may be renowned for its meat dishes, but you don't need to look too far to find delicious vegetarian-friendly meals: ask for *pad phak* (stir-fried vegetables), *pak boong* (water spinach), or *gang jay* (veggie curry). Vegetarian festivals also take place from September to October in Phuket *(p329)* and Trang *(p353)* and involve eating "jay" food, which is also vegan.

↑ Tucking into a tasty, spicy vegetarian pad thai lunch

↑ Toasting the early evening with a refreshing beer

TOP 5 FOODS FOR THE FEARLESS

Balut
Not for the squeamish, this is a cooked, fertilized bird's egg – embryo and all.

Hon mhai
Thais are famous for silk, but they also eat silkworms, seasoned and deep fried.

Larb mote daeng
A "salad" of red ants and their eggs, which have a pleasant citrusy flavor.

Durian
Banned in hotels, but still at large in Thai markets, Durian is the world's smelliest fruit.

Malang Tod
Fried insects, from scorpions to crickets, are a local specialty in Bangkok, and a great source of protein.

Home Brews

Great food is nothing without a delectable drink to wash it down with, and Thailand excels in this department, too. The leading beer brands, Chang and Singha, are supplemented by a burgeoning craft beer scene, with microbreweries popping up all over Bangkok and beyond. There's even an emerging Thai wine scene, with the highland vineyards of Khao Yai *(p172),* Hua Hin *(p316),* and Loei *(p277)* producing acclaimed drops.

Street Eats

There's no more authentic and immediate way to enjoy great Thai food than from a ramshackle street cart, and Bangkok is arguably the street food capital of the world. Yaowarat Road *(p116)* is Bangkok's beating street food heart, while bizarre and delicious delights are on offer every evening in Chiang Mai's Warorot Market *(p210),* and every Sunday at Phuket's Walking Street *(Thalang Rd).*

Eating delectable food *(inset)* on offer ↑ on Yaowarat Road

Beautiful Beaches
Immense stretches of white sand shaded by swaying palms provide Thailand's most gorgeous scenery. Walk along the pristine Railay-Phra Nang *(p342)* headland or explore Ko Muk *(p352)*, where an emerald cave opens onto a hidden beach.

Spectacular karst cliffs towering above the sandy Railay-Phra Nang

THAILAND FOR
NATURAL BEAUTY

From soaring karst mountains to tumbling waterfalls, and mighty rivers flowing through the world's oldest tracts of rainforest, Thailand's vast and impressive landscapes are one of its best attractions, and there are endless exciting options for exploring them.

TOP 4 NATIONAL PARKS

Khao Yai
Thailand's first national park is home to splendid waterfalls and the rare Indochinese tiger *(p172)*.

Doi Inthanon
A playground for hikers, bird-watchers, and plant spotters *(p214)*.

Phu Kradung
"Bell mountain," said to ring when struck with a staff, counts black bears and jackals among its residents *(p268)*.

Tarutao
This idyllic island group harbors some of the best diving in Thailand *(p350)*.

Wonderful Waterfalls
Nothing is more photogenic than a tumbling waterfall, and Thailand has them in bucketloads. Erawan Falls *(p180)* makes for a perfect shot, or if picnicking is your thing, Phuket's Bang Pae *(p327)* provides a serene backdrop.

Erawan Falls, famed for its emerald pools

Majestic Mountains

Those with a head for heights will have plenty to keep them on cloud nine in Thailand. Doi Chiang Dao *(p220)* is particularly picturesque, smothered in teak and pine forests and dotted with ancient caves and temples. It's worth joining a two-day hike to see the sun rise and set from the top of the peak. Thailand's tallest mountain, Doi Inthanon *(p214)*, also offers spectacular views over the forested landscape. Visit on a day trip from Chiang Mai *(p208)* – those in luck may even spot leopard cats, which amp up the beauty here.

$\rightarrow$
Orange and pink hues from the sun setting over the lush Doi Chiang Dao

Lush Lakes

From life-giving rivers to quiet lagoons, Thailand is as beautiful off dry land as it is on. The serene Red Lotus Lake near Udon Thani *(p261)* is as stunning as they come, and is best admired on a morning boat ride. For something more immersive, stay in a floating bungalow on Cheow Lan Lake in Khao Sok National Park *(p340)*.

$\leftarrow$
Lakeside cabins and long-tail boats on the idyllic Cheow Lan Lake in Khao Sok National Park

Teeming Jungles

Dense jungles brimming with unique fauna and foliage can be found across the whole stretch of Thailand. One of the world's oldest tracts of rainforest waits to be admired in Khao Sok *(p340)*: on a guided tour you can see elephants, monkeys, and tigers. In Krabi *(p339)*, forests are punctuated by stark karst formations, creating an otherworldly atmosphere.

$\rightarrow$
A spectacled langur monkey climbing in Khao Sok National Park

Volunteer With Rescued Elephants

Elephant tourism is a controversial ethical issue in many parts of Asia, but you can ensure your stay is helping rather than harming these gentle giants. Avoid elephant rides and shows and volunteer at sanctuaries like the Elephant Nature Park *(p221)* or Boon Lott's *(blesele. org)* near Sukhothai for a once in a lifetime experience.

→

Rescued elephant at one of Thailand's many rehabilitation centers

THAILAND FOR
WILDLIFE ENCOUNTERS

Home to the most beautiful and unusual plants and animals, Thailand offers no end of fascination for wildlife lovers. Beyond moments of awe, you can even help pave the way for more sustainable tourism.

ENDANGERED WILDLIFE

The diverse natural landscapes in Thailand make it the perfect habitat for a vast range of flora and fauna. Sadly, however, deforestation and poaching led to the extinction of many species in the 20th century, including Schomburgk's deer. The exotic pet trade threatens animals like gibbons, while many others, such as snakes, are killed out of fear. Thailand is home to close to 300 mammal species, of which about 40 are endangered.

A diver among coral reef at one of Ko Tao's dive sites ↑

Brave the Bugs

Among the gargantuan many-legged inhabitants in Thailand is the Atlas moth, the world's largest. The best place to marvel at its colossal wingspan of up to 12 inches (30 cm) is Khao Sok *(p340)*. There's also the fearsome Vietnamese centipede, which reaches up to 8 inches (20 cm) long – but be careful as they bite when aggravated.

$\rightarrow$

The stunning orange hues of the Atlas moth

Marvel at the World's Largest Flower

Head to the jungles of Khao Sok *(p340)* to admire Thailand's most unusual plant, the *Rafflesia kerrii*. This parasitic plant has no roots or leaves, but blooms out of its host plant once a year into the world's largest flower – up to 31 inches (80 cm) in diameter. It has an unpleasant smell, but makes for an unforgettable photograph.

$\leftarrow$

The giant and bizarre red *Rafflesia kerrii* found in Khao Sok National Park

Discover the World Beneath the Waves

Thailand's coastline and islands hold the promise of some of the world's most spectacular scuba diving. In beautiful spots like Ko Tao *(p306)* and Ko Chang *(p292)*, you can get up close with, and admire the beauty of, colorful bluespotted rays, giant whale sharks, and gentle turtles.

Monkey Around

Known as "Monkey Kingdom," the city of Lop Buri *(p181)* brims with macaques who delight in stealing visitors' lunch. The Monkey Buffet Festival satiates their appetite with a feast put on for them every November.

$\uparrow$ One of the cheeky inhabitants of Lop Buri perched on a statue

Discover the Ancient Art of Krabi Krabong

This ancient martial art was developed by Thai warriors, and practitioners fight using a sword and staff. Today you can expect to mostly see it in catch-all cultural shows, but a couple of reputable places are happy to teach, including the renowned Master Toddy's *(mastertoddy.com)* in Bangkok.

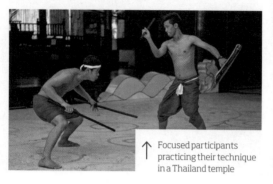

↑ Focused participants practicing their technique in a Thailand temple

THAILAND FOR
SPORTS FANS

Perhaps surprisingly, Thailand offers a wealth of variety to keep sports fans entertained, spanning traditional Thai martial arts, Southeast Asian ball sports, and international favorites. Whether you're looking to watch on the sidelines or get stuck in, you can expect a lively local spirit wherever you go.

Try Your Hand at Muay Thai

Thailand's national sport is related to boxing and kickboxing but distinct from both, with fighters using their fists, feet, elbows, and knees. Watching a tense bout is a memorable, heart-pounding experience in itself, but you can now take courses to learn the sport yourself. Tiger Muay Thai *(tigermuay thai.com)* in Phuket is an award-winning training camp and great for beginners, while Bangkok Fight Lab *(www.bangkokfightlab.com)* is a popular choice for those with more experience.

←

Two *muay thai* fighters in the boxing ring, with a tense crowd looking on

Catch a Soccer Game

Few places in the world have evaded the spell of "the beautiful game," and soccer unexpectedly rivals *muay thai* as the country's most popular sport. Most big towns and cities have a team and stadium, as well as soccer schools and youth football teams. Wherever you choose to watch or play a game, you can expect a family-friendly, cordial atmosphere.

←

SCG Muangthong United and Consadole Sapporo playing soccer at SCG Stadium in Nonthaburi

Take in a Thai Rugby Match

Rugby has surprisingly taken Thailand by storm, with established clubs competing in the Hong Kong Sevens. Most games are held in Bangkok, but watching a game at Pepper's Sports Bar *(p328)* immerses you in the cheerful local spirit. If you're looking to play, try Southerners Sports Club *(southerners-bangkok.com)* in Bangkok.

→

Playing a game of rugby in the country's mild climate

THAILAND'S FLOATING SOCCER PITCH

The charming fishing village of Ko Panyee in southern Thailand is famous for its floating soccer pitch. First built in the mid-1980s, the original ramshackle wood-and-nails construction has since been replaced with a modern plastic one, although it's still open-sided, so lost balls remain something of an issue. Remarkably, Panyee's youth team is one of the best in southern Thailand, and has helped keep young people in the town and support the local economy.

↑ Players competing in a *takraw* tournament

Enjoy Takraw

Wander around any town or city and it won't be long before you spot a group of people leaping acrobatically around a *takraw* net. The idea is to keep a woven rattan ball in the air, like volleyball, but with any body part except your hands. Join in with the locals at Benchasiri Park *(Sukhumvit Road, Bangkok)* and Sappan Hin Park *(Wichit, Mueang Phuket district, Phuket)*.

National Treasures

The biggest events in the Thai festival calendar see the whole country coming together as one in celebration. Songkran *(p210)*, the Thai New Year, takes the lead as the country's best festival, with widespread water fights and traditional parades, while Western New Year sees fireworks lighting up the sky. If you're looking to party hard, head to Pattaya *(p295)* during Songkran to take part in one of the biggest water fights imaginable. At Yi Peng in November, have your camera at the ready to snap the swarms of lanterns that are released into the sky for good luck. This coincides with the equally beautiful Loy Krathong *(p67)*.

$\rightarrow$

Dreamlike, fire-powered lanterns released into the sky for Yi Peng in Chiang Mai

THAILAND FOR
VIBRANT
FESTIVALS

Thais are a celebratory bunch, and their calendar is packed year-round with countless festivals all over the country. From the religious to the secular, nearly all of them are a riot of food, music, color, and smell, and promise to raise your spirit no matter when you visit.

Religious Celebrations

As a Buddhist country, Thailand's most atmospheric festivals are unsurprisingly religious. At Visakha Bucha *(p66)*, between May and June, head to Bangkok's great temples to take part in rituals and celebrate the Buddha's life. Phi Ta Khon *(p277)* in the summer sees revelers dress in flamboyant ghost costumes to commemorate the Buddha's enlightenment.

 $\leftarrow$

An imposing Buddha statue illuminated in Bangkok on Visakha Bucha

Local Festivities

There's no need to feel disappointment if you miss out on the large, countrywide festivals – the tiny towns in Thailand know how to party. If you're after ample photo opportunities, head to Bo Sang, which comes alive each January with thousands of paper umbrellas at the Umbrella Fair *(p222)*. For something more energetic, check out the incendiary Rocket Festival *(p258)* in May, which emanates a joyful community spirit as rockets light up the skies in northeast Thailand. Not for the faint-hearted, the Vegetarian Festival *(p329)* in Phuket sees performers skewer themselves with metal rods and walk on hot coals.

← Cycling through Bo Sang below the vibrant paper umbrellas decorating the town for the Umbrella Fair

Arty Parties

Thailand's rich folk arts tradition can best be seen at the country's dedicated festivals. At Phra Phutthabat Fair *(p67)*, an ancient temple hosts theater and folk music, but Bangkok's Wat Saket Fair in November is particularly spectacular, with performances held against the grand Golden Mount *(p106)*.

↑ Costumed dancers performing at Wat Saket Fair

▽ Dance Til Dawn at a Full Moon Party

No other feature of Thai nightlife has achieved such legendary status as Ko Pha Ngan's full noon parties. Once a month, the beach at Hat Rin *(p305)* comes alive with thumping beats, fire dancers, and booze buckets.

THAILAND FOR
ENTERTAINMENT

Thailand may be famous for its raucous nightlife, but if partying until dawn isn't your thing, there are plenty of other offerings. Take your pick from classical music shows, sophisticated riverside bars, authentic night markets, or a buzzing backpacker bar – Thailand has it all.

▷ Revel in Khao San Road Madness

For the quintessential backpacker experience, head to Khao San Road in Bangkok. Buy a pad thai and an ice-cold Chang and soak up the electric atmosphere amid the bars, bookshops, travel agents, and market stalls.

▽ Browse Chiang Mai Night Bazaar

Perhaps Thailand's most iconic market experience, this nightly extravaganza (p209) sells everything from samurai swords to football shirts. Keep an eye out for beautiful traditional Lanna handicrafts, and take the opportunity to try some exotic foods.

△ Party in Phuket's Beach Bars

On Phuket (p324), Thailand's largest island, there's no need to choose between feeling the sand between your toes and partying in stylish bars and nightclubs – here, they open out right onto the beach. Catch Beach Club (p328) is the place to be seen, and even offers a fantastic infinity pool.

▷ Relax at a Classical Show

There is no better way to experience Thailand's rich classical arts heritage than watching its many dance and music shows. Marvel at the grace of the dancers' movements at a *khon* (masked dance) (p63) or *lakhon* (p63) drama performance, enjoy some lighthearted *likay* (p62) folk theater, or discover the world of Thai classical music (p62). Most performance venues are conveniently clustered around Bangkok (p74) and Chiang Mai (p208).

INSIDER TIP
Catch Some Culture

Bangkok's National Theatre (Rachinee Rd) is a good place to watch a classical dance show; *khon* and *lakhon* performances are held on the first and second Sunday of the month, with tickets available on the door.

△ Unwind at Elegant Riverside Bars

The banks of the Chao Phraya River in Bangkok are lined with classy hotels, rooftop bars, and riverboat restaurants, where you can experience a calmer side to the city. ThreeSixty Jazz Lounge (p147) is a favorite spot, offering a 360-degree view of the city, an outdoor terrace, and jazz sessions every evening.

Party All Night

Thailand's islands give the big cities a run for their money when it comes to nightlife. Legendary full moon parties (*p305*) aside, Ko Phi Phi (*p334*) keeps things moving every night with SangSom Thai Rum buckets, while the bars in Ko Samui (*p310*) make for a more stylish night out.

→

Selling buckets of liquor and soft drinks to visitors for a full moon party

THAILAND FOR
ISLANDS
AND BEACHES

Thailand's 1,550 miles (2,500 km) of stunning coastline and hundreds of dreamy islands are among its greatest draws. With opportunities to dive on vibrant coral reefs, bliss out on pristine sand, or seek out a secret haven, Thailand's beaches and islands promise something for everyone.

Uncover a Hidden Gem

It's easy to find your own slice of paradise with a trip out to sea. Ko Kut (*p293*) in Ko Chang is one of Thailand's most secluded islands and offers stunning sunrises. Remote Ko Kradan (*p352*) is similarly idyllic, and not a beach party in sight.

→

Boats docked on the quiet and scenic island of Ko Kut

1,430
The estimated number of islands in Thailand to explore.

TOP 3
SWIMMING BEACHES

Hat Khlong Dao
The longest beach on Ko Lanta (p343) stretches for 3 miles (5 km) down the coast and backs on to vegetation-covered sand dunes. Its calm waters are perfect for a refreshing dip.

Japanese Garden
The smallest of the three tiny islets of Ko Nang Yuan (p307) is a beautiful spot for swimming and snorkeling, with magnificent coral.

Ao Thong Nai Pan
Cresting a secluded bay on the northeast coast of Ko Pha Ngan (p302), the shallow, warm waters here are ideal for a swim.

Dive In

Ko Tao (p306) makes for one of the best (and cheapest) places to learn to dive – check out Roctopus Dive (roctopus dive.com) to book a course. Qualified scuba divers should head to the Similan Islands (p338), home to multicolored corals, manta rays, and more.

↑ Exploring Thailand's clear, turquoise waters

Get Romantic

The combination of pristine white sand, towering palm trees, and azure sea of the Thai islands paints an impossibly romantic picture. The twin beaches of Ko Lipe (p351) make for the perfect couple's retreat, with luxury villas and lush backdrops. To escape the crowds, head to Ko Phi Phi's secluded bay, Ao Lo Bakao (p335). Lined with exclusive restaurants and bars, it has become a favorite honeymoon spot.

↑ Enjoying the sun setting (inset) over the idyllic beaches in Ko Lipe

Savor Southern Thai Delicacies

Thailand's food markets are a world unto themselves, and the south gives Bangkok a run for its money. Feast on barbecued squid at Phuket's Walking Street *(Thalang Rd)*, or try *kaeng tai pla* (salty fish curry) at Chaweng's Night Market *(14/102 Moo 2, Chaweng Beach Road)*.

←

Delicious grilled squid on a street stall along the seafront

THAILAND FOR
MARKETS

Market trading is a deeply ingrained aspect of Thai traditions and the backbone of local economies, from the capital to tiny rural towns. No trip to Thailand is complete without visiting its many markets, sampling unusual food, shopping for handicrafts, and immersing yourself in Thai culture.

Take Home Beautiful Handicrafts

Thai markets are often the best places to pick up traditional gifts. Chiang Mai's Night Bazaar *(p209)* is one of the best spots to browse high-quality Lanna and hill-tribe artifacts and take a true slice of Thailand home with you. If you're stopping in northeast Thailand, be sure to look out for gorgeous Lao textiles in Nong Khai, particularly Indochina Market *(p270)*.

INSIDER TIP
Strike a Deal

Learning a few Thai numbers is a great way to look like you know how to bargain – and may stop traders from trying to rip you off.

Float Your Boat

For the quintessential Thai shopping experience, visit a floating market. The lively Damnoen Saduak *(p152)* makes for an unforgettable experience as you travel on your own boat. The beautiful Bang Nam Pheung *(Phra Pradaeng district)* is a less touristy alternative.

$\rightarrow$

An abundance of colorful fruit for sale at the Damnoen Saduak Floating Market

Soak Up the Backpacker Buzz

Markets in Thailand's backpacker enclaves seem to absorb the manic energy of their occupants, reflected in the bewildering array of bizarre goods on offer. A popular stop on the backpacker trail, Khao San Road in Bangkok brims with eclectic stalls, while Ko Pha Ngan's Thong Sala Night Market *(p302)* is the place to shop for cheap clothes.

$\leftarrow$

Buzzing Khao San Road in the evening

Browse a Bit of Everything

Don't be put off by the chaos at the biggest markets: they are the best way to peruse fascinating items. With more than 15,000 stalls, Chatuchak Market *(p158)* provides an authentic market experience on a large scale, while a similar motley mix of goods fills Chiang Mai's Warorot Market *(p324)*.

$\uparrow$
A stall of crafts at one of Nong Khai's outdoor markets

$\rightarrow$
Choosing from an array of cacti at Chatuchak Market

Wet and Wild

Thailand's impressive stretch of coastline offers endless areas to scuba dive, but an oxygen tank is not always necessary: snorkel among sea otters and more in idyllic spots such as the Tarutao National Marine Park (p350). Inland, you should have a go at white-water rafting on the Mae Taeng, near Chiang Mai (p208).

A thrilling white-water rafting ride down the Mae Taeng

THAILAND'S
OUTDOOR ADVENTURES

Lovers of the great outdoors will find Thailand's vast landscape of dense jungles, heavenly waters, and sublime limestone stacks one big playground. With scuba diving, rock climbing, caving, and bungee jumping on offer, thrill-seekers and adventurers are spoiled for choice.

Trek Through Mysterious Jungles

Nothing brings out your inner adventurer like a jungle trek, and Thailand has no shortage of routes to explore. Khao Sok (p340) is home to a range of easy to challenging trails - great for spotting monkeys, elephants, and bears. For something more scenic, journey through the rainforests and limestone mountains of Krabi (p339), passing hot springs and emerald pools.

Roots engulfing an otherworldly pool in a forest at Krabi ↓

Did You Know?

Pattaya Bungy Jump is the highest bungee jump in the country, at 197 ft (60 m) above the ground.

Spread Your Wings

For an adrenaline rush like no other, request to do a backward jump at the immense Pattaya Bungy Jump *(pattayabungy.com)*. If you're after a more scenic ride, head to the Jungle Bungy Jump *(phuketbungy.com)* to see dense rainforest and a lush lagoon beneath you.

→

Enjoying the thrill of one of Thailand's colossal bungee jumps

Climb Like a Monkey

The limestone stacks which soar out of the sea in Krabi *(p339)* and Ko Phi Phi *(p334)* attract serious rock climbers, but there are options for everyone. Book a course with Krabi Rock Climbing *(krabirockclimbing.com)* or head to the countryside near Chiang Mai *(p208)* to join other newbies.

←

A climber tackling one of the difficult limestone rocks above the sea at Krabi

Journey into Caves

Thailand's forests and mountains are dotted with countless intriguing and picturesque caves. Drifting down waterways in Tham Lot *(p219)* on a bamboo raft is an unforgettable experience. Other caves, like Phraya Nakhon, north of Khao Sam Roi Yot *(p316)*, hide paths that lead to gilded pavilions.

→

Exploring ethereal rock formations at Tham Lot

Cook Up a Storm

Across the country you'll find cookery classes on hand to help you unlock the secrets of Thai food's delicate balance of spices and flavors. Bangkok's cooking schools, such as Chef LeeZ *(chefleez.com)*, attract pupils from all over the world. In southern Thailand, the popular Phuket Thai Cooking Academy *(phuketthaicooking academy.com)* is a fun way to sharpen your culinary skills.

Ingredients for perfecting a Thai green curry

THAILAND FOR
WELLNESS

Beautiful countryside, peaceful temples, and countless luxurious spas – not to mention delicious food – make Thailand a wellness wonderland. You can take some of the Thai wholesome wisdom home with you, too, with courses enabling you to perfect your pad thai or master a Thai massage.

Get Pampered in a Luxury Spa

Sultry temperatures, idyllic landscapes, and a sense of tranquility make Thailand the perfect place for disconnecting from the world, and its bevy of luxurious spas are ideal for doing just that. The vast array of options, from hotel spas to retreats, can be overwhelming, but indulgence is promised wherever you opt to relax. For a one-off day spa visit, consider Bangkok's bohemian Oasis Spa *(oasisspa.net)*. If you're after a longer remote retreat with stunning surroundings, try the Four Seasons Tented Camp *(fourseasons.com/golden triangle)*, accessible by traditional long-tail boat.

Relaxing by the palm-fringed pool in a luxurious spa resort

Become a Meditation Master

Getting to grips with the ancient art of meditation is no mean feat, but Thailand offers a range of inspirational courses and retreats that also give a valuable insight into Thai culture. Novices may find a one-off session at Wat Suan Mokkh (suanmokkh-idh.org) outside Chaiya (p318) a great introduction to calming the mind. For serious meditators, check in with your inner self at the 10-day silent retreat here, or discover the techniques of the Thai Forest Tradition at Wat Pah Nanachat (watpahnanachat.org).

→

Finding inner peace at a retreat in Thailand

Unleash Your Inner Yogi

Thailand is brimming with centers dedicated to the ancient Indian art of yoga, but there's no need to splash out on a fancy retreat to find inner peace. Align your *chakras* at The Yoga Retreat (yogaretreat-kohphangan. com) on Ko Pha Ngan (p302) or recharge at Ko Tao's (p306) Shambhala Yoga (shambhalayogakohtao.com).

Practicing yoga on a blissful Ko Pha Ngan beach

THAI MASSAGE

Traditional Thai massage (*nuat paen boran*) is said to date back to the time of the Buddha, and is related to both Chinese acupuncture and Indian yoga. Thailand's unique massage tradition combines yoga, reflexology, and acupressure with vigorous, rejuvenating results. Highly trained masseurs pull and stretch the limbs and torso to relieve various ailments, from general tension to viruses.

Try Your Hand at Thai Massage

There's no better way to learn about – and treat others to – the popular practice of Thai massage than engaging in the art yourself. Take a course or treat yourself at the most respected massage school in Bangkok, based in Wat Pho (p102), or the Thai Massage School of Chiang Mai (tmcschool.com).

↑ Students learning with massage masters at the famous school in Wat Pho

Laugh at a Lively Likay Show

A rambunctious form of folk theater, *likay* uses gaudy jokes, flamboyant costumes, and humorous improvization to tell traditional folk tales. It tends to be performed at temple fairs and festivals.
Where to go: Thailand Cultural Centre *(Ratchadaphisek Road, Bangkok)*

Characters in a *likay* show, Thailand's most popular dance-drama

THAILAND FOR
TRADITIONAL CULTURE

With thousands of years of history as a meeting point for myriad cultures, ideas, and artistic traditions, it's no surprise that the country has a rich and varied heritage. Immerse yourself in this impressive legacy with the vast repertoire of music, theater, and puppetry that flourishes across Thailand.

Discover the World of Thai Classical Music

The classical music traditions of Thailand began to take shape in the Sukhothai era, with instruments including xylophones, gongs, and the lute-like *chake*. There is no notation, but each musician improvises on a basic tune, treating their instrument like a character in a play. Watch out for a tuned percussion ensemble, or *piphat*, at theater performances or, surprisingly, even boxing matches *(p48)*.
Where to go: Sala Chalermkrung *(salachalermkrung.com)*, Bangkok; Vic Hua Hin *(vichuahin.com)*, Bangkok

Playing the *Gong Mon*, a traditional Thai instrument

Marvel at Graceful Dance Dramas

Two of the most esteemed expressions of Thai culture are *khon* and *lakhon*. Based on folklore, they feature slow movements set to music. Their lavish costumes make them particularly enjoyable.
Where to go: National Theatre, Bangkok *(Rachinee Rd)*; Old Chiang Mai *(oldchiang mai.com)*

↑ Highly stylized, angular movements of a stunning *khon* performance

Enjoy Thai Puppetry

There are two major threads to traditional Thai puppetry: *hun krabok*, which features ornately painted wooden hand puppets, with Chinese influences, and *nang talung (p355)*, or Thai shadow puppetry, thought to date back to 400 BC. *Nang talung* performances are especially prevalent in the Deep South, and last for many hours in the late evening.
Where to go: Wandering Moon Theatre *(wanderingmoon theatre.com)*, Chiang Mai

→ A beautifully decorated marionette and shadow puppet *(inset)*

THAILAND'S ETHNIC GROUPS

Thailand takes its name from the majority Tai ethnic group, who make up some 90 percent of the country's population. Within that broad categorization are tens of subdivisions, while myriad minority ethnic groups – numbering more than 60 – contribute to Thailand's cosmopolitan patchwork of peoples and cultures. This diversity extends to an estimated 62 languages that are spoken in the country.

CHINESE THAI PEOPLE

The most visible ethnic minority in the country are the Chinese, whose influence is often visible in the big cities and extravagant Chinese New Year. In fact, the Chinese population in Thailand is the biggest in the world outside China.

HILL TRIBES

The hills of northern Thailand are home to six ethnic groups: the Akha, Hmong, Lisu, Karen, Lahu, and Mien. They live semi-nomadic lives centered around slash-and-burn farming (whereby forests are burned to create nutrient-rich fields).

THAI MALAY PEOPLE

Thailand is home to a very large Malay population, many of whom live in the south near the Malaysian border. The majority of Thai Malays are Muslims, and many speak the Pattani Malay language.

THE ISAN (THAI-LAO)

Northeast Thailand is home to the Isan, ethnic Lao people, most of whom speak the Isan language. They have a vibrant culture – rocket festivals *(p258)* and Ok Phansa *(p66)* are a Lao pursuit – and their cultural practices include Khmer-style *kantrum* folk music and consumption of sticky rather than long-grain rice.

↑ Celebrating Chinese New Year in colorful, traditional outfits in the Hua Hin district of Thailand

↑ Dancers in richly colored Isan dress during the annual Ok Phansa festival

SPIRITUAL BELIEFS

The diversity of cultures found across Thailand's ethnic groups extends to spirituality, with many groups following distinct religious traditions.

Theravada Buddhism - Most of the population are Theravada Buddhists *(p40)*, including the majority of the Isan and ethnic Tai people.

Thai Chinese Religion - Many Thai Chinese practice a fusion of folk traditions, such as Taoism and Confucianism, with more formal religions, like Mahayana Buddhism.

Animism - Some hill tribes practice a form of animism, centered on shamanic ritualism and communion with the natural world. Ceremonies often involve offerings of sacrificed animals to ancestor spirits, nature deities, or both.

Islam - Most Thai Malays follow the Islamic faith. Today Islam in Thailand remains heavily influenced by Sufism, a mystical form of the religion involving ritual chanting, breathing and singing - a practice known as *zikr*.

1 Burning incense, an important Theravada Buddhism ritual.

2 Praying during Chinese New Year at a temple in Bangkok.

3 Animist hermits saying healing prayers in Chiang Mai.

4 A family of the Islamic faith.

↑ Akha women walking in a tea plantation

A YEAR IN
THAILAND

JANUARY

△ **Chinese New Year** (late Jan/early Feb). Dragon dances and street fairs can be seen countrywide.

Umbrella Fair (mid-Jan). A celebration of traditional paper and wood umbrella making in Bo Sang, with painting displays and music.

FEBRUARY

△ **Flower Festival** (first weekend). Beautiful blooms of the north are displayed on floral float parades in Chiang Mai.

Makha Bucha (Feb full moon). Merit-making and candlelit processions at temples across Thailand commemorate a spontaneous gathering of Buddhist disciples in India.

MAY

Rocket Festival (May–Jun). Homemade rockets are fired in the northeast to ensure plentiful rains amid a carnival atmosphere.

△ **Visakha Bucha** (May full moon). The most important date on the Buddhist calendar celebrates the birth, Enlightenment, and death of the Buddha with sermons and candlelit processions at temples nationwide.

JUNE

△ **Baba Wedding Festival** (mid-Jun). Old Town Phuket celebrates its unique Peranakan (Sino-Portuguese) heritage with parades, special local foods, and re-enactments of their elaborate wedding ceremonies.

SEPTEMBER

△ **Nan Boat Races** (Sep/Oct). Up to 60 oarsmen in brightly painted longboats sprint along the Nan River in the center of town.

Bangkok's International Festival of Dance and Music (early Sep–mid-Oct). Classical musicians, folk dancers, and more perform.

OCTOBER

△ **Vegetarian Festival** (early Oct). Devotees in trances engage in body-piercing and fire-walking, following abstinence from meat.

Ok Phansa (Oct full moon). Celebration of the Buddha's reappearance on Earth.

MARCH

△ **Poi Sang Long Festival** *(Mar/Apr)*. Teenage boys dress as princes in Mae Hong Son, in memory of the Buddha's origins.
Phra Phutthabat Fair *(first or second week)*. Celebration of the annual pilgrimage to Wat Phra Phutthabat in Saraburi.

APRIL

Chakri Day *(Apr 6)*. The founding of the Chakri dynasty by Rama I is commemorated, with the Royal Pantheon in Wat Phra Kaeo's grounds in Bangkok open to the public on this day only.

△ **Songkran** *(Apr 12–14)*. Traditional Thai New Year is celebrated nationwide, with water splashing and parades of Buddha images, which are taken to temples and ritually bathed.

JULY

Asanha Bucha *(Jul full moon)*. The second of the year's three major Buddhist festivals celebrates the anniversary of the Buddha's first sermon to his first five disciples.

△ **Candle Festival** *(Jul full moon)*. Marking the beginning of Khao Phansa (Buddhist Lent) are parades of carved candles displayed on floats and later presented to temples, held in the northeast.

AUGUST

△ **Hungry Ghost Festival** *(mid-late Aug)*. Chinese shrines come alive at this Chinese Mahayana Buddhist commemoration of the spirits of the dead, who are believed to emerge from the beyond during this time.

NOVEMBER

Golden Mount Fair *(first week)*. Thailand's largest temple fair is held at the foot of Bangkok's Golden Mount.

△ **Loy Krathong** *(Nov full moon)*. Thais pay homage to the goddess of rivers and waterways, Mae Khongkha, as people gather at rivers and lakes nationwide to float *krathongs* with candles and incense.

DECEMBER

△ **Phra Nakhon Si Ayutthaya World Heritage Fair** *(late Dec)*. Music and dance performances celebrate Ayutthaya's former glory.

A BRIEF
HISTORY

The history of Thailand is that of an area rather than of a single nation, and since 40,000 BC, numerous peoples have made their home in this region. Thailand today is the product of ancient Indianized kingdoms, the Chakri Dynasty, and military regimes that have all held sway over the centuries.

Prehistoric Thailand

By around 40,000 BC, hunter-gatherer communities were already living in semi-permanent settlements in the area of modern-day Thailand. Ancient seed and plant husks found in caves in northern Thailand have led to speculation that agriculture began to develop around 9000 BC, and a rice chaff left in Banyan Valley Cave in 3000 BC indicates the beginning of rice cultivation. Elaborate pottery and sophisticated bronze work began to be produced in the area of Ban Chiang in 2100 BC. This Bronze Age culture is believed by some historians to be the earliest in the world.

1. An antique map of Siam (Thailand), printed in c1888.

2. A prehistoric cliff painting at Pha Taem.

3. A *chedi* with Buddhas at Wat Chama Thewi in Lamphun.

4. The Khmer temple, Khao Phanom Rung.

Timeline of events

Early 6th century

Mon people from Burma establish Dvaravati culture. They have already inherited Buddhism from Indian missionaries.

7th century

Chamadevi becomes Queen of the Dvaravati Kingdom.

AD 661

Haripunchai said to be founded at Lamphun, northern Thailand, by Buddhist holy men.

7th century

Srivijaya civilization expands from Sumatra, now part of Indonesia.

9th century

Khmer Empire founded at Angkor.

The First States

From the first few centuries BC, many Hindu and Buddhist missionaries from India and Sri Lanka came to Southeast Asia, and distinctly Indianized kingdoms began to emerge over the next millennium. Originating in the Mon state of Burma, the Dvaravati Kingdom flourished between the 6th and 11th centuries in what is now the heart of Thailand, near the towns of Phetburi and Lop Buri. They later controlled parts as far north as Lamphun, near modern Chiang Mai. Between the 7th and 13th centuries, the Srivijaya Empire, originating in the island of Sumatra in modern Indonesia, flourished further south, near Nakhon Si Thammarat.

The Khmer Empire expanded from Cambodia, defeating the Dvaravati forces, and conquered most of mainland Southeast Asia during the 9th and 13th centuries. Their legacy includes many magnificent temples and intricate palaces, many of which are in present-day northeast Thailand. The Tai, from southern China, migrated to the area from the 11th century onward. It is from the Tai that most inhabitants of moder-day Thailand trace their ethnic and cultural heritage.

BAN CHIANG POTTERY

Pots found at Ban Chiang *(p258)* date from 3000 BC to AD 500. Until their discovery in 1966, this area of Southeast Asia was thought to have produced little of cultural merit in prehistoric times. These, and other finds, show that indigenous peoples were capable of producing beautiful works of art.

1001–1002

Reign of Khmer King Udayadityavarman, who invaded Haripunchai (Lamphun) following an attack on Lop Buri.

1115–55

Lop Buri tries to assert its independence from Khmer control.

10th–12th centuries

Srivijaya becomes involved in ruinous wars with the Indian Chola Dynasty.

11th–13th centuries

Lop Buri incorporated into Khmer Empire as a provincial capital.

11th–12th centuries

Population of Tai people increases in areas of present-day Thailand.

The Kingdom of Sukhothai

Centered around the city of Sukhothai (p188) in the Central Plains, Sukhothai was the first notable kingdom of the Tai people. The Khmers referred to the Tai as Siam, a name that came to be used for this and subsequent Tai kingdoms. During the Sukhothai period in the 13th century, Theravada Buddhism (p40) achieved new expression in innovative architecture and images of the Buddha finely cast in bronze. Sukhothai was made powerful by its most illustrious ruler, Ramkhamhaeng, but by 1320 was only a local power again.

The Kingdom of Ayutthaya

In the mid-14th century, Ayutthaya (p166) supplanted Sukhothai as the most powerful kingdom in Siam and by around 1438 had incorporated it into its empire. The Ayutthaya period saw military, legal, and administrative reforms and a flowering of the arts, as well as diplomatic and trade links with the West. By the mid-16th century Ayutthaya held sway over much of what is now Thailand, but its demise came after years of conflict with Burma, when in 1767 the capital was sacked.

↑ The notable Wat Mahathat in Sukhothai Historical Park

Timeline of events

1238–1448
Thai-speaking Sukhothai Kingdom expands its rule further south, dominating modern-day Thailand.

1259–1317
Reign of King Mengrai; northern principalities unified as the Lanna Kingdom.

1292
Chiang Mai founded as capital of Lanna Kingdom.

1350–1767
Ayutthaya Kingdom gradually brings Thailand under its control and becomes a major power. At its greatest extent around 1600, it rules parts of modern-day Cambodia, Laos, and Burma.

1767
Invading Burmese forces sack Ayutthaya, ending the kingdom.

Lanna and Burmese Kingdoms

The northern kingdom of Lanna was established at the same time as Sukhothai and endured for 600 years. Its first ruler, Mengrai, extended Lanna rule into Burma. Ayutthaya had driven the Burmese out of Lanna once before, but in 1615 the Burmese took back the Lanna capital, Chiang Mai. In the 1700s, newly allied Siamese and Lanna forces drove the Burmese out. Lanna remained autonomous into the 19th century.

The Chakri Dynasty

After the sack of Ayutthaya, Taksin, an army general, created a new capital at Thon Buri, on the west bank of the Chao Phraya. Within 10 years Siam was a regional power again. However, in 1782, Taksin was ousted by his military commander Chao Phraya Chakri, who was later pronounced King Rama I. Perhaps the greatest king of the Chakri dynasty, Chulalongkorn (1868–1910), or Rama V, carried on the modernization of Siam that his father, Mongkut, had started. Financial reforms were made, the government restructured, and slavery abolished. His diplomacy kept the colonial powers, Britain and France, at bay.

1 An illustration of the ruins at Sukhothai.

2 An ancient mural of the Buddha in Ayutthaya.

3 King Naresuan of Siam defeats the Burmese Crown Prince.

4 King Chulalongkorn.

Did You Know?

Written Thai came from Khmer script and was adapted by King Ramkhamhaeng of Sukhothai.

1768–1782

Under Taksin the Great, the briefly lived Thonburi Kingdom re-establishes Thai control. Taksin is toppled by General Chao Phraya Chakri, who founds a new dynasty.

1782

Beginning of the Chakri dynasty under King Rama I. The country is known as Siam.

1868–1910

Reign of King Chulalongkorn (Rama V). Employment of Western advisers to modernize Siam.

1804–1868

Reign of King Mongkut (Rama IV), who embraces Western innovations and modernization.

1884

Chiang Mai made a province of Siam, ending Lanna Kingdom.

Constitution and Coups

On June 24, 1932, a group of young intellectuals, bureaucrats, and low-ranking military officers led by law student Pridi Banomyong sent word to King Prajadhipok (Rama VII) that absolute monarchy had ended, but he was invited to continue to rule as a constitutional monarch. The revolutionaries, who called themselves the People's Party, proposed a set of political reforms, with the intention of moving Thailand from feudalism to democracy. However, one of the original conspirators, Lt. Plaek Phibunsongkhram, decided that the role of fascist dictator was more to his liking, and seized power in a *coup d'état* in 1938. He rolled back Peoples Party reforms, openly expressed support for the Nazis, and styled himself as The Leader. Sadly, this has become a trend, with Thailand among the world leaders for military coups – 20, of which 12 have succeeded.

The Bhumibol Era

At the time of the mysterious fatal shooting of his brother Ananda (Rama VIII) in 1946, Bhumibol Adlulyadej was a teen-ager, but was nonetheless made King Rama IX. Surrounded by

1 Rama V and his wife.

2 King Bhumibol Adlulyadej and Queen Sirikit celebrating his 60th anniversary on the throne.

3 King Maha Vajiralongkorn gracing magazine covers in Bangkok in 2018.

Timeline of events

1932
People's Party Revolution; Siam made a constitutional monarchy.

1935
Prajadhipok abdicates; Ananda Mahidol becomes king, but leaves Thailand.

1938
Phibunsongkhram becomes Prime Minister; renames Siam Thailand.

1946
King Ananda mysteriously killed in Royal Palace; his younger brother Bhumibol made king.

1959
General Sarit Thanarat becomes Prime Minister in coup, continuing a trend of coups.

3

rapacious military factions and importuning minor aristocrats, he retreated from political intrigue and started major rural development projects, mainly in poorer north and northeast parts of the country. As these projects gave tangible benefits to the rural poor without upsetting Bangkok elites, his power and reputation for probity and love of all Thais let him emerge as a stabilizing force in the country's political landscape, finding compromises among the various factions. Thais came to revere him as a demi-god, and the grief at his passing in October 2016, after 70 years on the throne, was palpable.

Thailand Today

In 2011, Yingluck Shinawatra was elected the first female Prime Minister of Thailand, following her brother Thaksin. However, protests against her regime took place, and in 2014, the military deposed her and established an interim government. Bhumibol's son, Vajiralongkorn, is now the tenth king of the Chakri Dynasty, though he has yet to gain the status held by his father. Although Thailand is still ruled by a military regime, Thais can generally get on with their lives without great interference.

BANGKOK OR KRUNGTHEP?

What the world knows as Bangkok is Krungthep to Thais, an abbreviation of the city's official name. It translates as many things, including city of angels and the happy city.

1965
US military starts constructing bases in Thailand to support war in Vietnam.

1976
Massacre of students at Thammasat University brings huge support for the Communist Party of Thailand (CPT). Students flee to northern jungles.

1980s
CPT a spent force; King offers students amnesty. Thailand enters a period of rapid economic growth.

2006
Thaksin deposed by military coup.

2019
Bhumibol's son, Vajiralongkorn, is crowned King.

EXPERIENCE
BANGKOK

Wat Arun illuminated at sunset

EXPLORE
BANGKOK

This guide divides Bangkok into five sightseeing areas: the four shown on this map and Beyond the Center. Find out more about each area on the following pages.

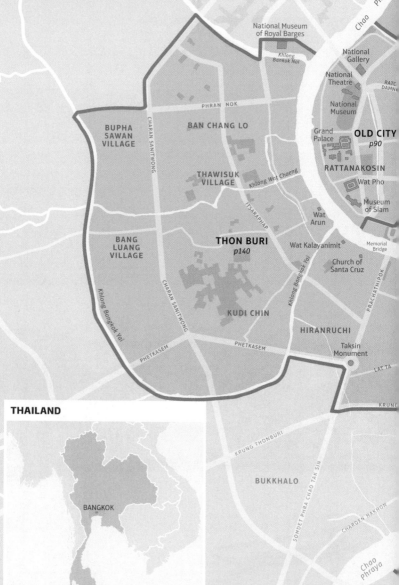

National Museum of Royal Barges

Chao Phraya

Khlong Bankok Noi

National Gallery

National Theatre

RATC DAMN

PHRAN NOK

National Museum

BUPHA SAWAN VILLAGE

CHARAN SANITWONG

BAN CHANG LO

Grand Palace

OLD CITY *p90*

RATTANAKOSIN

THAWISUK VILLAGE

Khlong Wat Chaeng

Wat Pho

ITSARAPHAP

Wat Arun

Museum of Siam

BANG LUANG VILLAGE

THON BURI *p140*

Wat Kalayanimit

Memorial Bridge

Khlong Bankok Yoi

Church of Santa Cruz

PRACHATHIPOK

Khlong Bangkok Yai

KUDI CHIN

HIRANRUCHI

PHETKASEM

PHETKASEM

Taksin Monument

LAT TA

KRUNG

THAILAND

BANGKOK

KRUNG THONBURI

BUKKHALO

SOMDET PHRA CHAO TAK SIN

CHAROEN NAKHON

Chao Phraya

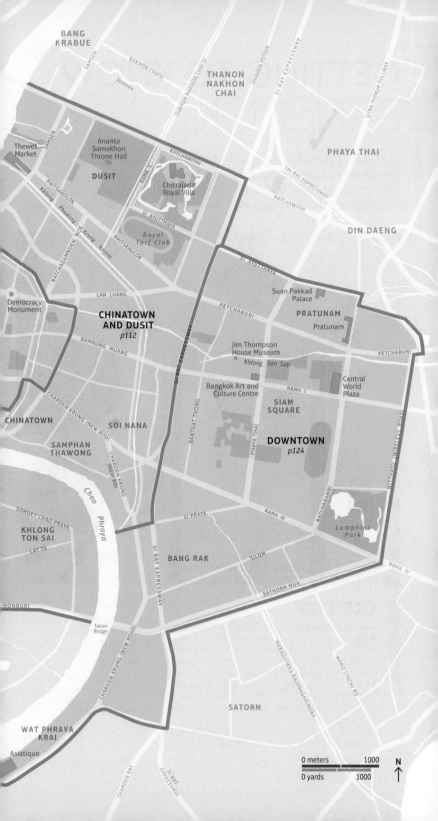

BANG
KRABUE

THANON
NAKHON
CHAI

PHAYA THAI

Thewet
Market

Ananta
Samakhon
Throne Hall

DUSIT

Chitralada
Royal Villa

DIN DAENG

Royal
Turf Club

Democracy
Monument

CHINATOWN
AND DUSIT
p112

Suan Pakkad
Palace

PRATUNAM

Pratunam

Jim Thompson
House Museum

Khlong San Sap

CHINATOWN

SOI NANA

Bangkok Art and
Culture Centre

SIAM
SQUARE

Central
World
Plaza

SAMPHAN
THAWONG

DOWNTOWN
p124

KHLONG
TON SAI

Chao
Phraya

Lumphini
Park

BANG RAK

SILOM

Taksin
Bridge

HONBURI

SATORN

WAT PHRAYA
KRAI

Asiatique

0 meters 1000

0 yards 1000

N

GETTING TO KNOW
BANGKOK

Bangkok is a sprawling patchwork of diverse areas, each with an essence and vibe of its own. The Chao Phraya River flows through the center of the city, where its historic and cultural heart lie, while the green spaces of outlying districts offer a peaceful retreat from the ceaseless bustle.

PAGE 90

OLD CITY

Perched on the eastern bank of the Chao Phraya, Bangkok's Old City expands eastward from the Grand Palace complex and the temples that line the river-front. Many of Bangkok's most famous and impressive attractions are clustered around this area, including the enormous Reclining Buddha at Wat Pho and the National Museum, one of the finest in Southeast Asia. The Grand Palace and Wat Phra Kaeo are the area's true star and together comprise one of Thailand's most-visited attractions. Away from the busy streets, Sanam Luang is often used for picnics and kite-flying.

Best for
Royal palaces, temples, and museums

Home to
Grand Palace, National Museum, Wat Pho

Experience
Watching craftsmen make traditional alms bowls in the Monk's Bowl Village

CHINATOWN AND DUSIT

A lively maze of narrow streets lined with shops and restaurants, the heart of Chinatown is Yaowarat Road, a curving street which bustles with gold shops and street stalls, sizzling with strange and delicious delicacies. It's here, more than anywhere else, that has earned Bangkok the title of street food capital of the world. Dusit, by contrast, is a peaceful area of stately boulevards connecting royal residences and parks, and is now where the royal family lives.

Best for
Street food, Chinese architecture, and royal residences

Home to
Yaowarat Road and Pak Khlong Market

Experience
Trying an unusual delicacy at the crowded street restaurants of Yaowarat Road

$\rightarrow$

PAGE 124

DOWNTOWN

Sprawling east from Chinatown and Dusit, downtown Bangkok is the heart of the city's modern business district and nightlife. Despite its ever-increasing bevy of gleaming skyscrapers, downtown is also home to one of the city's great green lungs in the form of Lumphini Park. For lovers of art and culture, this area satisfies every desire with the Bangkok Art and Culture Centre and the elegant Neilson-Hays Library. Any exploration of downtown should begin and end in the Mandarin Oriental Hotel, whose atmospheric bars and lounges evoke a bygone colonial Bangkok.

Best for
Shopping, nightlife, and high-end hotels

Home to
Jim Thompson House, Mandarin Oriental Hotel, Lumphini Park

Experience
Unwinding with a cocktail in the Mandarin Oriental Hotel's stylish Bamboo Bar

THON BURI

Facing the Old City on the western bank of the Chao Phraya River, the former capital Thon Buri is a snapshot of a time when Bangkok moved to a slower pace of life. Spectacular temples sit side-by-side with wooden houses perched above the *khlongs*, and barge is the preferred mode of transport. Thon Buri is home to one of the most beautiful temples in Thailand, Wat Arun, making this area a photographer's paradise. Weird and wonderful museums also abound, including the National Museum of Royal Barges and macabre Museums at the Siriraj Hospital.

Best for
Khlongs and unusual museums

Home to
Wat Arun, National Museum of Royal Barges, the Museums at the Siriraj Hospital

Experience
Spotting the sights along the river on the Chao Phraya Express Boat

BEYOND THE CENTER

Bangkok's attractions are not limited to the city center, with the pleasant towns of Ratchaburi and Nakhon Pathom to the west, both far enough to warrant a day trip, and many museums, markets, and parks closer to the city. Chatuchak Market, held weekly in the north of Bangkok, is one of the world's biggest markets, while Bang Krachao, nestled in a bend of the Chao Phraya in the south of Bangkok, is a haven of tree-lined canals and walking trails, perfect for some respite from the chaos of Bangkok's streets.

Best for
Floating markets and peaceful parks

Home to
Chatuchak Market, Ratchaburi, Bang Krachao

Experience
Souvenir shopping and navigating the madness of Chatuchak Market

←

 Panoramic view over the city from the Red Sky Bar.

② The Jim Thompson House.

③ A performance at Sala Chalermkrung Royal Theatre.

④ Train at Kanchanaburi.

4 DAYS

in and around Bangkok

Day 1

Morning Begin your tour of the buzzing capital at its most famous sight: the Grand Palace *(p94)*. Built in 1782, this complex is home to several important *wats*, including Wat Phra Kaeo, the holiest site in Thailand. Once you've admired the complex, jump on a Chao Phraya river cruise *(p88)* – the best way to explore further nearby sights.

Afternoon Have a leisurely lunch at Err *(p105)*, where street food dishes meet delicacies from the Thai countryside. Stroll around the colorful Pak Khlong Market *(p116)*, well known for its beautiful flowers, before catching a late afternoon performance of *khon* (masked dance) at the Sala Chalermkrung Royal Theatre *(www.salachalermkrung.com)*.

Evening Tuck into Thailand's signature dish, pad thai, at Thipsamai *(p105)*, known for producing the best in the country.

Day 2

Morning Learn about the life and work of Jim Thompson, an American expat who revitalized Thailand's silk production industry, at his former home, the beautiful Jim Thompson House *(p128)*. Stay for an early lunch at the stylish wine bar and restaurant on site.

Afternoon Visit Bangkok's Chinatown *(p113)* – one of the largest in the world – and gawp at Wat Traimit's *(p118)* magnificent Buddha image, made of 18-carat solid gold. Yaowarat Road *(p116)*, the heart of Chinatown, is a great place to pick up unique souvenirs, from gold trinkets to herbal remedies.

Evening Experience the classier side of Bangkok's nightlife in one of its towering rooftop bars, the Red Sky Bar *(999/99 Rama 1 Road)*, and soak up the impressive panoramic view of the bustling city below.

Day 3

Morning Take a three-hour train trip to Kanchanaburi *(p178)*, the site of the notorious Burma-Siam Railroad. Begin your visit at the Thailand-Burma Railroad Center and learn the devastating story of those who were forced to build the infamous bridge over the Khwae Yai River.

Afternoon Fuel up at homey restaurant On's Thai Issan *(p178)*, then visit the Kanchanaburi War Cemetery and Chong Kai Cemetery, where thousands of the prisoners and laborers who died in the construction of the railroad are buried.

Evening Unwind for dinner at the classy Blue Rice Restaurant *(p178)*, then browse the stalls of Kanchanaburi Night Market for a sweet dessert.

Day 4

Morning Take an hour-long train ride from Kanchanaburi to Tha Kilen, then take the short walk to nearby Prasat Muang Sing *(p181)*, a Khmer-style Buddhist temple. A small museum displays archeological finds from the site.

Afternoon Return to Kanchanaburi and stop for lunch at Mangosteen *(13 Maenamkwai Road, Tambon Ban Tai, Amphoe Mueang Kanchanaburi)*, a cafe and bookshop near the station.

Evening Settle in for the train journey back to Bangkok. On arrival, relax at the Mandarin Oriental's extremely glamorous Bamboo Bar *(p135)* with a cocktail while listening to their fantastic live jazz sets.

Tempting Street Food

Despite a strong government crackdown on unlicensed street vendors, you don't have to travel very far to find a roadside stand cooking up delicacies. To get to the heart of Bangkok's vibrant and authentic street food scene, head straight to buzzing Yaowarat Road *(p116)* in Chinatown, which is alive day and night with the sounds and smells of hundreds of street food stalls and restaurants.

$\rightarrow$

Succulent Thai satay, one of many delicacies found at roadside vendors

BANGKOK FOR
FOODIES

It's no surprise that Bangkok proudly claims the title of street food capital of the world, with hundreds of vendors in buzzing Chinatown selling tempting treats. But this city has more to offer in the way of Michelin-starred restaurants, unique food challenges, and entertaining food tours.

Dine in Style

Gourmet cuisine may not come to mind when you think of Bangkok, but the city is home to a swath of Michelin-starred restaurants. This is not all pretentious high cuisine, though. Our pick of these is the legendary hole-in-the-wall eatery Raan Jay Fai *(327 Maha Chai Rd, Khwaeng Samran Rat)*, which was awarded a star in 2018 and combines a shop-house location with luxury.

$\leftarrow$

Phad kee mao, a famous seafood dish served at Raan Jay Fai

Try Bizarre Foods

Trying new and unusual foods is a surefire way to experience Thai culture in all its glory, and Bangkok has no shortage of offerings. From deep-fried scorpions at street vendors on Khao San Road night market to pig's blood soup tasted at Sukhumvit Road *(p159)*, Bangkok is the top destination for the gastronomically intrepid. And who knows? You might even discover a new favorite.

↑ Cooking up a storm for hungry customers in Bangkok's Chinatown

A roasted scorpion on a skewer from one of the streetside stalls in Bangkok
↓

INSIDER TIP
Food Court Coupons

In the food courts of Bangkok's large markets and shopping centers, it is customary to purchase a value card. You can then peruse the many outlets and buy the food of your choice.

Take a Tuk-Tuk Tour

In the narrow, traffic-choked streets of Bangkok, tuk-tuks (auto rickshaws) are a fun and convenient way to get to the best eating spots. The city's leading food tours company, Bangkok Food Tours *(bangkokfoodtours. com)*, offers a midnight tuk-tuk tour which zips between the best eateries, taking in a range of tasty Bangkokian and Isan delicacies. You can also go behind the scenes to learn how cooks prepare classic street food dishes.

←
A tuk-tuk outside a night market in Chinatown's Yaowarat Road

Raise the Roof

At street level, the sights, sounds, and smells of Bangkok can be dazzling, so there's nowhere better to get a different perspective on the city than one of its elegant rooftop bars. A good place to start is the swanky Sky Bar on Silom Road *(p132)*, allegedly one of the highest rooftop bars in the world. The Octave Rooftop Lounge & Bar *(2 Sukhumvit Road Soi 57)* is the best choice for sunset views.

$\longrightarrow$

Drinks galore and splendid views at the Octave Rooftop Lounge & Bar

BANGKOK'S
DIVERSE NIGHTLIFE

No city in Southeast Asia has a nightlife as legendary as Bangkok. Whether you're looking to take part in the backpacker buzz around the city or chill out in a stylish rooftop riverside lounge with a creative cocktail, Bangkok's nightlife has something for every taste.

Step into a Stylish Superclub

Flip-flops and shorts may be in style in the backpacker dives of Khao San Road, but they won't cut it in the city's bevy of sleek superclubs. Onyx *(onyxbangkok.com)* welcomes EDM superstar DJs and thousands of well-heeled punters through its doors every night, while the darkly stylish Sing Sing Theater *(singsingbangkok.com)* combines Chinese-inspired decor with house, jazz, and burlesque performances.

$\longleftarrow$

Creative interior and fantastical costumes at Sing Sing Theater

Try a Creative Cocktail

With an expanding range of drinking options, Bangkok is home to some of the best cocktail bars in Southeast Asia. At Maggie Choo's, you can expect fruit and candy concoctions, while Bangkok's best bartenders elevate mixology to a fine art at Backstage Cocktail Bar.

← Pouring a tempting cocktail with a unique Thai twist

DRINK

New watering holes are always popping up in the city, with plenty of trendy bars to explore.

Rabbit Hole
⌂ 125 Thonglor
Sukhumvit 55
🆆 rabbitholebkk.com

Backstage Cocktail Bar
⌂ PlayHaus Thonglor
205/22-23 ☎ 0-6151-95891

Maggie Choo's
⌂ 320 Silom Rd
🆆 maggiechoos.com

↑ A traditional puppet show at the Aksra Theatre

Catch a Classical Cultural Show

Look beyond Bangkok's hectic bars, and there are many places to discover Thailand's classical arts. For an authentic classical music performance, head to the Sala Chalermkrung Royal Theatre *(salachalermkrung.com)*. The Aksra Theatre *(King Power Duty Free Complex, Soi Rang Nam)* is the best venue for Thai puppet shows.

A RIVER VIEW OF BANGKOK

The two great rivers of the north, the Ping and the Nan, join at Nakhon Sawan in the Central Plains to form the Chao Phraya ("river of kings"), Thailand's most important waterway. This vital transportation link drains some of the country's most fertile rice-growing land. The stretch shown here is actually a canal, built in the 16th century as a shortcut at a point where the Chao Phraya took a huge meander along what is now Khlong Bangkok Noi and Khlong Bangkok Yai. Along this busy "royal mile" you can catch glimpses of the Grand Palace, temples, and colonial buildings, and experience a flavor of old Bangkok's colorful riverfront.

Did You Know?

Bangkok was named the "Venice of the East" as many of its buildings were built on stilts above the river.

The Buddhaisawan Chapel *in the National Museum (p100) is home to the Phra Buddha Sihing, one of the most venerated Buddha images in Thailand after the Emerald Buddha. Elsewhere in the museum is a fabulous collection of arts and crafts from every period of Thai history.*

RIVERBOATS ON THE CHAO PHRAYA

The Chao Phraya is a major transportation artery, for both goods and people. Hefty rice barges, tiny boats laden with fruit and vegetables, and a variety of ferry services continually ply the river. No visitor to Bangkok should miss seeing the city from the water, and jumping on the Chao Phraya Express is one of the easiest and cheapest ways to do so. There are also cross-river ferries from almost every river pier, as well as countless long-tail boats that operate as buses.

Wat Rakhang *(p147) is a little visited but rewarding temple containing fine murals painted in the 1920s.*

↑ Sights along the scenic "river of kings" which flows through Bangkok

↑ Floating markets selling a colorful array of local produce

Sanam Luang *(p109), ("field of kings"), the venue for national ceremonies, is one of Bangkok's few open spaces.*

Wat Phra Kaeo *(p98) contains one of Thailand's most sacred Buddha images, the Emerald Buddha.*

Wat Pho *(p102), the city's oldest temple, dates from the 16th century. It is famed for its school of massage.*

Wat Arun *(p144) is delicately covered in pieces of broken porcelain.*

OLD CITY

As the spiritual and historical heart of Bangkok, the Old City is dense with temples and shrines. Known as Rattanakosin, this was the center of the new Siamese capital that Rama I founded in 1782 *(p71)*. The capital was moved from Thon Buri *(p140)* to east of the river as a defense against the Burmese *(p71)*, and Rama I ordered the digging of many canals to serve as moats, thus creating the artificial Rattanakosin Island. Fortifications were also built to prevent invasions, and remnants of a defensive wall can be seen between the Golden Mount and Wat Rachanadda. Rama I designed the city with the layout of the former capital of Ayutthaya *(p166)* in mind, and some of Thailand's finest Rattanakosin period architecture is within the Old City. The foremost example is the Grand Palace, where government offices were based. South of here is Wat Pho, one of the city's oldest temples, while to the north lies Sanam Luang ("field of kings"), the site where royal ceremonies and functions used to be held.

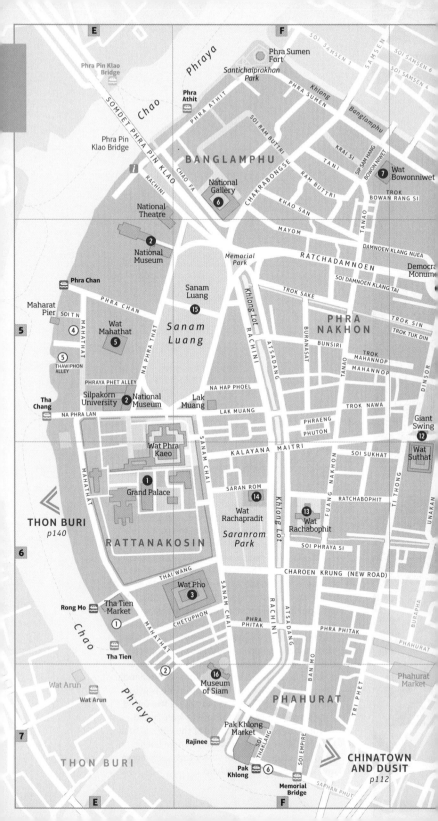

CHINATOWN
AND DUSIT
p112

The Queen's
Gallery

King
Prajadhipok
Museum

Mahakan
Fort

Loha
Prasat

8 Wat
Rachanadda

Wat Saket **9**

9
Golden
Mount

3

Bamrung
Muang Road
10

11
Monk's Bowl
Village (Ban Bat)

Corrections
Museum

Suan
omaninart

Ratchadamnoen
Boxing Stadium

DUSIT

OLD
CITY

OLD CITY

Must Sees
1 Grand Palace
2 National Museum
3 Wat Pho

Experience More
4 Democracy Monument
5 Wat Mahathat
6 National Gallery
7 Wat Bowonniwet
8 Wat Rachanadda
9 Wat Saket and the
Golden Mount
10 Bamrung Muang Road
11 Monk's Bowl Village
(Ban Bat)
12 Wat Suthat and
the Giant Swing
13 Wat Rachabophit
14 Wat Rachapradit
15 Sanam Luang
16 Museum of Siam

Eat
1 Eat Sight Story
2 Err
3 Thipsamai

Shop
4 Tha Chang Amulet
Market
5 Tha Maharaj
6 Yodipman River Walk

0 meters   400
0 yards   400

N

❶ 🎨 🏛

GRAND PALACE

พระบรมมหาราชวัง

📍 E6　🏠 Na Phra Lan Rd　🚌 1, 3, 25, 33, 39, 53　🚤 Chang, Tien　Ⓜ Sanam Chai
🕐 8:30am–3:30pm daily　⚜ Ceremonies　🌐 palaces.thai.net

This complex, generally referred to as the Grand Palace and Wat Phra Kaeo, encompasses Thailand's holiest temple and a lavish fairytale-esque palace that was once a residence for the king.

Construction of this remarkable site began in 1782, to mark the founding of the new capital and provide a resting place for the sacred Emerald Buddha (Phra Kaeo). Surrounded by walls stretching for 2,080 yards (1,900 m), the complex was once a self-sufficient city within a city. Built at the same time as Wat Phra Kaeo, the Grand Palace was the king's official residence from 1782 to 1946, although King Chulalongkorn (Rama V) was the last monarch to live here. Today, Chitralada Palace (p123) is the official residence of the royal family. Throughout the palace's history, many structures have been altered. While there are a few functioning government buildings here, such as the Ministry of Finance, most are unused. Important ceremonies are still held on the site.

↑ The stunning Dusit Throne Hall and its lush grounds

> **Construction of this remarkable site began in 1782, to mark the founding of the new capital and provide a resting place for the sacred Emerald Buddha (Phra Kaeo).**

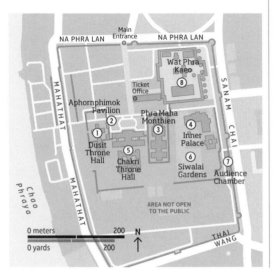

①

Dusit Throne Hall

For many, this building is the Grand Palace's crowning glory, featuring a four-tiered roof. This cross-shaped throne hall was originally built in 1784 as a reproduction of one of Ayutthaya's grandest buildings, Wat Phra Si Sanphet (p168). Five years later the hall was struck by lightning and rebuilt on a smaller scale. Crowned with a sumptuously decorated tiered spire, it is one of the finest and most impressive examples of traditional Thai and early Rattanakosin architecture. Inside is a masterpiece of Thai art: the original Rama I teak throne, inlaid with mother-of-pearl. In the south wing is an interesting window in the form of a throne. The hall is also used for various royal celebration ceremonies.

↑ An intricate and
impressively crafted
statue at the complex

② Aphornphimok Pavilion

King Mongkut (Rama IV) built this small but attractive wooden structure as a royal changing room for when he was giving audiences at the Dusit Throne Hall. The king would be carried on a palanquin to the pavilion's shoulder-high first step. Inside the building he would change into the appropriate apparel for the occasion. The pavilion's simple structure, complemented by its elaborate decoration, makes it a building of perfect proportions: indeed, it is considered a glory of Thai architecture. It inspired Rama V so much that he had a replica built at Bang Pa-in (p176).

↑ The elaborate Aphornphimok pavilion

③ Phra Maha Monthien Buildings

This cluster of connected buildings, located to the east of the Chakri Throne Hall, is the "Grand Residence" of the palace complex.

The focal point of the 18th-century Amarin Winichai Hall, the northernmost building of the group, is Rama I's boat-shaped Busabok Mala Throne surmounted by a nine-tiered white canopy. The hall is now used for state ceremonies.

Connected to the hall by a gateway through which only the king, queen, and royal children may walk is the Phaisan Thaksin Hall. This was used by Rama I as a private hall when dining with family, friends, and members of the royal court.

The third building is the Chakraphat Phiman Hall. It served as a residence for the first three Chakri kings. It is still the custom for a newly crowned king to spend a night here as part of his coronation.

④ Inner Palace

Behind a gateway to the left of the Chakri Throne Hall is the entrance to the Inner Palace, which is closed to the public. Until the time of Rama VII, the palace was inhabited solely by women of the royal family. Apart from sons, who had to leave the palace on reaching puberty, the king was the only male allowed to live within its walls. The palace functioned as a small city, with its own government and laws, complete with prison cells. Under the strict guidance of a formidable "Directress of the Inside," a small army of uniformed officers policed the area. In the late 19th century, Rama V built small Victorian-style palaces here for his favorite consorts. Because his successor, Rama VI, had only one wife, the complex was left virtually empty, and it eventually fell into disrepair.

One of the palace buildings that continues to function is the finishing school for the daughters of high-society Thai families. The girls are taught flower weaving, royal cuisine, and social etiquette.

⑤ Chakri Throne Hall

Also known as the Grand Palace Throne Hall, Chakri Maha Prasat was built in

Did You Know?

In 1809, a ceremony was performed in the Phaisan Thaksin Hall to mark the coronation of King Rama II.

Timeline

1782
△ Official founding of Thailand's new capital, Bangkok.

1783
▽ Work begins on Wat Phra Kaeo, Dusit Throne Hall, and Phra Maha Monthien.

1809
△ Rama II introduces Chinese details to the complex.

1840s
Women's quarter laid out as a city within a city.

↑ The impressive Chakri Maha Prasat, glowing as dusk descends over the Grand Palace complex

Neo-Classical style by the architect John Chinitz. Rama V commissioned the building in 1882 to mark the centenary of the Chakri dynasty.

On the top floor of the Central Hall are the ashes of royal monarchs, and the first floor – the only floor open to the public – acts as the main audience hall where the king entertains foreign monarchs.

Behind the Niello Throne in the Chakri Throne Room is the emblem of the Chakri dynasty: a discus and trident. The paintings in the room depict diplomatic missions, including Queen Victoria welcoming Rama IV's ambassador in London. The East Wing is used as a reception room for royal guests. The long hall connecting the Central Hall with this wing is lined with portraits of the Chakri dynasty. In the West Wing is the queen's personal reception room.

⑥
Siwalai Gardens

These beautiful gardens, which are sadly now closed to the public, lie east of the Inner Palace and contain the Phra Buddha Ratana Sathan, a personal chapel built by Rama IV. The pavilion is covered in gray marble and decorated with white and blue glass mosaics. The Neo-Classical Boromphiman Mansion in the gardens was built by Rama V

💬 INSIDER TIP
Dress Code

The stunning *wats* of the Grand Palace complex are among the most sacred in Thailand, and a strict dress code applies. Appropriate clothes can be borrowed from a booth at the main entrance.

as a residence for the Crown Prince (later King Rama VI). The building served as a temporary residence for several kings: Rama VII, Rama VIII, and Rama IX. Today it is used as a guest house for visiting dignitaries.

⑦
Audience Chamber

Visible from outside the palace walls, this chamber – Phra Thinang Sutthaisawan Prasat – is located between Thewaphithak and Sakchaisit gates. It was built by Rama I as a place to grant an audience during royal ceremonies and to watch the training of his elephants. Rama III strengthened the wooden structure with brick, and decorative features were added later. These include the crowning spire and ornamental cast-iron motifs.

1855
▽ New buildings epitomize fusion of Eastern and Western styles.

1880
▲ Chulalongkorn, the last king to make major additions, renovates Wat Phra Kaeo.

1925
Rama VII chooses to live in the less formal Chitralada Palace at Dusit. Grand Palace reserved for special occasions.

1932
Chakri Dynasty's 150th year celebrated at palace.

1982
Renovation of the complex.

(8)

WAT PHRA KAEO

วัดพระแก้ว

Serving as the royal chapel and sub complex of the greater Grand Palace, this complex impresses with its slender *chedis*, glittering mosaics, and the fearsome *yaksha* (giants) by the gates. The *wat* is Thailand's holiest temple, though there are no resident monks here.

When Rama I established the new capital of Bangkok in 1782 his ambition was to construct a royal temple along the lines of the grand chapels of previous capital cities. Symbolizing the simultaneous founding of the Chakri dynasty, this temple was to surpass its larger Sukhothai and Ayutthaya predecessors in the splendor of its design. The result of his vision was Wat Phra Kaeo, or Temple of the Emerald Buddha (officially known as Wat Phra Si Rattana Sasadaram), so called because the *bot* houses the Emerald Buddha image. Thought to have been crafted in Sri Lanka, this palladium was housed in Chiang Rai, Lampang, and Laos before Rama I brought it to Bangkok.

Did You Know?

Carved from a single piece of jade (not emerald), the Emerald Buddha is only 26 in (66 cm) tall.

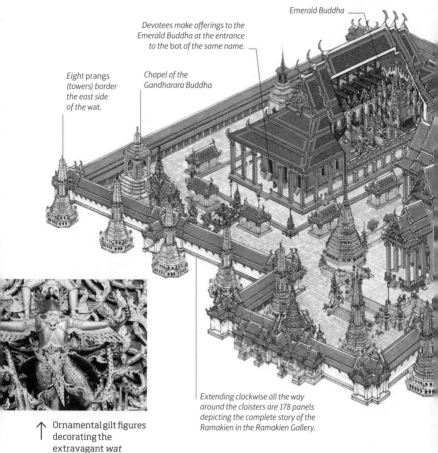

Emerald Buddha

Devotees make offerings to the Emerald Buddha at the entrance to the bot of the same name.

Eight prangs (towers) border the east side of the wat.

Chapel of the Gandharara Buddha

↑ Ornamental gilt figures decorating the extravagant *wat*

Extending clockwise all the way around the cloisters are 178 panels depicting the complete story of the Ramakien in the Ramakien Gallery.

The Bot

▽ The most sacred building within the palace complex, the *bot* was erected to house the most revered image of the Buddha. Inside, the surprisingly small Emerald Buddha sits in a glass case high above a golden altar.

Ramakien Gallery

◁ Lavishly painted and meticulously restored murals are divided by marble pillars inscribed with verses relating to the Ramakien *(p171)*.

Upper Terrace

The Phra Si Rattana Chedi is the most striking structure here, with golden tiles on the exterior.

Northern Terrace

Ho Phra Nak was originally constructed by Rama I in the late 18th century. Rama III, however, demolished the hall and built the present structure to house ashes of members of the royal family.

Auxiliary Library

▲ Also on the Northern Terrace is the Ho Phra Monthien Tham. Inside, Buddhist scriptures are stored in fine cabinets.

THE EMERALD BUDDHA

According to legend, in 1434 lightning struck the *chedi* of Wat Phra Kaeo in Chiang Rai, revealing a simple stucco image. The abbot of the temple kept it in his residence until the flaking plaster exposed a jadeite image beneath. Upon learning of the discovery, the king of Chiang Mai sent elephants to bring the image to him.

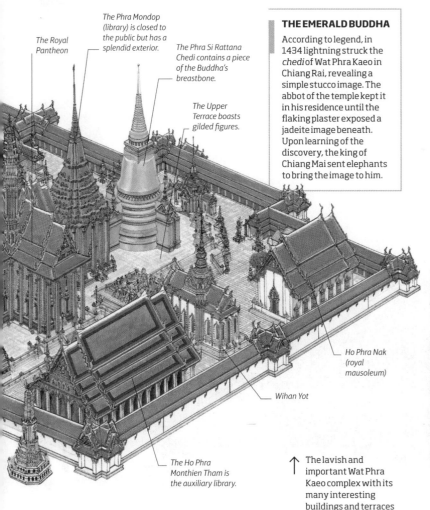

The Royal Pantheon

The Phra Mondop (library) is closed to the public but has a splendid exterior.

The Phra Si Rattana Chedi contains a piece of the Buddha's breastbone.

The Upper Terrace boasts gilded figures.

Ho Phra Nak (royal mausoleum)

Wihan Yot

The Ho Phra Monthien Tham is the auxiliary library.

↑ The lavish and important Wat Phra Kaeo complex with its many interesting buildings and terraces

❷ 🍴 ⏱ 🎨 🛍

NATIONAL MUSEUM

พิพิธภัณฑ์สถานแห่งชาติ

📍 E5 🏠 1 Na Phra That Rd 📞 0-2224-1333 🚌 15, 19, 32, 39, 53, 59, 70; AC: 506, 507, 508 🚢 Phra Athit Ⓜ Sanam Chai 🕘 9am–4pm Wed–Sun

Thailand's premier museum has one of the most comprehensive and largest collections in Southeast Asia and provides an excellent introduction to the arts, crafts, and history of Thailand.

The central 18th-century Wang Na Palace and Buddhaisawan Chapel, two of the museum's buildings, are works of art in themselves. The chapel contains the venerated Phra Buddha Sihing image, and an eclectic selection of artifacts, from ancient weaponry to shadow puppets. The collection is displayed in several buildings set around the Wang Na Palace. Art exhibits are arranged chronologically in the two wings, starting from the left (south) wing. Other attractions include galleries of history and prehistory. The labeling of the collection is not always helpful, so taking one of the frequent, free guided tours is recommended.

1887

The year Rama V decided to turn Wang Na into Thailand's first museum.

↑ The pristine temple-turned-museum complementing the orange sky

Admiring the large collection of Thai artifacts and treasures in one of the museum's two wings

Doors of Throne Hall

▶ Beautifully decorated black and gold lacquered doors mark the entrance to the Wang Na Palace and date from the 19th century. They are works of art in themselves, and their intricate designs and motifs show a strong Chinese influence.

Buddhaisawan Chapel

◀ Built in 1787, this beautiful building is one of the country's most precious treasures. It sits at the heart of the National Museum complex and is decorated with some of the best Rattanakosin-period murals in Thailand, as well as gilt Buddha images. Its hushed atmosphere makes it a calming space to visit.

Phra Buddha Sihing

▶ The history of this image, one of Thailand's holiest after the Emerald Buddha, is shrouded in legend. It probably dates from the 13th century and was brought here from Chiang Mai by Rama I in 1787.

Royal Funeral Chariots Gallery

▶ Several lavishly decorated, gilded teak chariots used in royal funeral processions can be seen in this gallery, including Racharot Noi, built in 1795. Each of the stunning gilded teak carriages weighs several tons.

3 🛈 Ⓜ 🛍

WAT PHO

วัดโพธิ์

📍F6 🏛Sanam Chai Rd 🚌AC: 25, 32, 44, 60, 508 ⛴Tien, Chang, Rachinee
Ⓜ Sanam Chai ⏰9am–5pm daily (Institute of Massage: 8:30am–6pm daily)
🌐watpho.com; watpomassage.com

With its awe-inspiring Reclining Buddha, resident monks, massage pavilions, a school, and a strong community spirit, Wat Pho is one of the most lively and lived-in Thai temples in Bangkok.

Officially known as Wat Phra Chetuphon, Wat Pho is not only Bangkok's oldest and largest temple but also Thailand's foremost center for public education. In the 1780s Rama I rebuilt the original 16th-century temple on this site and enlarged the complex. In 1832 Rama III built the Chapel of the Reclining Buddha, housing the stunning image, and turned the temple into a place of learning. Today Wat Pho is a traditional medicine center, of which the famous Institute of Massage – the most respected massage school in the city – is a part. Nearby on Chetuphon Road is the temple monastery, home to some 300 monks.

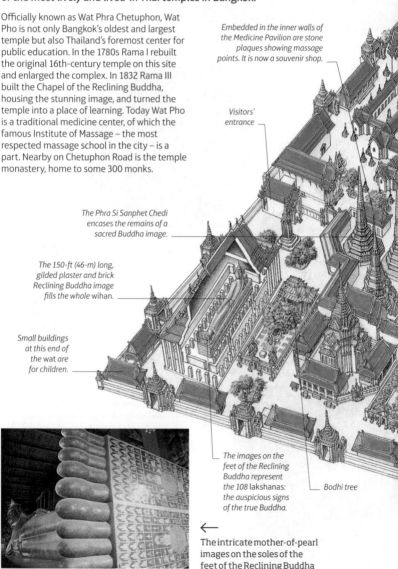

Embedded in the inner walls of the Medicine Pavilion are stone plaques showing massage points. It is now a souvenir shop.

Visitors' entrance

The Phra Si Sanphet Chedi encases the remains of a sacred Buddha image.

The 150-ft (46-m) long, gilded plaster and brick Reclining Buddha image fills the whole wihan.

Small buildings at this end of the wat are for children.

The images on the feet of the Reclining Buddha represent the 108 lakshanas: the auspicious signs of the true Buddha.

Bodhi tree

← The intricate mother-of-pearl images on the soles of the feet of the Reclining Buddha

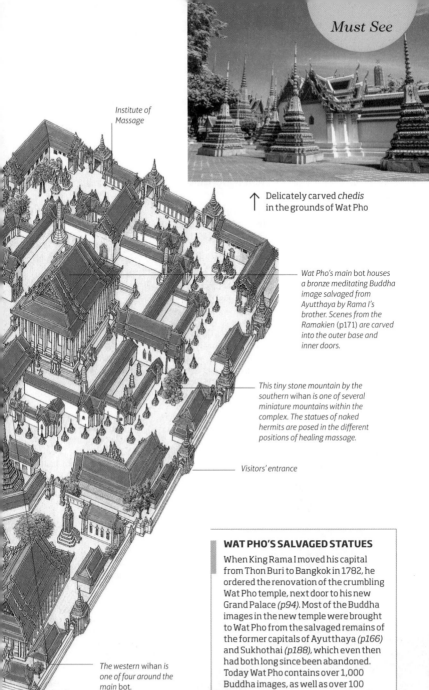

Institute of Massage

↑ Delicately carved *chedis* in the grounds of Wat Pho

Wat Pho's main bot *houses a bronze meditating Buddha image salvaged from Ayutthaya by Rama I's brother. Scenes from the Ramakien (p171) are carved into the outer base and inner doors.*

This tiny stone mountain by the southern wihan is one of several miniature mountains within the complex. The statues of naked hermits are posed in the different positions of healing massage.

Visitors' entrance

The western wihan is one of four around the main bot.

↑ The impressive Wat Pho complex and its large number of statues

WAT PHO'S SALVAGED STATUES

When King Rama I moved his capital from Thon Buri to Bangkok in 1782, he ordered the renovation of the crumbling Wat Pho temple, next door to his new Grand Palace *(p94)*. Most of the Buddha images in the new temple were brought to Wat Pho from the salvaged remains of the former capitals of Ayutthaya *(p166)* and Sukhothai *(p188)*, which even then had both long since been abandoned. Today Wat Pho contains over 1,000 Buddha images, as well as over 100 plaques made from stones recovered from a temple in Ayutthaya, and a *mondop* (p39) that features ancient scriptures written in palm leaves from Ayutthaya, though this section unfortunately cannot be visited.

EXPERIENCE MORE

Democracy Monument
อนุสาวรีย์ประชาธิปไตย

📍 G5 🏛 Ratchadamnoen Klang 🚌 AC: 503, 509, 511 🕐 Daily

A strong focal point during pro-democracy demonstrations, this monument (built in 1939) commemorates the revolution of 1932. Each feature symbolizes the date of the establishment of Thailand's constitutional monarchy, on June 24, 1932.

The four wing towers are each 79 ft (24 m) high. The 75 cannons indicate the year 2475 of the Buddhist Era (1932), and the pedestal, containing a copy of the constitution, is 10 ft (3 m) high, referring to the third month of the Thai calendar (June).

The structure was designed by Silpa Bhirasri, an Italian sculptor who took a Thai name and citizenship.

Wat Mahathat
วัดมหาธาตุ

📍 E5 🏛 3 Maharaj Rd 📞 0-2221-5999 🚌 AC: 203, 506 🚢 Chang Maharaj 🕐 Daily

This is a large, busy temple complex, interesting more for its atmosphere than for its architecture. Dating from the 1700s, the *wihan* and *bot* were both rebuilt between 1844 and 1851. The *mondop*, which gives the temple its name – "temple of the great relic" – has a cruciform roof, a feature rarely found in Bangkok.

The *wat* is the national center for the Mahanikai monastic sect, and it holds one of Bangkok's two Buddhist universities. There is also a herbal medicine market, and, on weekends, stalls selling a range of goods.

💬 INSIDER TIP
Me Time

If you want to give meditation a try, free daily classes are held at Wat Mahathat, in Thai and English, at 7am, 1pm, and 6pm in Section Five, near the monks' quarters. You can also have your fortune told.

National Gallery
หอศิลป์แห่งชาติ

📍 F4 🏛 4 Chao Fa Rd 📞 0-2281-2224 🚌 AC: 506 🚢 Phra Athit 🕐 9am–4pm Wed–Sun

Thailand's main art gallery, housed in the old mint building, was established in 1977. It concentrates on modern Thai and international art. Initially the gallery suffered from lack of funds, but in 1989 further wings were added. The high-ceilinged, spacious halls now attract exhibitions

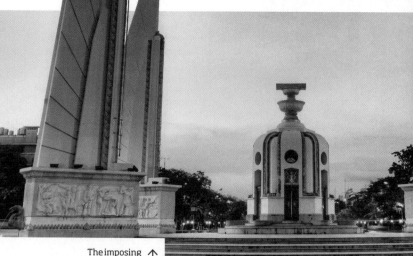

The imposing Democracy Monument in the center of Bangkok ↑

Intricate design and golden hues of the stunning Wat Bowonniwet

from all over Asia. Temporary shows of prominent Asian artists are often better than the permanent exhibits. Modern art can also be found at the Bangkok Art and Culture Center (*p136*). Check out the *BKK 101* magazine for other exhibitions in the city.

 7

Wat Bowonniwet
วัดบวรนิเวศน์

9 F4 **A** 248 Phra Sumen Rd **C** 0-2281-5052 **🚌** 12, 15, 56; AC: 511 (Express) **🕐** 8am–5pm daily

In quiet, tree-filled grounds, this mid-19th-century temple was constructed by Rama III. The style bears his trademark Chinese influence. A central gilded *chedi* is flanked by two symmetrical chapels. The interior murals are attributed to monk-painter Khrua In Khong, who is famous for the introduction of Western perspective into Thai temple murals. As court painter to King Mongkut (Rama IV) he was exposed to Western ideas and adapted these to a Thai setting. The result was a series of murals that on first glance look wholly Western, but that portray the same Buddhist allegories found in traditional Thai murals. The images are all the more remarkable for the fact that Khrua In Khong never traveled to the West. The main Buddha image, Phra Buddha Chinasara, is

EAT

Eat Sight Story
At this old pier, enjoy superb Thai curries and stir-fries, and views of Wat Arun.

9 E6 **A** 45/1 Maharaj Rd **W** eatsightstorydeck. com

 ⑧ⓑⓑ

Err
Trendy eatery serving a rustic menu, showcasing dishes from Thailand's cities and countryside.

9 E7 **A** 394 Maharaj Rd **W** errbkk.com

 ⑧ⓑⓑ

Thipsamai
Often described as the home of Thailand's best pad thai, including the classic version – rice noodles, shrimp, tofu, and vegetables.

9 G5 **A** 313–315 Maha Chai Rd **W** thipsamai.com

 ⑧ⓑⓑ

one of the best examples from the Sukhothai period.

King Mongkut served as abbot here during his 27 years in the monkhood and founded the strict Tammayut sect of Buddhism, for which the temple is now the head-quarters. Since Mongkut, many Thai kings have served their monkhoods at the *wat*, including King Bhumibol (Rama IX). The temple also houses Thailand's second Buddhist university.

37

The number of spires at Wat Rachanadda, representing 37 virtues.

8

Wat Rachanadda
วัดราชนัดดา

📍G5 🏛Maha Chai Rd
🚌2, 44, 59; AC: 79, 503, 511
🕐9am–4pm daily

The most interesting feature at Wat Rachanadda (often spelled Ratchanaddaram) is the metal monastery. Originally conceived as a *chedi* to complement the temple, it evolved into an elaborate meditation chamber modeled on a 3rd-century BC Sri Lankan temple (the original is now ruined). Passages dissect each level, running north to south and east to west. The meditation cells are at each intersection.

In the temple's courtyard is Bangkok's best amulet market. Tourists may face disapproval if they attempt to take talismans home as souvenirs. Across the road, behind the old city walls, is the Doves' Village, where singing doves are sold for competitions.

9

Wat Saket and the Golden Mount
วัดสระเกศและภูเขาทอง

📍G/H5 🏛Chakkaphatdi Phong Rd 🚌8, 15, 37, 47, 49; AC: 38, 543 🕐7:30am–5:30pm daily

Built by Rama I in the late 18th century, Wat Saket is one of the oldest temples in Bangkok. Visitors come to climb the artificial hill topped with a golden tower within the grounds. Rama III built the first Golden Mount, but the soft soil led to its collapse. King Chulalongkorn (Rama V) provided the necessary

The Golden Mount's distinctive tower *(inset)*, with a golden Buddha statue in Wat Saket's tropical gardens ↓

 GREAT VIEW
The Golden Mount

It's well worth the hike up the Golden Mount for panoramic views over Bangkok and to explore the gilded Wat Saket, adorned with striking murals depicting Buddhist realms of hell.

technology to create the 250-ft (76-m) high representation of the mythical Mount Meru seen today. It is believed to house relics of the Buddha presented to Rama V by the Viceroy of India. A circular staircase lined with monuments and tombs leads to the top, where there is a sanctuary. The octagonal building opposite, Mahakan Fort, is one of 14 original watchtowers of the city walls.

↑ Putting the final touches to a Buddha statue at a workshop on Bamrung Muang Road

Until the 1960s the Golden Mount was one of the highest points in Bangkok. Today, it still forms a prominent landmark, although it is dwarfed by skyscrapers.

During the 19th century the grounds of Wat Saket served a macabre function as a crematorium. The bodies of the poor were sometimes left for vultures and dogs. By contrast, a fair with dancing and a candle procession is now held in the grounds in November.

AMULETS

The Thais are a highly superstitious people – those who do not wear some form of protective or lucky amulet are firmly in a minority. Amulets come in myriad forms and are sold in specialty markets. Although many are religious in nature – such as tiny Buddha images and copies of sacred statues – others are designed for more practical purposes, such as model phalluses to ensure sexual potency. Amulets are such a big business that there are even magazines dedicated to them.

10

Bamrung Muang Road
ถนนบำรุงเมือง

Q G5 AC: 508

Bamrung Muang, like Charoen Krung, was an elephant trail until the 20th century, when it became one of Thailand's first paved roads. The stretch between Maha Chai Road and the Giant Swing provides an enlightening peek into the thriving business behind the Buddhist practice of merit-making. The road is lined with shops selling religious paraphernalia: monks' robes, votive candles, and Buddha images. Monks shop here for temple essentials; other people buy offerings and shrines for the home. Although the religious objects look enticing, they are not intended as souvenirs: images of the Buddha cannot be taken out of the country without an export license.

11

Monk's Bowl Village (Ban Bat)
บ้านบาตร

Q G6 A Bamrung Muang Rd, Soi Ban Bat AC: 508

Monks' bowls were first used 2,500 years ago and are still widely used today in Buddhist countries for early morning alms-gathering (p40). Such bowls have been made at Monk's Bowl Village in Bangkok since the late 18th century. The village once stretched as far as Wat Saket, but modern developments have reduced the village to three homes and a cluster of small workshops. This area may be hard to find amid the maze of sois, but the bowls are sold at Wat Suthat (p108).

The process of bowl making is time consuming and requires eight pieces of metal, representing the eight spokes of the wheel of Dharma. The first strip is beaten into a circular form to make the rim. Three pieces are then beaten to create a cross-shaped skeleton. Four triangular pieces complete the sides. After being welded in a kiln, the bowl is shaped, filed smooth, and fired again to give an enamel-like surface.

At the center of the maze of alleyways next to the village hall is an unusual shrine, constructed from old Chinese cylinder bellows, that is dedicated to the "Holy Teacher and Ancestor."

↑ Craftsman welding in his workshop at Monk's Bowl Village

People praying inside
the Buddhist temple
of Wat Suthat

⓵③ Wat Rachabophit
วัดราชบพิตร

📍F6 🏛 Fuang Nakhon Rd
📞 0-2222-3930 🚌 2, 60;
AC: 501, 502, 512 🚢 Tien
🕐 8am–5pm daily

The circular form of Wat
Rachabophit is a successful
architectural blend of East
and West. The whole complex
is decorated with porcelain
tiles, which were made in China.
The focal point is the central,
Sri Lankan-style, gilded *chedi*,
whose full height from the
terrace is 140 ft (43 m).

Inside the *wat* are four
Buddha images, each facing
one of the cardinal points.
Leading off from the circular
gallery are the *bot* to the
north, the *wihan* to the south,
and two lesser *wihans* to the
east and west: an unusual
layout for a Thai *wat*.

The 10 door panels and 28
window panels of the *bot* are
decorated with mother-of-
pearl inlay that illustrates the
insignia of five royal orders.
The moldings over the door
depict King Chulalongkorn's
seal. The carved, painted
guards on the doors are
distinctively *farang* (European).

⓵② Wat Suthat and the Giant Swing
วัดสุทัศน์และเสาชิงช้า

📍 G5 🏛 Bamrung Muang Rd
🚌 10, 12, 19, 35, 42, 56, 96
🕐 8:30am–4pm daily
(*wihan*: Sat & Sun only)

There are several superlatives
for Wat Suthat, a temple
that was begun by Rama I
in 1807 and completed by
Rama III. Its *wihan* (shrine hall
containing Buddha images) is
the largest in Bangkok. The art

and architecture beautifully
exemplify Rattanakosin style.
Its central Buddha, at 26 ft (8
m) high, is one of the largest
surviving Sukhothai bronzes.
This image was moved from
Wat Mahathat in Sukhothai
(*p188*) to Bangkok by Rama I.
The murals in the immense
wihan are some of the most
celebrated in Thailand.
Amazingly intricate, they
depict the Traiphum (Buddhist
cosmology) and were restored
in the 1980s. The teak doors to
the *wihan* are carved in five
delicate layers and stand 18 ft
(5.5 m) high. (One made by
Rama II is now housed in the
National Museum.) The cloister
around the outside of the
wihan is lined with 156 golden
Buddha images.

The square in front of Wat
Suthat used to feature the
Giant Swing, the remains of a
swing used for a Brahmin
ceremony. After standing for
224 years, this was moved in
2007 to Devasathan Brahmin
temple and replaced by a
new swing made from six
100-year-old teak trees.

THE SWING IN ACTION

Sao Ching Cha, the
"Giant Swing" at Wat
Suthat, was built in
1784 by Rama I. During
ceremonies - Brahmin
in origin - teams of
four would swing in
180-degree arcs up to
82 ft (25 m) high. One
participant would try
to bite off a sack of gold
hung from tall poles.
The event, linked to the
god Shiva swinging in
the heavens, caused
many deaths and was
abolished in 1935.

→

The public square of
Sanam Luang, in front
of the Grand Palace

14

Wat Rachapradit
วัดราชประดิษฐ์

F6 **Saran Rom Rd** **0-2223-8215** **AC: 501, 502, 512** **Tien** **8am–6pm daily**

This peaceful temple was built in the mid-19th century by King Mongkut (Rama IV) and his East-meets-West taste in architecture is apparent in the choice of building materials. The main *wihan*, for instance, is covered in forbidding gray marble. The interior murals were painted in the late 19th century and depict festivals of the Thai lunar calendar. Striking carvings adorn the doors, eaves, and gables.

15

Sanam Luang
สนามหลวง

F5 **Ratchadamnoen Nai Rd** **82; AC: 25, 59, 60, 80** **5am–10pm daily**

Originally a royal cremation ground, and still used in this capacity occasionally – as for the funeral of King Rama IX in 2017 – Sanam Luang is a sacred spot for Thais. Throughout the year, it serves as one of

Bangkok's great green lungs: a venue for kite-flying, picnics, and resting in between visiting sites like Wat Mahathat (*p104*) and the Grand Palace (*p94*).

16

Museum of Siam
พิพิธภัณฑ์สยาม

F7 **Sanam Chai Rd** **12, 47; AC: 3, 82** **Thien** **10am–6pm Tue–Sun & pub hols** **museumsiam.org**

The interesting Museum of Siam is in the former Ministry of Commerce – a handsome Italianate building that was designed by Mario Tamagno. The project was finished in 1922 and was converted into its present incarnation in 2007. A Milanese architect, Tamagno was also the designer of other important Bangkok landmarks, including the Ananta Samakhom Throne Hall (*p121*).

The museum is spread over three floors and features permanent interactive exhibits that explore what it means to be Thai through ancient and contemporary history. Buddhism, village life, and politics and communication are some of the themes that are examined here.

SHOP

Tha Chang Amulet Market
Amulets are big business in Thailand, as the Thais are highly superstitious. This is a great place to browse charms, though be aware that there are rules on exporting Buddhist artifacts.

E5 **1 Sanam Phra**

Tha Maharaj
Perfect for a break in between touring the Old City, this riverside mall hosts rotating pop-ups, such as arts and crafts and farmers' markets.

E5 **1/11 Maharaj Rd**

Yodipman River Walk
Lovely waterfront shopping arcade, with a good selection of souvenir shops and cafes to relax in after plenty of shopping.

F7 **Chakkraphet Rd**

A SHORT WALK
AROUND SANAM LUANG

Distance 2 miles (3 km) **Time** 40 minutes
Nearest riverboat pier Tha Chang

Sanam Luang (p109) ("field of kings" or "royal ground") is one of the few sizable open spaces in Bangkok. It is the traditional site for royal cremations, the annual kite-flying festival, and the Royal Plowing Ceremony. Spiritually speaking, this area is one of the luckiest in the city, with the Grand Palace, the Lak Muang (City Pillar) shrine, and the Amulet Market bordering Sanam Luang. Neighboring streets overflow with salesmen hawking lotions, potions, and amulets for luck, love, or protection from evil spirits. Astrologers gather to chart your stars or read your palm, and fortune tellers gather near Wat Phra Kaeo. Notable sights include Wat Mahathat and the National Museum. If visiting the area between February and April, look out for fiercely contested kite fights.

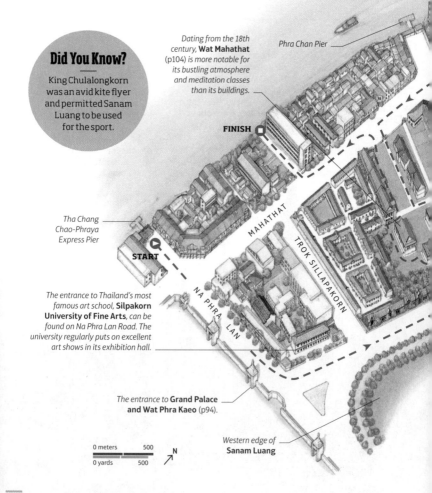

Did You Know?

King Chulalongkorn was an avid kite flyer and permitted Sanam Luang to be used for the sport.

Dating from the 18th century, **Wat Mahathat** (p104) is more notable for its bustling atmosphere and meditation classes than its buildings.

Phra Chan Pier

FINISH

Tha Chang Chao-Phraya Express Pier

START

The entrance to Thailand's most famous art school, **Silpakorn University of Fine Arts**, can be found on Na Phra Lan Road. The university regularly puts on excellent art shows in its exhibition hall.

MAHATHAT

TROK SILLAPAKORN

NA PHRA LAN

The entrance to **Grand Palace and Wat Phra Kaeo** (p94).

Western edge of **Sanam Luang**

0 meters   500
0 yards   500

N

← Thammasat University campus

Locator Map
For more detail see p92

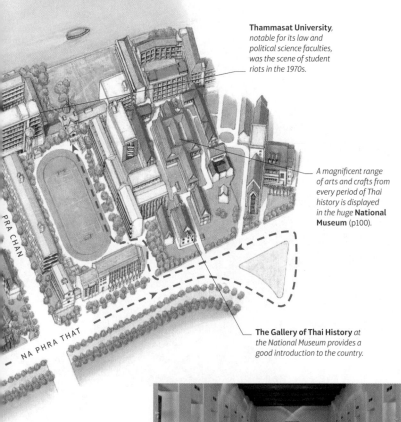

Thammasat University, *notable for its law and political science faculties, was the scene of student riots in the 1970s.*

*A magnificent range of arts and crafts from every period of Thai history is displayed in the huge **National Museum** (p100).*

PRA CHAN

NA PHRA THAT

The Gallery of Thai History *at the National Museum provides a good introduction to the country.*

→ Ancient artifacts displayed in the National Museum

CHINATOWN AND DUSIT

Bangkok's Chinese residents originally lived in the area where the Old City is today. When Rama I decided to move his capital across the river in 1782, the entire community was relocated. Since then the district around Yaowarat and Sampeng roads has been the focus of Chinese life in the city, although now it is also home to a small Indian community. Once the financial center of Bangkok, Chinatown remains a thriving, bustling, noisy area.

Dusit, north of Chinatown, is the center of Thai officialdom and an oasis of relative calm in a chaotic city. The district was established by King Chulalongkorn as an alternative to Rattanakosin Island *(p91)*, and political power is concentrated in the area. Treelined avenues, *khlongs*, old buildings, and the low skyline have all been preserved here. King Chulalongkorn laid out the district along European lines, with grand vistas, broad boulevards, and a geometric road grid surrounding his palaces. A century later it is still the royal quarter, and in 2017, many sites – including Vimanmek Mansion and Dusit Park – were taken back for private use by the royal family.

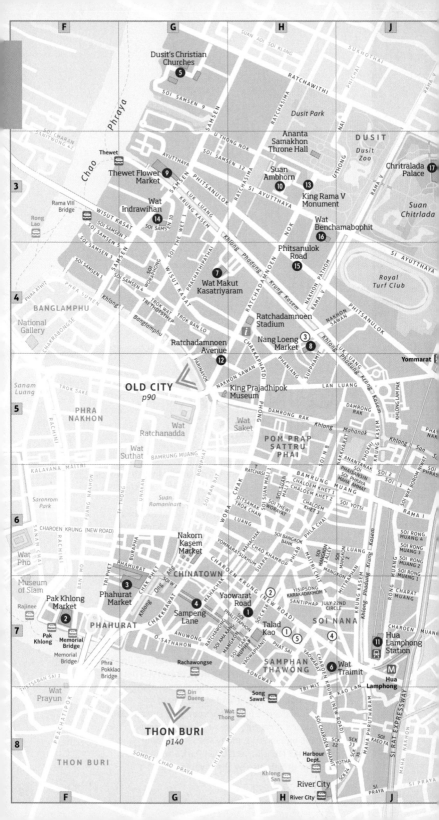

CHINATOWN AND DUSIT

Experience

1. Yaowarat Road
2. Pak Khlong Market
3. Phahurat Market
4. Sampeng Lane
5. Dusit's Christian Churches
6. Wat Traimit
7. Wat Makut Kasatriyaram
8. Nang Loeng Market
9. Thewet Flower Market
10. Suan Ambhorn
11. Hua Lamphong Station
12. Ratchadamnoen Avenue
13. King Rama V Monument
14. Wat Indrawihan
15. Phitsanulok Road
16. Wat Benchamabophit
17. Chitralada Palace

Eat

1. Lek & Rut
2. Jek Pui Curry
3. Nuea Toon Nang Loeng

Drink

4. 23 Bar & Gallery
5. Red Rose Jazz Lounge

DOWNTOWN p124

CHINATOWN AND DUSIT

0 meters 700

0 yards 700

N

Colorful neon signs lighting up the bustling Yaowarat Road ↑

EXPERIENCE

EAT

Lek & Rut
At this stall, waiters navigate bikes, cars, and tuk-tuks to deliver superb seafood.

⦿ H7 ⌂ Phadung Dao Rd
☏ 66 81 637 5039

Jek Pui Curry
Famous for the fire engine-red stools, Jek Pui serves some of the best curry in Chinatown.

⦿ H7 ⌂ 25 Mangkon Rd
☏ 66 2 222 5229

Nuea Toon Nang Loeng
Delve into braised beef served in a rich broth with rice or noodles at this family-run favorite.

⦿ H4 ⌂ Nang Loeng Market ☏ 66 2 282 0608

1

Yaowarat Road
ถนนเยาวราช

⦿ H7 🚌 4, 25, 40, 53, 73; AC: 1, 7 ⛴ Ratchawong Pier

This long, bustling artery connects Wat Traimit in the east to Chakphet Road in the west. Thought to resemble the curve of a dragon's body, it is believed to be an auspicious area, and the hundreds of gold shops, herbal vendors, restaurants, and cafes that line the road pay testament to that theory. Most of all, Yaowarat Road is the heart of Bangkok's street food scene, with weird and wonderful delicacies sizzling on roadside stalls and sidewalks clustered with plastic tables and chairs.

2

Pak Khlong Market
ตลาดปากคลอง

⦿ F7 ⌂ Maharaj Rd 🚌 AC: 501, 512 ⛴ Rachinee, Pak Khlong Ⓜ Wat Mangkhol
🕓 24 hours daily

Known for offering the best array of fresh flowers in Thailand, Pak Khlong Market

---

is a one-stop florist's dream. Deliveries arrive from 1am and by dawn the display has roses, orchids, lotus, jasmine, and Dutch tulips. The widest variety of blooms can be seen at 9am. Visitors can buy beautiful bouquets or floral basket arrangements.

3

Phahurat Market
ตลาดพาหุรัด

⦿ G7 ⌂ Phahurat Rd
🚌 6, 37, 88; AC: 3, 82
Ⓜ Wat Mangkhol

This predominantly Indian market offers all the tastes, sights, and smells of Mumbai. The main bazaar, which spills out around Phahurat and Chakphet roads, specializes in fabrics. Downstairs, cloth merchants sell anything from tablecloths to wedding saris. The dimly lit upstairs section is devoted to traditional Indian accessories such as sandals and ornate jewelry. In the surrounding streets are many delicious "hole-in-the-wall" Indian restaurants and samosa stalls. Off Chakphet Road is Siri Guru Singh Sabha, a traditional Sikh temple.

THE CHINESE IN THAILAND

The first Chinese immigrants arrived in Thailand as merchants in the 12th century. During the late 18th and early 19th centuries, Chinese immigration was encouraged in order to help rebuild the economy. By the mid-19th century half of Bangkok's population was of pure or mixed Chinese blood. The Chinese still dominate the commercial sector, and their traditions and beliefs remain strong in their communities.

CHINESE SHOP-HOUSES

Shop-houses are a common feature of Chinatown. The family lives on the first floor while the ground floor is devoted to the family business, whether it is a small workshop or a store selling, for example, food or household goods.

LENG NOI YEE TEMPLE

This important Mahayana Buddhist shrine also incorporates elements of Taoism and Confucianism. The temple, with its glazed ceramic gables topped by Chinese dragons, is the focal point of the annual Vegetarian Festival in Bangkok.

TRADITIONS

"Hell's Bank Notes" are a form of *kong tek* – paper replicas of real objects, burned to provide for the dead during their next life. Sign painting is also a big art tradition. Good luck messages, written in gold, are said to ward off evil and sickness. They are displayed during the Chinese New Year.

DIM SUM

Bite-size snacks, including shrimp toast and pork dumplings, are big business in Chinatown and can be sampled in many of the area's Chinese restaurants.

> ## Did You Know?
> Dim sum means "touch the heart" and is often regarded as "Chinese brunch."

↑ Painting gold messages on red paper for Chinese New Year, a Chinese tradition

↑ Tempting range of dim sum on offer for a traditional breakfast

Hoards of hungry diners sampling the food at Sampeng Lane market

known as Wat Noi. Some Cambodian refugees settled here in the late 17th century and still live in the parish. They take part in religious festivals here, hence the church's nickname, the Cambodian Church.

Wat Noi houses the Wat Mae Phrae Museum (no set opening times), which contains a statue of the Virgin Mary. The statue is venerated in an annual ceremony held each October.

 4

Sampeng Lane
สำเพ็ง

📍 G7 🏠 Soi Wanit 1
🚌 1, 7, 9 75, 110
⛴ Ratchawong Pier
🕐 8am–6pm daily

Running parallel and to the south of Yaowarat Road is Sampeng Lane, a narrow cluster of alleyways packed with a variety of market stalls selling clothes, textiles, electronics, knock-off jewelry, and the endless variety of assorted miscellany that Thai markets specialize in. There's also plenty of food on offer, from delicious barbecued pork to piles of deep-fried insects – although eating space is at even more of a premium here than on Yaowarat Road (p116). Be prepared to be swept along by the liveliness of this quint-essential Thai experience.

 5

Dusit's Christian Churches
โบสถ์ดุสิตคริสเตียน

📍 G2 🚌 3, 9, 30, 53; AC: 506; MB: 8, 10

By the bank of the Chao Phraya River, just south of Ratchawithi Road, is a small group of Christian churches.

The first of these, St. Francis Xavier Church, is near Krung Thon Bridge. Built in the early 1850s, it is notable for the statue of the saint atop its triple-arched portico frontage. Among its congregation are members of the local Viet-namese Catholic community, who settled here in 1934.

Just south is the smaller Church of the Immaculate Conception. It was originally constructed in 1674 during King Narai's reign by Father Louis Laneau for the early Portuguese community. It was then rebuilt in 1847 by French missionaries, and within its grounds is a smaller church

6

Wat Traimit
วัดไตรมิตร

📍 H7 🏠 Tri Mit Rd 🚌 1, 4, 11, 25, 53, 73; AC: 501, 507 Ⓜ Wat Mangkhol 🕐 9am–5pm daily

Also called the Temple of the Golden Buddha, Wat Traimit houses the world's largest solid gold Buddha. The gleaming 13-ft (4-m) high 13th-century Sukhothai image is made

of 18-carat gold and weighs five tons. The Buddha was discovered by accident in 1955. While extending the port of Bangkok, workers for the East Asiatic Company unearthed what appeared to be a plain stucco Buddha. The image was kept at Wat Traimit under a makeshift shelter for 20 years, until a crane dropped it while moving it to a more permanent shelter. The plaster cracked, revealing the gold Buddha beneath.

The statue had likely been encased in stucco to hide it from Burmese ransackers – a common practice during the Ayutthaya period (p70). Local Chinese residents come here to worship the Golden Buddha and to make merit (p40) by rubbing gold leaf on the temple's smaller Buddha images.

 Wat Makut Kasatriyaram
วัดมกุฎกษัตริยาราม

📍G4 ⬜330 Krung Kasem Rd 🚌12, 516 ⏰6am-6pm daily

Built in 1868 (and restored to its former glory in 2007), this peaceful, beautiful white

wat was commissioned by – and named for – King Mongkut, who reigned from 1851 to 1868 and is in many ways considered the father of modern Thailand for his modernizing cultural and technological reforms. He was also, however, a Buddhist monk – he was ordained in 1824 and served in this capacity for 27 years until his coronation as king – and this temple now stands as a monument to this chapter of his life. Notable features include an ornate gilded door, a central statue of the Buddha in the meditation posture, and a large chedi.

 Nang Loeng Market
ตลาดนางเลิ้ง

📍H4 ⬜Nakhon Sawan 6, Wat Sommanat 🚌5, 171 🚉Yommarat (skytrain) ⏰8am-3pm Mon-Sat

Dating back well over 100 years, Nang Leong Market remains one of the best

← Stairs leading up to the gleaming exterior of Wat Traimit

Did You Know?

The Sala Chalerm Thani Cinema, outside Nang Leong Market, is Thailand's oldest cinema.

places to be in Bangkok if you're hungry. As a designated market rather than a busy street, there's more space to eat than on Yaowarat Road (p116), with long metal benches at the center of the Food Court. One of the best markets for an authentic Thai experience, it's also the best place for traditional dishes – try kanom bueang yuan, a Vietnamese-inspired rice crepe filled with tofu and vegetables, or treat yourself to traditional Thai desserts, including kanom gluay (banana cake) or khao mahk (fermented rice pudding). Just outside the market, be sure to check out the Sala Chalerm Thani Cinema, built from wood in 1918. While it no longer functions as a working cinema, it is made entirely of wood and holds the title of one of the world's first wooden cinemas.

9

Thewet Flower Market

ตลาดดอกไม้เทเวศน์

⦿ G3 🏠 Krung Kasem Rd; National Library: Samsen Rd 🚌 AC: 506 🕙 9:30am-7:30pm daily

One of Bangkok's premier plant and garden markets flanks both sides of Khlong Phadung Krung Kasem, west of Samsen Road. It stocks a huge range of goods, including ornamental garden pots, orchids, trees, and pond bases. Although Thewet Market is not as vast as Chatuchak Market (p158), its prices are generally lower. It is a pleasant place to browse, even if you buy nothing. Around the corner is the National Library, which contains a large collection of books in Thai and English.

↑ A selection of flowers growing at the Thewet Flower Market

10

Suan Ambhorn

สวนอัมพร

⦿ H3 🏠 Uthong Nai Alley 🚌 🏠 Ramathibodi Hospital (skytrain) 🕙 8am-6pm daily

This pleasant park is a nice spot for a breather when you're taking in the sights of Dusit – a serene place that perfectly encapsulates the peaceful atmosphere of this royal district when contrasted with the bustle of neighboring Chinatown. Centered around its large pond and fountains, the park is commonly used to host civic events, such as celebrations of royal birthdays and coronations. Universities also use the area for graduation ceremonies. The park is surrounded by many royal monuments, including Dusit Palace (now closed to the public) and the popular King Rama V Monument.

11

Hua Lamphong Station

สถานีรถไฟหัวลำโพง

⦿ J7 🏠 Rama IV Rd 🚌 4, 21, 25, 29, 34, 40, 48, 109; AC: 501, 507, 529 Ⓜ Hua Lamphong 🌐 railway.co.th

King Chulalongkorn (Rama V), a great champion of modernization, was the instigator of rail travel in Thailand. The first railroad line, begun in 1891, was a private line from Paknam to Hua Lamphong. Today, the historic station is Bangkok's main rail junction. From here, trains leave for the north, northeast, the central

← A decorative pond with fountains in the gardens at Suan Ambhorn

Hotel as Ratchadamnoen Klang ("middle"). It then passes the Democracy Monument (p104) and 1930s mansions – a vista featured in the movie *Good Morning, Vietnam* (1987).

Just across from Khlong Banglamphu, Ratchadamnoen Nok ("outer") turns north into the Dusit area. This stretch, shaded by trees, is flanked by ministries, the main TAT headquarters, and Ratchadamnoen Boxing Stadium. Just before the ornate double bridge over Khlong Phadung Krung Kasem is the Thai-influenced modern building of the United Nations Economic and Social Commission for Asia and the Pacific (ESCAP).

The avenue ends at the domed Ananta Samakhom Throne Hall, which looms up beyond the Chulalongkorn Equestrian Statue in the parade ground, the site of December's Trooping of the Colors ceremony.

Up until the passing of King Bhumibol in 2016, the avenue had been splendidly decorated and illuminated in December as part of his birthday festivities.

INSIDER TIP
Dusit Park Closure

Dusit Park's royal attractions, such as Vimanmek Mansion and the Throne Room, are now closed to the public after being taken back for private use by the royal family.

is this impressive bronze equestrian statue that depicts and honors King Rama V – also known as King Chulalongkorn – on horseback. Erected in 1908, the statue was created to commemorate the 40th year of the king's reign, which at that time was the longest of any Siamese monarch. It's said that he set his heart on an equestrian statue during his travels in Europe, where he had admired similar sculptures in Italy and France.

Today, Thais often visit the statue to pay their respects on Tuesdays, the weekday on which the king was born, and in particular on October 23, the date on which he passed away in 1910.

Did You Know?

Hua Lamphong's half-dome structure was designed in an Italian Neo-Renaissance style.

plains, and the south. The city's other station, Bangkok Noi, serves only the South.

Ratchadamnoen Avenue
ถนนราชดำเนิน

 G5 🚌 15, 33, 39, 70, 159, 201; AC: 157, 170, 183, 503, 511

Planned by King Mongkut (Rama IV) in the style of a European boulevard, this thoroughfare has three parts.

The avenue's first section, Ratchadamnoen Nai ("inner"), starts at Lak Muang and skirts Sanam Luang (p109), before veering east at the Royal

King Rama V Monument
พระบรมรูปทรงม้า

🔲 H3 🏛 Dusit Royal Plaza 🚇🚊 Ramathibodi Hospital (skytrain)

Standing at the center of Dusit's Royal Plaza in front of the parliament building

→ Cast in bronze, an equestrian statue honoring King Rama V

> While admittedly not the most beautiful of Buddha images because of its rather flattened features, it stands out against the sky.

→

Sunrise at the beautiful marble temple, Wat Benchamabophit

 14

Wat Indrawihan
วัดอินทรวิหาร

📍 G3 🚇 Wisut Kasat Rd
🚌 3, 53; AC: 506 ⏰ Daily

You cannot miss the reason for Wat Indrawihan's fame: an impressive 105-ft (32-m) standing Buddha. The statue was commissioned in the mid-19th century by King Mongkut (Rama IV) to enshrine a relic of the Buddha from Sri Lanka. (Relics such as fragments of bone and hair are housed in countless Buddhist monuments worldwide.)

While admittedly not the most beautiful of Buddha images because of its rather flattened features, it stands out against the sky. Its enormous toes make a bizarre altar for the many offerings presented, including garlands of flowers.

Inside the *bot* (ordination hall) of Wat In (a popular abbreviation for the temple) are hundreds of Bencharong (five-color) funerary urns. Traditional-style, modern murals can also be seen inside the *bot*. In another, smaller building, "lucky" water is sold in plastic bags.

15

Phitsanulok Road
ถนนพิษณุโลก

📍 H4 🚌 16, 23, 201, 505

A number of important state institutions are located along this major avenue, which cuts through the heart of Dusit. Traveling northwest past the Mission Hospital at the Sawankhalok Road end, the first of interest is Ban Phitsanulok. This mansion has been the official residence of the prime minister since it was restored in 1982. It was originally built in 1925 by Rama VI for Major General Phraya Aniruttheva. Designed by the architects who built the Ananta Samakhom Throne Hall, it is a riot of Venetian Gothic, with floral-shaped mullioned windows, spindly crenellations, and a sweeping curved wing. It is not open to the public, and guests rarely stay overnight, because it is supposedly haunted.

On the opposite side of the road is the grassy oval of the Royal Turf Club. Now closed, this was once one of Bangkok's two major horse-racing tracks – the other is the Royal Bangkok Sports Club (*p135*). Government House, to the west, just past the Nakhon Pathom Road turning, is a fanciful, cream-colored Neo-Venetian style building. It is now used to house the prime minister's office, and it is closed to the public.

16

Wat Benchamabophit
วัดเบญจมบพิตร

📍 H3 🚇 69 Rama V Rd
📞 0-2281-2501 🚌 3, 16, 23, 505 ⏰ 8:30am–5:30pm daily

European influence on Thai architecture is exemplified by Wat Benchamabophit, the last major temple to be built in central Bangkok. In 1899 King Chulalongkorn (Rama V) commissioned his brother Prince Naris and the Italian architect Hercules Manfredi to design a new *bot* and cloister for the original Ayutthaya-period temple which stood on the site. The nickname for the new *wat* ("Marble Temple") is derived from the gray Carrara marble used to clad the walls.

Laid out in cruciform with cascading roof levels, the *bot* is elegantly proportioned. It contains another successful fusion of traditions: intricate Victorian-style stained-glass windows depicting scenes from Thai mythology. In the room of the ashes of Rama V is the most revered copy of Phitsanulok's Phra Phuttha

---

💬 INSIDER TIP
Gem Scam

Wat Benchamabophit is one of the target areas for practitioners of the gem scam, a confidence trick whereby scammers will pressure visitors to buy discounted gems or jewelry, which turn out to be fake.

Chinarat, with a pointed halo. Displayed in the cloister are 53 different Buddha images – originals and copies of images from around Thailand and other Buddhist countries, assembled by Rama V.

Within the *wat* is one of the three sets of doors inlaid with mother-of-pearl that were salvaged from Wat Borom Buddharam in Ayutthaya. The building in which Rama V lived as a monk features murals depicting events that occurred during his reign.

Wat Benchamabophit is a particularly popular location for witnessing monastic rituals, from Buddhist holiday processions to the daily alms round (p41), during which merit-makers donate food to the monks lined up outside the *wat* along Nakhon Pathom Road (p156). These events are a reversal of the usual practice where the monks go out in search of alms.

Chitralada Palace
พระตำหนักจิตรลดา

📍 J3 🏛 Ratchawithi & Rama V rds 🚌 18, 28; AC: 510 🚫 To the public

The official residence of the king and queen is an early 20th-century palace set in extensive grounds, east of the former Dusit Zoo (closed in 2018). Although the palace is hidden from view, the buildings, once used by King Bhumibol (Rama IX) for agricultural and industrial experiments are visible. In 1993 he became the first monarch in the world to earn a patent – interestingly for a waste water aerator.

The grounds also contain the Chitralada School, for children of the royal family. The perimeter of the palace is lit from the late King Rama IX's Birthday (Dec 5) to New Year.

DOWNTOWN

The center of Bangkok's vast and continually expanding downtown is the area spanning Silom and Ploenchit roads. The business district originated in the 19th century in the Old Farang quarter of Charoen Krung Road, where charming colonial buildings have been conserved around the Oriental Hotel. While most of Bangkok's trade centered on the canals in the 19th century, the downtown areas were not part of this trading circuit given their distance from the Chao Phraya River. Today's concrete canyon of Silom was instead rural farmland and a center for growing rice and fruit. After the building of Charoen Krung Road in 1861 – the first paved road in Bangkok – many of the canals slowly started to be replaced by roads. A newly industrialized economy led to Silom becoming Thailand's major financial quarter. In the 1960s, Patpong also became the home of the city's notorious red-light district, but the area today is surprisingly safe and vibrant.

DOWNTOWN

Must See

❶ Jim Thompson House

Experience More

❷ Mandarin Oriental Hotel
❸ Charoen Krung (New) Road
❹ Assumption Cathedral
❺ Neilson-Hays Library
❻ Silom Road
❼ Chulalongkorn University
❽ Maha Uma Devi Temple
❾ Patpong
❿ Erawan Shrine
⓫ Lumphini Park
⓬ Royal Bangkok Sports Club
⓭ Asiatique
⓮ Suan Pakkad Palace
⓯ Bangkok Art and Culture Centre
⓰ Siam Square
⓱ Pratunam
⓲ Wat Pathum Wanaram

Drink

① Vesper
② Bamboo Bar
③ CRU Champagne Bar

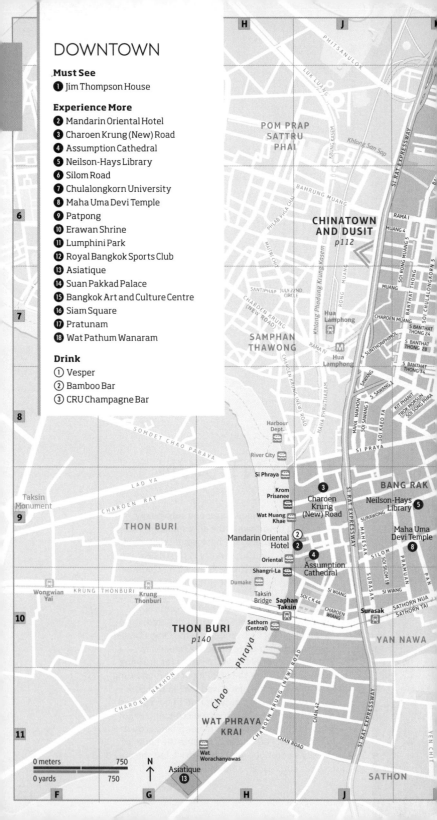

POM PRAP
SATTRU
PHAI

Khlong San Sap

CHINATOWN
AND DUSIT
p112

SAMPHAN
THAWONG

Hua
Lamphong

Hua
Lamphong

BANG RAK

THON BURI

Taksin
Monument

Wongwian
Yai

Krung
Thonburi

Mandarin Oriental
Hotel

Oriental

Shangri-La

Dumake

Taksin
Bridge

**Saphan
Taksin**

Sathorn
(Central)

THON BURI
p140

Harbour
Dept.

River City

Si Phraya

Krom
Prisanee

Wat Muang
Khae

❸
Charoen
Krung
(New) Road

Neilson-Hays
Library ❺

Maha Uma
Devi Temple
❽

❹
Assumption
Cathedral

Surasak

YAN NAWA

WAT PHRAYA
KRAI

Wat
Worachanyawas

Asiatique
⓭

SATHORN

0 meters   750

0 yards   750

N
↑

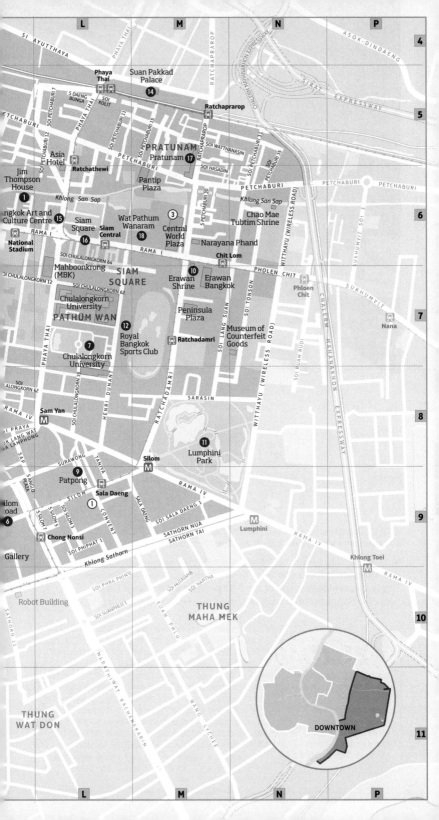

JIM THOMPSON HOUSE

บ้านจิมทอมป์สัน

🜢 K6 🏠 6 Soi Kasemsan 2, Rama I Rd 🚌 15, 48, 204; AC: 508 🚇 National Stadium (skytrain) 🕐 9am–5pm daily 🌐 jimthompsonhouse.com

In a flower-filled garden opposite the ancient silk weavers' quarter of Ban Khrua is the former home of American entrepreneur Jim Thompson. This leafy compound is one of the best-preserved traditional Thai houses in Bangkok and among the finest museums in the country.

> 💬 **INSIDER TIP**
> **Jim Thompson Art Center**
>
> Don't miss a look around the Jim Thompson Art Center. Located in the same compound as the house, this great modern gallery space hosts exhibitions by celebrated local artists.

The entrepreneurial American is perhaps best known for his unlikely role in reviving the art of Thai silk weaving *(p263)* following its demise during World War II. Having settled in Bangkok after the war, he became fascinated by these intricate textiles, and began supplying them to major fashion houses around the world. In 1959 Thompson dismantled six teak houses in Ban Khrua and Ayutthaya province and reassembled them here in a rather unconventional layout. Thompson was an avid collector of antiquities and artworks from all over Southeast Asia. His distinguished array, which spans 14 centuries, is displayed attractively, and left much the same as it was when he mysteriously disappeared in 1967. Unlike many other domestic museums, this feels like a lived-in home.

↑ Lush foliage surrounds the teak buildings of the Jim Thompson House

WHO WAS JIM THOMPSON?

An architect by profession, Thailand's most famous American came here in 1945 as the Bangkok head of the Office of Strategic Services (OSS), a forerunner of the CIA. In 1948 he founded the Thai Silk Company Ltd., turning the ailing industry into a thriving business once again. Thompson became something of a social celebrity in Bangkok and finally achieved mythical status following his disappearance on Easter Sunday 1967 while walking in the Cameron Highlands in Malaysia. Explanations for his vanishing range from falling from a path or having a heart attack to more sinister suggestions of CIA involvement.

Teak Houses

▶ The distinctive teak houses that form the main structure of the compound were erected with some walls reversed so that exterior carvings now decorate the interior walls. The oldest building dates from 1800.

Jataka Paintings

Eight early 19th-century paintings in the house show scenes from the *Vessantara Jataka*, one of the most popular *apadānas* (collection of biographical stories) of Theravada Buddhism. These paintings depict Prince Vessantara as an incarnation of the Buddha.

Drawing Room

▶ Thompsons ornate drawing room is certainly a sight in itself. It is home to a 14th-century U Thong sandstone head of the Buddha, while the 18th-century carved wooden figures in the alcoves depict ancient Burmese spirits.

Burmese Carvings

▽ A carved wooden figure of an animist Nat spirit is among Thompson's extensive collection of Burmese images. When Buddhism developed in Burma, it incorporated the preexisting worship of Nat spirits.

Dvaravati Torso of the Buddha

Dating back to the early Dvaravati period (7th century), this ancient torso, carved from limestone, is celebrated as one of the oldest surviving Buddha images in Southeast Asia. The tight-fitting monastic robe is intended to reveal a sexless body.

Diners taking in the magical view from a terrace at the Mandarin Oriental Hotel ↑

EXPERIENCE MORE

Mandarin Oriental Hotel

โรงแรมโอเรียนเต็ล

◘ J9 **⌂** Oriental Ave, off Charoen Krung Rd
🚌 35, 75 **⛴** Oriental
ⓦ mandarinoriental.com/bangkok

Repeatedly voted the world's best hotel for its service and attention to detail, the Mandarin Oriental was Thailand's first large hotel. It was established in 1876 and completely rebuilt in 1887. More wings have since been added. The hotel owes much of its charm to the Armenian Sarkies brothers, creators of the luxurious Raffles Hotel in Singapore, and features lavish decor and a spectacular setting on the banks of the Chao Phraya River.

The original, white-shuttered wing contains the renowned Authors' Suites. Somerset Maugham was one such author who stayed here in the 1920s. Recovering from a bout of malaria, he wrote of the "dust and heat and noise and whiteness and more dust" of Bangkok, though his perception of the city was to change once he was able to explore the *wats* and *khlongs*.

Classic, English-style high tea is served in the Authors' Lounge of the hotel, a riot of potted plants and wicker chairs. A teak barge shuttles back and forth to the Sala Rim Naam on the opposite bank,

WESTERN WRITERS IN BANGKOK

Western impressions of Thailand were for a long time influenced by one author – Anna Leonowens. A teacher at the court of King Mongkut (Rama IV), Leonowens wrote the book that inspired the musical *The King and I*. However, its portrayal of the king as a comic figure stirred up anger in the country, and the book is now regarded as an unreliable historical source. Less controversially, Joseph Conrad wrote about his journey up the Chao Phraya in *The Shadow Line*, and Somerset Maugham described his impressions of Thailand in *The Gentleman in the Parlour*. These are just two of the Western authors commemorated by suites at the Oriental Hotel. Others include Noël Coward, Gore Vidal, Graham Greene, and Barbara Cartland.

one of Bangkok's oldest thoroughfares. Linking the Customs House and trading companies, the road was once the center of Bangkok's European community. At their insistence it became Thailand's first paved highway.

Still home to the gem and antique trades, today the road is choked with traffic pollution and noise, but side streets, lined with trees and old wooden buildings, can be blissfully serene. Along the road is the imposing General Post Office, now occupied by the Thailand Creative & Design Center. The coin and stamp stalls (open Sundays) outside the post office and the Bangrak Market (open daily), selling clothing and fruit, give the area vibrancy.

Assumption Cathedral
โบสถ์อัสสัมชัญ

◉ J9 ⌂ Oriental Lane, off Charoen Krung Rd 🚌 35, 75 🕐 Daily

This Romanesque-style brick edifice was built in 1910 on the site of an earlier cathedral. Its rose window is flanked by twin squat towers. The richly ornamented Rococo interior is dominated by a lofty, barrel-arched blue ceiling patterned with gold starbursts. The cathedral faces a tree-shaded piazza, the site of several other Western-style buildings.

one of the hotel's eight highly acclaimed restaurants. Performances of traditional dance are staged here as guests dine. The hotel runs a respected school of Thai cookery so you can take some of the secrets of Thai cuisine home with you, and guests get free fitness classes to help burn off those extra calories.

Charoen Krung (New) Road
ถนนเจริญกรุง

◉ J9 🚌 1; AC: 504

Skirting the Chao Phraya River, from Wat Pho through Chinatown and on to Yannawa, Charoen Krung, or New Road (as it is often also called), is

→

The simple yet elegant building housing the Neilson-Hays Library

Neilson-Hays Library
ห้องสมุดเนลสันเฮยส์

◉ K9 ⌂ 195 Surawong Rd 🚌 16, 93 🕐 9:30am–5pm Tue–Sun 🌐 neilsonhays library.com

Housed within an elegant building beside the British Club is the Neilson-Hays Library. Its 20,000 volumes form one of Southeast Asia's finest English-language collections.

The library was built in 1921 in honor of Jennie Neilson-Hays, who was the mainstay of the Bangkok Library Association between 1895 and 1920. The internal domed rotunda is used as a modern art gallery, and each Saturday morning sees a fantastic children's story time, held in English and great for families. Creative writing workshops are on offer for young adults, while arts and crafts classes are among the other kids' activities regularly held here. Internationally renowned authors often visit the library to give talks.

> INSIDER TIP
> **Yoga at Neilson-Hays Library**
>
> On Saturdays, after the children's story time sessions, yoga classes for children and adults are held in the library's Children's Corner.

6
Silom Road
ถนนสีลม

📍 K9 🚌 AC: 177, 504, 514, 532, 544 Ⓜ Silom 🚇 Saladaeng (skytrain)

The commercial heart of Bangkok, Silom Road is becoming a polluted canyon of skyscrapers, shopping malls, and elevated railroad lines, though the area used to consist of orchards flanking a canal. One feature that remains unchanged is the thousands of barn swallows that nest here from October to March.

Toward the river end of the road, and also on parallel Surawong Road, are several gem and silk shops, as well as

shopping complexes like the lovely Silom Village, housed in 19th-century teak houses. Near Patpong is the Dusit Thani Hotel that overlooks Lumphini Park (*p135*) and the local nightlife. Close by is Convent Road, home to the Gothic-style Anglican Christ Church, built in 1904.

7
Chulalongkorn University
มหาวิทยาลัยจุฬาลงกรณ์

📍 L7 🏛 Phaya Thai Rd ☎ 0-2215-0871 🚌 16, 40, 47, 50; AC: 501; MB: 1

Dedicated to the modern-minded king who founded it, this is Thailand's oldest, richest, and most prestigious university. Chulalongkorn's central gardens, between the busy Phaya Thai and Henri Dunant roads, are the site of

several attractive buildings and a pond that is often used during the festival of Loy Krathong (*p67*).

The **Imaging Technology Museum**, south of the lake, features hands-on photographic displays and brilliant exhibitions of high-quality photography from Thailand and other countries. Nearby are an auditorium, used mainly for classical concerts, a contemporary art gallery, which stages various temporary exhibitions, and a **Museum of Natural History**.

Imaging Technology Museum
 ☎ 0-2218-5583
🕐 10:30am-3:30pm Mon-Fri

Museum of Natural History
 🕐 10am-3:30pm daily

8
Maha Uma Devi Temple
วัดศรีมหาอุมาเทวี

📍 K9 🏛 Corner of Silom and Pan rds 🚌 AC: 76, 502, 504 🕐 7am-6pm daily

Tamils founded this colorful Hindu temple during the 1860s. They were part of an influx of Indians who decided to move to Bangkok when India was handed over to the British Crown in 1858.

The main temple building is topped by a gold-plated copper dome above a 20-ft (6-m) high facade depicting various Hindu gods. Always buzzing with activity, and often with live Indian music, the temple is also the focus for Deepavali (Festival of Lights) celebrations in November. An oil-lamp ritual is held most days at noon, and on Fridays at 11:30am

Did You Know?

State Tower on Silom Road is home to the world's highest alfresco restaurant.

←

The vast urban landscape surrounding bustling Silom Road

there is a *prasada* (vegetarian ceremony), in which blessed food is distributed to devotees. Although some Thais might call the temple Wat Khaek ("Indians' temple"), a common cultural heritage means that many local Thais and Chinese also regularly worship here. The Hindu deities Shiva and Ganesh feature in Thai Buddhism, and Hindus regard the Buddha as one of the incarnations of Vishnu.

Patpong
พัฒน์พงษ์

L9 **Silom Rd, Patpong 1 and 2** **AC: 76, 177, 504, 514** **Silom** **Sala Daeng (skytrain)**

The private streets of Patpong 1 and 2, named after the one-time owner, Chinese millionaire Khun Patpongpanit, comprise what is probably the world's most notorious red-light district. In the 1960s

↑ The neon-lit bars and clubs lining the streets of Patpong

the area was the home of Bangkok's entertainment scene – the go-go bars sprang up to satisfy airline crews and US GIs on leave during the Vietnam War. Since the 1970s, the sex shows have been sustained mainly through tourist patronage. A less visible gay scene exists in adjacent Soi Silom 4.

The tourist police department monitors Patpong, and the area is surprisingly safe. A night market, with stalls selling souvenirs and original and fake fashions, gives the area a thin veneer of respectability. A bookstore in the center of Patpong is one of Southeast Asia's major outlets for books on feminism. These days, most visitors are drawn to the now infamous Patpong area out of curiosity rather than to indulge in its adult entertainment scene.

⑩

Erawan Shrine
ศาลพระพรหมเอราวัณ

📍 M7 🏠 Ratchadamri Rd
🚌 AC: 501, 504, 505
🚉 Rachadamri, Chit Lom,
or Siam Center (skytrain)

Drivers take their hands off
the steering wheel to *wai* (a
gesture of respect) as they
pass the Erawan Shrine, such
is the widespread faith in the
luck that this landmark brings.

The exuberant
Erawan Shrine and
its central gold
statue *(inset)* in
front of the Grand
Hyatt Erawan Hotel

The construction of the
original Erawan Hotel in the
1950s, on the site that is now
occupied by the Grand Hyatt
Erawan Hotel, was plagued
by a series of mishaps. In
order to counteract the bad

spirits believed to be causing
the problems, this shrine
dedicated to Indra and his
elephant mount, Erawan, was
erected in front of the hotel.
Ever since, the somewhat
gaudy monument has been
decked with garlands, carved
wooden elephants, and other
offerings in the hope of, or
thanks for, good fortune. By
the shrine are women dressed
in traditional costume. Anyone
wishing to express gratitude
for good fortune can pay the
dancers a fee, and they will do
a thank-you dance around it.

Close to the shrine, and
along Ploenchit and Sukhumvit
roads *(p159)*, are several of
Bangkok's most upscale shopping complexes, including
Sogo, Siam Center, World
Trade Center, Gay Sorn Plaza,
Amarin Plaza, Le Meridien,
and the swankiest of them
all, the Siam Paragon – where
you can even buy a Ferrari.

> ### BANGKOK'S MODERN ARCHITECTURE
>
> An endless mass of concrete towers, gaudy mockclassical
> edifices, and rows of shop-houses give Bangkok the
> overall impression of a sprawling urban jungle rather
> than the Oriental splendor visitors expect. Nonetheless,
> there are some modern buildings within the city that
> were designed by visionary architects. Postmodern
> architecture is particularly noticeable along Sathorn Tai
> and Silom roads - look out for striking buildings such as
> the Baiyoke Towers I and II. Thailand's most famous, and
> witty, modern landmark is the Bank of Asia's head office,
> nicknamed the "Robot Building." Sophisticated examples
> of Thai Modernism by Westerners are the roof of the
> Siam InterContinental, designed to resemble a traditional
> "Mongkut" crown, and the gardens of the Sukhothai
> Hotel, which evoke the serene waterscape of the old
> capital of the same name *(p188)*. In the 21st century,
> Bangkok's skyline continues to change, with additions
> such as the Siam Paragon, Central World, and the King
> Power Maha Nakorn, Thailand's highest building.

11

Lumphini Park
สวนลุมพินี

 M8 14; AC: 50, 507
Ⓜ Silom, Lumphini
Ⓡ Sala Daeng (skytrain)
🕐 5:30am–9pm daily

Named after the Buddha's birthplace in Nepal, Bangkok's main greenbelt sprawls around two boating lakes. Dominating the Silom Road (p132) corner of the park is a statue of Rama VI.

The best time to visit is early morning, when it is used by Thais for jogging and by Chinese for practicing t'ai chi ch'uan. The park is a relaxing place to stroll and observe elderly Chinese playing chess, and impromptu games of *takraw* (p49).

12 🖉

Royal Bangkok Sports Club
ราชกรีฑาสโมสร

🕐 L7 🏠 Henry Dunant Rd
🚌 16, 21; AC: 141 🕐 9am–6pm alternate Sun for races only Ⓦ rbsc.org

Considered to be Thailand's most exclusive social institution, the RBSC has a waiting list to prove it. It offers a wide range of sports to its members – including rugby, soccer, and field hockey – who form some of the top Thai teams in these sports.

Nonmembers may watch horse races at the club, the country's principal race course.

Gambling is virtually a national institution in Thailand, and on race days thousands of bettors flock to the track. As the start of the race draws near, betting becomes furious, and huge electronic screens track the odds on each horse and the total money wagered. Visitors are welcome to join in but may need help to fill out Thai-language betting slips.

 13

Asiatique
เอเชียทีค

🕐 G11 🏠 Chareonkrung Soi 72–76 🚌🚌 🕐 4pm–midnight daily Ⓦ asiatique thailand.com

With an atmospheric setting in the former dock warehouses of the East Asiatic Company, Asiatique is a modern development that brings together the bustle of a Thai night market with the accessibility of a modern shopping mall. The wide array of retailers includes edgy fashion brands, upscale international restaurants, and cheap noodle stands. The Joe Louis Thai Puppet Theatre is also a big entertainment draw. The easiest way to reach Asiatique is by the free ferry from Sathorn Pier.

DRINK

Vesper
Named for the martini created by James Bond in the 1953 novel *Casino Royale*, Vesper is a cocktail bar fit for 007, with a sleek interior and creative cocktails.

🕐 L9 🏠 10/15 Convent Rd, Silom
Ⓦ vesperbar.co

Bamboo Bar
The city's most glamorous hotel (p130) is also home to some of its most beloved bars. Bamboo hosts international jazz performers every night of the week, and the cocktails are award-winning.

🕐 J9 🏠 Mandarin Oriental, 48 Oriental Ave
Ⓦ mandarinoriental. com/bangkok

CRU Champagne Bar
The new kid on Bangkok's rooftop bar scene is incredibly glamorous, with panoramic city views, caviar on the menu, and, of course, champagne on ice.

🕐 M6 🏠 Centara Grand, 999/9 Rama Rd 1
Ⓦ champagnecru.com

→
Bustling Asiatique and its famous Ferris wheel

14

Suan Pakkad Palace
วังสวนผักกาด

◉M5 **⌂352 Si Ayutthaya Rd** **🚌AC: 201, 513** **Ⓜ Phaya Thai (skytrain)** **🕐9am–4pm daily** **🌐suanpakkad.com**

This palace, a group of five traditional teak houses, was originally the home of Prince and Princess Chumbhot. The houses were assembled in the 1950s within a lush garden landscaped out of a cabbage patch – suan pakkad in Thai – that gives the palace its name. Each building has been converted into a museum, and together they house an impressive private collection of art and artifacts that once belonged to the royal couple.

The eclectic assortment ranges from Khmer sculpture, betel-nut sets, and pieces of antique lacquered furniture, to Thai musical instruments and exquisite shells and crystals. More important, perhaps, is the first-class collection of whorl-patterned red and white Bronze Age pottery, excavated

Did You Know?

The idea to open the Bangkok Art and Culture Centre was suggested 13 years before it was built.

from tombs at Ban Chiang (p258) in northeast Thailand. The highlight for most visitors, though, is the Lacquer Pavilion, which was built from two exquisite temple buildings retrieved by Prince Chumbhot from Ayutthaya province.

Charmingly detailed black and gold lacquered murals inside each edifice depict scenes from the Buddha's life and the Ramakien (p171). They also portray ordinary Thai life from just before the fall of Ayutthaya in 1767. These murals are some of the only ones to survive from the Ayutthaya period. Scenes include foreign traders exchanging goods and gruesome depictions of hell.

15

Bangkok Art and Culture Centre
หอศิลปวัฒนธรรมกรุงเทพ

◉L6 **⌂939 Rama I Rd** **🚌AC: 15, 16, 501, 508, 529** **Ⓜ National Stadium (skytrain)** **🕐10am–9pm Tue–Sun for special exhibitions and performances** **🌐bacc.or.th**

The Bangkok Art and Culture Centre opened in 2008 and offers an insight into Thai culture and society among the shopping temples of Pratunam. This striking 11-story building is home to galleries, cafes, small shops, performance spaces, and a library.

The interior is reminiscent of the Guggenheim in New York with its huge white spiral walkways. The center displays over 300 contemporary works of art by excellent Thai and international artists and hosts regular exhibitions alongside an exciting events program. The agenda spans music, cinema, theater, and education, with international dance troupes, photography exhibitions, and art therapy programs just a few highlights of the ever-changing calendar.

Siam Square
สยามสแควร์

◉L6 ◈Rama I Rd ☒AC: 25, 501, 508 ⊞Siam (skytrain)

Street shopping is fast disappearing in Bangkok as shopping malls proliferate. The principal exception to this phenomenon is the network of *sois* (alleys) collectively known as Siam Square, between Chulalongkorn University *(p132)* and the Siam Center. The square is packed with independent shops and stalls selling music, books, accessories, and clothing – much of it by young Thai designers.

Rama I Road, on one side of the square, is the showcase for Thailand's movie industry. Three grand theaters – the Scala, the Lido, and the Siam – are here. On the western edge of the square, on Phaya Thai Road, is the Mahboonkrong Center (MBK), which houses a department store and various shops and stalls. Across Ploenchit Road are the Siam Center, Discovery, and Paragon shopping malls. Beyond here is the National Stadium, Thailand's main arena for soccer and other sports events. The future of the entire district is uncertain: it is feared the land may be redeveloped when its lease expires.

 GREAT VIEW
Cityscape from Baiyoke Tower

Pratunam's Baiyoke Tower II is the third-tallest building in Thailand, and between the 77th and 84th floors are restaurants, bars, and observation decks affording unbeatable views over Bangkok.

←

Visitors admiring artwork hung in the Bangkok Art and Culture Centre

Decorated statue in the grounds of Wat Pathum Wanaram ↑

Pratunam
ประตูน้ำ

◉M5 ☒12; AC: 504

Pratunam district is worth a brief visit. The lively and colorful Pratunam Market is a vast maze of stalls, stores, and workshops, trading mostly in clothing and fashion accessories. Just west of the market is the Modernist Baiyoke Tower, which reigned briefly as the tallest building in Bangkok from 1987 until 1995. Despite evidence of settling in the surrounding ground, permission was granted for construction of the adjacent Baiyoke Tower II, which was completed in 1997.

Wat Pathum Wanaram
วัดปทุมวนาราม

◉M6 ◈Rama I Rd ☒AC: 25, 501, 508 ⊞Siam Center (skytrain) ⊙9am–4pm daily

It's a pleasant surprise to discover such an oasis of calm in this bustling area. The main reason for visiting the Pathum Wanaram temple is to see Phra Meru Mas, a reconstruction of the crematorium of the late Princess Mother. Following her cremation at Sanam Luang in March 1996, her remains were transferred to these grounds in an elaborate procession. The crematorium is a rare example of ancient craftmanship, featuring ornate stencils and lacquered sculptures. It represents Mount Meru, the heavenly abode of the gods.

A SHORT WALK
OLD FARANG QUARTER

Distance 1.5 miles (2 km) **Time** 20 minutes
Nearest riverboat pier Wat Muang Kae

This area was Bangkok's original port and foreign commercial district in the 19th century. In 1820 Portugal was granted land in Bangkok, which resulted in the construction of the Portuguese Embassy. Embassies of other countries, such as France, soon followed. As you walk around, look out for the amalgam of Western and Eastern architectural styles created by these outside influences. Charoen Krung (New) Road cuts through the Old Farang Quarter and is home to gem traders, tailors, and antiques dealers. The Quarter's back-streets are surprisingly quiet.

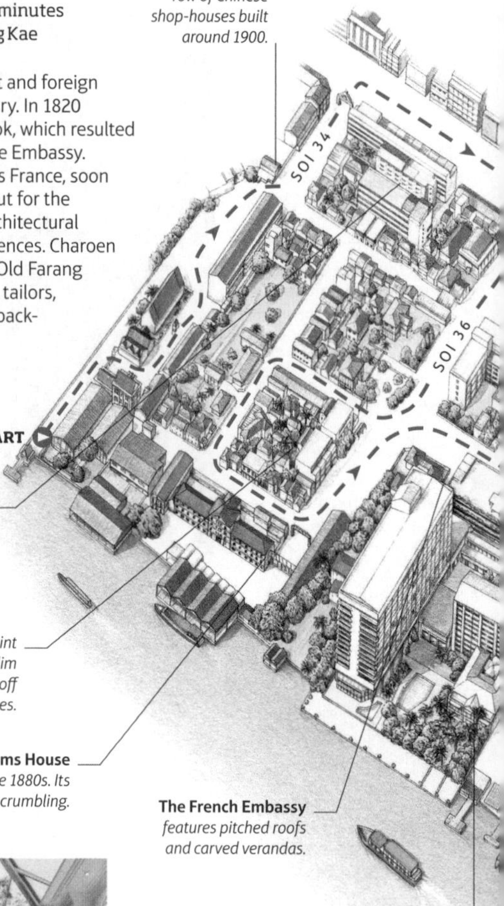

Harmonique restaurant *is one of a row of Chinese shop-houses built around 1900.*

SOI 34

SOI 36

START

House of Gems *is a tiny shop/museum selling rocks and fossils. Geological oddities – such as dinosaur droppings and tektites (glassy meteorites) – can be seen here.*

The Haroon Mosque *is a quaint stucco building with a Muslim graveyard. It faces Mecca and is off a street lined with wooden houses.*

The Old Customs House *was built in the 1880s. Its exterior is now crumbling.*

The French Embassy *features pitched roofs and carved verandas.*

The world-renowned **Mandarin Oriental Hotel** *(p130) was established in 1876 by two Danish sea captains. In 1958 a new structure (the Tower Wing) was added, and in 1976 the 10-story River Wing opened.*

←

The elegant Authors' Lounge, one of many rooms at the Mandarin Oriental Hotel

↑ The lavish interior and vaulted ceiling of Assumption Cathedral

Locator Map
For more detail see p126

The China House, *one of Bangkok's most expensive restaurants, is in a building dating from the reign of King Vajiravudh (r. 1910–1925). Next door, the Commercial Co. of Siam was built in the same era.*

CHAROEN KRUNG

CENTRAL AVENUE (SOI 40)

ORIENTAL LANE

SILOM

FINISH

SOI 42/1

SOI 42

0 meters 50
0 yards 50

N

The elegant **Assumption Cathedral** (p131) *was built in 1910. The Rococo interior features a high, vaulted ceiling and a striking marble altar.*

Bangrak Market

Wat Suan Phu *is distinguished by its carved wooden buildings and the Phra Bodhisattva Kuan-Im, a Chinese shrine over a carp pond.*

The East Asiatic Company *building is a Venetian-style edifice constructed in 1901.*

Shangri-La Hotel

THON BURI

Known originally as Ban Kok ("village of the wild plum"), Thon Buri was the capital of Thailand for 15 years between 1767 and 1782 *(p71)*. After the destruction of the Ayutthaya Kingdom, it was thought that the new location on the west side of the Chao Phraya River – difficult for Burmese armies to access – would help to avoid further invasions. The location was also ideal for carrying out seaborne trade and commerce, and inhabitants lived and traded on its centuries-old network of canals. The new king of Siam, Taksin, encouraged business with Chinese merchants, resulting in large numbers of Chinese settling permanently in Thon Buri. When Rama I overthrew Taksin and moved his capital across the river, its original name followed, and, though Thais refer to the capital as Krung Thep, it remains known as Bangkok to foreigners. Thon Buri wasn't linked by bridge to Bangkok until 1932 and was officially incorporated into the city only in 1971. Today this area preserves a distinct identity, offering a sleepier version of Bangkok proper. Its most important and prominent landmark is Wat Arun.

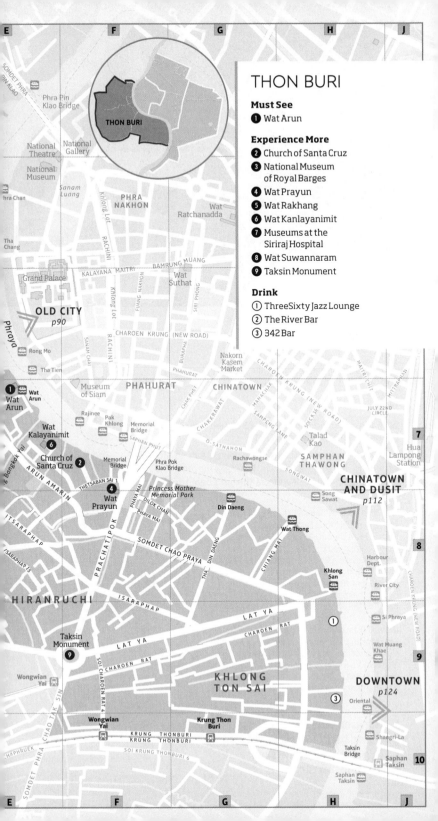

THON BURI

Must See
1. Wat Arun

Experience More
2. Church of Santa Cruz
3. National Museum of Royal Barges
4. Wat Prayun
5. Wat Rakhang
6. Wat Kanlayanimit
7. Museums at the Siriraj Hospital
8. Wat Suwannaram
9. Taksin Monument

Drink
1. ThreeSixty Jazz Lounge
2. The River Bar
3. 342 Bar

The beautifully illuminated Wat Arun reflected in the river ↑

WAT ARUN

วัดอรุณ

♦E7 ♦Arun Amarin Rd ■19, 57, 83 ■Tien to Wat Arun
♦7am–5pm daily ♦watarun.net

A striking Bangkok landmark, Wat Arun is named after Aruna, the Indian god of dawn. Fittingly, morning is a great time to visit, as it reflects the light beautifully.

Wat Arun owes its name to the legend that, in October 1767, King Taksin arrived here at sunrise from the sacked capital, Ayutthaya. He soon enlarged the tiny temple that stood on the site into a Royal Chapel to house the Emerald Buddha (p99). Rama II and Rama III were responsible for the size of the current temple: the main *prang* (tower) is 260 ft (79 m) high and the circumference of its base is 768 ft (234 m). In the 19th century King Mongkut (Rama IV) added the ornamentation created with broken pieces of porcelain. The monument's style, deriving mainly from Khmer architecture (p254), is unique in Thailand. The central *prang* is the mythical Mount Meru, and its ornamental tiers are worlds within worlds.

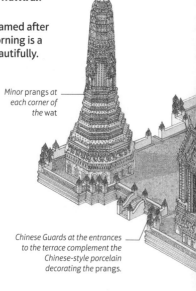

Minor prangs at each corner of the wat

Chinese Guards at the entrances to the terrace complement the Chinese-style porcelain decorating the prangs.

> **Wat Arun owes its name to the legend that, in October 1767, King Taksin arrived here at sunrise from the sacked capital.**

The central monument of Wat Arun symbolizes Hindu-Buddhist cosmology ↑

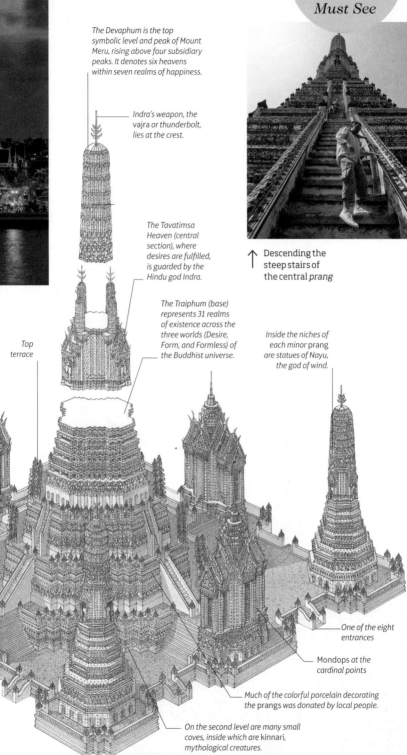

The Devaphum is the top symbolic level and peak of Mount Meru, rising above four subsidiary peaks. It denotes six heavens within seven realms of happiness.

Indra's weapon, the vajra or thunderbolt, lies at the crest.

The Tavatimsa Heaven (central section), where desires are fulfilled, is guarded by the Hindu god Indra.

The Traiphum (base) represents 31 realms of existence across the three worlds (Desire, Form, and Formless) of the Buddhist universe.

Top terrace

Inside the niches of each minor prang are statues of Nayu, the god of wind.

↑ Descending the steep stairs of the central *prang*

One of the eight entrances

Mondops at the cardinal points

Much of the colorful porcelain decorating the prangs was donated by local people.

On the second level are many small coves, inside which are kinnari, mythological creatures.

145

EXPERIENCE MORE

② Church of Santa Cruz
โบสถ์ซางตาครู้ส

📍 F7 🏠 Soi Kudi Chin
🚌 2, 8 to Pak Klong Talad then ferry or express boat to Saphan Phut pier ⏰ 6am and 7pm Sun (for Mass)

This pastel-yellow church is one of the most prominent reminders of the community of Portuguese merchants and missionaries who lived here during the mid-19th century. The church was built in the late 18th century, when Thon Buri was the capital of Thailand. It was rebuilt by Bishop Pallegoix in 1834, and again in 1913. The church is known in Thai as Wat Kuti Chin ("Chinese monastic residence"), from the Chinese influences in its architecture.

Although only a few houses of Portuguese origin remain in the muddle of alleyways surrounding the church, the Portuguese legacy can still be seen in the private Catholic shrines that are tucked away among the traditional Thai shop-houses.

③ 🖱 National Museum of Royal Barges
พิพิธภัณฑ์เรือพระที่นั่ง

📍 D4 🏠 Khlong Bangkok Noi 📞 0-2424-0004 🚌 7, 9, 19 🚤 Long-tail from Chang pier ⏰ 9am–5pm daily

Housed within a huge warehouse-like structure is a collection of Thailand's most ostentatious boats, the royal barges. Paintings of fabulous Ayutthayan barges engaged in battles and stately processions, together with archive photographs of royal barge ceremonies in Bangkok over the last 150 years, have provided some of the most splendid visions of Thailand presented to the world via postcards and brochures. Nowadays, though, the vessels are rarely seen cruising the Chao Phraya River, since they have been housed at the museum

since 1967. The barges are reproductions of some built 200 years ago by Rama I, who had copied a range of Ayutthayan originals.

In 1981 most of the royal barges underwent an expensive face-lift. They came out in all their gilded glory during the 1982 Bangkok Bicentennial celebrations, for the late King Bhumibol's 60th birthday in 1987, and for the Golden Jubilee of his reign on November 7, 1996. For such auspicious occasions more than 50 barges sail in a lengthy procession down the Chao Phraya. Most of the 2,000 oarsmen – dressed in traditional uniforms – are sea cadets, a fitting crew for boats that were once the naval fleet.

The vessel that stands in the center of the museum, *Supphanahongsa* ("golden swan"), is the most important royal barge. Made from a single piece of teak, it is over 165 ft (50 m) long and weighs 15 tons. When in action it requires a highly trained crew of 64 oarsmen. The mythical, swanlike bird Hongsa rears up from its prow. *Anantanagaraj*, a barge bearing a multiheaded *naga* and a Buddha image, is reserved for conveying monks' robes. *Narai Song Suban Rama IX* was the first barge to be built (1994) during King Bhumibol's reign. It is 145 ft (44 m) long and can carry 50 people.

← Close-up detail of exquisite royal barges kept at the National Museum of Royal Barges

Ferry plying the Chao Phraya River with Wat Rakhang in the background

4

Wat Prayun

วัดประยูร

📍F7 🏛Pratchatipok Rd
🚌6, 43 ⛴Express boat to
Saphan Phut pier 🕐7am-
4:30pm daily

The unusual artificial hill at the entrance to this temple was created on a whim of Rama III. While reading by candlelight, the king observed the inte-resting wax formation of the melting candle. He then asked one of his courtiers, Prayun Bunnag, to create a hill in the same shape. The hill is dotted with bizarre shrines, miniature *chedis*, *prangs*, grottoes, and tiny temples, but is perhaps most memorable for its ornamental pond, filled with hundreds of turtles. Devotees buy the turtles nearby and then release them into the pond. This act of setting free confined creatures (more commonly caged birds) is a way of gaining merit for future lives.

The temple *bot* features many doors and window shutters decorated with mother-of-pearl. The large *chedi* has a circular cloister surmounted by smaller *chedis*.

5

Wat Rakhang

วัดระฆัง

📍E5 🏛Soi Wat Rakhang
🚌57, 83 ⛴Chang pier
🕐Daily

Wat Rakhang was the last major temple to be constru-cted by Rama I in the early 19th century. The fine murals in the main *wihan*, painted between 1922 and 1923 by a monk named Phra Wanawatwichit, include scenes of Bangkok. Although the capital has changed since then, the Grand Palace (*p94*) just across the river from Wat Rakhang is easy to identify. The murals show the palace under an imaginary attack. There is also an elaborate depiction of a royal barge procession.

The raised wooden library (*ho trai*) of Wat Rakhang, in the west of the compound, was used as a residence by Rama I before he became king. The building's eave supports, delicately carved bookcases, and gold and black doors are period masterpieces. Inside the library are murals depicting scenes from the Ramakien (*p171*) and a portrait of Rama I.

DRINK

ThreeSixty Jazz Lounge

Rooftop lounge with floor-to-ceiling windows affording 360-degree panoramas. Live jazz.

📍H9 🏛Millennium Hilton Hotel, 123 Charoen Nakorn Rd
🌐hilton.com

The River Bar

This canopy-covered bar combines great cocktails with river views.

📍E5 🏛Peninsula Hotel, 333 Charoen Nakorn Rd
🌐peninsula.com/ bangkok

---

342 Bar

Not the swankiest, but 342 Bar has views of the Grand Palace on the opposite bank.

📍H9 🏛342 Soi Wat Rakhang 🌐baan wanglang.com

⑥ Wat Kanlayanimit
วัดกัลยาณมิตร

📍 E7 🏠 Soi Wat Kanlaya 🚌 2, 8; AC: 2 to Pak Klong Talad, then ferry ⏰ 8:30am-4:30pm daily

This dilapidated temple complex is one of the five temples built in Bangkok by Rama III (ruled 1824–51). Rama liked Chinese design, as can be seen from the statuary around the courtyard and the Chinese-style polygonal *chedi*. The immense *wihan* contains a large sitting Buddha image.

Near the *wat*, on the other side of Khlong Bangkok Yai, is Wichai Prasit Fortress, built to guard the river approach to Thon Buri when Ayutthaya was the dominant city in Thailand.

Did You Know?

At one of the Siriraj Hospital museums, the museum founder's skeleton is on display.

⑦ Museums at the Siriraj Hospital
พิพิธภัณฑ์โรงพยาบาลศิริราช

📍 D5 🏠 Arun Amarin Rd 🚌 81, 91 🚤 Phrannok and Wang Lang ⏰ 10am-5pm Mon, Wed-Sun 🌐 si.mahidol.ac.th/museums

The six medical museums located at this hospital are not for the faint hearted and provide an eye-opening museum experience. The fascinating Museum of Forensic Medicine is the best known and the one to begin with. It houses macabre objects, such as the preserved figure of Si Oui, a man who suffocated and ate seven children. Thai parents often threaten their naughty children with his ghost.

In the Congdon Museum of Anatomy are still-born Siamese twins. Such twins are so named because the famous Chan and In, who toured the world in the mid-19th century, were from Siam, as Thailand was then known. The Sood Sangvichien Prehistoric Museum contains

HIDDEN GEM
Baan Silapin

Nestled in a maze of little alleyways, Baan Silapin, or the Artist's House *(Soi 28, Wat Kuhasawan)*, is a traditional wooden canalside house full of wooden sculptures, bizarre masks, and quirky artworks. It even holds puppet shows.

artifacts and fossils from Thailand's ancient past, including the skeleton of Lampang Man, a *Homo erectus* who lived between one million and 500,000 years ago.

⑧ Wat Suwannaram
วัดสุวรรณาราม

📍 C4 🏠 Charan Sanit Wong Rd, Khlong Bangkok Noi 🚤 Hire a long-tail from any pier ⏰ Daily

Wat Suwannaram was constructed by Rama I on the foundations of a temple dating from the Ayutthaya era *(p166)*. It was renovated

→

Taksin Monument, at the center of the Wong-wian Yai traffic circle

by Rama III and finally completed in 1831. The temple complex provides a graceful example of early Rattanakosin architecture, in which a few traces of the Ayutthaya style still linger. The well-restored murals of the main *wihan*, some of the best of the early 19th century, are attributed to two renowned painters of the third reign, Luang Vichit Chetsada and Krua Khonpae.

Western perspective had not permeated Thai mural painting at the time: scenes are depicted as aerial views with figures shown at the same size whether they are in the foreground or background. On the side panels are depictions of the last 10 tales of the *jataka* (the Buddha's previous lives). On the south wall are the Buddhist cosmological kingdoms, and the entrance wall is dominated by a lively scene of the Buddha's victory over Mara. Notice the hairstyles of the third reign (1824–51):

the heads of both sexes are shaven to leave a small patch of hair at the top. Also, look for a Christian cross on a hermit's hut, evidence that missionaries were active in Thailand at the time.

 9

Taksin Monument
อนุสาวรีย์พระเจ้าตากสิน

⑨ F9 🏛 Pratchathipok Rd
🚌 **21, 40, 43, 82**

Located on the Wong-wian Yai traffic circle, this 20th-century statue commemorates King Taksin, who moved the capital to Thon Buri after the Ayutthaya were destroyed by the Burmese in 1767.

In 1950 the commission to design the monument was given to Professor Silpa Bhirasri, the Italian "father" of Thai modern art who took a Thai name and citizenship. The striking equestrian statue took three years to complete and was finally unveiled in 1954. Each year, on December 28 – the anniversary of King Taksin's coronation – many Thais come to pay homage at the statue.

 ←

The pristine, Chinese-style Wat Kanlayanimit temple complex

BEYOND THE CENTER

Many interesting sights lie outside central Bangkok. Older provincial towns include Nakhon Pathom, a large center in the Dvaravati Kingdom, and Ratchaburi, which was was sacked twice during the Ayutthaya period. Two of Thailand's most notable floating markets are also in this area. The hubs of communities in Thailand for centuries, Damnoen Saduak and Khlong Mayom are reminiscent of an age when districts were built at the sides of rivers and trade relied on these waterways. The Chatuchak Market has been operating since 1942 after the Prime Minister Plaek Phibunsongkhram ordered each province to have its own market. It ended up becoming the biggest in Thailand.

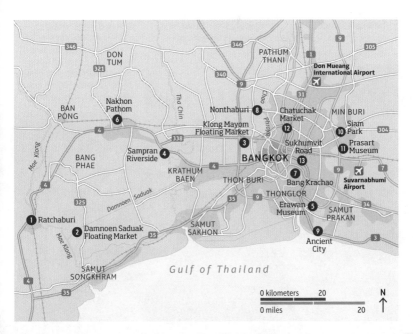

EXPERIENCE

 1

Ratchaburi

ราชบุรี

🅰 **Ratchaburi province** 🚉
🚌 **ℹ Phetchaburi; 0-3247-1005**

Originally an estuarial port at the mouth of the Klong River, Ratchaburi is now 19 miles (30 km) from the ocean. During the Ayutthaya period the town was sacked twice, in 1765 and 1767, by invading Burmese armies en route to besiege the capital city of Ayutthaya.

Nowadays, Ratchaburi is a pleasant place to stop on the way to Kanchanaburi and the Western Seaboard. Some stay

---

 PICTURE PERFECT
Khao Chon Waterfall

Near Bo Khlueng springs, in Suan Phung, Khao Chon Waterfall is one of Ratchaburi's most photogenic attractions. At 3.1 miles (5 km) long, its water cascades over nine tiers of rock.

---

overnight if visiting Damnoen Saduak Floating Market the next morning.

The town has few sights, but Wat Mahathat is worth a visit. Its *prang*, allegedly modeled on the main *prang* at Cambodia's Angkor Wat, dates from the 15th century, although the temple complex may have been founded as early as the 8th or 9th century. Inside the *prang* are traces of murals from the 15th century, as well as partially restored stucco work.

Artifacts in the **Ratchaburi National Museum** include archeological finds such as fine Khmer sculptures and stucco decorations excavated from Muang Khu Bua, a Dvaravati site south of Ratchaburi.

The countryside around the town includes the scenic lake, caves and mountains of Khao Ngu, and the Bo Khlueng hot springs, home to several pools where you can go for a dip.

Ratchaburi National Museum

⊘ 🅰 Woradej Rd 🕐 9am–4pm Wed–Sat 🔤 national museums.finearts.go.th

---

 2

Damnoen Saduak Floating Market

ตลาดน้ำดำเนินสะดวก

🅰 **1 mile (2 km) W of Damnoen Saduak, Ratchaburi province**
🚉🚌🚐 🕐 **4–11am daily**
ℹ **Phetchaburi; 0-3247-1005**

This floating market is a labyrinth of narrow *khlongs* (canals) organized almost exclusively for tourists. The small wooden boats are paddled mainly by female traders, some of whom are dressed in traditional blue farmers' shirts – *mo hom* – and conical straw hats. The fresh produce comes straight from the farm.

The floating market actually consists of three sections. The largest, Ton Khem, is on Khlong Damnoen Saduak. On the parallel *khlong* is Hia Kui, where structures anchored to the banks function as warehouses selling souvenirs. To the south, on a smaller *khlong*, is Khun Phitak, the least crowded.

The best way of getting around the three markets is by boat: trips can be taken along the *khlongs*. It is best to arrive between 7am and 9am, when it is in full swing.

→

Inside the elephant structure that houses the Erawan Museum collection

 3

Klong Mayom Floating Market

ตลาดน้ำคลองลัดมะยม

 15 30/1 Bang Ramat Rd
🚇 Krungsri Ayudhya
🕐 9:30am–4:30pm Sat, Sun, & pub hols

One of Bangkok's three famous floating markets, Khlong Lat Mayom is abuzz each weekend with boat and riverside stalls cooking up a storm – and, unlike many Thai floating markets, locals outnumber tourists here. Try *pla pao* (salt-crusted grilled fish), or *hoi tod* (mussel or oyster omelette), before heading in to explore the rest of the market. Displays of flowers, plants, and tropical fruits are particularly extensive.

 4

Sampran Riverside

สามพราน ริเวอร์ไซด์

🅿 Off Hwy 4, 20 miles (32 km) W of Bangkok
🚌 MB: 15; AC: to Nakom Pathom or Suphan Buri
🕐 8am–6pm daily
🌐 sampranriverside.com

This well-manicured garden, west of Bangkok, is a great place to walk or cycle through, take a boat ride on the river, swim, and even play tennis. The daily shows of culture, held at 1:30pm and 2:45pm, are particularly popular and showcase traditional Thai dancing, ancient sword fighting, and Thai boxing. Also within the grounds are a model Thai village, a hotel, and great restaurants.

 ←

A boat trip among the stalls at Damnoen Saduak Floating Market

 5

Erawan Museum

พิพิธภัณฑ์ช้างเอราวัณ

🅿 99/9 Moo 1, Bangmuangmai Samut Prakan province 🚌 25, 142, 365; AC: 102, 507, 511, 536
🕐 8am–5pm daily
🌐 erawan-museum.com

A monumental three-headed bronze elephant stands astride the Erawan Museum, making it visible for miles around (and also holding the title of the biggest hand-carved sculpture in the world). The 14 floors inside hold a large collection of ancient religious objects, including a number of priceless Buddha statues.

The exterior of the building's lower story is decorated with tiny pink enamel tiles in the style of Thai Benjaron ceramics. An elaborate double staircase, which takes you up inside the body of the elephant, dominates the upper levels. There is also an elevator that travels up one of the hind legs. Outside, the tranquil gardens contain ponds and fountains in a variety of styles.

EAT

Baan Rabiang Nam
Riverside restaurant serving Thai food.

🅿 Soi 23, Wat Khae Nok, Nonthaburi 🌐 baan rabiangnam.com

Ⓑ Ⓑ Ⓑ

Kung Ob Phu Kow Fai
Famous for superb seafood. Don't miss the volcano prawns.

🅿 885 Phet Kasem Rd, Nakhon Pathom
📞 0-3424-1109

Ⓑ Ⓑ Ⓑ

Suan Thip Baan Chao Phraya
Exquisite dishes served in a teak pavilion

🅿 9 Sukhaprachasan 2, Nonthaburi
🌐 suanthip.com

Ⓑ Ⓑ Ⓑ

Traders selling fruit and colorful flowers at Damnoen Saduak Floating Market

Nakhon Pathom

นครปฐม

🏛 Nakhon Pathom province
🚉🚌 ℹ Bangkok, 0-2250-5500; Kanchanaburi, 0-3451-1200

Some 42 miles (67 km) to the west of Bangkok, Nakhon Pathom was a major center of the Dvaravati Kingdom, which thrived from the 6th to the 11th centuries AD.

The highlight of the town is the Phra Pathom Chedi, on Phetkasem Highway. This huge monument, housing a large standing Buddha image, is one of the most important places of pilgrimage in Thailand. The original *stupa* (a non-Thai *chedi*) on this site is thought to have been built sometime between the 2nd century BC and the 5th century AD. It commemorated the first Buddhist missionaries

in Thailand, allegedly sent here from India in the 3rd century BC. The building fell into decay in the 11th century and was not restored until the early 19th century, when King Mongkut had the old shrine encased in a *chedi*. The spire was completed by King Chulalongkorn. The *chedi* dominates the town and, at 395 ft (120 m) in height, is the tallest Buddhist *stupa* in the world.

Southeast of the *chedi* is the **Phra Pathom Chedi National Museum**, which has a fascinating collection of locally excavated pieces from the Dvaravati period.

West of the *chedi* is the early 20th-century **Sanam Chandra Palace**. The peaceful and pretty grounds are a good place from which to view the palace's unique and unusual mix of architectural styles.

Phra Pathom Chedi National Museum
♿ 🏛 Khwa Phra Rd
📞 0-3427-0300 🕐 Wed–Sun

Sanam Chandra Palace
♿ 🏛 Off Phetkasem Hwy
📞 0-3427-0222 🕐 Tue–Sun

Did You Know?

Nakhon Pathom is well known for growing some of the best pomelo fruits in Thailand.

🔍 HIDDEN GEM
Thonglor

Bangkok's newest hipster hangout is 6 miles (10 km) from Bang Krachao and packed with voguish bars, reclaimed art spaces, and an array of restaurants, both Thai and international.

Bang Krachao

บางกระเจ้า

🏛 Phra Pradaeng district
🚢 Bang Krachao pier

Sitting on an artificial island in a bend of the Chao Phraya, Bang Krachao is a green oasis in the south of Bangkok. Far from the traffic-choked streets of the city center, Bang Krachao is a car-free area of walking trails and bike paths, covered by vegetation and bisected by bridges crossing over little canals. In stark contrast to the gleaming skyscrapers across the river, the jungle of Bang Krachao is dotted with little

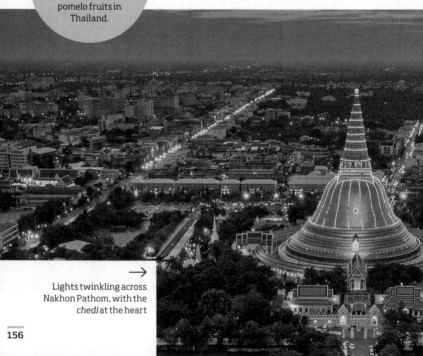

→ Lights twinkling across Nakhon Pathom, with the *chedi* at the heart

wooden houses, adding to the impression that you're in the country. Boats depart for Bang Krachao from the riverbank near Wat Khlong Toey Nok.

↑ A woman selling food from her boat on the canals of Nonthaburi

---

8

Nonthaburi
นนทบุรี

🏠 **Nonthaburi province**
🚆🚌🚤 **ℹ️ Bangkok (1672);**
Ayutthaya, 0-3524-6076

Approximately 6 miles (10 km) north of Bangkok, Nonthaburi offers a relaxing slice of provincial life. The town is best reached by riverboat from one of Bangkok's express piers. The journey takes 50 minutes and offers interesting sights, the first of which is the Royal Boat House near Wat Sam Phraya pier, where some of the royal barges are kept. Others are housed at the National Museum of Royal Barges (p146). Past the Krung Thon Bridge is a community of rice barges on the east bank, and shortly before Nonthaburi pier is Wat Khian, which is half-submerged in the river.

Nonthaburi has a pleasant, provincial atmosphere that contrasts with the chaos and pollution of the capital just down the river. The town is particularly well known for the quality of its durian fruit – reflected in the unusual decoration of the lampposts on the promenade. A round-trip boat ride from Nonthaburi along Khlong Om will take you on a slow-paced journey through durian plantations and past riverside houses. The tiny river island of Ko Kret, accessible only by boat,

is home to a community of craftsmen, who are famous for their distinctive style of pottery. Another worthwhile excursion from Nonthaburi is the river journey to Wat Chalerm Phrakiet, on the west bank of the Chao Phraya. The *wat* occupies the site of a 17th-century fortress, built by Rama III in the 19th century for his mother. A particularly striking feature is the intricate detailing, including porcelain tilework, on the doors, gables, and window frames of the *bot*. Behind is a *chedi*, added by Rama IV.

9

Ancient City
เมืองโบราณ

🏠 Sukhumvit Rd, Bangpu, Samut Prakan province 🚌 AC: 511 to the end of the line, then take the 36 mini-bus 🕐 8am–5pm daily 🌐 ancientcitygroup.com

Muang Boran, or "Ancient City," is an outdoor cultural theme park financed and created in the early 1970s by the art-loving philanthropic owner of Thailand's largest Mercedes-Benz dealership.

The peaceful grounds, shaped roughly like Thailand itself, display replicas of important monuments in Thailand as well as actual buildings and sculptures that have been restored to their former grandeur. Replicas are one third real size. All the Thai art periods are represented, including a few mythical and literary ones such as at the Garden of Phra Aphaimani, inspired by a 19th-century verse play. Some of the buildings are reconstructions of monuments destroyed centuries ago in battle.

10

Siam Park
สวนสยาม

🏠 203 Suan Siam Road, Khan Na Yao district 🚌 AC: 519 🕐 10am–6pm Mon–Fri, 9am–7pm Sat, Sun & pub hols 🌐 siamparkcity.com

Siam Park is a great place to cool off from the heat of the Thai sun. Its attractions include waterslides, a gentle whirlpool, and an artificial lake. Facilities are well maintained, and there are restaurants and lifeguards. There is also an amusement park with fairground rides and a small zoo. Bangkok families descend upon the park in numbers on the weekend.

11

Prasart Museum
พิพิธภัณฑ์ปราสาท

🏠 9 Soi Krungthepkretha 4a, Bang Kapi district 📞 0-2379-3601 🚌 MB: 10 🕐 9:30am–3pm Tue–Sun

The privately owned Prasart Museum is relatively unknown, but the journey out to this elegant museum,

INSIDER TIP
Free Map

In the very likely event that you feel lost while wandering around Chatuchak Market, pick up a free map from one of the information kiosks that are dotted around the site.

set in landscaped tropical gardens, will be worthwhile for anyone who loves Thai art. The collector, Prasart Vongsakul, started to acquire Thai antiques in 1965 when he was only 12 years old.

12

Chatuchak Market
ตลาดนัดจตุจักร

🏠 Chatuchak district 🚌 AC: 38, 502, 503, 509, 510, 512, 517, 518, 521, 523 Ⓜ Kampangphet 🚉 Mo Chit (skytrain) ℹ Bangkok (1672) 🕐 7am–6pm Sat & Sun 🌐 chatuchak.org

Thailand's biggest market is staged in a northern suburb of Bangkok, between the Northern Bus Terminal and Bangsu Railroad Station. This chaotic mass of over 15,000

↑ A stall crammed with souvenirs at the weekend Chatuchak Market

stalls occupies the space of over five football fields. It is always full of eager shoppers, many of whom spend a whole day browsing among the merchandise displays.

The huge variety of goods for sale ranges from seafood to antiques, and from Siamese fighting fish to jeans. The plant section offers a good introduction to Thai flora, while the food stalls display every ingredient of Thai cuisine. The antique and hill-tribe sections sell a good selection of artifacts and textiles, both fake and genuine, from Thailand and neighboring countries.

↑ The Prasart Museum, set in a beautiful spot on the edge of a lake

The market has been called the "wildlife supermarket of the world," due to the sale of some endangered species. Despite efforts to stop this, it is still continuing.

Aim to arrive at the market early, before the heat and the crowds become overbearing, and be aware of pickpockets.

Sukhumvit Road
ถนนสุขุมวิท

🏠 **Phra Khanong district** 🚇
🚌 AC: 38, 501, 508, 511, 513

This road begins at the eastern end of Bangkok's downtown and continues all the way to the Cambodian border in Trat province (p297). The area has numerous moderately priced hotels and restaurants, and a few attractions.

Foremost of these is the **Siam Society**, founded in the early 1900s to research and preserve Thai culture. In the grounds are two traditional teakwood northern Thai houses that comprise the country's only genuine ethnological museum. Also on the grounds is a reference library on Thai culture, open to visitors. The *Journal of the Siam Society* is one of Asia's most respected publications on art history, culture, and society.

Next to the Eastern Bus Terminal, the **Bangkok Planetarium**, with its hands-on exhibitions, may be of some interest to those people who have time to spare while waiting for a bus. Farther out toward Samut Prakan, the large King Rama IX Park, with its lush botanical gardens and area for water sports, is one of the city's most pleasant green oases.

Siam Society
🏠 131 Soi Asoke, Sukhumvit Rd, Soi 21 ⏰ Tue-Sat 🌐 siam-society.org

Bangkok Planetarium
♿ 🏠 928 Sukhumvit Rd ⏰ Tue-Sun 🌐 sciplanet.org

SHOP

Bangnamphueng Floating Market
Off the beaten tourist trail, riverside stalls at this floating market sell traditional handicrafts, street food and *gac*, an orange fruit uncommon elsewhere in Bangkok.

🏠 Bangnamphueng Rd, Bang Krachao ⏰ 8am-3pm Sat & Sun

Tao Hong Tai Ceramics
Buy hand-made Thai pottery and see master potters at work at this part showroom, part factory.

🏠 Phet Kasem Rd, Ratchaburi ⏰ 8am-5pm daily 🌐 thtceramic.com

Nonthaburi Market
This fresh produce market is a full-on sensory experience.

🏠 Pracharat Rd, Nonthaburi ⏰ 5am-9am daily

EXPERIENCE
THAILAND

The idyllic Erawan Waterfall in Kanchanaburi

SOUTH CENTRAL PLAINS

For centuries, the broad flood plain of the Chao Phraya, which bisects the South Central Plains north to south, has been Thailand's rice basket as well as its most densely populated region. The river remains a vital link between the country's cultural heartland and its present-day capital.

The old capital of Ayutthaya was one of the greatest mercantile centers in Asia during the 14th–18th centuries. Its fabulous temples and palaces, built around the confluence of the Chao Phraya, Lop Buri, and Pasak rivers, were regarded with wonder by foreigners. In 1767 it was sacked by the Burmese, and the capital was forced to move downstream to Bangkok.

Kanchanaburi, to the west of Bangkok, is another area steeped in history. During World War II the Japanese built a railroad from here to the Three Pagodas Pass near Burma, along an old Burmese invasion route. Little of the railroad was ever used, but at Kanchanaburi there are poignant reminders of this grueling episode, when thousands of Asian laborers and Allied POWs died.

Ban Pueng
Klueng

Katokkra

Lee Tong Ku

Ban Lan
Ma Nai

Settlement

Ban Jakae

Huai Kha Khaeng

Ban Bueng
Charoen

Kyondaw

Nong
Chang

Payathonzu

5

Three Pagodas Pass

5

HUAI KHA
KHAENG

333

SANGKHLA
BURI **7**

THUNG YAI
NARESUAN
WILDLIFE
SANCTUARY

Ban Rai

323

Khao Laem
Reservoir

Krasiaw
Reservoir

Dan Chang

Thong Pha Phum

CHALOEM
RATTANAKOSIN
NATIONAL PARK

Thong Pha Phum
National
Park

Huai Khamin
Falls

6

333

Si
Nakharin
Dam

Si Sawat

Nong Pru

3086

Si Nakharin
National
Park

Erawan Falls

Bo Phloi

323

Hellfire
Pass

10

ERAWAN
NATIONAL PARK

3

SAI YOK
NATIONAL
PARK

Nam
Tok

324

Pa Kar Ri

Myitta

Sai Yok

323

KANCHANABURI **8**

Dawei

PRASAT
MUANG
SING

13

Ban
Kao

Khwae Yai

M Y A N M A R

Ban Pong

Min Dat

Ban Tako Lang

Chom Bueng

8

Suan Phueng

Ratchaburi

Ban
Tha Yang

Ban Pong
Krathing Lang

4

0 kilometers   25

0 miles   25

N

Huai Kha Khaeng

Huay Thap Salao

Khwae Noi

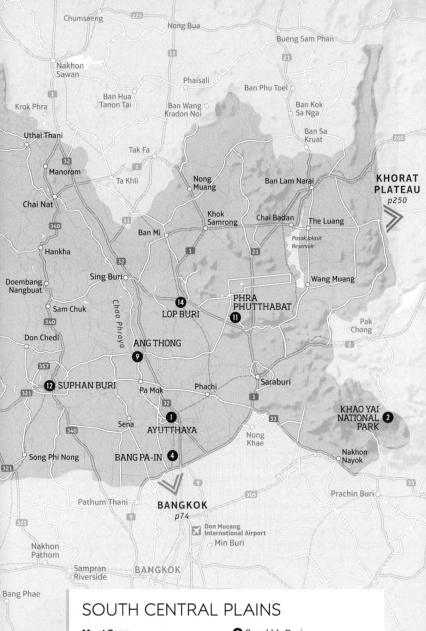

SOUTH CENTRAL PLAINS

Must Sees

1. Ayutthaya
2. Khao Yai National Park

Experience More

3. Sai Yok National Park
4. Bang Pa-in
5. Thung Yai Naresuan and Huai Kha Khaeng
6. Chaloem Rattanakosin National Park
7. Sangkhla Buri
8. Kanchanaburi
9. Ang Thong
10. Erawan National Park
11. Phra Phutthabat
12. Suphan Buri
13. Prasat Muang Sing
14. Lop Buri

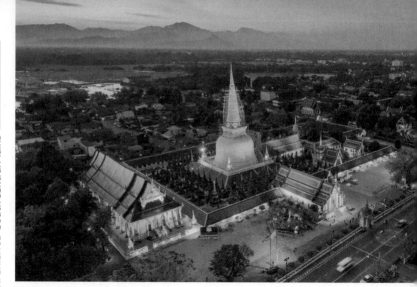

AYUTTHAYA

อยุธยา

B5 ⓐ Off Bang Ain Rd ⓑ Naresuan Rd ⓒ ⓘ 108/22 Mu 4, Tambon Phratuchai Amphoe, Ayutthaya; 0-3524-6076

Founded around 1350 by Ramathibodi I (1351–69), Ayutthaya stands at the confluence of the Chao Phraya, Lop Buri, and Pasak rivers. The town's most imposing sites are to be found on its central island. However, a short *samlor* ride by bridge over any of the rivers, which more or less encircle it, will bring you to many more sites of interest. The main part of modern Ayutthaya sprawls to the east of the island, over the Pasak River and beyond. Today, ruins stand among the modern buildings of the provincial town, which has a great selection of restaurants and hotels.

① 🖊

Wat Ratchaburana
วัดราชบูรณะ

ⓐ Cheekun Rd ⓒ Daily

Across the road from Wat Mahathat, Wat Ratchaburana was built in the 15th century by King Borommaracha II (1424–48) on the cremation site of his two brothers, who died in a power struggle. Both had wanted to succeed their father, Intharacha I (1409–24), to the throne. Robbers looted the crypt in 1957 and escaped with a cache of gold artifacts, only a few of which were recovered. A narrow staircase descends to the crypt where you can see the remains of Ayutthayan frescoes.

Timeline

1351
△ Ayutthaya is established and Ramathibodi I becomes king.

1507–15
△ Ayutthaya is at war with Lanna.

1564
△ Burmese invade the Kingdom of Ayutthaya.

1766–67
△ Burmese forces, after taking Chiang Mai, besiege Ayutthaya.

↑ Illuminated Wat Phra Mahathat, towering above Ayutthaya

style of architecture. Other buildings were subsequently added by his successor, Ramesuan (1388–95). The temple was host to a range of important royal ceremonies in the Ayutthaya era.

② Wat Phra Mahathat

วัดมหาธาตุ

🏛 Corner of Cheekun Rd and Naresuan Rd ⏰ Daily

Wat Phra Mahathat is one of the largest and most important *wat* complexes in Ayutthaya, as well as the most photographed. Though the exact date is unknown, it was almost certainly founded in the late 14th century by King Borommaracha I (1370–88), and follow the Khmer

③ Chan Kasem Palace

วังจันทรเกษม

🏛 Uthong Rd, opposite the night market ⏰ 9am-4pm Wed-Sun

In the northeast corner of the main island stands the Chan Kasem Palace or Wang Na. It was built in 1577 by the illustrious Naresuan, the son of King Maha Thammaracha (1569–90), before he became king. When Naresuan came to the throne in 1590, the palace became his permanent residence. The buildings seen today, however, date from the reign of King Mongkut (1851–68), as the palace was razed by the Burmese in 1767. It houses a large collection of Buddha images and impressive historical artifacts. Behind the Chan Kasem Palace is the Pisai Sayalak Tower, once used as an astronomical observatory by King Mongkut.

 PICTURE PERFECT
Buddha Head

Don't leave Wat Phra Mahathat without getting an iconic shot of the head of a Buddha image, which is being slowly reclaimed by the roots of a banyan tree - an interesting addition to any photo album.

④ Wat Thammikarat

วัดธรรมิกราช

🏛 Uthong Rd ⏰ Daily

At this picturesque site are the dilapidated remains of a large, early Ayutthayan, octagonal *chedi* surrounded by stucco and brick lions, or *singhas*, by far the most photographed part of the temple. Beside the *chedi* is the interesting ruin of a *wihan*, slowly succumbing to weeds and trees. A beautiful U Thong Buddha head recovered from here is now in the fantastic Chao Sam Phraya National Museum (*p168*). The temple makes for a delightful place to sit and relax while passing through Ayutthaya.

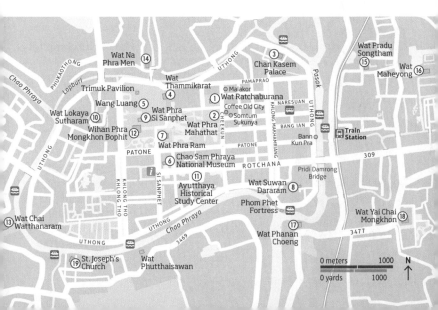

(5)
Wang Luang
วังหลวง

⬛ Uthong Rd 🕐 Daily

West of Wat Thammikarat, Wang Luang is the northern extension of the palace built by King Borommatrailokanat (1448–88) in the mid-15th century. Successive monarchs added a number of pavilions and halls. Wang Luang was razed by the Burmese in 1767. The best preserved of the former royal palace buildings is the Trimuk Pavilion, built during the reign of King Chulalongkorn (1868–1910).

(6)
Chao Sam Phraya National Museum
วังจันทรเกษม

⬛ Intersection of Rotchana Rd and Si Sanphet Rd 📞 0-3524-4570 🕐 9am–4pm Wed-Sun

Among the exhibits at this museum is a small collection of gold artifacts, including a jewel-encrusted sword, gold slippers, and jewelry. Discovered in the crypt of Wat

→

Decorative interior of Wat Suwan Dararam, with its beautiful wall paintings (inset)

Ratchaburana's central *prang* when it was looted in 1957, they are among the few items from the *wat* to have survived the sack of Ayutthaya by the Burmese. Other artifacts include bronze Buddha images and wooden door panels from *wats* around Ayutthaya.

(7)
Wat Phra Ram
วัดพระราม

⬛ Si Sanphet Rd 🕐 Daily

A chronicle relates that Wat Phra Ram was built in 1369 on the cremation site of King Ramathibodi by his son, Ramesuan. The elegant *prang* is the result of renovation by King Borommatrailokanat. The *prang* is decorated with *garudas*, *nagas*, and walking Buddha images. Wat Phra Ram is a peaceful temple to walk around and casts beautiful and photogenic reflections in the nearby lily ponds.

←

Lavish and delicately carved gold Buddha statue in Chao Sam Phraya National Museum

(8)
Wat Suwan Dararam
วัดสุวรรณดาราราม

⬛ Near Pomphet 🕐 Daily

This temple was completely destroyed by the Burmese but later rebuilt by Rama I. The *ubosot* is usually locked, but it is worth requesting the key to see the murals commissioned by Rama VII, depicting key scenes from the time of King Naresuan. Nearby is a section of the old city defenses.

(9)
Wat Phra Si Sanphet
วัดพระศรีสรรเพชญ์

⬛ Si Sanphet Rd 🕐 9am–5pm daily

Founded in the 15th century by King Borommatrailokanat as a state temple, Wat Phra Si

> Wat Phra Ram is a peaceful temple to walk around and casts beautiful photogenic reflections in the nearby lily ponds.

Sanphet was later added to by his son, Ramathibodi II, who built two *chedis* to house the relics of his father and brother. The third *chedi* was built by Borommaracha IV to house the remains of Ramathibodi II. The site was extended by subsequent rulers until the Burmese sack of 1767. The temple was partially renovated in the 20th century, and many of its treasures are now kept in museums.

---

⑩

Wat Lokaya Sutharam
วัดโลกยสุธาราม

⌂ W of main island ⏱ Daily

This *wat* is the site of a 140-ft (42-m) long, whitewashed reclining Buddha image. Large Buddha images such as this do not always depict the Buddha's death, but sometimes, as in this instance, an occasion when the Buddha grew 100 times in size to confront the demon Rahu. The image now lies in the open air, the original *wihan*, having been destroyed by the Burmese; 24 octagonal pillars are all that remain of this *wihan*. The *wat* also houses the ruins of a *bot* and *chedis*.

⑪

Ayutthaya Historical Study Center
ศูนย์ศึกษาประวัติศาสตร์อยุธยา

⌂ Rotchana Rd ☎ 0-3524-5123 ⏱ 9am–5pm daily

This study center houses interesting audiovisual displays depicting Ayutthaya's history and trading relations. Another part of the study center stands in what was the Japanese quarter at the time when Ayutthaya was at the height of its power.

---

⑫

Wihan Phra Mongkhon Bophit
วิหารพระมงคลบพิตร

⌂ Si Sanphet Rd ⏱ Daily

This *wat* contains one of Thailand's largest bronze Buddha images. Now gilded, it probably dates from the late 15th century, though it has undergone numerous restorations. In 1767 Burmese invaders destoyed much of the *wihan* and damaged the image's head and right hand. The image was left open to the sky until the 1950s, when the *wihan* was rebuilt.

EAT

Malakor
Classic Thai food served either in the lovely wooden dining room, or outside in view of the illuminated ruins of Wat Ratchaburana, which sit diagonally across the road.

⌂ Cheekun Rd ☎ 0-9177-96475

Ⓑ Ⓑ Ⓑ

Coffee Old City
Occupying a prime spot directly opposite Wat Phra Mahathat, this cafe serves good coffee, pastries, and sandwiches, as well as Thai curries, and stir-fries. Western and Thai breakfasts are also on offer.

⌂ Cheekun Rd ☎ 0-8988-99092

Ⓑ Ⓑ Ⓑ

Somtum Sukunya
Another great option close to Wat Phra Mahathat, serving classic Thai dishes. It specializes in zingy *som tam* (papaya salad).

⌂ 11/7 Ho Rattanachai Rd ☎ 0-8916-37342

Ⓑ Ⓑ Ⓑ

Bann Kun Pra
One of Ayutthaya's most popular guesthouses also has a riverside restaurant that serves good Thai food, the specialty being seafood.

⌂ 48 U Thong Rd ☎ 0-3524-1978

Ⓑ Ⓑ Ⓑ

↑ The sun setting behind the iconic Wat Chai Watthanaram

completely disappeared. Its doors are from the early 19th century. In the adjacent *bot* is a gilded Buddha image, probably from the reign of King Prasat Thong.

---

⑮ Wat Pradu Songtham
วัดประดู่ทรงธรรม

 N of railroad station, E of main island **Daily**

This active temple features a monks' quarter, bell tower, and sermon hall. Inside the *wihan* of Wat Pradu Songtham are the remains of interesting murals dating from the early Rattanakosin period (1782– 1932). These recount the life of the Buddha and also show images of daily life, including a performance of the Ramakien at a fair. Outside is a bell tower topped by a small *chedi* from the late Ayutthaya period.

---

⑯ Wat Maheyong
วัดมเหยงค์

 E of main island **Daily**

The partially reconstructed ruins of Wat Maheyong date from the reign of King Borommaracha II (1424–48). The principal, bell-shaped *chedi* shows a clear stylistic link with earlier Sukhothai *chedis*, while all around the rectangular base are the remnants of stucco elephants. Other *chedis* at this site also show Sukhothai influence.

> GREAT VIEW
> **Ayutthaya Sunsets**
>
> One of the most spectacular sights in Ayutthaya is watching the sun set over Wat Chai Watthanaram from the western bank of the Chao Phraya, southwest of the main island.

⑬
Wat Chai Watthanaram
วัดไชยพัฒนาราม

W bank of Chao Phraya River, SW of main island **Daily**

This *wat*, located near St. Joseph's Church, was built by King Prasat Thong (1629–56) in 1630. It is one of Ayutthaya's most impressive temples and follows the architecture of the Khmer mountain temples of Angkor. The tall central *prang* represents Mount Meru, a mountain that is considered to be the center of the universe in Hindu and Buddhist cosmology. This *prang* is surrounded by eight smaller ones, decorated with stucco reliefs depicting images such as the Buddha preaching to his mother in the Tavatimsa Heaven.

⑭
Wat Na Phra Men
วัดหน้าพระเมรุ

Opp Royal Palace, nr Muang Canal **0-3525-2163** **Daily**

Across a bridge to the north of the main island is Wat Na Phra Men, one of the most beautiful of Ayutthaya's monasteries, and one of the few to survive the Burmese sacking of the city in 1767. Thought to date from the reign of Intharacha II (1488–91), it was restored during the reign of King Borommakot (1733–58), and again in the mid-19th century. In the *wihan* is a Dvaravati seated Buddha image, Phra Kanthararat, that was moved here from Nakhon Pathom *(p156)* in the mid-16th century. The murals covering the *wihan* walls have now almost

⑰

Wat Phanan Choeng
วัดพนัญเชิง

🏠 S of main island 🕐 Daily

Located on the banks of the Pasak River, this *wat* has been renovated over the years and houses the large 62-ft (19-m) tall, 14th-century, seated image of Phra Chao Phanan Choeng. It is the key reason for visiting the site and is even classed as the most beautiful image of the Buddha in Thailand. The *wihan* was built in the mid-19th century.

---

⑱

Wat Yai Chai Mongkhon
วัดใหญ่ไชยมงคล

🏠 E of main island 🕐 Daily

The *chedi* here, one of the largest in Ayutthaya, was built by King Naresuan (1590–1605) to celebrate his victory over the Burmese at Nong Sarai in 1593. Flanking steps up to the *chedi* are two *mondops* housing seated Buddha images. On the northeast side of the *wat* is a ruined *wihan* containing a reclining Buddha.

THE RAMAKIEN

The old capital of Ayutthaya was named for Ayodhya, a fictional kingdom in the Ramakien, the Thai version of the Indian Ramayana and an allegory of the triumph of good over evil. The hero, Rama, is a paragon of virtue - the ideal king. The villain, the demon king Tosakan, is a tragic character of great dignity. This epic tale is thought to have become established after the Thais occupied Angkor in the 15th century. It has been an inspiration for painting and classical drama. All the Chakri kings have taken Rama as one of their names. While the Thai versions were written down during the Ayutthaya Kingdom *(p70)*, most editions were unfortunately lost in the Burmese invasion.

---

⑲

St. Joseph's Church
โบสถ์เซนต์ยอแซฟ

🏠 SW of main island on the Chao Phraya River 🕐 Daily

St. Joseph's Church, overlooking the Chao Phraya River, has been the site of Catholic worship for over 300 years. The original 17th-century structure was destroyed by the Burmese in 1767. The present attractive church was built during the 19th century.

A ten-minute walk east from St. Joseph's is **Wat Phutthaisawan**, also located on the riverbank. It has a restored 14th-century *prang* surrounded by a cloister filled with a range of impressive Buddha images.

Wat Phutthaisawan
 🏠 S of main island 🕐 Daily

Row of Buddha statues in orange robes at Wat Yai Chai Mongkhon ↑

2 ⊕ ⊕ ⊕

KHAO YAI NATIONAL PARK

อุทยานแห่งชาติเขาใหญ่

🅰 C4 🚪 Khorat, Nakhon Nayok, Saraburi & Prachin Buri provinces 🚉 Pak Chong, then bus or *songthaew* 🚫 In bad weather ℹ️ Off Hwy 1, NE of Bangkok; 08-6092-6529

Thailand's best place for wildlife and outdoor adventures is also the oldest national park in the country. With photographic gems to uncover, cascading waterfalls, and a host of trekking opportunities, Khao Yai is an essential part of any visit to Thailand.

PICTURE PERFECT
Haeo Narok Waterfall

Lush surroundings and 592 ft (150 m) of cascading water make Khao Yai's largest waterfall an idyllic shot for any photo album.

Established in 1962, Khao Yai was then Thailand's sole national park. Today there are well over 100, but this one remains popular. Set over 770 sq miles (2,000 sq km), the park has a wide variety of habitats, including submontane evergreen forests and grasslands. There are also several mountains of around 3,300 ft (1,000 m), including Khao Khieo. The abundant wildlife includes many endangered mammals such as elephants, gibbons, tigers, and Malaysian sun bears, as well as more than 300 bird species. It's advisable to hire a guide for trips to more remote parts. The surrounding area offers luxurious resorts, golf courses, and even vineyards.

↑ The serene Haeo Suwat waterfall surrounded by abundant foliage

← A group of elephants marching through the park

Lam Takhong River

Rainfall in Khao Yai National Park is usually in excess of 120 inches (3,000 mm) per year. Streams swollen by the rains flow off forested slopes forming rivers, among them the Lam Takhong River. Wildlife living around this river includes kingfishers, cormorants, elephants, and macaques.

Haeo Suwat Waterfall

Located along the upper reaches of the Lam Takhong River, this waterfall is one of many dotted around Khao Yai. From March through May each year many varieties of orchids can be seen flowering around the waterfall. Relaxing by the falls is a splendid way to spend an afternoon in the park.

↑ The impressive Haeo Narok waterfall, one of many in the park, tumbling down the face of a three-tiered cliff

STAY

Muthi Maya Khao Yai
One of the finest of a swath of hotels on Khao Yai's northern fringes, the lovely villas here overlook the forest with private pools.

⌂ 1/3 Moo 6, Thanarat Rd, Moo Si
🌐 kirimaya.com

Ⓑ Ⓑ Ⓑ

Khao Yai Cottage
Quaint rooms and charming surroundings with a close proximity to everything the park has to offer.

⌂ 888 Thanarat Rd, Tambon Mu Si
📞 0-8191-96771

Ⓑ Ⓑ Ⓑ

EXPLORING THE PARK

Trekking Paradise

Khao Yai is one of the best places in Thailand for trekking, with hundreds of square miles of jungles and mountains to explore and tumbling waterfalls to cool off in. There are five main trekking trails in Khao Yai which it's possible to explore without a guide. Trail 1, the shortest, connects the visitor center with the stunning Kong Kaew waterfall, while Trail 2 leads you to the famous Haeo Suwat and Pha Kluay Mai falls. At the end of Trail 4 is a viewpoint over the Sai Sorn Reservoir, while trails 3 and 5 finish up at the Nong Phak Chi observation tower, which is one of the best places in the park – and, by extension, anywhere in Thailand – to spot wildlife. There is a sixth trail, at 5 miles (8 km) long, which finishes at the Haeo Suwat waterfall, but jungle trekking guides are required.

It's a good idea to wear proper hiking boots and trousers when exploring the park – especially in the rainy season – as leeches have been known to be a problem. You can also buy leech socks in the visitor center.

Photography Heaven

With its abundant splendid waterfalls, evergreen forests, and numerous watchtowers from which to take social media-worthy shots, Khao Yai is the perfect spot for budding photographers. The

> **The submontane evergreen forest here contains deciduous trees such as chestnuts.**

---

3 million

The estimated number of wrinkled-lipped bats who live in Khao Luk Chang Bat Cave.

---

submontane evergreen forest here contains deciduous trees such as chestnuts, which make for fantastic close-up photographs. It grows at Khao Yai's highest altitudes, 3,300 ft (1,000 m) to 4,450 ft (1,351 m) above sea level. Khao Yai's two watchtowers offer great views of the landscape and the forest scenery, and are the best chances of getting atmospheric, panoramic shots – especially at sunset, outside of the rainy season.

Nong Phak Chi Watchtower, 1.5 miles (2.5 km) north of the visitor center, is easily accessible from the main road. It's popular for good reason: aside from offering

360-degree views, it's the best option for bird and wildlife photography.

Wildlife Encounters

Wildlife watching in Khao Yai is also among the best in Thailand, with some of the country's rarest creatures living across the park's diverse range of habitats.

This includes a population of wild elephants and even one of the country's largest hornbill populations, among hundreds of bird, reptile, and mammal species. While you can see plants and animals on a self-guided trek, the best way to spot wildlife is to join a tour led by an expert. Day trips are available, while night safaris give you increased chances of seeing elephants, gibbons, and monkeys, among other creatures.

The Khao Luk Chang Bat Cave is another impressive wildlife attraction. Some 2.7 miles (4.5 km) north of the park, you can see a long cloud of bats flying out from the cave during sunset.

→

Getting the perfect shot of the park during the spectacular sunrise

WILDLIFE IN THE PARK

Endangered Species
Khao Yai is home to about 20 of the 500 or so tigers left in Thailand. These noble animals can be found surprisingly close to the park's headquarters.

White-Handed Gibbon
These beautiful, tailless apes use their long arms to move swiftly and agilely through the trees.

Siamese Fireback Pheasant
Thailand's national bird, this pheasant spends its days on the ground where it feeds on small insects, seeds, and fruit. It roosts in the trees at night.

Sambar Deer
The largest species of deer in Thailand, Sambar are mostly forest dwellers. Though hunted by tigers and leopards, humans are its main predator. It is now common only in well-protected conservation areas.

Earthball Fungus
This parasitic fungus is found in humid evergreen forests all over Southeast Asia. Unlike many parasites, its presence encourages the growth of its host.

1 A rare Indochinese tiger dwelling in the park.

2 A white-handed gibbon relaxing in the trees.

3 Handsome pair of Siamese fireback pheasants.

4 Sambar deer in the forest.

5 An earthball fungus.

EXPERIENCE MORE

3

Sai Yok National Park
อุทยานแห่งชาติไทรโยค

A4 **Kanchanaburi province Park HQ off Hwy 323, 62 miles (100 km) NW of Kanchanaburi** **From Kanchanaburi** **Kanachanaburi; 0-3451-1200**

Sai Yok was the site of a large Japanese army barracks and POW labor camp during World War II. The stunning 190-sq mile (500-sq km) Sai Yok National Park was established in 1980 and today is renowned for its tranquil river scenery and the impressive Sai Yok Yai waterfall, which tumbles into the Khwae Noi River near to

Did You Know?

The caves of Sai Yok National Park are home to the world's smallest mammal, Kitti's hog-nosed bat.

the park headquarters. There are some well-maintained hiking trails in the park and accommodations are available in park bungalows or on pleasant houseboats. Boats can be chartered – at some expense – to some nearby caves. One of the more recommended is Dao Daung Cave, accessible by long-tail boat along the river and hiking.

4

Bang Pa-in
บางปะอิน

B5 **Phra Nakhon Si Ayutthaya province** **Ayutthaya; 0-3524-6076** **palaces.thai.net**

Visitors to Bang Pa-in stop off, for the most part, just to visit **Bang Pa-in Palace**, whose exuberant 19th-century buildings stand in stark contrast to those of nearby Ayutthaya. It is thought that a royal palace was first built at Bang Pa-in by King Prasat Thong (1629–56), to mark the birth of his son and successor, King Narai. With the defeat of

Ayutthaya by the Burmese in 1767 the site fell into ruin; the present buildings date from the reigns of Mongkut (1851–68) and Chulalongkorn (1868–1910).

The beautiful pavilion, Phra Thinang Aisawan Thipha-at (meaning "divine seat of personal freedom"), at the center of an ornamental lake, was built for Chulalongkorn in 1876, together with the Phra Thinang Warophat Phiman ("excellent and shining abode"), to the left. Behind are the terra-cotta- and white-striped lookout tower, Ho Withun Thasana, built by Chulalongkorn in 1881, and the Chinese-style mansion, Phra Thinang Wehat Chamrun, built as a gift for him by an association of Chinese merchants in 1889. Visitors can cross a canal by cable car to the impressive structure of Wat Niwet Tham Prawat, which was built by Chulalongkorn in 1877–8.

Bang Pa-in Palace
 Bang Pa-in district **0-3526-1044** **8am–5pm daily**

Boat filled with tourists visiting the Sai Yok Yai waterfall ↑

5 Thung Yai Naresuan and Huai Kha Khaeng
ทุ่งใหญ่นเรศวรและเขตรักษาพันธุ์สัตว์ป่าห้วยขาแข้ง

A/B4 **Kanchanaburi, Tak and Uthai Thani provinces** **From Kanchanaburi** **Kanchanaburi; www. thenationalparks.com/huai-kha-khaeng-wildlife-sanctuary**

These two huge, adjacent wildlife sanctuaries, covering 2,400 sq miles (6,220 sq km) and surrounded by a further 2,320 sq miles (6,000 sq km) of protected forest, form one of the most important and impressive conservation areas in Southeast Asia. They are listed jointly as a UNESCO World Heritage Site and are home to some of Thailand's largest remaining wild elephant herds, as well as several endangered carnivores, such as tigers, clouded leopards, and Malaysian sun bears. The enormous gaur, a species of wild cattle, and the country's last wild buffalo herds also live within the sanctuary. Rare species of gibbon can also be seen, as well as green bee eaters.

→ Green bee eater, native to Huai Kha Khaeng wildlife sanctuary

6 Chaloem Rattanakosin National Park
อุทยานแห่งชาติเฉลิมรัตนโกสินทร์

B4 **From Kanchanaburi to Nong Preu, then *songthaew*** **Daily** **Off Hwy 3086, 60 miles (97 km) NE of Kanchanaburi; 0-3451-1200**

This beautiful and isolated national park is one of Thailand's smallest, at just 23 sq miles (59 sq km). The main trail runs beside a stream that passes through a cavern, Tham Than Lot Noi, to emerge in a thickly forested, steep-sided ravine. The path continues for 8,200 ft (2,500 m), climbing steeply beside the Trai Trung falls to Tham Than Lot Yai, a limestone sinkhole, and a small Buddhist shrine. On weekday mornings you may find that you are the only visitor in this delightful spot.

---

7 Sangkhla Buri
สังขละบุรี

A4 **Kanchanaburi province** **From Kanchanaburi** **Kanchanaburi; 0-3451-1200**

In the center of Sangkhla Buri is a market where, among other things, you can buy curries and samosas, as well as books written in the Mon language. However, the main attraction of this isolated trading town, which is populated by Mon and Karen tribespeople (*p64*) as well as Thais, is its serene lakeside location. The lake, which you can explore by rowing boat, is actually a large reservoir,

formed by the damming of the Khwae Noi River. Sometimes, late in the dry season, drowned remains of old villages and forests can be seen sticking up out of the calm surface of the lake's waters.

The north shore of the lake is overlooked by the unusual *chedi* of Wat Wangwiwekaram. It replaced an older Buddhist temple that is now partially submerged by the reservoir, making for an eerily haunting sight; in the dry season the whole thing is above water and accessible. You can reach the *wat* on foot by crossing a wooden bridge that spans the wide, shallow inlet of the lake. A large settlement, consisting mainly of Mon tribespeople, has grown up in close proximity to the *wat*. An interesting daily market is held here in the early morning.

TOP 3 FOODS TO TRY AT SANGKHLA BURI MARKET

Roti ong
A Mon dish of roti stuffed with spiced chickpeas.

Yam Mon
The Burmese answer to a Thai noodle salad.

Mon curries
Rich, spicy, and often made with mutton or beef.

EAT

On's Thai Issan

The chef and owner serves up delicious traditional Thai food with a twist: everything is vegetarian or vegan. Cookery classes are also available.

 B5 🏠 268/1 Mae Nam Kwai Rd, Kanchanaburi 🌐 onsthaiissan.com

Ⓑ Ⓑ Ⓑ

Maad Mee

The superb Thai food at this restaurant has made it popular with locals and visitors alike. Try the *gaeng khua* with pandan-leaf-wrapped meatballs.

 B4 🏠 8/18 Phra Sri Mahosote Rd, Lop Buri 📞 0-3641-2883

Ⓑ Ⓑ Ⓑ

Kui Mong

Homey, no-frills restaurant packed with locals every lunchtime. The signature jumbo river shrimp are absolutely enormous.

 B4 🏠 328 Khokram, Suphan Buri 📞 0-3558-7256

Ⓑ Ⓑ Ⓑ

Blue Rice Restaurant by Apple & Noi

Friendly restaurant with an attached guesthouse. Try the signature dish – massaman curry – or one of their other excellent set-dinner options.

 B5 🏠 153/4 Sutjai Bridge, Thamakham, Mahardthai Rd, Kanchanaburi 📞 0-3451-2017

Ⓑ Ⓑ Ⓑ

Modern-day locomotive traveling along the Burma-Siam Railroad ↑

8

Kanchanaburi

กาญจนบุรี

🅰 B5 🏠 Kanchanaburi province 🚌 🚆 ℹ️ Saeng Chuto Rd, Kanchanaburi; 0-3451-1200

Though surrounded by many limestone hills and expanses of sugarcane, Kanchanaburi is best known for the infamous Burma-Siam, or Thai-Burma, Railroad. Constructed in 1942–3, it crosses over the Khwae Yai River just to the north of Kanchanaburi town center. At the small station beside the bridge are a number of steam locomotives dating from the period. A memorial to those who died during the war was erected by the Japanese administration in 1944. Today, 47 miles (77 km) of the railroad remain, and the trip along it from Kanchanaburi to Nam Tok is one of the most interesting in Thailand. The **Thailand-Burma Railroad Center** charts the history of this railroad. The building of it tragically cost the lives of more than 100,000 Asian laborers and 12,000 Allied prisoners of war.

The **Kanchanaburi War Cemetery** contains the graves of almost 7,000 mostly British and Australian prisoners and is one of two war cemeteries in the town. The smaller of the two cemeteries, **Chong Kai Cemetery**, contains 1,740 graves and lies on the north bank of the Khwae Noi River, a short ferry ride from the center of town. Nearby is Wat Tham Khao Pun, overlooking the river and the Burma-Siam Railroad, which at this point heads south toward Ban Kao and Prasat Muang Sing. In the grounds of the *wat* complex a network of narrow passages leads through a cave system filled with Buddha images.

In the **JEATH War Museum**, housed in Wat Chai Chumphon, visitors can see three replicas of the bamboo huts used to house prisoners of war in the camps that sprang up along the Burma-Siam Railroad during the war. The huts display paintings, sketches, and photographs of life in the

> Though surrounded by limestone hills and expanses of sugarcane, Kanchanaburi is best known for the infamous Burma-Siam Railroad.

victims' relatives visit each year. Accommodations here include riverside raft houses.

South of Kanchanaburi, on a hill overlooking the Mae Klong Dam, sit two temples. Wat Tham Sua features a huge golden Buddha statue, while Wat Tham Khao Noi has a beautiful Chinese pagoda.

Thailand-Burma Railroad Center
- 🏛 73 Jaokunneu Rd
- 🕐 9am–5pm daily
- 🌐 tbrconline.com

Kanchanaburi War Cemetery
- 🏛 Saeng Chuto Rd 🕐 8am–5pm daily

Chong Kai Cemetery
- 🏛 Ban Kao Rd 🕐 Daily

JEATH War Museum
- 🏛 Wisuttharangsi Rd
- 📞 0-3451-1263 🕐 8:30am–4:30pm daily

camps and along the railroad line. JEATH is an acronym for Japan, England, Australia and America, Thailand, and Holland, some of the countries whose nationals worked on the railroad. Many survivors and

Ang Thong
อ่างทอง

- 🅰B4 🏛 Ang Thong province
- 🚌 ℹ Ayutthaya; 0-3524-6077

This small town is a useful base from which travelers who are interested in Thai images of the Buddha can visit three little known but rewarding sites nearby. To the south of Ang Thong, Wat Pa Mok houses a reclining Buddha image from the 15th century. Wat Khun In Pramun is to the northwest. In its grounds is a huge reclining Buddha image, about 165 ft (50 m) long, dating from the Ayutthaya period.

At Wat Chaiyo Wora Wihan, to the north of Ang Thong, a *wihan* houses a third enormous, seated image of the Buddha from the Rattanakosin period, called the Phra Maha Phuttha Phim.

THE BRIDGE OVER THE KHWAE YAI RIVER AND THE BURMA-SIAM RAILROAD

The first railroad bridge over the Khwae Yai River, near Kanchanaburi, was built of wood, using Allied and Asian slave labor. In 1943 it was abandoned for an iron bridge, which was repeatedly bombed by the US Army Air Force from late 1944. It was put out of commission in 1945. The bridge was part of an immense project, the 255-mile (414-km) Burma-Siam Railroad, conceived by the Japanese after the Allies blockaded sea routes in 1942. Built under appalling conditions, it operated for only two years. Around 60,000 Allied prisoners of war and 300,000 Asian laborers were forced to work 18-hour shifts on its construction, with many losing their lives to malaria and maltreatment. The present-day bridge was rebuilt as part of Japanese war reparations.

Did You Know?

The Erawan Falls are named after, and said to resemble, the three-headed elephant from Hindu mythology.

10 Erawan National Park

อุทยานแห่งชาติเอราวัณ

B5 Kanchanaburi province; Park HQ off Hwy 3199, 40 miles (65 km) NW of Kanchanaburi From Kanchanaburi Kanchanaburi; 0-3451-1200

In the lush forest of the Erawan National Park, the nearest park to Kanchanaburi and covering 210 sq miles (550 sq km), are the beautiful Erawan Falls, which drop through a series of cascades and shady rock pools. While park rangers still find occasional tiger prints, visitors are more likely to see pig-tailed and rhesus macaques, and some 80 bird species. The Visitors' Center offers a slide show about the park, and there is a pleasant, 1-mile (2-km) hiking trail which climbs up beside the falls. This is one of Thailand's most popular national parks, and it can get very crowded. The large limestone cavern of Tham Wang Badan, situated on the west side of the park, contains many colorful stalactites and stalagmites.

11 Phra Phutthabat

พระพุทธบาท

B4 Saraburi province From Saraburi, then *samlor* 7am-6pm daily Ayutthaya; 0-3524-6077

In the early 17th century, King Song Tham of Ayutthaya sent a group of monks to Sri Lanka to pay homage to a Footprint of the Buddha. (According to legend, these Footprints show where the Lord Buddha walked upon the Earth.) The monks were surprised to be told by the Sri Lankans that, according to scriptures, there was a Footprint in Thailand. Song Tham, on hearing this, ordered a search for the Footprint. It was found by a hunter pursuing a wounded deer – the animal vanished into the undergrowth only to re-emerge healed. On closer inspection, the hunter found a water-filled pool shaped like a footprint. He drank from it and was miraculously cured of a skin disease. The king, on learning of this, had a temple built on the site, which subsequently became one of the most sacred places of worship in Thailand.

Today, the 5-ft (1.5-m) long Footprint, Phra Phutthabat, lies in an ornate *mondop*, restored in the late 18th century after the earlier buildings were destroyed by the Burmese in 1765. A museum here displays offerings by pilgrims, who flock to the sight each year. Phra Phutthabat is also the name of the small town here.

↑ The central sanctuary of the Prasat Muang Sing ruins

12 Suphan Buri

สุพรรณบุรี

B4 Suphan Buri province Suphan Buri, 0-3553-6030; or Ayutthaya, 0-3524-6077

Suphan Buri found fame with the rise of Ayutthaya in the 14th century. Near the center of town is the beautiful *prang* of Wat Phra Si Rattana Mahathat, restored in the Ayutthaya

← The generous flow and emerald pool of the Erawan Falls

Banhan-Jamsai Tower

The tallest observation tower in Thailand (not including the viewing platforms of Bangkok's monster skyscrapers) is the Banhan-Jamsai Tower, which looms 404 ft (123 m) above Suphan Buri.

period and again in the 20th century. At Wat Pa Lelai, on the edge of Suphan Buri, is a Buddha image from the Dvaravati period. To the east is San Chao Pho Lak Muang, a Chinese shrine. Wat Phra Rup, on the other side of the Suphan Buri River, houses a reclining Buddha image and a carved wooden Footprint of the Buddha.

Near the center of town is the Dragon Descendants Museum, built to celebrate 5,000 years of Chinese history. The building itself takes the form of a stunning fiberglass dragon. Inside, exhibits cover aspects of Chinese culture, from creation myths to the Cultural Revolution.

13

Prasat Muang Sing
ปราสาทเมืองสิงห์

B5 **Off Hwy 323, 27 miles (43 km) W of Kanchanaburi, Kanchanaburi province** **From Kanchanaburi to Tha Kilen, then** *songthaew* **Daily** **Kanchanaburi; 0-3451-1200**

The ruins of Muang Sing, beside the Khwae Noi River, date from around the 13th century and mark the westernmost point of expansion of the Khmer Empire. Earthen ramparts surround an inner wall of laterite that forms a rough rectangle. Near the center of this are the ruins of the Buddhist sanctuary, Prasat Muang Sing. Like most Khmer temples it faces east, in alignment with the city of Angkor.

Although the Muang Sing temple complex looks Khmer, some art historians believe it was actually built by artisans in imitation of the occupying Khmers – the sanctuary, for example, lacks the stylistic details that are normally associated with Khmer sites. It was probably built after the reign of Jayavarman VII (1181–1220) as the Khmer Empire began to decline.

14

Lop Buri
ลพบุรี

B4 **Na Phra Kan Rd** **Phra Narai Maharat Rd** **City Hall, Narai Maharaja Rd, Amphoe Mueang; 0-3677-0096-7**

The ancient city of Lop Buri is famous for its Khmer temples, but also for the macaques who have made it their home. With no fear of humans, they focus on stealing people's food and bags, particularly those of tourists at Prang Sam Yot.

> **The ruins of Muang Sing, beside the Khwae Noi River, date from around the 13th century and mark the westernmost point of expansion of the Khmer Empire.**

A SHORT WALK
LOP BURI

Distance 1.2 miles (2 km) **Time** 20 minutes
Nearest station Na Phra Kan Rd

One of Thailand's oldest cities, Lop Buri (p181) was known as Lavo in the Dvaravati period (p69) and subsequently became an important outpost of the Khmer Empire (p69). The Khmer *prang* on the grounds of Wat Phra Si Rattana Mahathat, and those of Prang Sam Yot, date from this time. Lop Buri reached its political peak during the 17th century, when the Ayutthayan King Narai (1656–88) preferred to stay at Lop Buri rather than his official palace at Ayutthaya. Today, the thriving modern town of Lop Buri, also known as "monkey town," lies to the east of the old city. You can expect to meet macaques on your stroll around the city, but keep an eye on any valuables that they may be keen to steal.

0 meters   75
0 yards   75

N

The wihan at **Wat Sao Thong Thong** *was altered by King Narai so it could be used as a Christian chapel.*

The market sells vegetables and other foodstuffs.

WICHAYEN

PHARA RAM

RUE DE FRANCE

START

RATCHADAMNOEN

SORASAK

Abandoned after King Narai's death, parts of **King Narai's Palace**, *including the Chanthara Phisan Hall, were later restored by King Mongkut (p71).*

PRATUCHAI RD

Somdej Phra Narai National Museum *is housed in the partially restored, colonial-style Phiman Mongkut Hall of King Narai's Palace. It has a superb collection of Lop Buri Buddha images, and collections of art.*

←
An imposing stucco Buddha at Wat Phra Si Rattana Mahathat

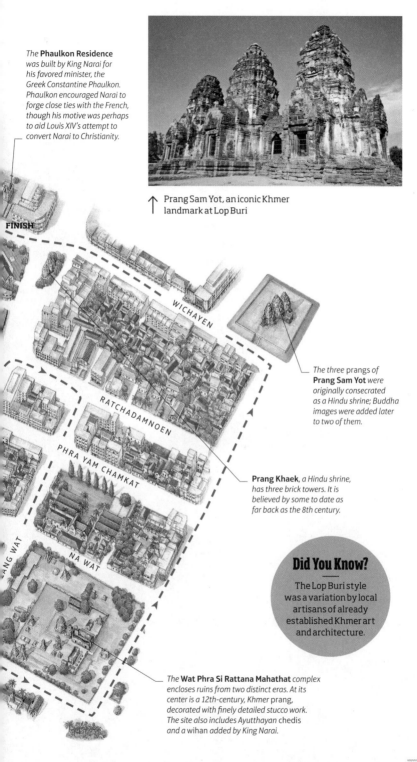

The **Phaulkon Residence** *was built by King Narai for his favored minister, the Greek Constantine Phaulkon. Phaulkon encouraged Narai to forge close ties with the French, though his motive was perhaps to aid Louis XIV's attempt to convert Narai to Christianity.*

FINISH

↑ Prang Sam Yot, an iconic Khmer landmark at Lop Buri

WICHAYEN

RATCHADAMNOEN

PHRA YAM CHAMKAT

NA WAT

ANG WAT

The three prangs of **Prang Sam Yot** *were originally consecrated as a Hindu shrine; Buddha images were added later to two of them.*

Prang Khaek, *a Hindu shrine, has three brick towers. It is believed by some to date as far back as the 8th century.*

Did You Know?

The Lop Buri style was a variation by local artisans of already established Khmer art and architecture.

The **Wat Phra Si Rattana Mahathat** *complex encloses ruins from two distinct eras. At its center is a 12th-century, Khmer prang, decorated with finely detailed stucco work. The site also includes Ayutthayan chedis and a wihan added by King Narai.*

NORTH CENTRAL PLAINS

The landscape here has for centuries been typified by gentle, rolling hills and rice farms, and its major attractions are ancient city ruins, relics of an illustrious past when competing princedoms and city-states fought each other for land and power.

In the 13th century, during the reign of King Ramkamhaeng *(p70)*, one city, Sukhothai, came to dominate the region to such an extent that its influence was felt far beyond Thailand's present borders. But its power was short-lived, and by the mid-14th century the region was once more a collection of fiefdoms. The capital was moved from Sukhothai to Phitsanulok, until the Kingdom of Ayutthaya became the most powerful, delegating Phitsanulok to the "second capital."

The hillier areas, in the west and northeast of the region, are the setting for a number of national parks and wildlife sanctuaries. These have provided a much needed refuge for endangered plant and animal species *(p46)* whose habitats are threatened by the impact of illegal logging and the widespread loss of land to agriculture.

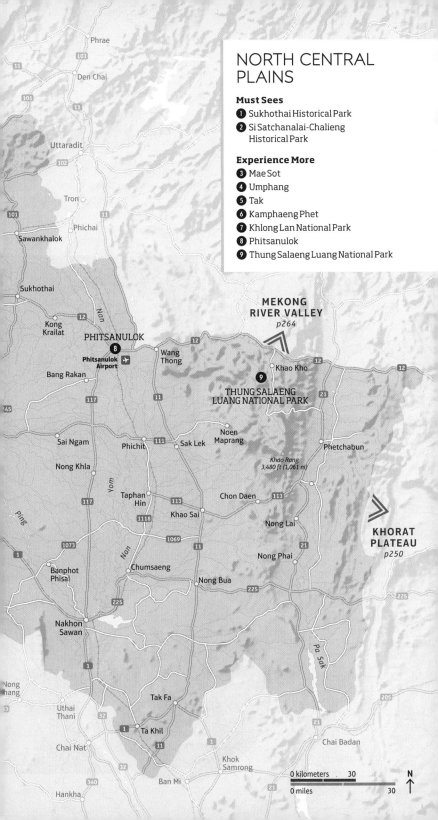

NORTH CENTRAL PLAINS

Must Sees

❶ Sukhothai Historical Park

❷ Si Satchanalai-Chalieng Historical Park

Experience More

❸ Mae Sot

❹ Umphang

❺ Tak

❻ Kamphaeng Phet

❼ Khlong Lan National Park

❽ Phitsanulok

❾ Thung Salaeng Luang National Park

MEKONG RIVER VALLEY
p264

KHORAT PLATEAU
p250

PHITSANULOK

Phitsanulok Airport

THUNG SALAENG LUANG NATIONAL PARK

Khao Rang 3,480 ft (1,061 m)

0 kilometers   30

0 miles   30

N

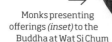

1 🔪 🍽 🛍

SUKHOTHAI HISTORICAL PARK

อุทยานประวัติศาสตร์สุโขทัย

🅐 B3 📍 8 miles (13 km) W of New Sukhothai, Sukhothai province
📞 0-5569-7241 🚌 New Sukhothai, then *songthaew* 🕐 6am–9pm daily

The UNESCO World Heritage site of Old Sukhothai is a potent reminder of the ancient Sukhothai Kingdom. The abandoned city seen today is the best preserved and most popular site in Central Thailand.

The Sukhothai Kingdom (*p70*) arose in the early 13th century and came to dominate the Central Plains of Thailand. The ruins of Old Sukhothai make up the historical park, which has around 40 temple complexes spread over a large area. The layout, as with many major Thai cities (*muangs*), follows fixed principles: a large, central *wat* complex surrounded concentrically by walls, river, rice fields, and, beyond, forested mountains.

Exploring the Park

The park is divided into five zones. At its center is the walled Royal City, or the central zone, protected by moats and ramparts. The most important ruins, including Wat Mahathat, are within this inner compound. The four zones outside of this center are split into north, south, east, and west, but feature equally impressive ruins, including the monumental Buddha at Wat Si Chum – one of the most photographed sights here. One way to see the ruins of the Royal City is by bicycle: shops beside the old east gate rent them for a small fee.

The Royal City

Entering from the east, the first *wat* within the city walls is Wat Traphang Thong, which is situated on an islet in a small lotus-filled lake. The Sri Lankan-style *chedi* dates from the mid-14th century, and a small *mondop* beside it enshrines a stone Footprint of the Buddha, still worshipped by resident monks. The Ramkamhaeng National Museum houses photographs, taken around 1900–1920, of Sukhothai's ruins prior to renovation.

> **Did You Know?**
>
> The layout of the city and its temples is based on mythological patterns.

→ Monks presenting offerings (*inset*) to the Buddha at Wat Si Chum

↑ A series of stunning water lilies in a pond within Sukhothai Historical Park

EAT

Nham Khang Sukhothai

An elegant restaurant with Thai food and, in the evenings, performances of classical music and *Ram thai* (traditional dance).

🏠 214 Moo 3, Old Sukhothai 🌐 legend hasukhothai.com

ⓑⓑⓑ

Junshine

The spring rolls here are particularly good. Vegetarian versions of most dishes are also available.

🏠 169/9 Charot Withi Thong Rd, Old Sukhothai 📞 0-6428-24247

ⓑⓑⓑ

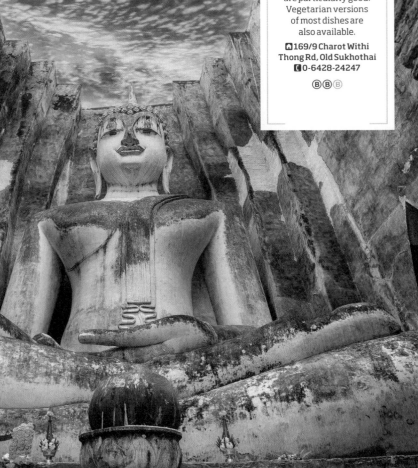

Wat Mahathat

At the heart of the moated Royal City is Wat Mahathat, once the spiritual center of the Sukhothai Kingdom. The central *chedi* was founded by Si Intharathit (c1240–70), first king of Sukhothai, and rebuilt in the 1340s by Lue Thai (1298–1346) to house relics of the Buddha. Buildings were added to the complex by successive kings. Nearby, Wat Takuan has a restored, Sri Lankan bell-shaped *chedi*. Several Buddha images found in the vault of the *chedi* are thought to date from the early Sukhothai period. To the southwest, at Wat Si Sawai, are three 12th–14th-century Khmer-style *prangs*.

→
Wat Mahathat's peaceful grounds and lush foliage

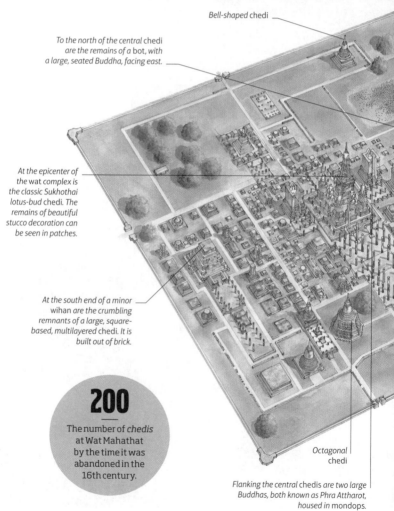

Bell-shaped *chedi*

To the north of the central *chedi* are the remains of a bot, with a large, seated Buddha, facing east.

At the epicenter of the *wat* complex is the classic Sukhothai lotus-bud *chedi*. The remains of beautiful stucco decoration can be seen in patches.

At the south end of a minor wihan are the crumbling remnants of a large, square-based, multilayered *chedi*. It is built out of brick.

200
—
The number of *chedis* at Wat Mahathat by the time it was abandoned in the 16th century.

Octagonal *chedi*

Flanking the central *chedis are two large Buddhas, both known as Phra Attharot, housed in* mondops.

Wat Mahathat, the most important *wat* complex in Sukhothai

Perimeter wall

Ornamental pond

Aligned with the central group of chedis is the main wihan. The only remains today are columns that once supported a roof and a seated Buddha image.

0 meters 25
0 yards 25
N ↑

Highlights Beyond the Royal City

Must See

East of the Royal City

▽ Wat Chang Lom, a bell-shaped *chedi* similar to one at Si Satchanalai *(p192)*, has 36 brick and stucco elephants around its base. It represents mythical Mount Meru, supported by elephants. Beyond is Wat Chedi Sung, a beautiful *chedi* with a high, square base typical of the late Sukhothai era.

North of the Royal City

▽ Wat Phra Phai Luang, a Khmer-style complex, is thought to be part of the original mid-13th-century settlement, built when this region was part of the Khmer Empire. Only one of the three laterite *prangs*, decorated with stucco fragments, is extant. Nearby, the *mondop* of Wat Si Chum has an immense seated Buddha peering through an opening.

The Outer Sights

▷ Along a low ridge of hills, around 2 miles (3.5 km) west of the ramparted Royal City, is another string of ruins that form part of the Sukhothai Historical Park. Most important of these is Wat Saphan Hin, where a 41-ft (12.5-m) high Buddha image, Phra Attharot, similar to the Buddha images of the same name at Wat Mahathat, stands on a low summit. There is another large image, similar to Phra Attharot, at Wat Phra Yun, though the head and hands are missing. Closer to the west city wall is Wat Pa Mamuang, of archeological importance for the inscriptions discovered here relating to King Loe Thai. At Wat Chedi Si Hong, the laterite brick *chedi* is lined with elephants.

2

SI SATCHANALAI-CHALIENG HISTORICAL PARK

อุทยานประวัติศาสตร์ศรีสัชนาลัย-ชะเลียง

🅱️B3 📍41 miles (67 km) N of New Sukhothai, Sukhothai province
🚌From New Sukhothai to Si Satchanalai, then *samlor*
🕐8:30am-4:30pm daily ℹ️0-2250-5500

Containing the ruins of the old cities of Si Satchanalai and Chalieng, this UNESCO World Heritage Site is steeped in history. A peaceful ambience, ancient *wats*, and lush greenery make it a delightful visit.

During the 13th century, the mighty Sukhothai Kingdom consolidated its power in the Central Plains by building a number of satellite cities. The most important was Si Satchanalai. Today, its ruins lie on the right bank of the Yom River, 4 miles (7 km) south of modern Si Satchanalai. One of the best examples of a Thai *muang* (city-state), it was laid out along fixed cosmological lines – temple complexes lay at its heart, surrounded by city walls, rivers, and forest. The ruins of Chalieng, half a mile (1 km) to the southeast, are thought to be an earlier Khmer settlement, an outpost of that empire dating from the time of Jayavarman VII (1181–1220).

While the ruins of Si Satchanalai are not as grandiose as those of Sukhothai *(p188)*, they are in some ways more interesting – Si Satchanalai is considered by historians to be the apogee of Thai city planning. The ruins have not been as extensively restored, and attract fewer visitors. Nonetheless, they evoke a once powerful city that, although not a seat of government of the Sukhothai Kingdom, was the city of the deputy king and an important commercial center in the 14th and 15th centuries. Its most important trade was in ceramics *(p195)*, for which it was renowned all over Southeast Asia and China.

Exploring the Park

Today, the ruins at Si Satchanalai cover an area of roughly 18 sq miles (45 sq km) and are surrounded by a moat 40 ft (12 m) wide. A good way to tour the site is by bicycle; there is a bicycle rental store located halfway between Si Satchanalai and Chalieng. An information center located in front of the Ram Narong Gate houses a small exhibition of artifacts found at the site and photographs of its monuments.

↑ The ruins of Wat Phra Si Rattana Mahathat, in the park's Chalieng zone

The ruins evoke a once powerful city that, although not a seat of government of the Sukhothai Kingdom, was the city of the deputy king.

Si Satchanalai Wats

Wat Khao Phnom Phloeng

▷ On a low, wooded hill north of Wat Chang Lom, this was once the site of ritual cremations. Also among the ruins is a seated Buddha.

↑ The Sri Lankan-style *chedi* of Wat Nang Phaya within the walled city

Wat Chang Lom

▲ At the heart of the moated city a huge Sri Lankan-style, bell-shaped *chedi* forms the centerpiece of Wat Chang Lom.

Wat Nang Phaya

▲ The *wihan* here is decorated with fine stucco reliefs from the Ayutthaya period. Its grille-like windows are also typical of Ayutthaya.

Wat Suwan Khiri

▲ On a hilltop, farther west, all that remains of this *wat* is a single *chedi*, though it offers great views of the city.

Wat Chedi Chet Thaeo

▲ To the south of Wat Chang Lom is Wat Chedi Chet Thaeo, around whose central lotus-bud *chedi* are many smaller ones in different styles.

Sri Lankan Influence

During the Sukhothai period, Theravada Buddhism, which had developed in Sri Lanka, arrived in Thailand. With it came Sri Lankan, bell-shaped *chedis*, reliquary towers symbolizing the teachings of the Buddha. The three-tiered base, which can be seen around the park, symbolizes hell, earth, and heaven. A second layer of symbolism designates the base as the Buddha's folded robes, the *stupa* as his alms bowl, and the spire as his staff.

Did You Know?

Wat Chang Lom is thought to be the first Sri Lankan-style *chedi* of the Sukhothai Kingdom.

The remaining ↑
Sri Lankan-style *chedi*
of Wat Suwan Khiri

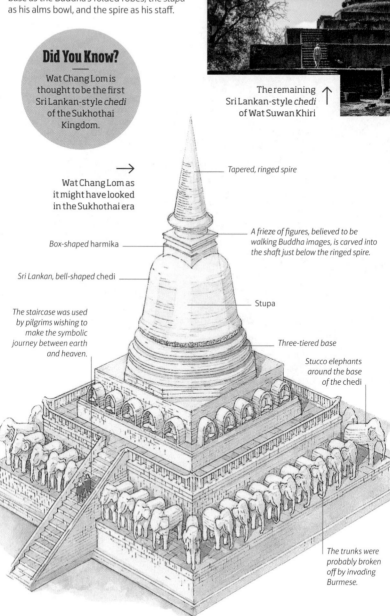

→
Wat Chang Lom as it might have looked in the Sukhothai era

Tapered, ringed spire

A frieze of figures, believed to be walking Buddha images, is carved into the shaft just below the ringed spire.

Box-shaped harmika

Sri Lankan, bell-shaped chedi

Stupa

The staircase was used by pilgrims wishing to make the symbolic journey between earth and heaven.

Three-tiered base

Stucco elephants around the base of *the* chedi

The trunks were probably broken off by invading Burmese.

EXPERIENCE MORE

3

Mae Sot
แม่สอด

A3 **Tak province**
🚆🚌 **𝒊 Tak; 0-5551-4341**

Trade in Myanmar hardwoods and gemstones, both legal and smuggled, has brought considerable wealth to this small town. Today Mae Sot retains the feel of a frontier town and makes a relaxing stopover for travelers. Gem traders, usually ethnic Chinese, are often huddled on Mae Sot's sidewalks, negotiating with buyers from Bangkok and other parts of Thailand. Because of its location and trading history, Mae Sot has a distinct Myanmar flavor, evident in architecture and market goods.

Trilingual shop signs can be seen on the streets, Myanmar-language publications are sold in shops, and streets are always busy with locals. Traders haggle during the morning food market, one of Thailand's most picturesque and colorful.

North of the market is Wat Chumphon Khiri, which has a magnificent Myanmar *chedi* decorated with golden mosaic tiles. On the southeast side of town is the Muslim quarter; at its center is the small Nurul Islam Mosque. Dotted around the town are a number of other temples that have Karen and Shan characteristics.

4

Umphang
อุ้มผาง

A4 **Tak province**
🚌 Mae Sot, then *songthaew*
𝒊 Tak; 0-5551-4341

Part of Umphang's charm lies in the journey, as the road from Mae Sot is one of Thailand's most scenic. The village – its

↑ Thi Lo Su, one of many waterfalls in Umphang Wildlife Sanctuary

population consisting largely of Karen tribespeople – is surrounded by the lush forests of **Umphang Wildlife Sanctuary**, rich in birdlife and small mammals. Larger inhabitants include elephants, tapirs, and the elusive clouded leopard.

Umphang is popular for rafting and hiking, but its isolation has kept most of the tourist hordes away. The landscape is dotted with caves, rapids, cascades, and small Karen settlements. The stunning Thi Lo Su waterfall, often described as the highest waterfall in Thailand at some 820 ft (250 m), is an easy hike from the park headquarters, via beautiful bamboo forest. Agencies in Umphang or Mae Sot can arrange treks; avoid school vacations, when this region becomes very crowded.

Umphang Wildlife Sanctuary
⊘ **□** 93 miles (150 km) S of Mae Sot on Hwy 1090
□ Daily

5

Tak
ตาก

 B3 🏠 Tak province ✈️ 🚌
ℹ️ Taksin Rd, Tak; 0-5551-4341

During much of the 13th century, Tak was a western outpost of the Sukhothai Kingdom. After the death of King Ramkamhaeng and the subsequent collapse of the Sukhothai Empire, the town came under the influence of the Lanna Kingdom to the north. Today Tak sprawls along the left bank of the Ping River, and much of the Lanna influence can still be seen in the teak houses hidden in quiet lanes at the southern end of town. The houses here date from the late 19th and early 20th centuries.

Wat Bot Mani Sibunruang also shows northern influences with its finely decorated, Lanna-style *bot* and a small *sala* containing a much revered Buddha image called Luang Pho Phutthamon. Nearby is a statue of King Taksin, a former governor of Tak, who, after the sacking of Ayutthaya by Myanmar in 1767, established a new capital at Thon Buri, now part of Bangkok (p140).

The 40-sq-mile (105-sq-km) Lan Sang National Park, 9 miles (15 km) west of Tak, has tracks leading to several beautiful waterfalls. These are best visited during or soon after the rainy season; at other times of year there is little water. To the north of Lan Sang National Park is the Taksin Maharat

HIDDEN GEM
Phra Ruang Hot Springs

A short way off the main road, 15 miles (25 km) north of Kamphaeng Phet, is this lovely landscaped park, with little bathhouses built around a collection of five natural hot springs.

> Today Tak sprawls along the left bank of the Ping River, and much of the Lanna influence can still be seen in the teak houses hidden in quiet lanes at the southern end of town.

National Park, the highlight of which is a steeply descending trail to the huge *ton krabak yai*, or big krabak tree, which is some 165 ft (50 m) tall, and has a girth of 50 ft (16 m).

6

Kamphaeng Phet
กำแพงเพชร

 B3 🏠 Kamphaeng Phet province 🚌 ℹ️ Tak; 0-5551-4341

On the east bank of this settlement lie the impressive remains of the Old City, dating from the early 15th century, and which once formed part of a satellite city to the mighty Sukhothai (p188). Within its walls is the **Kamphaeng Phet National Museum**. In this collection are several fine 16th-century bronzes of Hindu deities, including a standing image of Shiva and torsos of Vishnu and Lakshmi. The Old City walls also enclose two important ruins from the late Sukhothai period. Close to the National Museum, Wat Phra Kaeo is the Old City's largest site, containing the ruins of several *wihans*, a *bot* at the eastern end, a *chedi* from the late Sukhothai period, and the laterite cores of a number of Buddha images. At the western end are three more partly restored Buddha images. Neighboring Wat Phra has a fine late Sukhothai, octagonal-based *chedi*. One admission charge covers all ruins in the Old City.

The modern town of Kamphaeng Phet sprawls to the south of the Old City. Comprising mostly commercial buildings, it also has a riverside park and a few traditional wooden houses, as well as tourist-oriented facilities.

A *samlor* ride northwest of the Old City are the **Aranyik Ruins**, the area of many forest *wats* once used by a meditational order called the Forest Dwelling Sect. Built during the 14th to 16th centuries, the sheer number of ruins at Aranyik attest to the popularity of the sect, which achieved prominence in Thailand during the Sukhothai era. With the assistance of UNESCO, parts of the site have now been restored and landscaped.

The *wihan* at Wat Phra Non, near the entrance, once contained a large reclining Buddha, but this is so badly damaged as to be almost indiscernible. Nevertheless, a number of laterite columns from the *wihan* are still standing. On

each side of the *mondop* at Wat Phra Si Iriyabot are images of the Buddha in different postures, though all are damaged. In the ruined *bot* of Wat Sing (found in the northern part of the Aranyik site) is the laterite core of a Buddha image.

Most impressive of the Aranyik *wats* is Wat Chang Rop, consisting mostly of the remains of a very large, square-based *chedi*, flanked by the forequarters of elephants in laterite. On a few of these, the original stucco decoration has been restored but little of the Sri Lankan-style bell-shaped *chedi* is still standing.

In the modern part of town, other interesting monuments, such as the Sukhothai brick *chedi* of Wat Kalothai, are unceremoniously tucked away in unassuming streets and quiet lanes. Unfortunately, many such sites have now fallen into a state of disrepair, but their sheer quantity remains an indication of the importance of Kamphaeng Phet during the Sukhothai and Ayutthaya periods.

Kamphaeng Phet National Museum

⊘ 🏠 Old City, behind Wat Phra Kaeo ◷ 8:30am-4pm Wed-Sun 🆆 finearts.go.th

Aranyik Ruins

⊘ 🏠 NW of Old City ◷ Daily

Temple remains and detail of intricate Buddha images *(inset)* in Kamphaeng Phet
↓

EAT

Baan Nichapa
A riverside setting, terraced pavilion, and Thai menu.

🅰B3 🏠47/17 Ban Wan Yang Rd, Kamphaeng Phet 🆆maeping mangoriverside.com

Ⓑ Ⓑ Ⓑ

Tasty Restaurant
Stylish and modern restaurant serving a range of Thai classics.

🅰B3 🏠115-119 Tesa 1, Kamphaeng Phet 📞0-5571-2594

Ⓑ Ⓑ Ⓑ

Tori
Japanese decor is the setting for tasty sushi, sashimi, and curries.

🅰B3 🏠124 Ratruamchi Rd, Kamphaeng Phet 📞08-5961-3609

Ⓑ Ⓑ Ⓑ

Khlong Lan National Park
อุทยานแห่งชาติคลองลาน

🅐B3 ℹ️ Kamphaeng Phet province; Park HQ 4 miles (6 km) off Hwy 1117, S of Kamphaeng Phet; 0-5576-6002 🚌 From Kamphaeng Phet to Klonglan, then *songthaew*

This 116-sq-mile (300-sq-km) national park was formed in 1982. Formerly, the area was controlled by Communist insurgents, and inhabited by a number of hill tribes.

The highlight of the park is the Khlong Lan waterfall, which is easily accessible from the park headquarters. It falls 310 ft (95 m) into a pool ideal for a refreshing swim. At the foot of the road leading up to the waterfall is a small market selling Hmong handicrafts – a government rehabilitation scheme for the hill tribes relocated from the park.

The adjacent Mae Wong National Park is good for hiking and bird-watching. A tiger conservation project run by the WWF (*wwf.or.th*) is also located here. An old road running through the center of the park, now overgrown, makes a good hiking trail. Simple bungalow accommodations are also available.

Phitsanulok
พิษณุโลก

🅐B3 🄰 Phitsanulok province ✈️🚍🚌 ℹ️209/7-8 Borommatrailokanat Rd, Phitsanulok; 0-5525-2742/3

An important transportation hub, connecting Bangkok and the Central Plains to northern Thailand, there has been a settlement here from as early as the mid-14th century, when Wat Phra Si Rattana Mahathat was built on the bank of the Nan River. Initially, this *wat* complex, also called Wat Yai, probably housed a Sukhothai lotus-bud *chedi*, which was later replaced by the tall Ayutthayan *prang* that can be seen today. It was built by the Ayutthayan king Borommatrailokanat (1448–88), who ruled from Phitsanulok after 1463 in order to wage a military campaign against the Kingdom of Lanna.

Inside the west *wihan* is the revered Buddha image Phra

THAILAND-MYANMAR BORDER REFUGEES

There are nine official refugee camps on Thailand's western border, which are home to about 100,000 Myanmar refugees. The Karen tribespeople, Myanmar's largest ethnic minority, have long occupied an area straddling Myanmar and Thailand. The British were supposed to grant the Karen an autonomous homeland within Myanmar after World War II, which didn't happen. Following pro-democracy demonstrations in Myanmar in 1988, and the subsequent crackdown, opposition MPs and ethnic minorities fled east to refugee villages, where the Karen organize their struggle for an independent state.

↑ Thung Salaeng Luang bathed in early morning mist

Phuttha Chinarat, made of gilded bronze and dating from the 14th century. It attracts pilgrims from all over Thailand.

Sergeant Major Thawee's Folk Museum houses a small collection of rural folk crafts, including wood and bamboo animal traps, farm tools, and basketry. Across the street is the affiliated **Buddha Foundry**, where visitors can watch bronze Buddha images being forged.

Sergeant Major Thawee's Folk Museum

 🏠 26/43 Wisuth Kasat Rd 📞 0-5521-2749 ⏰ 8:30am–4:30pm Tue–Sun

Buddha Foundry

🏠 26/43 Thanon Wisuthi Kasat ⏰ Mon–Sat

---

9 🏞️

Thung Salaeng Luang National Park

อุทยานแห่งชาติทุ่งแสลงหลวง

🅐 C3 🏠 Phitsanulok province; Park HQ off Hwy 12, 50 miles (80 km) E of Phitsanulok 🚌 From Phitsanulok to Nakhon Thai, then *songthaew* ℹ️ Phitsanulok, 0-5525-2742/3

With its open fields and lush forest, this 487-sq-mile (1,262-sq-km) park offers good hiking and bird-watching. Barking deer can also be seen, and elephants are sometimes found at the salt licks (a place where animals can lick mineral nutrients). The cascades of Kaeng Sopha lie 6 miles (9 km) from the park headquarters. Farther west are the Poi falls and smaller Kaeng Song rapids.

East at Khao Kho is a notable rehabilitation project for the Hmong, displaced through association in anti-Communist fighting in the 1970s–80s. King Bhumibol took great interest in the program and had a palace nearby.

SHOP

Borderline
Combining cafe, art gallery, and handicrafts shop, this fair-trade outlet supports Myanmar migrants and refugees. Products include brightly patterned bags and woven tablecloths.

🅐 A3 🏠 674/14 Intharakeeree Rd, Mae Sot 🌐 borderline collective.org

---

Phitsanulok Night Market
An unusual array of clothes and accessories stalls populate this busy market, along with foot massage stalls and fantastic food outlets serving northern delicacies.

🅐 B3 🏠 4 Phuttabucha, Phitsanulok

NORTHWEST HEARTLAND

Northwest Thailand is the heartland of Lanna Thai people *(p71)*. The ancient city of Chiang Mai, superbly sited in the Ping River Valley, was once the capital of the Lanna Kingdom. In the 12th–18th centuries this kingdom, strongly influenced by Myanmar *(p71)*, ruled over what is now northern Thailand. In the early 19th century, Rama V began to strengthen the links between the north and his capital of Bangkok in an effort to avoid colonial threats. Northern Thailand was integrated with Bangkok following the construction of Chiang Mai's railroad in 1921, and shortly after this, the northern provinces were finally considered part of the Siam Kingdom.

In the west, close to the Myanmar border, the remote towns of Mae Hong Son and Mae Sariang are in some ways more Myanmar than Thai. North of Chiang Mai, the streets of Chiang Dao are lined with two-story teak buildings, a reminder that the surrounding countryside was once rich in teak forests. To the south of Chiang Mai, Lanna influence can again be seen within Lampang and Lamphun. The latter city also has surviving traces of the older Kingdom of Haripunchai *(p68)*.

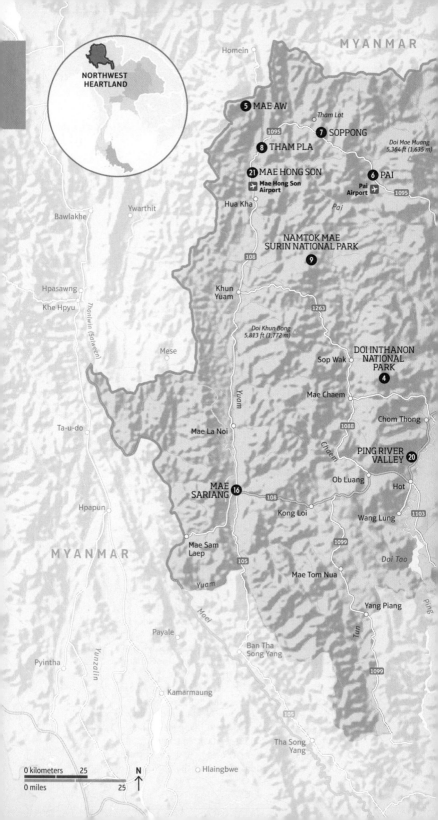

NORTHWEST HEARTLAND

Must Sees

1. Wat Phra That Lampang Luang
2. Doi Suthep
3. Chiang Mai
4. Doi Inthanon National Park

Experience More

5. Mae Aw
6. Pai
7. Soppong
8. Tham Pla
9. Namtok Mae Surin National Park
10. Doi Chiang Dao
11. San Kamphaeng
12. Uttaradit
13. Phrao
14. Mae Taeng Valley
15. Bo Sang
16. Mae Sariang
17. Doi Saket
18. Lamphun
19. Lampang
20. Ping River Valley
21. Mae Hong Son

The *nagas* at the main staircase, leading to the *wat*'s entrance ↑

 🛍

WAT PHRA THAT LAMPANG LUANG

วัดพระธาตุลำปางหลวง

🅰 B2 🏠 Off Hwy 1, 11 miles (18 km) SW of Lampang, Lampang province 🚌 Lampang, then *songthaew* or taxi 🕐 7:30am–5pm daily ℹ Lampang; 0-5421-8823 or 0-5422-6812

One of the most famous temples in northern Thailand, this *wat* is also one of the most attractive, distinctive for the graceful architecture and richly colored interiors of its many buildings.

GESTURES OF THE BUDDHA

Buddha images throughout Thailand mostly follow strict rules laid down in the 3rd century AD. There are four basic postures: standing, sitting, walking (the daily activities of the Buddha) and reclining (associated with the Buddha's final moments on earth). These can be combined with hand and feet positions.

The main buildings of Wat Phra That Lampang Luang were constructed in the late 15th century on the site of an 8th-century fortress. This had been built on a mound to protect it from attack and was further fortified by three parallel earthen ramparts separated by moats. The ramparts are still visible in the village around the present *wat*. In 1736 a local hero, Tip Chang, successfully defended the temple from the Burmese. The revered Phra Kaeo Don Tao image, allegedly carved from the same jadeite block as the Emerald Buddha (*p99*), is kept in one of the museums behind the main complex. Three museums lie in the gardens just outside the southern gate, all featuring a variety of Buddha images and figures. Antiques and handicrafts are also available from market stalls outside of the *wat*.

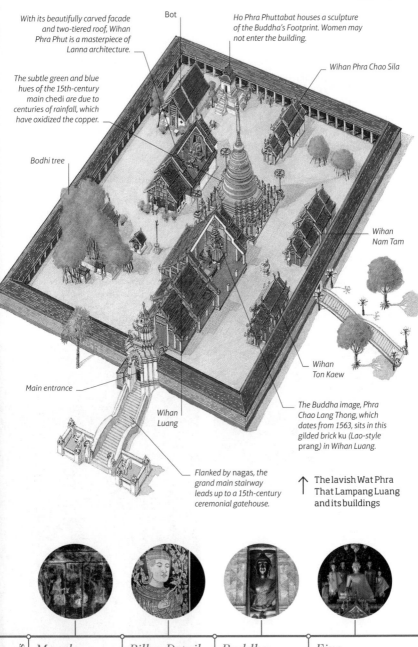

With its beautifully carved facade and two-tiered roof, Wihan Phra Phut is a masterpiece of Lanna architecture.

The subtle green and blue hues of the 15th-century main chedi are due to centuries of rainfall, which have oxidized the copper.

Bodhi tree

Bot

Ho Phra Phuttabat houses a sculpture of the Buddha's Footprint. Women may not enter the building.

Wihan Phra Chao Sila

Wihan Nam Tam

Wihan Ton Kaew

Main entrance

Wihan Luang

Flanked by nagas, the grand main stairway leads up to a 15th-century ceremonial gatehouse.

The Buddha image, Phra Chao Lang Thong, which dates from 1563, sits in this gilded brick ku (Lao-style prang) in Wihan Luang.

↑ The lavish Wat Phra That Lampang Luang and its buildings

Site Highlights

Murals
▲ Faded murals in Wihan Nam Tam depict 16th-century life and scenes from the *jataka* - folk tales from India.

Pillar Detail
▲ The black lacquered pillar, inlaid with gold, in Wihan Luang typifies the intricate decoration of the complex.

Buddha Statue
▲ A huge Buddha image sits inside the 13th-century Wihan Phra Phut, the oldest building.

Five Buddhas
▲ Inside the huge, open-sided Wihan Luang are five impressive seated Buddha images.

2 🍴 🖥 🛍

DOI SUTHEP

ดอยสุเทพ

309

The number of steps in the sweeping staircase that leads to Wat Phra That Doi Suthep.

🅰 A2 ⏱ 10 miles (16 km) NW of Chiang Mai, Chiang Mai province 🚈🚌 Chiang Mai then *songthaew* ℹ Chiang Mai; www.doisuthep.com

This thickly forested mountain in the twin-peaked Doi Suthep-Doi Pui National Park is an easy day trip from Chiang Mai. Often shrouded in fog, it is a serene and spiritual place.

Perched atop the 5,250-ft (1,601-m) bucolic summit of Doi Suthep is Wat Phra That Doi Suthep, one of the most revered Buddhist shrines in northern Thailand. From Chiang Mai, a paved road snakes up the hillside to a village with restaurants and souvenir shops. From here, you can choose between a steep climb or the funicular to the *wat*, from which there are breathtaking views over the national park and Chiang Mai city to the southeast. Enshrining sacred relics, the *wat*, founded in the 14th century, is regarded by many as the symbol of Lanna Thailand (*p71*). At the top of the *naga* staircase lies the white elephant monument, one of the most important shrines here. According to legend, in the 1930s King Ku Na's elephant selected the site of the *chedi* by marching up the mountain, trumpeting and turning three times. As well as its dazzling central *chedi*, the *wat* is home to a decorative bell tower that is distinctive for its multi-colored, layered roof. The mountain is also popular with birdwatchers and trekkers. Other attractions on Doi Suthep include waterfalls, a Hmong village and the picturesque English-style gardens of Phuping Palace.

WILDLIFE AROUND WAT PHRA THAT DOI SUTHEP

With its rich and varied wildlife, Doi Suthep-Doi Pui National Park is a great attraction for nature lovers, and trekkers are likely to spot a number of wild plant, bird, and mammal species while hiking the park's many trails. Despite the deforestation of the western side of the park due to agriculture and tourism, the park is rich in plants, butterflies, and birds such as the green cochoa. Though human activity has resulted in many indigenous mammals being killed or driven from their homes, 60 species still live here, including the Burmese ferret badger.

Wat Phra That Doi Suthep on the leafy mountain summit of Doi Suthep ↑

① The striking gold-plated Lanna structure of the central *chedi* of Wat Phra That Doi Suthep is a 16th-century extension of the original. The four multi-tiered gold umbrellas around it are adorned with intricate filigree.

② A Burmese *naga* statue at the staircase leads to the temple of Wat Phra That Doi Suthep.

③ The gold Buddha images in the *wihan* are the most important in the *complex*.

↑ The serene surroundings of Wat Chiang Man, one of Chiang Mai's many iconic temples

③

CHIANG MAI

เชียงใหม่

🅰B2 **🏠Chiang Mai province** **✈2 miles (3 km) SW of Chiang Mai** **🚉Charoen Muang Rd** **🚌Chiang Mai Arcade** **ℹ105/1 Chiang Mai-Lamphun Rd; 0-5324-8604**

Thailand's second most important city, Chiang Mai (literally, "new city"), was chosen in 1292 by King Mengrai to replace Chiang Rai *(p232)* as the capital of his Lanna Kingdom *(p71)*. It was during this period and the subsequent reign of King Tilok that many fine *wats* were built within the walled city. Today, visitors are drawn to Chiang Mai not only for its temples, but also for its excellent shopping and trekking facilities.

Wat Chedi Luang
วัดเจดีย์หลวง

🏠Phra Pok Klao Rd **🕐Daily**

Within the compound of this temple is the spot where King Mengrai was killed by lightning in 1317. The revered Emerald Buddha *(p99)* image was briefly housed in the *wat* in the 15th century – a previous attempt to bring it to Chiang Mai failed. The

towering *chedi*, once 295 ft (90 m) high, was damaged by an earthquake in 1465.

Wat Phra Sing
วัดพระสิงห์

🏠Samlan Rd, near Suan Dok Gate **🕐Daily**

Construction of this temple, the largest in Chiang Mai, began in 1345, though the *bot*

---

dates from 1600. The Wihan Lai Kham ("gilded hall"), decorated with murals of everyday life, houses the revered golden Phra Buddha Sihing. Like its namesakes in Bangkok *(p100)* and Nakhon Si Thammarat *(p348)*, the image is said to have originated in Sri Lanka.

Wat Chiang Man
วัดเชียงมั่น

🏠Off Ratcha Phakhinai Rd **🕐Daily**

King Mengrai dedicated this residence as a *wat*, the city's oldest, while his new capital was being built. It features Lanna teak pillars and a *chedi* surrounded by stone elephant heads. The *wihan* houses the Phra Kaeo Kao, thought to have been carved in Northern India in the 6th century BC.

---

④
Tha Phae Gate
ประตูท่าแพ

📍 **Moon Muang Rd**

Tha Phae Gate marks the beginning of Tha Phae Road, the commercial hub of Chiang Mai. Located here are bookstores, department stores, and handicraft shops. Farther east, the road becomes Highway 106, along which are shops and factories selling silk, celadon, and other crafts.

---

⑤
Wat Suan Dok
วัดสวนดอก

📍 **139 Suthep Rd** 📞 **0-5327-8304** 🕐 **6am–10pm daily**

The city's western gate, Suan Dok Gate, marks the start of Suthep Road, along which three important temples – including Wat Suan Dok – are situated. The temple was built in 1383 to house relics of the

Buddha, while the open-sided *wihan* was restored in the 1930s. The small *chedis* contain ashes of members of Chiang Mai's former royal family. Farther along Suthep Road is the 14th-century Wat U Mong. Some of the original tunnels leading to the monks' cells can be explored. This temple and nearby Wat Ram Poeng offer meditation courses.

---

⑥
Night Bazaar
ไนท์บาซาร์

📍 **Chang Khlan Rd**
🕐 **6–11pm daily**

With its wide range of goods at competitive prices, this easily rivals Bangkok's Chatuchak Market *(p158)*. Inside are endless stalls selling hill-tribe crafts, leather goods, and clothing. The top floor specializes in antiques. Beware of fakes, especially at the stalls outside the market. This is also a good place to try Chiang Mai's Myanmar-influenced cuisine. Shops on Wualai Road, south of Chiang Mai Gate, sell the best silverware and textiles.

TOP 3 · CHIANG MAI ART VENUES

One Nimman
📍 **1 Nimmanhaemin Rd**
🌐 **onenimman.com**
This fashionable center has shops and cafes, as well as a contemporary art gallery and regular cultural events.

Chiang Mai University Art Center
📍 **239 Nimmanhemin Rd**
🌐 **finearts.cmu.ac.th**
The university's Fine Arts Faculty oversees this gallery, which hosts exhibitions of contemporary art by artists from Thailand and across the world.

Sangdee Art Gallery
📍 **5 Siri Mangkalajarn Rd**
🌐 **sangdeeart.com**
With a gallery, music venue, bar, and cafe, this is a favorite hangout for Chiang Mai's bohemian set and a great place to get a feel for the city's arts scene.

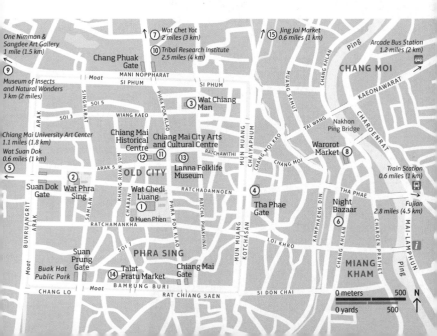

⑦
Wat Chet Yot
วัดเจ็ดยอด

🅰 Thanon Nimmanhemin

Wat Chet Yot, distinctive for its seven-spired chedi, is set in spacious grounds. Its stuccoed design is based on the Mahabodhi Temple of Bodhgaya in India, where the Buddha is said to have achieved Enlightenment.

⑧
Warorot Market
ตลาดวโรรส

🅰 N of Tha Phae Rd ⏱ Daily

During the day, this huge covered market sells local food, clothing, souvenirs, bags, and hill-tribe crafts, often at lower prices than the Night Bazaar. Fruits, spices, and tasty dishes are also avail-able. To beat the crowds, head here early. By night, Warorot Market is the site of a colorful flower market and an abundance of tempting food carts.

⑨
Museum of Insects and Natural Wonders
พิพิธภัณฑ์แมลงโลกและสิ่งมหัศจรรย์ธรรมชาติ

🅰 72 Srimankalajarn Rd, Nimman 🚌 12 Huay Keaw ⏱ 9am-5pm daily 🌐 thailandinsect.com

The quirky passion project of entomologist Dr. Rampa Rattanarithikul and her husband, this museum contains half a century's collection of more than 10,000 species of insect, including butterflies, beetles, and stick insects, alongside fossils, shells, and stones.

SONGKRAN FESTIVITIES

Celebrated nationwide, but most exuberantly in and around Chiang Mai, Songkran *(p67)* is one of Thailand's major festivals and marks the start of the Buddhist New Year in April. This holiday has evolved from a purely religious event, in which Buddha images are bathed with water to purify them, into a much greater celebration of water. Nowadays, buckets of water are thrown over everyone in the streets.

⑩
Tribal Research Institute
พิพิธภัณฑ์ชาวเขา

🅰 Chiang Mai University, off Huai Kaew Rd ☎ 0-5321-0872 ⏱ 8:30am-noon & 1-4:30pm Mon-Fri

On the grounds of Chiang Mai University is the Tribal Research Institute. Its small museum details the history of the area's ethnic minorities. Treks to hill-tribe villages can be arranged here.

⑪
Chiang Mai City Arts and Cultural Centre
หอศิลปวัฒนธรรมเมืองเชียงใหม่

🅰 Phra Pok Klao Rd 🚌 Pratu *(songthaew)*, Tha Phae Gate ⏱ 8:30am-5pm Tue-Sun 🌐 cmocity.com

In the heart of the Old City, this museum tells the story of centuries of Chiang Mai's impressive history – from first settlements to Chiang Mai

←

Tucking into local delicacies at Warorot Market in the evening

↑ Admiring the intricately detailed murals at the Lanna Folklife Museum

today – through a range of interesting artifacts, photos, and videos. Tickets to access the Chiang Mai City Arts and Cultural Centre also give visitors access to the Chiang Mai Historical Centre and the Lanna Folklife Museum, both nearby.

---

⑫

Chiang Mai Historical Centre
หอประวัติศาสตร์เมืองเชียงใหม่

🏠 **Phra Pok Klao Rd** 🚌 **Pratu (*songthaew*), Tha Phae Gate** 🕐 **8:30am-5pm Tue-Sun** 🌐 **cmocity.com**

Located next door to the Chiang Mai City Arts and Cultural Centre, this is a great museum for families, with its interactive displays and archeological reproductions that look into the history of Chiang Mai. The beautiful building itself is enough to warrant a visit here, and there is also a delightful garden.

Did You Know?

Warorot Market is also referred to as Chiang Mai's "little Chinatown."

---

⑬

Lanna Folklife Museum
พิพิธภัณฑ์พื้นถิ่นลานนา

🏠 **Phra Pok Klao Rd** 🚌 **Pratu (*songthaew*), Tha Phae Gate** 🕐 **8:30am-7pm Tue-Sun** 🌐 **cmocity.com**

Across the road from the Chiang Mai City Arts and Cultural Centre, and housed in a beautiful colonial building which was once the municipal courthouse, this museum offers a rich insight into traditional Lanna culture and history. The 18 different exhibits across two floors display tribal costumes and dioramas depicting traditional arts. Information is offered in Thai, Chinese, and English.

---

⑭

Talat Pratu Market
ตลาดประตูเชียงใหม่

🏠 **Bamrungburi Rd** 🚌 **Pratu (*songthaew*), Tha Phae Gate** 🕐 **4am-noon & 6pm-midnight daily**

Regarded as the best place for street food in Chiang Mai, this market bustles morning and night. It's much calmer during the day and is a great place to try traditional northern foods; look out for *gaeng hang lay* (Burmese pork curry) and *tam khanun* (jackfruit salad).

---

⑮

Jing Jai Market
ตลาดนัดวันอาทิตย์เจเจ

🏠 **45 Assadathon Rd** 🕐 **Shopping complex: 10am-6pm daily; Market: 6-9am Wed & Sat, 6am-noon Sun**

Known as the JJ Market, this place is relaxed for most of the week and offers a shopping complex to explore. It comes alive as a market on Wednesdays and weekends with organic food and coffee stalls. It's a great place for breakfast, with a range of cafes to pass the time in. The area is best reached by taxi.

EAT

Fujian
Atmospheric 1930s-style Chinese restaurant famed for its dim sum lunches, with an all you can eat option if you're really hungry. The evening menu is classic Chinese, complemented by an excellent wine list.

🏠 **Dhara Dhevi Resort, Sankampaeng Rd, 51/4 Moo 1** 🌐 **dharadhevi. com**

🅑🅑🅑

Huen Phen
An Old City institution, Huen Phen has been serving superb Lanna food for the past four decades. The specialty is *khao soi*, a curry noodle soup of Burmese origin.

🏠 **112 Rachamankha Rd** 📞 **0-5381-4548**

🅑🅑🅑

A SHORT WALK
CHIANG MAI

Distance 2 miles (3 km) **Time** 30 minutes
Nearest station Charoen Muang Rd

Often called the "Rose of the North," Chiang Mai boasts an exquisite location, circled by mountains. The city may be brimming with stylish boutique hotels and trendy restaurants, but the rich green countryside and relatively relaxed, slow pace of life here brings a more peaceful atmosphere than Thailand's capital city. Chiang Mai thrives on its crafts trade, as seen in the wide range sold at Warorot Market and the Night Bazaar. This walk takes in its stunning *wats* and historic sites, though be sure to also check out its bustling markets and lively nightlife as part of your visit.

Wat Muen Ngon Kong *has exquisite lattice-work and a Lanna chedi topped by a Burmese finial.*

Did You Know?

Though a fraction of the size of Bangkok, Chiang Mai boasts almost as many *wats* as the capital.

START

SAMLAN

SOI 7

Wat Phra Chao Mengrai *has a decorated ceremonial gate.*

A typica northern Thai temple, **Wat Pan Waen** *is set within peaceful compounds, which provide relief from the city heat. The doors of the wihan are decorated with religious images.*

FINISH

← Admiring the architecture and golden hues of Wat Phra Sing

Wat Phra Sing was built in 1345 to house King Kham Fu's ashes. The Wihan Lai Kham is a superb Lanna structure with carved and gilded pediments. Murals inside depict everyday life in 19th-century Chiang Mai.

↑ An array of beautiful colored lanterns at Wat Phan Tao

RATCHADAMNDEN

CHABAN

RATCHAMANKHA

SOI 2

Wat Chang Taem

The well-preserved Lanna wihan is notable at **Wat Phan Tao**. Its roof, supported by columns, is decorated with Lanna cho fas, which means "tassle of the air" and is a Thai architectural detail.

The spacious, triple-roofed wihan of **Wat Chedi Luang** houses panels depicting scenes from the jataka – folk tales from India.

0 meters 100
0 yards 100
N

④ 🚗 🍴 🛍

DOI INTHANON NATIONAL PARK

🔺A2 🏠Off Hwy 1009 (off Hwy 108), S of Chiang Mai 📞0-5328-6728-9
🕐6am–6pm daily 🚌From Chom Thong to Mae Klang falls, then *songthaew*
to Doi Inthanon summit ℹ️Chiang Mai; 0-5324-8604

Home to the highest mountain and waterfall in Thailand, Doi Inthanon National Park is a picturesque oasis. Animal and nature lovers will find the forested landscape and its inhabitants a delight.

Only 36 miles (58 km) from Chiang Mai, the 105-sq mile (272-sq km) Doi Inthanon National Park is a popular destination for one-day excursions. The park has many types of habitat and a wide range of mammals, such as leopard cats, pangolins, and flying squirrels. The area is also popular for bird-watching, being home to nearly 400 bird species, many from North Asia (including mountain hawk eagles and Eurasian woodcocks). Karen and Hmong peoples (*p64*) also live here. Falling over 820 ft (250 m), the Mae Ya waterfall is one of the most beautiful sights here. In contrast to the rest of Thailand, the climate on Doi Inthanon can be chilly, so visitors to the park are advised to take warm clothing.

The majestic grounds of
the Doi Inthanon National ↑
Park at sunrise

Did You Know?

Doi Inthanon, Thailand's highest mountain, is 8,400 ft (2,565 m) high.

① Visitors to the park are treated to impressive views. On a clear day it is possible to see for many miles over the forested landscape.

② The Hmong have been here since the 1890s. Their slash-and-burn agriculture has led to deforestation, but programs to reduce this are now underway.

③ Beautiful wild orchids are abundant on Doi Inthanon.

TOP 4 FLORA AND FAUNA

Sphagnum Moss
Doi Inthanon's cool climate allows plants such as mosses, ferns, and lichens to thrive. At the mountain's summit, sphagnum mosses form a bog, the only habitat of this kind in Thailand.

White-Crested Laughing Thrush
This bird takes its name from its distinctive white crest. Its common habitat is the forest crowning the upper slopes of Doi Inthanon.

Timber Beetle
For protection, this beetle's markings ape the warning coloration of wasps. Its larvae are hatched in the trunks or branches of trees.

Orchids
On the higher slopes of the mountain, pink and white orchids can be seen draped over the branches of trees.

The majestic Mae Ya waterfall surrounded by gorgeous foliage

EXPERIENCE MORE

⑤

Mae Aw
แม่ออ

 A1 🏠 Mae Hong Son province 🚌 Mae Hong Son 🛈 Mae Hong Son; 0-5361-2982-3

Situated in the mountains near the Myanmar border, Mae Aw is a remote settlement built by members of the Kuomintang, or KMT (Chinese Nationalist Army).

Apart from the superb views, the village itself is particularly interesting for its Chinese-style architecture, unique arts and crafts, and restaurants serving local cuisine. Tea is a staple crop here and choice Chinese-style oolong teas (p239) are available for sampling and purchase at the cafes and plantations here. There are several guesthouses and homestays available, making overnight stays an interesting option. Tours are offered, but the area is also accessible by motorcycle or a 4WD vehicle.

THE HISTORY OF OPIUM IN THAILAND

Opium was first grown in northern Thailand in the late 19th century, when hill tribes arrived from southern China. Grown on poor soil at high altitudes and easily transported, it was their most profitable cash crop. Opium production was outlawed in Thailand in 1959, but flourished during the Vietnam War. It was during this lucrative period that power struggles erupted for control of the Golden Triangle's (p248) poppy fields. The KMT and the Shan United Army, based in Burma (now Myanmar), were the largest of the many contenders, including the Thai, Burmese, and Lao armies. Opium production has been cut by more than 80 percent since the 1960s, and most hill tribes now grow other crops, but Thailand is still used as a channel for opium produced in nearby countries.

⑥

Pai
ปาย

 A1 🏠 Mae Hong Son province 🚌 From Mae Hong Son 🛈 Mae Hong Son; 0-5361-2982-3

Set in a beautiful valley, Pai has become one of the region's most popular destinations. Although still a haven for backpackers, Pai is attracting larger resorts. Halfway between Chiang Mai and Mae Hong Son, the old Shan settlement is home to hill tribes and is known for trekking and rafting.

The yellow and white tiles and multilayered roofs of Wat Klang, between the bus station and the Pai River, are typical of Shan temples. The hilltop Wat Phra That Mae Yen, just east of Pai, was also built by the Shan. The carved wooden doors of the main wihan depict scenes from nature and human life.

 Wooden raft navigating the Tham Lot cave system, near Soppong

⑦ Soppong
สบป่อง

🅐 A1 🏠 Mae Hong Son province 🚌 From Mae Hong Son 🛈 Mae Hong Son; 0-5361-2982-3

The village of Soppong is perched 2,200 ft (700 m) up in the mountains. With its fine views, surrounding teak forests, and air of tranquility, Soppong has become a popular resort. Many trekkers pass through here on the way to visit local hill-tribe villages populated by Lisu and Shan (a minority originally from Myanmar). The village itself has a thriving daily market.

Tham Lot, north of Soppong, is one of the largest cave systems in Southeast Asia. The three adjoining caverns form a vast subterranean canyon, which is cut through by a large stream. Boats carry visitors through the cavern with stops to view interesting geological formations.

⑧ Tham Pla
ถ้ำปลา

🅐 A1 🏠 Mae Hong Son province; off Hwy 1095, 11 miles (17 km) N of Mae Hong Son 🚌 Mae Hong Son 🛈 Chiang Mai; 0-5324-8604

Located north of Mae Hong Son, this scenic spot can be visited on a day trip from the town. Tham Pla ("fish cave") is actually a pool and stream at the base of a limestone outcrop, so named because

 Lanterns decorate the charming waterside village of Mae Aw

of the huge carp that live in it. Visitors make merit by buying papaya to feed to the fish. The peaceful surrounding gardens are perhaps the site's most attractive feature.

⑨ Namtok Mae Surin National Park
อุทยานแห่งชาติน้ำตกแม่สุรินทร์

🅐 A2 🏠 Mae Hong Son province Park HQ 2 miles (2.5 km) off Hwy 108, 5 miles (8 km) N of Mae Hong Son 🚌 From Khun Yuam then *songthaew* 🛈 Mae Hong Son; 0-5361-2982-3 🕐 Daily

This small park is the highlight of the area south of Mae Hong Son. Much of its lowland forest provides a habitat for the Malaysian sun bear, Asiatic black bear, and barking deer. Bird species include drongos and hornbills.

Mae Surin waterfall, which at 330 ft (100 m) is one of the highest in Thailand, is reached from the Khun Yuam district on a dirt road. Also accessible from this road is Thung Bua Thong ("wild sunflower meadow"), which blooms in November and December.

Raft trips along the Pai River, which flows through the park, can be arranged at guesthouses in the area.

EAT

Silhouette
Housed within the Reverie Siam Resort, Silhouette serves Mediterranean food in an evocative colonial-style dining room.

🅐 A1 🏠 476 Viengtai, Pai 🌐 reveriesiam.com

Ⓑ Ⓑ Ⓑ

Na's Kitchen
Owner Na does everything here: takes orders, cooks, cleans tables, and washes dishes. That means things take a while, but it's worth the wait.

🅐 A1 🏠 Ratchadamrong Rd, Pai 📞 08-1387-0234

Ⓑ Ⓑ Ⓑ

Boomelicious Cafe
This hip cafe has an industrial-chic vibe. The Western menu encompasses all-day brunches and burgers.

🅐 A1 🏠 Soi 1 Corner Plaza, Pai 📞 08-6329-3014

Ⓑ Ⓑ Ⓑ

 10

Doi Chiang Dao
ดอยเชียงดาว

⚑A1 🕙7.5 miles (12 km) W
of Chiang Dao, Chiang Mai
province 🚌From Chiang
Mai to Chiang Dao, then
songthaew 🛈Chiang Mai;
www.chiangmai-thai.com

At 7,200 ft (2,195 m), this is
the third-largest mountain
in Thailand. Home to several
Lisu and Karen villages, Doi
Chiang Dao features both
tropical and pine forests.
Today, this peak and the
surrounding area, characterized by rugged limestone
scenery and dense teak forest,
are more of an attraction than
the nearby town, Chiang Dao.

Running for some 8.5 miles
(14 km) under the mountain
is a network of caves, **Tham
Chiang Dao**, best reached
from Chiang Dao town. Most

of the caves house statues of
the Buddha that, over the
years, have been left by Shan
pilgrims from Myanmar. The
highlight of the bat-inhabited
caves, however, is their huge
stalactites and stalagmites.
Lanterns and guides can be
hired in order to make the
most of these impressive
features. The tours take
visitors along an illuminated
walkway through the caves.

Near the caves is a temple,
Wat Tham Chiang Dao, with a
Buddhist meditation center
and a small room displaying
gongs and other instruments.

East of Doi Chiang Dao,
and dominated by the peak,
is Chiang Dao town, with its
splendid traditional teak
buildings along the main
street. It was founded in the
18th century as a place of
exile for *phi pop*, ("spirit
people"), who were suspected
of being possessed by evil
spirits. In fact, the symptoms
of their true illnesses, such as
malaria, had been mistaken
as signs of madness.

Tham Chiang Dao
🚶🚶 ⚑Off Hwy 107, 3 miles
(5 km) NW of Chiang Dao
🕙Daily

> 💬 INSIDER TIP
> ### Trekking Around
> Chiang Dao
>
> Treks around Chiang
> Dao and Mae Taeng
> often combine visits to
> hill-tribe villages with
> a raft trip through
> stunning scenery.
> Treks can be arranged
> by guesthouses or
> trekking companies.

Did You Know?
—
The northern Thailand
landscape is renowned
for its excellent
trekking country.

 11

San Kamphaeng
สันกำแพง

⚑B2 🕙9 miles (13 km) E of
Chiang Mai, Chiang Mai
province 🚌From Chiang
Mai 🛈Chiang Mai; 0-5324-
8604

This village, with its old,
wooden buildings and narrow
streets, is renowned for its
silk and handicraft products.
There are many factories
here selling good-quality
silk, teak furniture, silverware,
lacquerware, jade, or celadon.
Prices can be high, though
bargaining often reduces
the cost significantly. An
interesting feature of most
of the silk factories is their
exhibits of the silk-making
process. The whole procedure

A stunning pink and orange sky over the mountain range of Doi Chiang Dao

The main temple of interest is Wat Tha Thanon.

To the west of Uttaradit is Wat Phra Boromathat, which is also known as Wat That Thung Yang. Its *wihan* is an example of the Lao Luang Prabang architectural style.

 13

Phrao
พร้าว

🅰 B1 🏠 Chiang Mai province 🚌 From Chiang Mai 🛈 Chiang Mai; 0-5324-8604

This small market town is a meeting place for Thai traders and hill-tribe people. Phrao was previously relatively isolated, but today Highway 1150 connects it with Wiang Pa Pao *(p241)*, making it more accessible. Phrao is still off the main tourist track. The town's principal sight is its covered market, which sells textiles and fruit and vegetables.

14

Mae Taeng Valley
หุบเขาแม่แตง

🅰 A1 🏠 Chiang Mai province 🚌 Chiang Mai, then *songthaew* 🛈 Chiang Mai; 0-5324-8604

The area around Mae Taeng, especially the vicinity of the Taeng River to the northwest

of the town, is very popular with trekkers. The land has been terraced and irrigated to improve agricultural production, and the variety of crops grown has created an attractive contrast of landscapes. However, most trekkers come here not only for the peaceful surroundings but also to witness everyday scenes in the region's many Lisu, Karen, and Hmong villages. Other activities, including river rafting, can be combined with treks in the surrounding area.

Established in 1995, the **Elephant Nature Park**, in the beautiful Mae Taeng Valley, is home to dozens of rescued elephants. Founder Lek Chailert's efforts to save the endangered Asian elephant from extinction have received praise and awards from around the world.

Elephant Nature Park
⊕ 🏠 6 miles (10 km) W of Hwy 107 🕑 Daily 🌐 elephantnaturefoundation.org

---

is shown, from silk moths, through the unraveling of the cocoons, to the weaving of dyed silk thread on traditional wooden looms.

 12

Uttaradit
อุตรดิตถ์

🅱 B2 🏠 Uttaradit province 🚐🚌 🛈 Phrae; 0-5452-1118

Relatively free of modern development, Uttaradit features on few visitors' itineraries. Nevertheless, the town's location makes it a convenient staging post between the North Central Plains and northern Thailand. The town is made up of old teak buildings and narrow streets.

The tiny, delightful chapel of Wat Phra Boromathat, just outside Uttaradit

Individually painted parasols hand-crafted in the village of Bo Sang

Bunruang dates from 1939. The area around Mae Sariang is mountainous and forested, with many winding roads. Organized trips by boat or *songthaew* (which can be arranged in town) make the 30-mile (45-km) journey from Mae Sariang to Mae Sam Laep, a Karen settlement on the Myanmar border next to the Salawin River. This river was once infamous for drug running and gem smuggling. Today, Mae Sam Laep is a staging post for the (mostly illegal) teak log trade. Political troubles in Myanmar have made this area a zone for refugees, though some Myanmar minorities, such as the Lawa, have lived here longer than Thais.

Bo Sang
บ่อสร้าง

🅰B2 🕐6 miles (9 km) E of Chiang Mai, Chiang Mai province 🚌From Chiang Mai 🛈Chiang Mai; 0-5324-8604

Bo Sang is known throughout Thailand as the "umbrella village" on account of the decorative umbrellas produced here. The village is made up almost entirely of shops and factories involved in this craft.

Each umbrella has a wooden handle, bamboo ribs, and a covering of oiled rice paper, silk, or cotton. Craftsmen will usually personalize designs in bold colors. The annual fair includes competitions, exhibitions, and a beauty contest.

Other handicrafts, including silverware, lacquerware, and celadon (a grayish-green porcelain), are also sold here. Aside from its umbrella making, Bo Sang is also the heart of a farming community. In the wet season (June to October), the rice fields are a deep green color. From November to January, the fields dry out and turn golden. Farmers then thresh the rice.

Many houses in and around Bo Sang are traditional, wooden northern Thai structures with spacious rooms. They are typically built on stilts and set in small gardens.

Mae Sariang
แม่สะเรียง

🅰A2 🕐Mae Hong Son province 🚌 🛈Chiang Mai; 0-5324-8604

Mae Sariang is a pleasant town on the Yuam River. The area has historical links with nearby Myanmar, a fact that is reflected in Mae Sariang's architecture and by its large community of Myanmar Muslims. People of the Karen hill tribe – the area's main ethnic group – frequent the central market. Two temples near the bus station have Myanmar features: multi-layered roofs and vivid orange and yellow exterior ornamentation. Wat Chong Sung (also called Wat Uthayarom) was built in 1896, while Wat Si

PICTURE PERFECT
Umbrella Fair

The village of Bo Sang is known for hand-crafted parasols. Close-ups of the artisans at work can be shot year-round, but during the January fair the parade of local women riding bicycles while shading themselves with umbrellas is the shot to get.

Doi Saket
ดอยสะเก็ด

🅰B2 🕐Off Hwy 118, 10 miles (16 km) NE of Chiang Mai, Chiang Mai province 🚊🚌Chiang Mai, then *songthaew* 🛈Chiang Mai; 0-5324-8604

Forming a triangle with Bo Sang and San Kamphaeng, the mountain of Doi Saket is an ideal sight to combine with these two towns on a day trip from Chiang Mai.

The main reason for visiting Doi Saket is its hilltop temple, Wat Doi Saket, which offers stunning views of the Chiang Mai valley. The *wat* is reached by a steep staircase consisting of 300 steps, flanked on either side by a *naga*. The temple complex includes a modern *wihan*, painted in red and gold, and a white *chedi*. There is a huge, seated Buddha on the hilltop and seven smaller Buddhas, one to represent each day of the week.

Lamphun

ลำพูน

🏔 B2 🏛 Lamphun province
🚌 🚆 𝒾 Chiang Mai; 0-5324-8604

Lamphun is made up of large wooden houses beside the Kuang River and is characterized by its peaceful atmosphere, ancient temples, and surrounding rice fields.

Its most important temple is Wat Phra That Haripunchai. The present compound was probably founded in AD 1044 by King Athitayarai of Haripunchai, though the 150-ft (46-m) high central *chedi*, topped by a nine-tier umbrella of pure gold, is thought to date from 897. In the 1930s, the temple was renovated by Khrubaa Siwichai, one of the most revered monks in northern Thailand. An unusual structure is the rare, pyramid-shaped *chedi* in the northwest of the compound. The large *bot* houses a reclining Buddha

image, while a 15th-century Lanna Buddha is kept in the main *wihan*. Adjoining it is a 19th-century library, with a staircase flanked by *nagas*. To the right of the library is an open pavilion displaying a huge gong cast in 1860, alleged to be the largest in the world. Outside the main compound is a smaller *bot*, inside of which is a so-called "happy Buddha," a smiling Chinese-style image.

The nearby **Lamphun National Museum** has carvings and artifacts from many periods, especially the Lanna, Dvaravati, and Haripunchai kingdoms. Modern artifacts include an ornate black and gold howdah.

Wat Chama Thewi (or Wat Kukut), just west of Lamphun on Highway 1015, is noted for its two *chedis*, thought to be among the oldest in all of Thailand. Both built in 1218, they are the last surviving examples of Dvaravati architecture.

Lamphun National Museum

♿ 🏛 Inthayongyot Rd
🕐 8:30am–4pm
Wed–Sun

NAGAS: MYTHICAL SERPENTS

Naga figures are protective serpents. Acting as guardians against bad spirits, they often flank the walls of temples or the staircases up to them. The significance of *nagas* is deep-rooted throughout Buddhist Asia, though their meaning may vary slightly. In Buddhism their origins can be traced back to an episode in the *jataka* tales in which a *garuda*, or mythical bird, attacks and subdues a *naga* that is trying to harm the Buddha. The *naga* subsequently becomes the Buddha's guardian.

← The central *chedi* (inset) and a golden Buddha housed in a smaller structure at Wat Phra That Hariphunchai in Lamphun

SHOP

Indra Ceramics

Beautifully painted ceramic goods, including Lampang's trademark "chicken bowl."

🅰B2 🏠382 Vajiravudh Damnoen Rd, Lampang

Dee Dee Otop

Furniture and animal sculptures beautifully carved from native teak.

🅰B2 🏠Tumbol Maetha, Amphoe Mae Tha, Lampang

Kad Kong Ta Street Market

Browse handmade cottonware at this evening and weekend market on the riverbank.

🅰B2 🏠Talad Gao Rd, Lampang

 19

Lampang

ลำปาง

🅰B2 🏠Lampang province
✈🚉🚌 *i* Lampang; 0-5421-8823 or 0-5422-6812

The second-largest town in northern Thailand, Lampang is a good base for excursions and travel within northern Thailand. In the 19th century, British traders came here from Myanmar (then Burma) and turned the town into a teak production center, bringing workers with them. The result was the many teak houses and Burmese-style temples seen throughout the town. Teak furniture is just one of the traditional crafts still produced in Lampang; others are cottonware and ceramics.

Modern Lampang is known for its brightly colored horse-drawn carriages, introduced in the 19th century. One of the most important temples in northern Thailand is Wat Phra That Lampang Luang (*p204*), southwest of town, which is famous for its impressive 19th-century murals.

Lampang town focuses on the south side of the Wang River, although the main sights are found to the north of it. Of its temples, the most interesting is Wat Phra Kaeo Don Tao. The *wat* is thought to have been built about the same time the town was founded, but only the *chedi* survives. The *mondop* is notable for its nine-tier teak roof with intricate carvings and a bronze Buddha in the Mandalay style. Within the compound is the **Lanna Museum**, which displays religious Lanna artifacts.

Ban Sao Nak ("many pillars house"), southeast of Wat Phra Kaeo Don Tao, is a Lanna structure built in 1896. It takes its name from the 116 square teak pillars supporting the building. Now a museum, it is furnished with Myanmar and Thai antiques. The sumptuous decoration includes lacquerware, ceramics, and silverware.

A more recent attraction is Wat Chalermprakiat, built in 2004. Essentially just pagodas at the top of a mountain, it is a steep climb but offers a marvelous view of Lampang spread out below.

Lanna Museum
🏛 🏠Phra Kaeo Rd 🕐Daily

Ban Sao Nak
🏛 🏠Ratwana Rd 🕐Daily

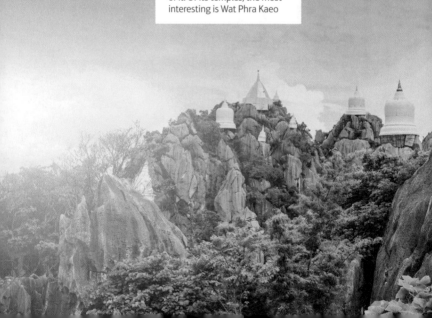

20

Ping River Valley
หุบเขาแม่น้ำปิง

B3 **Chiang Mai province** **Chiang Mai, then** *songthaew* **Chiang Mai;** 0-5324-8604

Nearly 370 miles (600 km) long, the Ping River is a major waterway in northern Thailand. It rises on the Myanmar border and flows on to the Bhumibol Reservoir before merging with the Wang, Yom, and Nan rivers. This becomes the Chao Phraya River at Nakhon Sawan, in the Central Plains. The valley is a rural area where traditional life can still be observed.

Chom Thong, just south of Chiang Mai, at the junction of Highway 108 and the road to Doi Inthanon National Park *(p214)*, is a small but busy town. It boasts one major sight, Wat Phra That Si Chom Thong. The *wat* was built to enshrine a relic of the Buddha and is still an important pilgrimage site for Buddhists. This *wat* is also widely considered to be one of the most beautiful in northern Thailand. The gilded *chedi*, built in 1451, is of Burmese design,

↑ Farmers working in a terraced rice field high on a ridge in the Ping River Valley

as is the mid-16th-century *bot*, which features intricate wood carvings depicting flowers, birds, and *nagas (p223)*.

The deep Chaem River Valley, west of Chom Thong, is known locally for its many varieties of butterfly and moth. Several villages, spread along the twisting road within the valley, are known collectively as the town of Mae Chaem. The town, once famous for weaving, is now modernizing rapidly. Its main temple, Wat Pa Daet, is worth visiting for its well-preserved Lanna buildings and murals.

At the southern end of the valley is the small town of Hot. Originally located 10 miles (15 km) farther downstream, the town was relocated to its present site in 1964, when the land was flooded to form the Bhumibol Reservoir. Ruins of the original town can still be seen beside the reservoir. Excavation of the site has turned up amulets, stucco carvings, and gold jewelry. Modern-day Hot, meanwhile, is an important market town and a useful staging post for journeys westward to the town of Mae Sariang.

←

Protruding through peaks, the pagodas of Wat Chalermprakiat, Lampang

21

Mae Hong Son
แม่ฮ่องสอน

A1 **0.5 miles (1 km) NW of Chong Kham Lake** **Khumlum Phraphat Rd** **Mae Hong Son; 0-5361-2982-3**

This isolated provincial capital retains its pre-modern charms and offers several worthy sights of historic significance. It lacks the raucous party scene that makes it neighbor Pai so attractive to some. It is also a good base from which to start treks in unvisited hill-tribe villages, or boat trips on the Pai River. In the center of town, Chong Kham Lake is flanked by two temples built in the distinctive Burmese style, Wat Chong Kham and Wat Chong Klang. For a great view of the town, climb the steps to Wat Doi Kong Mu.

 INSIDER TIP
Cruising on the Ping River

Chiang Mai province is best seen from a covered boat on the Ping River. Trips leave from Wat Chaimongkhol near the Night Bazaar in Chiang Mai; dinner cruises are also offered.

A SHORT WALK
MAE HONG SON

Distance 0.5 miles (1 km) **Time** 15 minutes
Nearest bus station Khumlum Phraphrat Rd

Beautifully located in a valley ringed by forested mountains, Mae Hong Son (*p225*) sprang up in 1831 from a small camp where elephants were tethered. The town was largely isolated until it was linked by a paved highway to Chiang Mai in 1965. The province has traditionally been dominated by nearby Myanmar, as shown by its architecture. Shan and Karen people, who make up most of the population, continue to move across the border to live in Mae Hong Son and its environs. If walking around the area in the cool season, you may need to wear a sweater or jacket here. The area is also known for the "long-neck women" of the Paduang, or Kayan, tribe, whose necks were lengthened from childhood by brass rings.

↑ Browsing a variety of Tai Lue fabrics at the Night Bazaar

The lively, pungent **Daily Market**, *which almost spills onto the airport runway, sells a range of fresh produce, Myanmar textiles, and trekking supplies.*

The **Night Bazaar** *sells crafts and Tai Lue fabrics.*

The teak **Wat Hua Wiang** *has a Burmese-style, multi-roofed design. The bot – in an advanced state of decay – houses an important brass image of Buddha, Phrachao Para La 'Khaeng, that was transported here from Burma.*

Traditional Shan teak houses can be seen along this street.

UDOM CHAONITHEN

PRADIT CHONG KHAM

STA

⏵ START

0 meters   25
0 yards   25

N ↑

🔘 FINISH

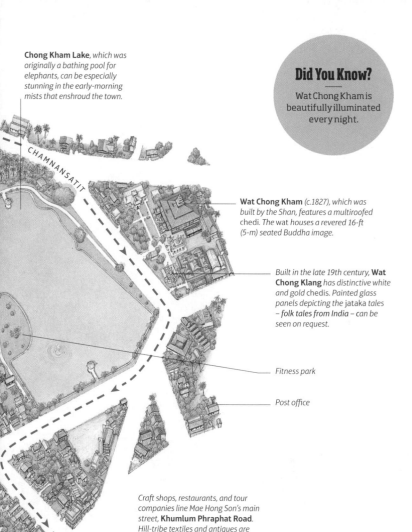

Chong Kham Lake, which was originally a bathing pool for elephants, can be especially stunning in the early-morning mists that enshroud the town.

CHAMNANSATIT

Did You Know?

Wat Chong Kham is beautifully illuminated every night.

Wat Chong Kham (c.1827), which was built by the Shan, features a multiroofed chedi. The wat houses a revered 16-ft (5-m) seated Buddha image.

Built in the late 19th century, **Wat Chong Klang** has distinctive white and gold chedis. Painted glass panels depicting the jataka tales – folk tales from India – can be seen on request.

Fitness park

Post office

Craft shops, restaurants, and tour companies line Mae Hong Son's main street, **Khumlum Phraphat Road**. Hill-tribe textiles and antiques are among the items for sale.

KHUMLUM PHRAPHAT

→ Wat Chong Kham reflected in the Chong Kham Lake at night

FAR NORTH

The Far North of Thailand is known as the Golden Triangle – the meeting point of Thailand, Myanmar, and Laos and an area historically associated with opium production. Since the 1980s, cash crops, including cabbage, tea, and coffee, began to replace poppies grown for opium production, and fields of these new crops are a common sight in northern Thailand today. The fertile flood plains of the Mekong, which touch the tip of the Far North before running east into Laos, contrast with the breathtaking beauty of the mountains in the west and east of the area. Here can be found remote villages inhabited by hill tribes such as the Mien and Akha, who still preserve their traditional way of life. There are also settlements populated by ex-Chinese Nationalist soldiers and their descendants, who migrated here after Mao Zedong's Communist army won the Chinese civil war in 1949. Chiang Rai is the main town in the Far North, and was very briefly made the capital of Thailand by King Mengrai in the 13th century, before Chiang Mai took the title.

FAR NORTH

Must Sees
1 Chiang Rai
2 Wat Phumin

Experience More
3 Nan
4 Mae Sai
5 Tha Ton
6 Fang
7 Mae Salong (Santikhiree)
8 Doi Tung
9 The Golden Triangle Apex (Sop Ruak)
10 Wiang Pa Pao
11 Chiang Khong
12 Chiang Saen
13 Phayao
14 Mae Saruai
15 Ngao
16 Nong Bua
17 Phrae
18 Doi Phu Kha National Park

THE GOLDEN
TRIANGLE APEX
(SOP RUAK)
9

12
CHIANG
SAEN

Huay Xai
1129
Ban Huoeisay

11 CHIANG KHONG

Pak Tha

L A O S

Mekong

Ban Hok

Chom Phu

1020

Ta Luang

Thoeng

15 NGAO

1021

Chiang Kham

Ban Pung

3

Ban Huay
Sanei

Mekong

2W

Xieng Hon

Muang Ngoen

1

Ing

Chun

Song Khwae

1148

1091

021

118

Pong

1091

Chiang Muan

Sa Lap

*Mae Yom
National Park*

103

Pa Lao Klang

Nan Rai Dao

Song

Rong Kwang

Phea
Muang Phi

101

17 PHRAE

Wat Phra That Chaw Hae

✈ **Phrae Airport**

Den Chai

11

taradit

117

Nan

101

Bo Yuak

DOI PHU KHA
NATIONAL PARK

Pua

18

*Doi Phu Kha
6,496 ft (1,980 m)*

Sainyabuli

Phiang

Nam Puy

NONG BUA **16**

1169

1081

Santisuk

✈ Nan Nakhon Airport

WAT
PHUMIN
2 **3** NAN

Ban Namo

*Doi Luang
4,491 ft (1,369 m)*

101

Wiang Sa

Pang Mon

Sao Din

Na Noi

1083

Na Mun

Huay Noi Ka

Ban
Suvannaphun

L A O S

Mekong

Pak Lai

6

Fak Tha

117

Ban Buamthon

211

Chiang
Khan

*Sirikit
Reservoir*

Wang Pha
Chan

Nam Pat

Nam Hoy

Ban
Nakok

Kaen Thao

**MEKONG RIVER
VALLEY**
p264

0 kilometers   30

0 miles   30

N
↑

FAR NORTH

The gloriously decorated Wat Phra Sing on a sunny afternoon

CHIANG RAI

เชียงราย

B1 5 miles (8 km) N of Chiang Rai Off Prasopsuk Rd; 4 miles (6 km) S of Chiang Rai Kok River pier Singkhlai Rd, Chiang Rai; 0-5371-7433

This town was founded in 1262 by King Mengrai, who decided that the site would be ideal for the capital of the Lanna Kingdom (p71). However, the capital was transferred to Chiang Mai 34 years later, and Chiang Rai declined in importance. The modern town may lack the charm and architectural interest of Chiang Mai, but it has a number of sights worthy of attention.

Wat Phra Sing
วัดพระสิงห์

Singhakhlai Rd
6am–5pm daily

Built in the late 14th century, Wat Phra Sing is a typical northern wooden structure, with low, curved roofs. The main *wihan* houses a replica of the Phra Sing Buddha in Chiang Mai's Wat Phra Sing (p208). Also of interest are the carved medallions below the windows of the *bot*, which depict animals. Around the Bodhi tree are Buddha images.

Wat Phra Kaeo
วัดพระแก้ว

Trirat Rd 8am–5pm daily

This is the city's most revered temple. According to legend, lightning struck and cracked the *chedi* in 1354, revealing a plaster-cast statue encasing the Emerald Buddha (actually made of jadeite). Today Thailand's most holy Buddha image is housed in Wat Phra Kaeo in Bangkok (p98). A replica, presented in 1991, is now kept here. The *wat* dates

from the 13th century and is also notable for its fine *bot*, decorated with elaborate wood carving, and the Phra Chao Lang Thong, one of the largest surviving bronze statues from the early Lanna period (p71).

Wat Phra That Doi Thong
วัดพระธาตุดอยทอง

At-am Nuai Rd, Doi Chom Thong Hill 6am–5pm daily

This fine temple, built in the 1940s, is located on a hilltop outside the town. It is on this spot that King Mengrai is said to have decided upon the location of his new capital. In the *wihan* is the city's

 PICTURE PERFECT
Clock Tower

A short walk south of Wat Phra Sing, this distinctive golden tower is lit up at night. Try and take a shot of tuk-tuks and motorbikes driving past as it changes from gold to green to pink.

original *lak muang*, or "city pillar," traditionally erected in Thailand to mark the founding of a new city.

of flooding and pollution, reflect the concern of Thais at the rapid growth of their cities, an issue of particular relevance in Chiang Rai.

 ④

Wat Chet Yot
วัดเจ็ดยอด

🏠 Chet Yot Rd 🕐 6am-9pm daily

This small temple, named for its unusual, seven-spired *chedi*, is similar in appearance to its namesake in Chiang Mai (*p210*). The front veranda of the main *wihan* has an interesting mural depicting astrological scenes.

⑤

Wat Mungmuang
วัดมุงเมือง

🏠 Uttarakit Rd 🕐 8am-4:30pm daily

A rotund Buddha image with one hand raised in the *vitarkha mudra* position (where the thumb and fore-finger form a circle) dominates this *wat*. The murals in the main *wihan*, depicting local mountain scenery and scenes

⑥

Hill Tribe Museum
พิพิธภัณฑ์ชาวเขา

🏠 620-625 Thanalai Rd 🕐 8:30am-6pm daily (from 10am Sat & Sun) 🌐 pdacr.org

This museum and crafts center was established in 1990 by the non-profit Population and Community Development Association (PDA), also known for raising awareness of Thailand's AIDS problem. In addition to informing tourists of the plight of Thailand's various hill tribes (*p64*), volunteers at the center work with the tribespeople, educating them on how to cope with threats to their traditional lifestyle from a rapidly modernizing society. The center displays and sells fine, traditional hill-tribe crafts (*p36*). These can also be bought at the market and in shops around the center of Chiang Rai.

Must See

EAT

Salungkham
Wonderful Thai cuisine served in the relaxing interior or in the pretty garden.

🏠 834/3 Phaholyothin Rd 📞 0-5371-7192

Ⓑ Ⓑ Ⓑ

Yunnan
The specialty here is Yunnanese dishes, although Thai staples are also on offer.

🏠 211/5 Khwae Wai Rd 📞 0-5371-3263

Ⓑ Ⓑ Ⓑ

Cabbages & Condoms
Thai food and some delicious local specialties. Profits go to promote safe sex.

🏠 620/25 Thanalai Rd 📞 0-5371-9167

Ⓑ Ⓑ Ⓑ

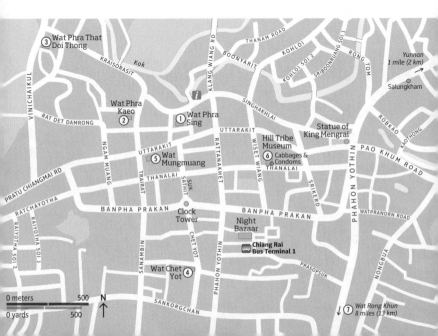

WAT RONG KHUN

🏠 8 miles (13 km) S of Chiang Rai 📞 0-5367-3579 🚌 From Chiang Rai
🕐 8am–5pm daily (to 5:30pm Sat & Sun)

Known as the "White Temple," this spectacular, unconventional *wat* is a combination of art exhibit and temple. Renovated in 1997 by artist-turned-architect Chalermchai Kositpipat, it remains unfinished, but is one of the most photogenic temples in Thailand.

Buddhist Symbolism

From a distance, Wat Rong Khun takes the traditional shape of a Thai *wat* (albeit an incredibly ornate one), but rather than the traditional gold, it is gleaming white – an effect enhanced by the fragments of mirrored glass which stud every surface. Originally built as a center of learning and meditation, Wat Rong Khun is rooted in Buddhist teachings and symbolism. Scenes from Buddhist mythology are depicted in striking, often startling, detail. Visitors enter the temple across a bridge, which passes over a reflective lake and a sculptural "sea" of outstretched arms, evoking the yearning of wretched souls in hell. The inside of the *ubosot* (main chapel) could not be more different from the outside, with walls covered in colorful murals. These depict mythical creatures and the Buddha alongside, strangely, celebrities and popular culture figures, from Keanu Reeves in the Matrix to Superman. This juxtaposition is typical of the artist's work, as he used to

 INSIDER TIP
Prayer Plates

You can earn some karmic merit by adding your name to a metal plate for a fee of 30 baht, which will then be hung from either a canopy walkway or one of the "trees" that dot the temple grounds. There is also a wishing well nearby.

Rather than the traditional gold, Wat Rong Khun is gleaming white – an effect enhanced by the fragments of mirrored glass.

be a movie poster designer. Somewhat disappointingly, photography is prohibited inside, although there is a souvenir shop and a museum showcasing Kositpipat's work.

Future Plans

The projected completion date for the temple is 2070, and eventually the site will include a total of nine structures. In addition to the *ubosot*, it will feature a hall to enshrine Buddhist relics, a meditation hall, monks' living quarters, and an art gallery. Kositpipat has so far spent more than 40 million baht on renovations for the temple. The building was damaged by an earthquake in 2014, but construction and further expansion is pushing on. The protracted progress is unlikely to be of much concern to Kositpipat, who is said to believe that his work on the temple will be rewarded with eternal life.

Spectacular detail and artistry of the *ubosot* and surrounding statues ↓

Bridge of the Cycle of Rebirth

▶ Passing over the bridge, which is surrounded by a pit of outstretched arms, represents escape from the painful cycle of life, death, and rebirth.

The Ubosot

▼ The temple's main building has a three-tiered pavilion-like structure typical of northern Thai temples, but it uses a pure white color, rather than the more conventional gold, to symbolize the purity of the Buddha. The use of glass, meanwhile, symbolizes the Buddha's wisdom and teachings. The *ubosot* traditionally serves as the monks' ordination hall.

Crematorium

▶ The temple's preoccupation with death is not merely artistic; one of the newer buildings is a working crematorium, also built in white.

The Golden Bathrooms

◀ At many Thai temples, gold is used as a symbol of beauty and purity; here, the gaudy golden building represents the earthly and profane. Appropriately, this is where you'll find the bathrooms, which are considered the most spectacular in the whole of Thailand.

Art Murals

▶ Colorful murals inside the ubosot depict the Buddha and mythical creatures from religious folklore alongside pop culture figures like Elvis.

2

WAT PHUMIN

วัดภูมินทร์

⬛C2 ⬛Phumin village, south bank of Nan River, Phakong Rd, center of Nan town ⬛⬛ ⬛8:30am–4:30pm daily

Notable for its impressive murals, cross-shaped design, elaborate coffered ceiling, and carved doors and pillars, Wat Phumin is one of the most beautiful temples in northern Thailand.

Wat Phumin was founded in 1596 by the ruler of Nan, and was renovated in the mid-19th century and again in 1991. The highlight is undoubtedly its murals, which were originally thought to have been painted by Thai Lue artists during the 19th-century renovation. But the apparent depiction of French troops, unknown in the area before the French annexation of part of Nan province in 1893, suggests a date in the mid-1890s. Three main themes can be picked out from the murals. The life of the Buddha, as seen in the famous Story of the Buddha mural, is a prominent theme in the collection. The *jataka* tale of his incarnation as Khatta Kumara, violently illustrated in the Descending Serpents mural, is also a repetitive feature, as well as scenes depicting everyday life in Nan.

↑ The peaceful temple, picturesque against the sunset

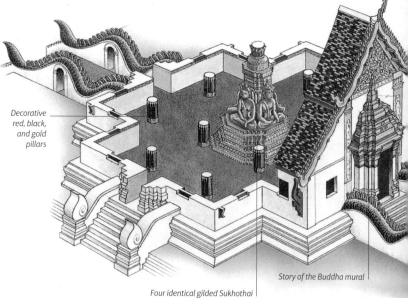

Decorative red, black, and gold pillars

Story of the Buddha mural

↑ The ornate design of Wat Phumin, with its unique snake carvings

Four identical gilded Sukhothai images sit back-to-back facing the cardinal points.

EXPERIENCE MORE

STORY OF THE BUDDHA MURAL

The mural on the northern wall above the main door is particularly outstanding. Located at the very top of the image is the Buddha, and on a lower plane are his disciples. In the bottom half, Khatta Kumara and his friends are depicted on their way to a city with a palace, which Khatta later rebuilds after its destruction by snakes and birds.

Nagas
(serpents) flank the steps at the front and back of the building.

Main entrance

Nan
น่าน

🅐 B/C2 🅰 Nan province ✈ 🚌
ℹ Chiang Rai; 0-5374-4674

Nan is a prosperous town on the Nan River. Its relative isolation, bordering Laos, has allowed it to keep a peaceful charm. It is home to the Thai Lue people, originally from Laos, and the textile handicrafts here are well-made and authentic.

Wat Phumin (*p236*), in the south of town, is without doubt the most important sight in Nan. Just north of it (on Highway 101) is the **Nan National Museum**, which is housed in an impressive former royal palace dating from 1903. The first floor is dedicated to the ethnic groups of Nan province, including the Hmong and Mien hill tribes. The upper floor has a comprehensive selection of artifacts relating to the history of the region, including weapons. Notable items include a "black" elephant tusk weighing 40 lb (18 kg), supported by a sculpted *khut* (mythological eagle). Thought to date from the 17th century, the tusk is actually dark brown.

Nearby is Wat Chang Kham Wora Wihan, with a magnificent 14th-century *chedi* resting on sculpted elephant heads. The *wat* also holds a pure gold Buddha image in the Sukhothai style (the largest

↑ Artifacts relating to the history of Nan at the Nan National Museum

of its type in Thailand). It was discovered when a trader offered the monks a large sum for a plaster image. During the transportation the image crashed to the ground revealing the golden Buddha inside. The deal was cancelled and the image is now in a glass case in the temple's manuscript library.

Among Nan's other temples is Wat Suan Tan, in the northwest of town, with a 130-ft (40-m) *chedi*, crowned by a white *prang* (a rounded, Khmer-style tower that is very rarely seen in northern Thailand). Housed in the *wihan* is a bronze Buddha image, Phra Chao Thong Thip. The image was made to the order of the king of Chiang Mai in 1449 after he conquered Nan. According to legend, the monarch gave the city's craftsmen just one week to make it.

Southeast of Nan is the revered Wat Phra That Chae Haeng. Dating from 1355, the temple is set in a square compound on a hilltop overlooking the Nan valley. Its gilded Lanna *chedi* is just over 180 ft (55 m) high and can be seen from several miles around.

Nan National Museum
⊗ 🅰 Hwy 101 🄲 0-5471-0561 🕘 9am–4pm Wed–Sun

Did You Know?

Since the end of the 19th century, boat races have taken place on the river at Nan every year.

Did You Know?

Mae Sai was where 12 teenagers were saved by divers in 2018 after being trapped in a cave for 18 days.

in the light. Farther south are more caves, **Tham Pum** and **Tham Pla**, with lakes inside.

Tham Luang

 △ Off Hwy 110, 3.5 miles (6km) S of Mae Sai **◐** Daily

Tham Pum and Tham Pla

△ Off Hwy 110, 8 miles (13km) S of Mae Sai **◐** Daily

 Hill-tribe women harvesting the abundance of tea crops on a clear day in Mae Salong

a striking golden topknot. The temple dominates the town from its hillside location to the west, offering splendid panoramic views.

4
Mae Sai
แม่สาย

△ B1 **△** Chiang Rai province **▦** **ℹ** Chiang Rai; 0-5371-7433

The northernmost town in Thailand, Mae Sai is separated from Myanmar (Burma) only by a bridge. The town bustles with traders from the neighboring country who come here to sell their wares, including gems and jade items, mostly made in Myanmar.

To visit the town of Tachilek, in Myanmar, visitors have to exit Thailand at the border bridge in Mae Sai. Mynamar Immigration charges a 500-*baht* fee for a temporary visa that allows a 24-hour stay. Most people simply look around the market and return to Mae Sai. Beware of buying counterfeit goods, since Thai customs may confiscate them.

South of Mae Sai is **Tham Luang**, a large cave complex with crystals that change color

5
Tha Ton
ท่าตอน

△ B1 **△** Chiang Mai province **▦** From Chiang Mai to Fang, then *songthaew* **ℹ** Chiang Mai; 0-5324-8604

Located on a bend in the Kok River, picturesque Tha Ton is essentially a staging post for riverboats that make regular trips from here to Chiang Rai. Excursions can be arranged at guesthouses in town, and may often be combined with visits to nearby tribal villages or hot springs. Committed mountain bikers can follow the trail on the north side of the river all the way to Chiang Rai, or shorter trips can be arranged through the guesthouses. Tha Ton's chief tourist attraction is Wat Tha Ton, which is notable for a huge white Buddha with

6
Fang
ฝาง

△ B1 **△** Chiang Mai province **▦** From Chiang Mai **ℹ** Chiang Mai; 0-5324-8604

This town was founded as a trading center in 1268 by King Mengrai, who took advantage of the site's location at the head of a valley. At the start of the 19th century the town was destroyed by Burmese raiders, and it lay deserted until 1880. Today Fang is effectively a border town between the areas inhabited by Thais and hill tribes. The local Mien, Karen, and Lahu tribes sell their goods at Fang's market, and this has made it an important trading center.

Fang is characterized by teak houses. The influence of nearby Myanmar is seen in many structures, such as Wat Jong Paen, located in the north of town. The most impressive

temple in Fang, it features a splendid Myanmar-style, multiroofed *wihan*.

Drug trading in the Fang area has been significant in the past, and fighting between rival drug factions in Myanmar still occasionally spills across the border. It is wise to check the situation with the local tourist office before venturing on a guided trek.

Mae Salong (Santikhiree)

แม่สลอง

🅰 B1 **🏠 Chiang Rai province** **🚌 Chiang Rai, then *songthaew*** **📱 0-5371-7433**

One of the main settlements in northern Thailand, the hillside town of Mae Salong is also one of the most scenic. Mae Salong was founded in 1962 by the Kuomintang (KMT), or Chinese Nationalist Army, following their defeat in China by Mao Zedong in 1949. It became a

center for exiled Chinese soldiers, who used it as a base for incursions into China. The Thai military agreed to let the KMT stay if they helped to suppress Communism, which they believed would become rife among the hill tribes at the time of the Vietnam War. In return for their help, the KMT were allowed to control and tax the local opium trade *(p218)*. As a result, the area around Mae Salong was relatively lawless and dangerous until the 1980s.

When Khun Sa, the opium warlord, retreated to Myanmar in the early 1980s, the Thai government began to have some success in pacifying the area. This was helped when, soon after the end of this turbulent period, Mae Salong was officially renamed Santikhiree ("hill of peace"), in an attempt to rid the town of its former image. However, many still refer to the area as Mae Salong.

Rising above the town is a 3,950-ft (1,200-m) peak, Doi Mae Salong. A temple has been built at the summit, giving spectacular views of the surrounding rolling hills, which are dotted with hill-tribe villages. Akha and Mien

villagers frequent the market in Mae Salong, but the town's main population is made up of the descendants of KMT soldiers. The sight of low, Chinese-style houses made of bamboo and the sound of Yunnanese (a Chinese dialect) give the impression that Mae Salong is more of a Chinese than Thai town.

A road built to Mae Salong in the early 1980s made the settlement less isolated. Opium production is now clamped down on, having been replaced by cash crops such as cabbage, tea, and Chinese herbs and medicines. All of this produce is sold in the town's market.

OOLONG TEA

All tea (excluding herbal infusions) is made from a single plant species, *Camellia sinensis*, which originated in the Lower Himalayas. Differing processes produce many types of tea; oolong tea, developed in China, lies between black and green in flavor and color. Considered as the most delicate and complex of teas, its flavor profile is close to floral, and varies by subspecies. Oolong is drunk without additions of milk or sugar.

The imposing Wat Tha Ton with its lavish decorations

Colorful flowers growing in the lush garden at Doi Tung Royal Villa ↑

 8

Doi Tung
ดอยตุง

B1 Chiang Rai province From Mae Chan or Mae Sai to turn-off for Doi Tung, then *songthaew* to summit Chiang Rai; 0-5371-7433

The mountain of Doi Tung is an impressive limestone outcrop dominating the Mekong flood plain near Mae Sai. The narrow road snakes through monsoon forest, winding its way up to the 5,900-ft (1,800-m) peak.

A major pilgrimage site at the top of the mountain, the *chedis* are at the heart of Wat Phra That Doi Tung, which was renovated in the early 1900s. Also here is a large, rotund Chinese-style Buddha image. Pilgrims throw coins into its navel to make merit. The area around Doi Tung has been the site of opium production, the poppy fields guarded by hill

tribespeople and the KMT. The area has become the focus for a rural development project aimed at increasing central government control over the area. In 1988 **Doi Tung Royal Villa** was built on the mountain as part of a plan to increase tourism in the area and to discourage nearby hill tribes from producing opium. Originally a summer residence for the mother of the late King Bhumibol, the villa has an attractive flower garden and a restaurant. While the plan has succeeded, local villagers have become dependent on hand-outs from the development project and from tourists.

Doi Tung is now connected to the other main settlements of the area by good roads. These make fascinating driving into areas that were once the preserve of drug barons. A Thai army presence has reduced drug trading substantially, but visitors are advised not to leave main roads.

Doi Tung Royal Villa

 Hwy 1149 7am-5:30pm daily; gardens: 6am-6pm

9

The Golden Triangle Apex (Sop Ruak)
สามเหลี่ยมทองคำ

B1 42 miles (68 km) NE of Chiang Rai, Chiang Rai province From Chiang Saen Chiang Rai; 0-5371-7433

The apex of the Golden Triangle is the point at which the borders of Thailand, Myanmar, and Laos meet, near the village of Sop Ruak. The "Golden Triangle" referred to a much wider region – the area of northern Thailand, Myanmar, and Laos in which opium was produced (p218). Nowadays, though, the term refers to a much smaller area and is associated with Sop Ruak village.

Sop Ruak, taking advantage of its location, is a popular tourist spot, with many good shops, tempting restaurants, and luxry hotels. The **House of Opium** in the center of the

> The apex of the Golden Triangle is the point at which the borders of Thailand, Myanmar, and Laos meet, near the village of Sop Ruak.

village displays artifacts relating to opium production. But the area's main attraction is the Mekong. Boat trips give views of Laos and of the Golden Triangle Paradise Resort. The resort and casino were built in Myanmar, as gambling is illegal in Thailand.

House of Opium

 ⌂ 212 House of Opium, SE of Sop Ruak village center ⏱ 7am–7pm daily 🌐 houseof opium.com

---

🔟

Wiang Pa Pao
เวียงป่าเป้า

⛰ B1 ⌂ Chiang Rai province 🚌 🚐 Chiang Mai or Chiang Rai, then *songthaew* 🛈 Chiang Rai; 0-5374-4674

This important market town is picturesquely located in a long, thin valley surrounded by mountains. The town is composed mainly of two-story teak buildings, typical of northern Thailand, and has quiet backstreets shaded by teak trees. Many hill-tribe villagers who live in the area, especially Lisu and Akha, come to trade at its market. Wiang Pa Pao's main tourist attraction is Wat Si Suthawat, to the east of the main road through town. This spacious old temple, with distinctive, curled *nagas* flanking the sweeping staircase that leads up to the main *wihan*, is surrounded by teak trees.

⓫

Chiang Khong
เชียงของ

⛰ B1 ⌂ Chiang Rai province 🚌 🚐 🛈 Chiang Rai; 0-5374-4674

On the banks of the Mekong River, Chiang Khong town is all that remains of the much larger territory of Chiang Khong, most of which was lost to the French in 1893, when they claimed it as part of French Indochina (the rest of this land now forms part of Laos). A growing border town, especially since the construction of a bridge to the town of Huay Xai on the Loa side, Chiang Khong is largely dominated by events in Laos. The town was one of the key points of arrival for refugees after the Communist victory in Laos in 1975. There is a large Thai Lue community here too, and shops sell their distinctive, multicolored textiles. Chiang Khong's main temple is the 13th-century Wat Luang, in the town center.

←

The sun setting behind golden Buddha statues at Wat Si Suthawat, Wiang Pa Pao

THAILAND'S TEAK INDUSTRY

The use of teak *(Tectona grandis)* in Thailand dates back centuries. Its favorable properties, including strength and resistance to pests, made it a natural choice for use in buildings, and its fine grain lent itself to intricate carving. Overlogging has led to tragic deforestation, and most commercial teak logging and export was banned in 1989. Pockets of teak may still be seen in its natural habitat - low-lying deciduous forests of up to 1,950 ft (600 m) in elevation, with rich, moist soil - or in large new plantations. Thailand's use of teak is evident in rural parts of the country, as in the old wooden houses of provincial towns such as Phrae *(p245)* and Ngao *(p243)*.

Chiang Saen

เชียงแสน

B1 **Chiang Rai province** **Chiang Rai; 0-5374-4674**

One of the oldest towns in Thailand, Chiang Saen is set beautifully on the bank of the Mekong River. The town was founded in 1328 by Saenphu, the grandson of King Mengrai, as a powerful fortification. There is evidence, however, from some of Chiang Saen's monuments, that suggests the town may be much older. In 1558, Chiang Saen was captured by the Burmese. It was liberated by King Rama I in 1804, who burned it to the ground to prevent its recapture. The present town was established in the early 1880s. Today, Chiang Saen is a quiet and peaceful settlement boasting an impressive number of monuments that survived the razing. The Fine Arts Department in Bangkok lists 66 ruins inside the walled town and 75 beyond.

The largest temple in Chiang Saen is Wat Phra That Chedi Luang. Its 190-ft (58-m) octagonal *chedi*, built between the 12th and the 14th centuries, is a classic Chiang Saen (more commonly known as Lanna) structure. Beside the temple is a small market selling traditional textiles and souvenirs made by the Thai Lue, an ethnic minority from China who came to the area in the 18th century. Also nearby is the Chiang Saen National Museum, with a collection of stone carvings from the Lanna period, Buddha images, and artifacts relating to hill-tribe culture *(p64)*.

GREAT VIEW
Wat Phra That Pha Ngao

Just south of Chiang Saen is the hilltop Wat Phra That Pha Ngao. This temple, with a white pagoda, offers stunning views of the river and the Golden Triangle region.

The grand Wat Pa Sak among teak trees in Chiang Saen

 Boatman rowing
across the freshwater
lake at Phayao

and new agriculture, including
flower production, is replacing
traditional crops such as rice.

15

Ngao
งาว

 ◮B2 ⌂ Lampang province
🚌 From Lampang or Chiang
Rai 🛈 Lampang; 0-5422-
1813

Like many towns in northern
Thailand, Ngao's historical
association with the teak trade
is evident in its buildings. The
suspension bridge over the
Yom River offers wonderful
views of the town, with its
teak houses on stilts backing
onto the fertile river valley.

Ngao's principal temple
is Wat Dok Ban, on the east
side of town. It is distinctive
for its wall surrounded by
about 100 kneeling angel
figures of different colors.

More than 50 species of
birds have been observed in
the Mae Yom National Park
(p245), northeast of Ngao, as
well as mammals, including
the serow (a type of antelope).

The town's most attractive
temple is Wat Pa Sak ("teak
forest temple"), located
outside the old walls to the
west. The monument consists
of seven separate ruined
structures set among teak
trees, which give the *wat* its
name. The *chedi*, built in 1295,
is the oldest in town. It is
carved with flowers and
mythological beasts.

On a hill to the northwest of
Chiang Saen is Wat Phra That
Chom Kitti, which may date
from the 10th century. The
temple has little of architectural interest, but gives
splendid views of the town
and the Mekong.

13

Phayao
พะเยา

◮B1 ⌂ Phayao province 🚌
🛈 Chiang Rai; 0-5374-4674

This quiet provincial capital,
spectacularly sited beside a
large lake, was possibly first

settled in the Bronze Age.
Later abandoned, it was
resettled in the 12th century,
when it became an independent city state. Today, Phayao
is divided into two parts. The
older district is confined to the
promontory jutting into the
lake. With its narrow streets
and traditional teak houses,
it is more pleasant than the
newer part.

The lavish Wat Si Komkam,
situated just north of town by
the lake, dates from the 12th
century. Its modern *wihan*
houses an impressive 16th-
century, 52-ft (16-m) Buddha
image. The *wihan* is
surrounded by 38 heads of
the Buddha in the Phayao style
(distinguished by their
rounded heads and
pointed noses)
dating from the
14th century.

14

Mae Saruai
แม่สรวย

◮B1 ⌂ Chiang Rai province
🚌 Chiang Rai, then
songthaew 🛈 Chiang Rai;
0-5371-7433

Situated on a plain between
mountains and jagged
limestone outcrops, this small
market town is a popular
meeting place for hill tribes,
particularly Akha (p64). Mae
Saruai is modernizing rapidly,

> ### Did You Know?
>
> Wat Si Komkam
> in Phayao has the
> largest Lanna-era
> Buddha statue in
> the country.

 A serow in Mae
Yom National
Park, near Ngao

EAT

224 Bar & Bistro
Homey, modern cafe serving a large menu of Thai and Western food, from rice and noodle dishes to fish and chips, pizza, and steak. Desserts include American pancakes.

🅰C2 🅐Phra Wa-Phra Ta Rd, Nong Bua
📞0-9522-69698

Pan Jai
One of the best places in Phrae to try classic northern cuisine, Pan Jai specializes in *khanom jeen:* spicy rice noodles served, in this case, with pork.

🅰B2 🅐2 Wira Rd, Phrae
📞0-5462-0727

Gingerbread House Gallery & Cafe
Great coffee and cakes and well-presented Thai food are on offer at this cafe-restaurant, which includes a gallery and a shop selling handmade textiles.

🅰B2 🅐94/1 Chareon Muang Rd, Phrae
📞0-5452-3671

Baan Dhalia
Sip a glass of wine as you admire the view over the river while sampling Italian and Mediterranean dishes.

🅰B1 🅐Anantara Golden Triangle Resort, 229 Moo 1, Chiang Saen
🌐anantara.com/en/golden-triangle-chiang-rai/restaurants

 Inside Wat Nong Bua, known for its murals on the temple walls

16
Nong Bua
หนองบัว

🅰C2 🅐Nan province
🚌Nan, then *songthaew*
ℹ️Chiang Rai; 0-5374-4674

This picturesque town, on a flat, fertile plain beside the Nan River, is characterized by traditional teak houses on stilts and neat vegetable gardens. It is one of a number of towns in Nan province inhabited by the Thai Lue, an ethnic minority related to the Tai people of southern China, who began to settle in the region in 1836.

Wat Nong Bua, which was built in 1862, has features typical of a Thai Lue temple, including a two-tiered roof and a carved wooden portico. Its murals are thought to be the work of the same artists who painted those at Wat Phumin (p236). Though the murals at Wat Nong Bua are more faded than Wat Phumin's, their depictions of 19th-century life are just as fascinating. As at Wat Phumin, scenes from the *jataka* tales (stories that are native to India and depict the Buddha's previous 10 lives) are also featured here.

To the west of town is a textile factory, where Thai Lue fabrics are made using hand-operated looms. The distinctive fabrics are for sale in the adjacent store.

INSIDER TIP
Mae Yom National Park

In the Song district north of Phrae, this forested National Park offers bungalows and camping facilities. The Yom River flows through the park, and rafting and house-boats are available.

Nong Bua is the site of a two-day festival held every three years in December (2020, 2023, and so on), during which the villagers pay homage to their ancestors.

Phrae

แพร่

🅐 B2 🏛 Phrae province
✈ 1 mile (1.5 km) SE of Phrae
🚌 Off Yantarakitkosok Rd
ℹ Lampang; 0-5422-2214-5

Although the town of Phrae is often bypassed by travelers, it is well worth a visit. Its location on the Yom River made it ideal for transporting teak logs to mills in Bangkok.

Many of the teak barons' homes remain and a few are open to the public, notably Vongburi House, which dates to 1897. The golden teak house, built in Thai-European style, offers ornate woodworks, and family artifacts.

Phrae is famous for *maw hom*, the distinctive blue clothing worn by farmers throughout Thailand. It is produced from local cotton, dyed with a species of indigo.

18

Doi Phu Kha National Park

อุทยานแห่งชาติดอยภูคา

🅐 C1 🚗 Off Hwy 1080, 42 miles (85 km) NE of Nan; 0-5473-1623 🚌 Nan, then *songthaew*

Ranged around the 6,550-ft (2,000-m) peak of Doi Phu Kha, this is one of the youngest national parks in Thailand. In the late 20th century the area was widely considered a hotbed of Communist infiltration. Some of the hill-tribe villagers here were suspected of sympathizing with the Communists and were kept isolated from visitors.

Doi Phu Kha has two main attractions, the most obvious being its beautiful scenery, such as caves and waterfalls. The visitors' center provides information on forest walks and bird-watching.

Situated in the park are tribal villages, particularly of Mien and Hmong *(p64)*, and of lowland ethnic minorities such as the Htin and Thai Lue.

There are few good roads or tourist facilities in the park, which means that the more adventurous will be rewarded by an area relatively free of development.

White-bellied erpornis *(inset),* a local resident of the stunning Doi Phu Kha National Park ↓

A SHORT WALK
PHRAE

Distance 0.5 miles (1 km) **Time** 15 minutes
Nearest bus station Off Yantarakitkosok Rd

With its distinctive charm and identity, Phrae *(p245)* is appealing yet surprisingly seldom visited. The town was built beside the Yom River in the 12th century and remained an independent city state until it came under Ayutthayan control. In the 18th century, the town was taken by Myanmar and later became a base for Myanmar and Lao teak loggers. Myanmar influence is obvious in Phrae's temples, which also have Lanna features. The town prospers on agricultural produce from the surrounding fertile valley, as shown by the growing commercial district outside the walled town. This route takes in all the main highlights, but remains of the old city walls can also be seen in the northeast of town.

*The octagonal Lanna chedi at **Wat Luang** is notable for its elephant caryatids. Swords, jewelry, and photographs are displayed in the museum.*

ST.

KHAMLUE 1

KHAMLUE

KHUMDERM

LUKMUANG

FINISH

*Several architectural styles are blended at **Wat Phra Ruang**. The cruciform bot is more characteristic of temples in nearby Nan (p237). The Lao wihan has delicately carved doors and the chedi is Lanna.*

PHRA RUANG

NARIRUT

↑ Buddhist monk praying at the lavish Wat Luang

0 meters 100
0 yards 100

N →

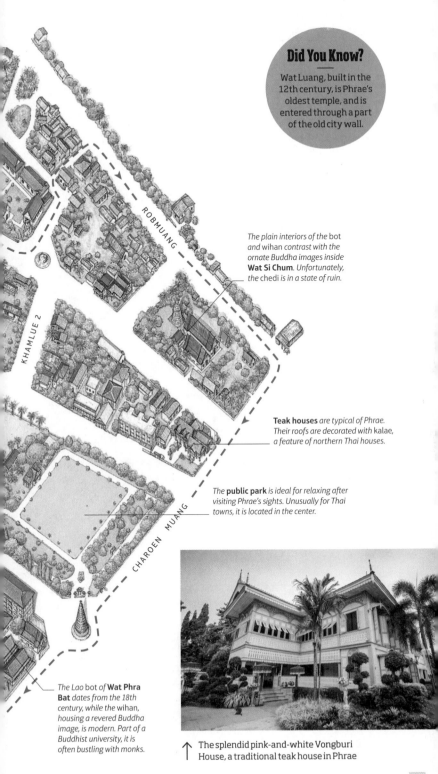

The plain interiors of the bot and wihan *contrast with the ornate Buddha images inside* **Wat Si Chum**. *Unfortunately, the chedi is in a state of ruin.*

ROBMUANG

KHAMLUE 2

Teak houses *are typical of Phrae. Their roofs are decorated with* kalae, *a feature of northern Thai houses.*

The **public park** *is ideal for relaxing after visiting Phrae's sights. Unusually for Thai towns, it is located in the center.*

CHAROEN MUANG

The Lao bot of **Wat Phra Bat** *dates from the 18th century, while the wihan, housing a revered Buddha image, is modern. Part of a Buddhist university, it is often bustling with monks.*

↑ The splendid pink-and-white Vongburi House, a traditional teak house in Phrae

A DRIVING TOUR
GOLDEN TRIANGLE

Length 125 miles (200 km) **Stopping-off points** Mae Sai, Chiang Saen, and Chiang Khong all have restaurants, guesthouses, and gas stations.

The Golden Triangle (p240) is a 75,000 sq-mile (195,000 sq-km) area spanning parts of Thailand, Laos, and Myanmar. The area is historically connected to the opium and heroin trades (thus "golden"), but it has much more to interest visitors. This tour takes in its best features: superb views of the "apex" of the Golden Triangle, where the three countries meet; hill-tribe villages nestling amid stunning mountain scenery; and the ancient towns of Chiang Saen and Chiang Khong. Smaller roads may be difficult for travel, especially in the wet season, June through September, so it is best to use the numbered roads displayed on the map here.

*Wat Phra That Doi Wao, on a hilltop outside **Mae Sai** (p238), is the town's best temple. The bot has carvings of the Buddha.*

*The impressive **Doi Tung** is the site of the Doi Tung Royal Villa (p240), which has a colorful flower garden.*

*Small sculptures of people decorate the village gates of **Saam Yekh Akha**.*

***Doi Mae Salong**, the site of the Chinese settlement of Mae Salong (p239), is set amid rolling scenery.*

Mae Sai

Doi Nang Non 2,723 ft (830 m)

Doi Tung 4,547 ft (1,389 m)

Doi Tung

Pong Pha

1149

1

Mae Kham

Mak

1130

Saam Yekh Akha

Doi Mae Salong

Pha Dua

Mae Chan

1130

1089

107

Tha Ton

1089

Mae Chan

Tha Sut

1

START

Kok

5023

Chiang Rai International Airport

1

Kok

*Located near the Myanmar border, **Tha Ton** (p238) is a staging post between the lowlands and the mountains.*

Chiang Rai

*The Mien village of **Pha Dua** sells textiles and handicrafts. You may also see elaborate rituals and ceremonies based on the local hill tribe's religion (p64).*

↑ Tha Ton's splendid countryside and mountains in the morning mist

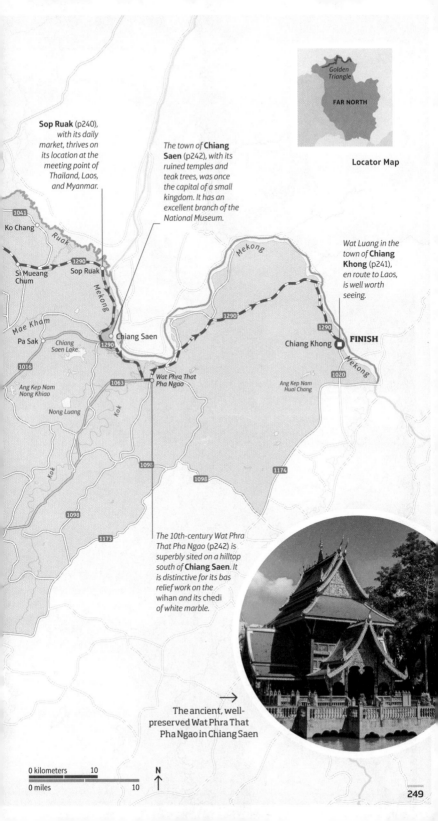

Sop Ruak (p240), with its daily market, thrives on its location at the meeting point of Thailand, Laos, and Myanmar.

The town of **Chiang Saen** (p242), with its ruined temples and teak trees, was once the capital of a small kingdom. It has an excellent branch of the National Museum.

Wat Luang in the town of **Chiang Khong** (p241), en route to Laos, is well worth seeing.

Locator Map

Golden Triangle

FAR NORTH

Ko Chang

Sì Mueang Chum

Sop Ruak

Mae Kham

Pa Sak

Chiang Saen Lake

Chiang Saen

Ang Kep Nam Nong Khiao

Nong Luang

Wat Phra That Pha Ngao

Ang Kep Nam Huai Chang

Chiang Khong

FINISH

Mekong

Ruak

Kok

The 10th-century Wat Phra That Pha Ngao (p242) is superbly sited on a hilltop south of **Chiang Saen**. It is distinctive for its bas relief work on the wihan and its chedi of white marble.

→ The ancient, well-preserved Wat Phra That Pha Ngao in Chiang Saen

0 kilometers 10

0 miles 10

N ↑

KHORAT PLATEAU

The vast, sandstone Khorat Plateau dominates the northeast, a region that the Thais call Isan. The plateau, which is about 660 ft (200 m) above sea level, takes up almost a third of Thailand's land mass. Though one of the most infertile areas of Thailand, the Khorat Plateau is rich in culture and historic sites from the days when the Khmer Empire held sway over the region. In the 9th century AD, the Khorat Plateau came under Cambodian control, which was to endure until the end of the 13th century. It was during this particular period that the region's splendid Khmer temples were built. The magnificent stone temples at Phnom Rung and Phimai, which once stood on a road linking the plateau with the Khmer capital of Angkor, have now been evocatively restored.

To the north, at Ban Chiang, lies a site that has revolutionized archeologists' views of prehistoric Southeast Asia. The northeast is now thought to be one of the first areas in the world where rice growing, bronze making, and silk weaving were pioneered. Silk production has flourished again since the mid-20th century, and modern-day weaving villages sell a wide range of silk and cotton goods.

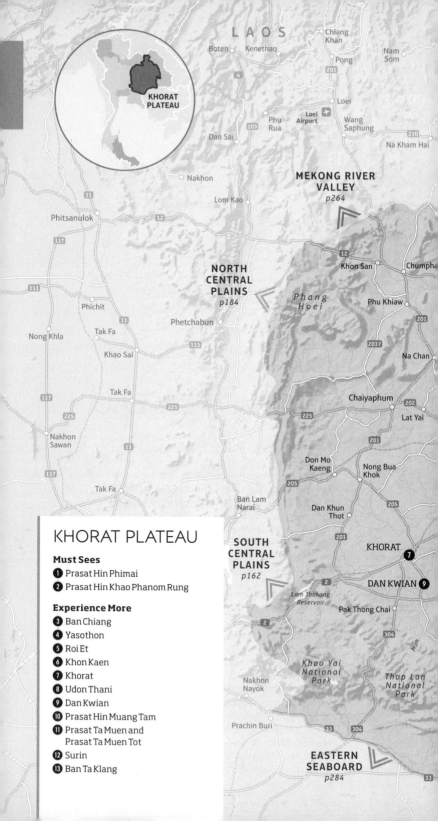

LAOS

Chiang
Khan

Boten   Kenethao

Pong   Nam
Som

**KHORAT
PLATEAU**

Loei

Loei
Airport   Wang
Saphung

Phu
Rua   Na Kham Hai

Dan Sai

Nakhon

**MEKONG RIVER
VALLEY**
p264

Lom Kao

Phitsanulok

Khon San   Chumpha

**NORTH
CENTRAL
PLAINS**
p184   *Phang
Hoei*   Phu Khiaw

Phichit

Phetchabun

Na Chan

Nong Khla   Tak Fa

Khao Sai

Chaiyaphum

Tak Fa   Lat Yai

Nakhon
Sawan

Don Mo
Kaeng   Nong Bua
Khok

Tak Fa   Ban Lam
Narai   Dan Khun
Thot

**SOUTH
CENTRAL
PLAINS**
p162   **KHORAT** ❼

DAN KWIAN ❾

*Lam Thakong
Reservoir*   Pak Thong Chai

*Khao Yai
National
Park*   *Thap Lan
National
Park*

Nakhon
Nayok

Prachin Buri

**EASTERN
SEABOARD**
p284

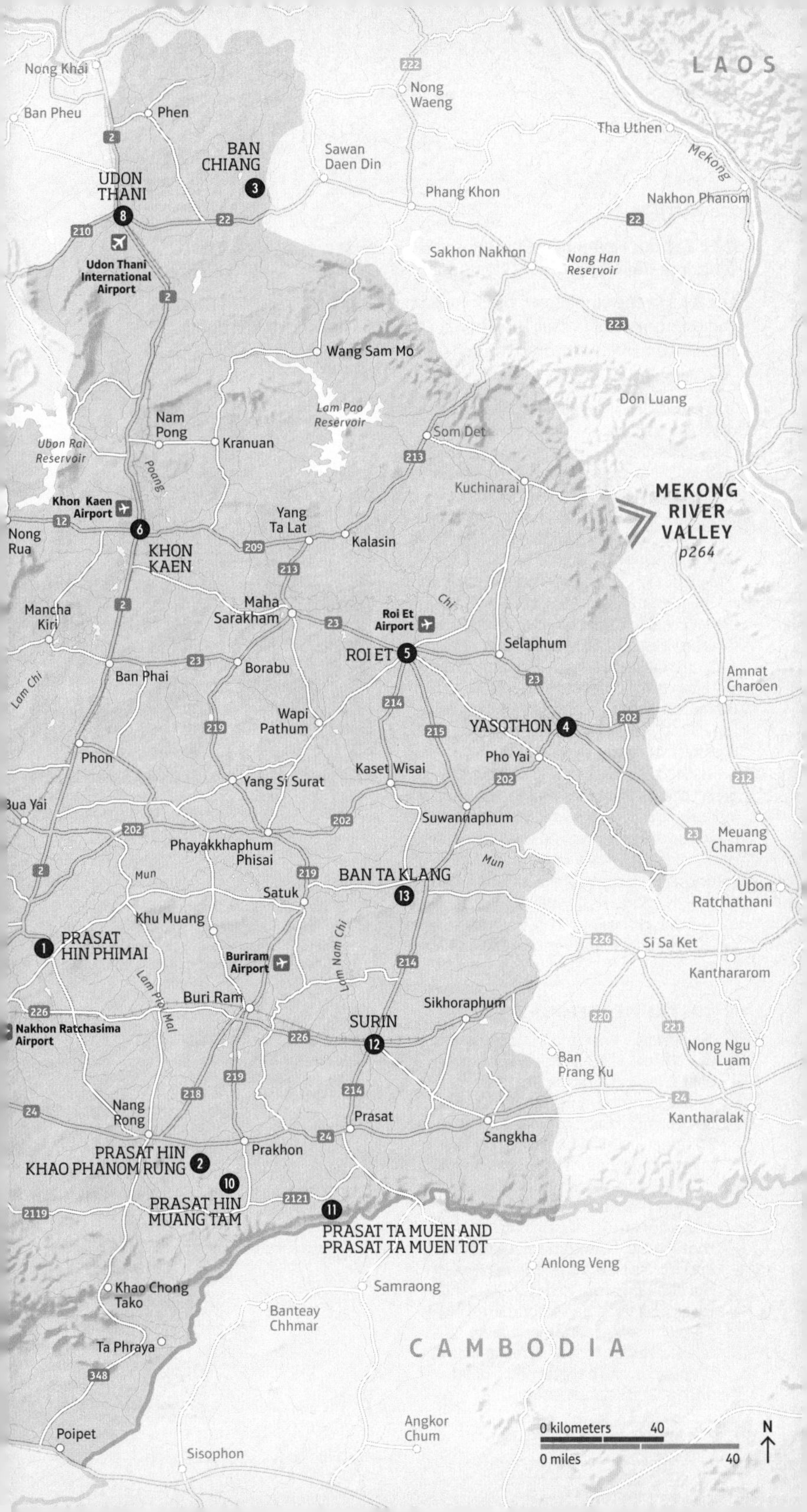

LAOS

Nong Khai

Ban Pheu

Phen

222

Nong Waeng

Tha Uthen

Mekong

Sawan
Daen Din

2

BAN
CHIANG
3

UDON
THANI
8

210

22

Phang Khon

Nakhon Phanom

22

Udon Thani
International
Airport

2

Sakhon Nakhon

Nong Han
Reservoir

223

Wang Sam Mo

Lam Pao
Reservoir

Som Det

Don Luang

Nam
Pong

Ubon Rai
Reservoir

Pong

12

213

Kuchinarai

MEKONG
RIVER
VALLEY
p264

Khon Kaen
Airport

6

KHON
KAEN

Kranuan

Yang
Ta Lat

209

Kalasin

213

Chi

Nong
Rua

Mancha
Kiri

2

Maha
Sarakham

23

Roi Et
Airport

Selaphum

Amnat
Charoen

Lam Chi

Ban Phai

23

Borabu

ROI ET
5

23

202

212

Phon

219

Wapi
Pathum

214

215

YASOTHON
4

202

Pho Yai

23

Meuang
Chamrap

Bua Yai

202

Yang Si Surat

202

Kaset Wisai

Suwannaphum

Mun

Ubon
Ratchathani

2

Phayakkhaphum
Phisai

219

BAN TA KLANG
13

226

Si Sa Ket

Mun

PRASAT
HIN PHIMAI
1

Satuk

Khu Muang

Lam Nam Chi

214

Kanthararom

226

Nakhon Ratchasima
Airport

Buri Ram

Buriram
Airport

Sikhoraphum

220

221

Nong Ngu
Luam

24

218

219

226

SURIN
12

Ban
Prang Ku

24

Kantharalak

Nang
Rong

PRASAT HIN
KHAO PHANOM RUNG
2

10

PRASAT HIN
MUANG TAM

Prakhon

2121

214

Prasat

24

Sangkha

2119

11

PRASAT TA MUEN AND
PRASAT TA MUEN TOT

Khao Chong
Tako

348

Ta Phraya

Banteay
Chhmar

Samraong

Anlong Veng

CAMBODIA

Poipet

Sisophon

Angkor
Chum

0 kilometers   40

0 miles   40

N

PRASAT HIN PHIMAI

ปราสาทหินพิมาย

🅰C4 🅾Center of Phimai town, Khorat province 📞0-4447-1568 ➡🅿
🚆Khorat, then *songthaew* 🕐7am-6pm daily ℹ️Khorat; 0-4421-3666

Located in the small town of Phimai, on the banks of the Mun River, the monumental Prasat Hin Phimai is one of Thailand's finest and most extensively restored Khmer temple complexes.

There is no definitive date for the construction of this temple, but the central sanctuary is likely to have been completed during the reign of Suryavarman I (1001–49). The word *prasat*, which is used to refer to the central sanctuary, also describes the temple complex as a whole. The white sandstone edifice of the central sanctuary is topped with a rounded *prang*, the style of which may have influenced the builders of Angkor Wat in Cambodia. Prasat Hin Phimai lies on what was once a direct route to the Khmer capital at Angkor and, unusually, is oriented in a southeasterly direction to face that city. Originally a Brahmanic shrine dedicated to Shiva, Prasat Hin Phimai was rededicated as a Mahayana Buddhist temple at the end of the 12th century. Its famous lintels and pediments depict scenes from the Ramayana, an ancient Indian epic and, unique among Khmer temples, Buddhist themes. Though Prasat Hin Phimai does not function as a working *wat*, it is sometimes the setting for Buddhist gatherings and celebrations. Restoration of the site was carried out by the Fine Arts Department, which oversees many temple restorations, in 1964–9.

↑ Lion on the *naga* bridge, leading to the main entrance of the complex

LOST KHMER TEMPLES

The Khmers, who ruled an area covering much of modern Cambodia and northeast Thailand from the 9th to 14th centuries, are now acknowledged to have been among the world's greatest architects. When Europeans first saw mysterious ruins in the forests far east of Ayutthaya, they thought they had found an ancient Chinese civilization. It was not until the 19th century that the history of the Khmers began to be uncovered. Many sites, such as Prasat Hin Phimai, can be visited in Thailand today; in Cambodia, restoration of Angkor, the old capital, is ongoing. Bas-reliefs depicting battles are common in these sites, and have helped scholars understand Khmer history.

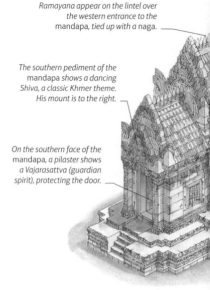

Rama and Lakshman from the Ramayana appear on the lintel over the western entrance to the mandapa, tied up with a naga.

The southern pediment of the mandapa shows a dancing Shiva, a classic Khmer theme. His mount is to the right.

On the southern face of the mandapa, a pilaster shows a Vajarasattva (guardian spirit), protecting the door.

↑ The impressive architecture of the central sanctuary towering over Prasat Hin Phimai

↑ A white stone Buddha in the central sanctuary, protected by an umbrella

Prang *(tower)*

Rama and his monkeys on the western pediment.

The centerpiece of the northern porch is this lintel depicting a three-headed, six-armed Vajarasattva. Below him crouch a group of dancing girls.

On the northern pediment is a scene from the Ramayana, which includes Vishnu holding a conch, a lotus, a discus, and a staff.

The God of Justice, on the eastern porch, judges a feud between good and evil.

Trilokayavijaya, the most important Mahayana Bodhisattva (Enlightened being), can be seen on the interior lintel of the eastern porch.

Seated atop a naga, or a mythical guardian spirit, is a reproduction of a 13th-century Buddha.

←

The intricately detailed central sanctuary and its various symbolic scenes and features

Mandapa *(hallway of main entrance)*

PRASAT HIN KHAO PHANOM RUNG

ปราสาทหินเขาพนมรุ้ง

△D4 **⌂31 miles (50 km) S of Buriram, off Hwy 24, Buriram province**
⊞From Khorat or Surin to Ban Ta Ko, then *songthaew* **⏰6am–6pm daily**
🛈Surin; 0-4451-4447

Crowning the extinct volcano of Khao Phanom Rung is the splendid temple complex Prasat Hin Khao Phanom Rung. Its superb carvings and buildings make it a fine example of Khmer architecture.

A Hindu temple, the impressive Prasat Hin Khao Phanom Rung, was built here to symbolize Shiva's abode on the heavenly Mount Krailasa – hence the processional way leading to the central sanctuary, its stairways and *naga* bridges extending in total for 655 ft (200 m). The temple's construction began early in the 10th century, and, like other Khmer sites, it lies on a route to Angkor Wat in Cambodia. Its buildings are aligned so that at Songkran (*p67*), the rising sun can be seen through all 15 doors of the western *gopura*. The complex is also home to a range of gift shops, some food stalls outside the entrance, and an information center where you can learn about the fascinating construction and restoration of the site.

> **Did You Know?**
>
> The complex has been submitted to UNESCO for deliberation as a World Heritage Site.

A Hindu temple, the impressive Prasat Hin Khao Phanom Rung was built here to symbolize Shiva's abode on the heavenly Mount Krailasa.

→

The Prasat Hin Khao Phanom Rung complex and its symbolic features

Site Highlights

Porch of Mandapa

▽ The pediment over this porch represents Shiva Nataraja, his arms splayed out in a dance of death.

Western Porch Pediment

This carving shows monkeys rescuing Sita in a chariot that is itself a model of the temple.

Nandin the Bull

▽ This image of the mythical mount of the Hindu deity Shiva is in the first, eastern chamber of the central sanctuary.

Processional Way

This processional walkway was built to symbolize the spiritual journey from earth to Hindu heaven.

Central Sanctuary

△ The corncob-shaped *prang* here is the cosmological summit of the processional way.

↑ One of the ornamental ponds located at the front of the entrance to the main temple

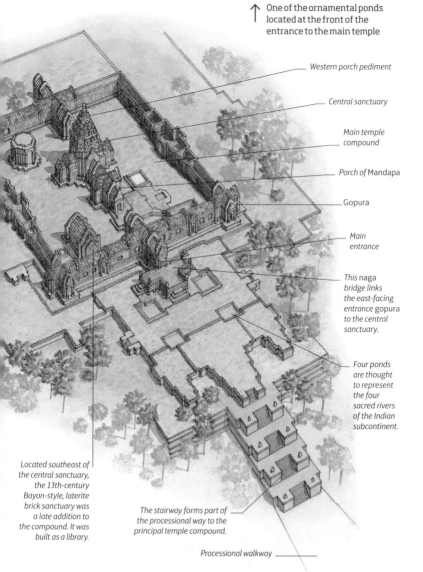

Western porch pediment

Central sanctuary

Main temple compound

Porch of Mandapa

Gopura

Main entrance

This naga bridge links the east-facing entrance gopura to the central sanctuary.

Four ponds are thought to represent the four sacred rivers of the Indian subcontinent.

Located southeast of the central sanctuary, the 13th-century Bayon-style, laterite brick sanctuary was a late addition to the compound. It was built as a library.

The stairway forms part of the processional way to the principal temple compound.

Processional walkway

EXPERIENCE MORE

Ban Chiang
บ้านเชียง

D3 ⌂ Udon Thani province ▦ From Udon Thani 𝘪 Udon Thani; 0-4232-5406

The principal attraction for visitors to Ban Chiang is its archeological site. It was discovered by accident in 1966 by an American sociologist who tripped over some remains. The finds provided archeological evidence that northeast Thailand may have been one of the world's earliest centers of bronze production. Spearheads from the site are thought to date from around 3600 BC, while ceramics, dating from between 3000 BC and AD 500, testify to a high degree of technical and artistic skill. Today, a collection of these artifacts is on display at the **Ban Chiang National Museum**.

31

The average number of years that the inhabitants of ancient Ban Chiang lived.

A short walk from the museum through dusty streets lined with wooden shop-houses, two covered excavation sites lie in the grounds of Wat Pho Si Nai. Here the main exhibits are graves containing skeletal remains and ceramics used for symbolic purposes in burial. Bodies were wrapped in perishable material and laid on their backs. Pots were then arranged along the edge of the grave and over the bodies.

Research associated with the discoveries at Wat Pho Si Nai indicates that the inhabitants of Ban Chiang were a strong, long-legged people with wide foreheads and prominent cheekbones.

Ban Chiang National Museum

◈ ⌂ On edge of Ban Chiang ☎ 0-4223-5040 ◷ 9am–4pm Wed–Sun

Yasothon
ยโสธร

D4 ⌂ Yasothon province ▦ 𝘪 Ubon Ratchathani; 0-4524-3770

Yasothon has one or two temples worth visiting, in particular Wat Thung Sawang and Wat Mahathat Yasothon.

In the center of the town, the latter is home to the Phra That Phra Anon *chedi*, thought to have been built in the 7th century to house the relics of Phra Anon, the closest disciple of the Buddha.

Yasothon is best known as the principal venue for the Bun Bang Fai or Rocket Festival. Due to harsh weather in northeast Thailand, this festival, which is to appease a Hindu rain god, is one of symbolic importance. Local people invest enormous sums of money in the construction of huge bamboo rockets. The gunpowder that goes into the rockets is pounded by young girls in the temple grounds, and it is Buddhist monks who possess the expertise of building and firing the rockets. The rockets are paraded on floats through the streets, surrounded by revelers, then shot into the clouds to "fertilize" them. The owners of those rockets that fail to go off are ritually coated in mud.

Artifacts from the Ban Chiang burial sites on display at the town's museum

The lakeside Chedi Maha Mongkol Bua, in Roi Et, and its gardens

Roi Et
ร้อยเอ็ด

D3 Roi Et province Khon Kaen; 0-4322-7714/5

Founded in 1782, Roi Et means "one hundred and one," a name that is thought to be an exaggeration of 11, the number of vassal states over which the town once ruled.

Today Roi Et is a charming provincial capital. The modern skyline is dominated by an immense brown and ocher image of the Lord Buddha, the Phraphuttha- rattana-mongkol-maha-mani, which is situated within the grounds of Wat Buraphaphiram. Measuring 225 ft (68 m) from its base to the tip of its flame finial, this giant standing Buddha is reputed to be one of the tallest in the world. The climb up the statue offers an impressive view of the town and surrounding area. Chedi Maha Mongkol Bua is another major landmark here, and its beautiful gardens are a peaceful spot to relax in. Silk and cotton are both good buys in Roi Et and can be found along Phadung Phanit Road.

Khon Kaen
ขอนแก่น

D3 Khon Kaen province 15/5 Prachasamoson Rd, Khon Kaen; www.khonkaen.com

Once the quiet capital of one of the poorest provinces in the northeast of Thailand, this place has changed into a bustling town. Located at the heart of the region, it has consequently been a focus of regional development projects – the town now boasts the largest university in the northeast, in addition to its own television studios. There are also a number of modern hotels and shopping complexes, all of which nestle rather incongruously among the town's more traditional streets and market places.

Places of interest include Khaen Nakhon Lake, an artificial lake beside which are some restaurants. Khon Kaen National Museum has examples of Ban Chiang artifacts.

STAY

The Pannarai
Modern but elegant hotel with spacious rooms decked out in regal red and gold.

D3 19/8 Sampanthamit St, Udon Thani the pannaraihotel.com

ⓑⓑⓑ

Centara Hotel & Convention Centre
Professional hotel with sleek rooms furnished in teak, and superb Isan and Cantonese cuisine.

D3 277/1 Prajaksillapakhom Rd, Udon Thani centara hotelsresorts.com

ⓑⓑⓑ

Hop Inn Roi Et
A short walk from the Buddha at Wat Buraphaphiram. Rooms are spotless and modern.

D3 377 Moo 6 Rob Mueang Soi 5, Rob Mueang Rd, Roi Et hopinnhotel.com

ⓑⓑⓑ

Sampling the street food at Khorat's Night Market in the old town

SHOP

Night Ban Koh
The preferred hangout for the young and trendy of Khorat, this market bustles every evening with food stalls and beer bars, and sells handicrafts. It's also a great stop for affordable clothes, accessories, and shoes, and you can even pick up plants.

🄰C4 🄰Sura Narai Rd, Khorat

Dan Kwian Pottery Village
Famed for its ocher-colored pottery, Dan Kwian is full of ceramics factories and shops. Items for sale include jewelry, elaborately decorated vases, chicken-shaped plant pots, leaf-shaped wind chimes, and traditional water jars.

🄰C4 🄰Khorat province

7

Khorat
โคราช

🄰C4 🄰Khorat province ↗
🚌🚆 🛈2102-4 Mittraphap Rd, Khorat; 0-4421-3666

In former times, Khorat, or Nakhon Ratchasima, was two separate towns, Khorakhapura and Sema; they were joined during the reign of King Narai (1656–88). Today Khorat is a business center. Its development stems from playing host to a nearby US air base during the Vietnam War. At first sight Khorat appears to the visitor as a sprawl of confusing roads and heavy traffic. The city center has little of interest save for the Night Market that sells good-value street foods and a range of local handicrafts.

At the city's western gate, Pratu Chumphon, is the Thao Suranari Monument, built in memory of Khunying Mo, a woman who successfully defended Khorat against an attack by an invading Lao army in 1826. While her husband, the deputy governor of Khorat, was away on business in Bangkok, Prince Anuwong of Vientiane seized the city. Khunying Mo and her fellow captives allegedly served the Lao army with liquor and were then able to kill them in their drunken stupor with whatever weapons were at hand. The Lao invasion was therefore held at bay until help arrived. Khunying Mo was given the title of Thao Suranari or "brave lady" from which the monument, built in 1934, derives its name. It shows Khunying Mo standing, hand on hip, on a tall pedestal. The base of the statue is adorned with garlands and ornamental offerings made by local people in their respect for her; a week-long festival, including folk performances of dancing, theater, and song, is also held in her honor each year in March.

Located in the grounds of Wat Suthachinda is Khorat's **Maha Weerawong National Museum**. The artifacts on display here range from skeletal remains of human corpses, Dvaravati and Ayutthaya Buddha images, ceramics, and wood carvings, and were donated to Prince Maha Weerawong, from whom the museum derives its name.

> Just outside Khorat, Wat Khao Chan Ngam is the site of prehistoric finds, while at Wat Thep Phitak Punnaram stands a large white Buddha overlooking the road.

Though quite a modern city, Khorat has a number of other ancient and important Buddhist temples. In the *wihan* of Wat Phra Narai Maharat is a sandstone image of the Hindu god Vishnu, originally found at Khmer ruins near to the city.

One of the most strikingly innovative modern Buddhist temples in northeast Thailand is Wat Sala Loi, or the "temple of the floating pavilion," standing on the banks of the Lam Takhong River. Designed in the form of a Chinese junk, the main *wihan* of this *wat* has won architectural awards. It was constructed entirely from local materials, including distinctive earthenware tiles made only at the nearby village of Dan Kwian. The original site on which Wat Sala Loi now stands dates back to the time of Khunying Mo, and her ashes are still buried here, a fitting resting place for the heroine without whom present-day Khorat would possibly not exist.

Just outside Khorat, Wat Khao Chan Ngam is the site of prehistoric finds, while at Wat Thep Phitak Punnaram stands a large white Buddha overlooking the road.

Maha Weerawong National Museum

 🏠 Ratchadamnoen Rd
🕒 9am–4pm Wed–Sun

8
Udon Thani
อุดรธานี

🅰️D3 🏠 Udon Thani province 🚆🚌🚐
ℹ️ Mukmontri Rd, Udon Thani; 0-4232-5406

During the Vietnam War, Udon Thani changed from a sleepy provincial capital into a booming support center for a nearby American air base. Udon today has retained a little of that past vibrancy, together with some rather nondescript streets, lined with coffee shops, nightclubs, and massage parlors. It has continued to grow as an industrial and commercial center within the region. The most attractive part of town is Nong Prachak Park, where

there are some excellent open-air restaurants. The town makes a good base for travelers wanting to visit nearby Ban Chiang.

About a 45-minute drive from Udon Thani, via a twisty road, the Red Lotus Lake is an amazing sight – particularly stunning early morning when the flowers are open.

9
Dan Kwian
ด่านเกวียน

🅰️C4 🏠 Khorat province
ℹ️ Khorat; 0-4421-3666

Southeast of Khorat is Dan Kwian, first inhabited in the mid-18th century by the Mon people traveling east from the Burmese border. Since then it has become famous for its rust-colored pottery, derived from the high iron content of the local clay.

Today Dan Kwian is essentially a collection of ceramics factories, many of which can export large items for tourists. Shops selling the local pottery line the highway at the entrance point to the village. Watch the potters crafting jars with traditional wooden wheels, and then pick up a gift or souvenir.

←
Tropical water lillies spreading out over the Red Lotus Lake near Udon Thani

Prasat Hin Muang Tam
ปราสาทหินเมืองต่ำ

D4 **Off Hwy 214, Buri Ram province** **From Surin to Prakhon Chai, then** *songthaew* **Surin; 0-4451-4447** **Daily**

Muang Tam, or "the lower city," stands at the foot of Khao Phnom Rung, an extinct volcano on top of which lies the Khmer site of Prasat Hin Khao Phnom Rung (p256). Muang Tam postdates the earliest stages of construction of the more elaborate and well-preserved temple above and was built in brick, sandstone, and laterite between the 10th and 12th centuries. Little remains, and at first sight Muang Tam appears to be nothing more than a heap of decaying brickwork.

> Muang Tam, or "the lower city," stands at the foot of Khao Phnom Rung, an extinct volcano on top of which lies the Khmer site of Prasat Hin Khao Phnom Rung.

The remains of four brick sanctuaries surround what would once have been a central temple containing religious icons. The reliefs on the Muang Tam lintels indicate that these icons are most likely to have been Hindu. The lintel over the northern sanctuary shows Shiva and his consort Parvati riding on Nandin the bull, another lintel depicts the four-headed Hindu god of creation, Brahma.

All the sanctuaries in the complex face east and are encircled by galleries (now collapsed). On each side there are also four *gopuras* or entrance pavilions. Beyond these lie four L-shaped ponds, decorated at each corner with majestic, multiheaded *nagas*.

The ancient remains of Muang Tam and an intricately carved relief *(inset)* on one of the sanctuaries'
↓ many lintels

Prasat Ta Muen and Prasat Ta Muen Tot
ปราสาทตาเมือนและปราสาทตาเมือนโต๊ต

D4 **Off Hwy 214, Surin province** **Surin, then preferably by organized tour** **Surin; 0-4451-4447** **Daily**

In the district of Ta Muen, in Surin province, the remains of two Khmer *prasats* stand 330 ft (100 m) apart. One, Prasat Ta Muen, is a laterite chapel marking what would once have been a resting place on the long, arduous road between Angkor and Prasat Hin Phimai (p254). The other, Prasat Ta Muen Tot, is more decayed and was originally a hospital to care for travelers along this route. Both were built by King Jayavarman VII (1181–1220).

Although both *prasats* are today largely in ruins, with their brickwork gripped and

overrun by the roots of towering fig trees, they are potent reminders of the powerful Khmer Empire that once held sway over the Khorat Plateau. Because of their location along the rather dangerous Cambodian border, Ta Muen and Ta Muen Tot are best seen as part of a tour organized by one of the guesthouses in Surin, and may require a military escort. They are not easily accessible to lone tourists and cannot be visited at times of disputes and skirmishes between the various rival factions in the area.

 Surin

สุรินทร์

🅐D4 🄰 Surin province 🚉🚌
🄸 Surin; 0-4451-4447

Surin is famous for its silk, its elephants, and its first ruler, Phraya Surin Phakdi Si Narong Wang, from whom it derives its name. A modern statue in the town depicts the leader dressed to go into battle. A member of the Suay tribe, Phraya Surin became ruler of Surin in 1760 when, according to legend, he was instrumental

SILK PRODUCTION

In Thailand, silk production was beginning to die out until an American, Jim Thompson, revived it in the 1940s. Today, all manner of silk products are available, with shirts and sarongs popular with visitors. The silk industry is centered mostly in the northeast, due to the suitability of soil in these areas for growing mulberry bushes, the main diet of the silkworm. Silk production in these areas is still very much based on traditional methods.

in recapturing an escaped royal white elephant (p119).

The process of silk production can be seen in the surrounding villages. There are over 700 patterns used by silk weavers in Surin province. Rhomboid designs are especially popular.

During the 1970s, when the Khmer Rouge seized control of, and terrorized, neighboring Cambodia, thousands of Cambodian refugees crossed the Banthat mountains into Surin province and took up residence there, alongside already established Lao refugees, Thais, and Suay tribespeople. Although most immigrants have been repatriated, some remain. The **Surin National Museum** is a good source on the history and geography of the area, and its ethnic groups.

Surin is also known for its annual Elephant Roundup, at the Surin Sports Park in mid-November. Do keep in mind before attending that these roundups are controversial and viewed by many as cruel due to the distressing training that gets the elephants ready for "shows."

Surin National Museum

🄰 Chitramboong Rd
🄲 0-4415-3054 🄾 9am–4pm
Wed–Sun

 Ban Ta Klang

บ้านตากลาง

🅐D4 🄰 Surin province
🄸 Surin; 0-451-4447

The Suay tribespeople make up the population of Ban Ta Klang, which is also known as the Elephant Village, a name that reflects the Suay people's history of training wild elephants. The Suay are thought to have migrated to Thailand from Central Asia in the early 9th century and to have been the first people to make use of elephants for building, in particular for the construction of Khmer temples. Nowadays, Ban Ta Klang is the primary training ground for the controversial annual Surin Elephant Roundup, but several NGOs (non-governmental organizations) have successful projects here to improve elephant welfare.

> **Did You Know?**
>
> Surin is also well-known for producing Thailand's iconic jasmine rice.

MEKONG RIVER VALLEY

Some 1,250 miles (2,000 km) from its source in the Tibetan Himalayas, having passed through China, Myanmar (Burma), northern Thailand, then Laos, the Mekong River reaches Chiang Khan in northeast Thailand. From here the river forms the border with Laos until it flows into Cambodia. The Mekong River Valley's relatively fertile land means fruit and vegetables are produced here on a marketable scale. Furthermore, due to its distance from Bangkok, the area has escaped widespread development and remains one of the most beautiful, unspoiled regions in the country.

Lively Nong Khai is the most important border town in the region and the access point to the Lao capital, Vientiane. The construction, in 1994, of the Friendship Bridge – a crossing point for tourists and traders going from Nong Khai to Vientiane – was a huge factor in an increase in trade between Thailand and Laos. However, the Cambodian border with Thailand has been the scene of skirmishes between rival factions and, as a result, it is not always possible to reach the most magnificent Khmer monument, Prasat Khao Phra Wihan.

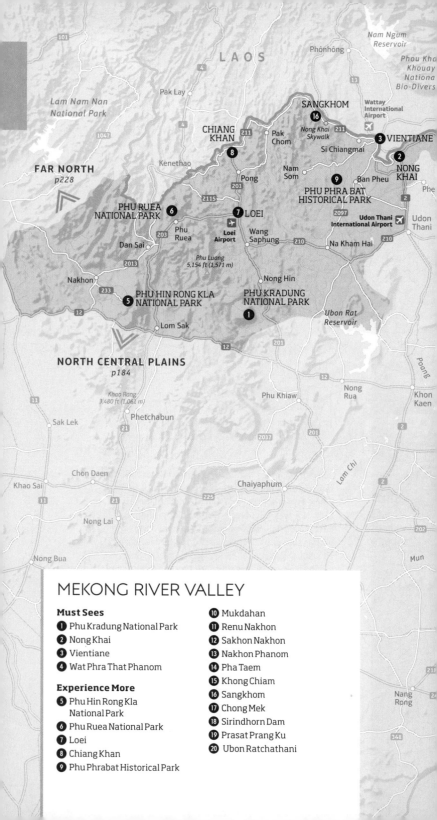

MEKONG RIVER VALLEY

Must Sees

1 Phu Kradung National Park
2 Nong Khai
3 Vientiane
4 Wat Phra That Phanom

Experience More

5 Phu Hin Rong Kla
National Park
6 Phu Ruea National Park
7 Loei
8 Chiang Khan
9 Phu Phrabat Historical Park
10 Mukdahan
11 Renu Nakhon
12 Sakhon Nakhon
13 Nakhon Phanom
14 Pha Taem
15 Khong Chiam
16 Sangkhom
17 Chong Mek
18 Sirindhorn Dam
19 Prasat Prang Ku
20 Ubon Ratchathani

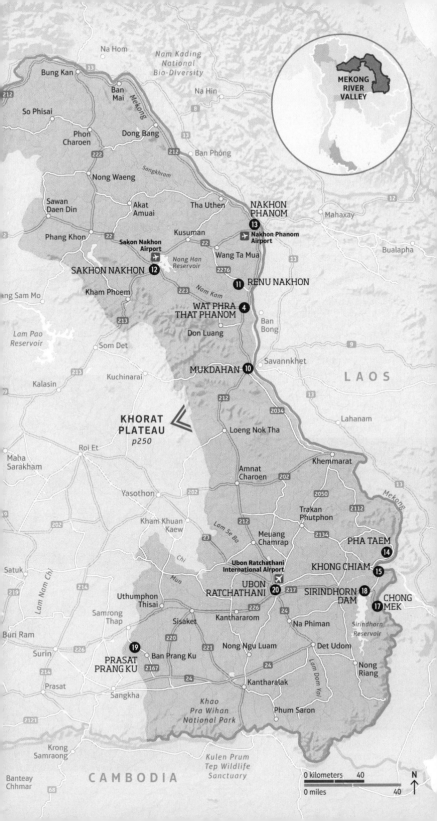

❶ ⬡ ▱ 🛍

PHU KRADUNG NATIONAL PARK

อุทยานแห่งชาติภูกระดึง

▲C3 **◉**Loei province; Park HQ about 5 miles (8 km) off Hwy 2019 **🚌**To Pha Nok Kao then *songathaew* **🕐**Mid-Jul–early Sep **🛈**Loei; 0-4281-1405

Cloaked in legend, the extensive Phu Kradung National Park is a treat for explorers in northern Thailand. Offering spectacular viewpoints and majestic waterfalls, the park is also home to an abundance of indigenous wildlife.

There are two tales connected to Phu Kradung, or "bell mountain": the first is that the sound of a bell, said to be that of the god Indra, once rang out from its peak; the second is that the mountain rings like a bell when struck with a staff. This steep-sided, flat-topped mountain is now a national park covering 135 sq miles (348 sq km), its 37-mile (60-km) plateau 4,450 ft (1,350 m) above sea level. This plateau has a climate cool enough for plants that cannot survive in other parts of Thailand; many animals also live in its forests and grasslands.

Waterfalls, most impressive in October, are dotted all over Phu Kradung. One example is the Phone Phop waterfall, named for the first World Champion Thai boxer, Phone Kingphet, who stumbled upon it and chose the plateau as a training ground because its cool climate prepared him for fights abroad.

Did You Know?

The rare "Tao Poo Loo" turtle can occasionally be spotted in streams high up in the park.

← Water rushing down the multiple rock terraces that form Phone Phop waterfall

① Tall pine trees blanket areas of the park and are beautiful to photograph at sunset. These giants are essential to the ecological system of Phu Kradung.

② Carnivorous pitcher plants, common in the area, gather nutrients lacking in the local acidic soil by "eating" insects.

③ Thailand has two species of wild dogs. The handsome Asian jackal, which lives on Phu Kradung, has a bushy tail. The other species is the red dog.

TOP 3 VALLEY VIEWPOINTS

Pha Lom Sak
This unusually shaped sandstone ledge is situated 9 km (6 miles) from the visitor center, on the southern edge of the plateau. It provides beautiful vistas over the rolling hills. The ledge can get very busy in the summer months.

Pha Nok An
"Swallow cliff," situated 1 km (0.6 miles) from the eastern edge of the plateau, offers breath-taking sunrise views. Its name refers to the many families of swallows who build their nests under the cliff's overhang.

Pha Mak Duk
Sweeping sunset views can be captured at this lesser-known lookout, 3 km (1.8 miles) from the visitor center.

NONG KHAI

หนองคาย

▣D2 ◻ Nong Khai province ▢ 2 miles (3 km) W on Kaeo Worawut Rd ▦ Praserm Rd ℹ Udon Thani; 0-4232-5406

Now one of the busiest commercial centers in the northeast, this once sleepy border town benefits from lively border trade with Laos. Nong Khai's main attraction for travelers is still its peaceful riverside character. Its streets and *sois* are lined with traditional wooden shop-houses, and its most vibrant neighborhood is around the Sadet riverboat pier, with its market and adjacent restaurants overlooking the Mekong River. It offers a growing number of restaurants, shopping centers, and banking facilities.

Indochina Market
ตลาดอินโดจีน

◻ Off Rimkhong Rd, Tha Sadet ◯ Daily

Also known as Tha Sadet Market, this market remains the focus of lively, local trade carried out between Thailand and Laos. Reciprocal visa arrangements allow merchants from either country to visit Vientiane (p272) or Nong Khai for up to three days. Merchandise that can be bought here includes clothing, foodstuffs, pestles and mortars, fishing nets, and tables woven from bamboo.

Friendship Bridge
สะพานมิตรภาพ

Though always a major crossing point for those bound for Vientiane, Nong Khai gained significance as a commercial border post with the opening of this bridge in 1994. Built with Thai, Lao, and Australian cooperation, it links Ban Chommani on the western outskirts of Nong Khai to Tha Na Laeng on the opposite bank. By the foot of the bridge, on the Thai side, is a stretch of sand known as Chommani beach, a popular spot for picnicking.

Prap Ho Monument
อนุสาวรีย์ปราบฮ่อ

◻ Janjopthit Rd

A symbol of municipal pride, this was built to honor those who held off Ho Chinese invasions in 1855 and 1877. Built in 1886, and bearing Thai, Lao, Chinese, and English inscriptions, it is the site of celebrations on March 5.

TOP 5 EVENTS IN NONG KHAI

Walking Street
A riot of music and food along the riverfront each Saturday.

Candle Festival
Candles are paraded on floats to signal the start of Buddhist Lent.

Long Boat Race Festival
Held in October to mark the end of Ok Phansa (Buddhist Lent).

Naga Fireball Festival
Fireballs rise up from the Mekong in October.

Chinese Dragon Festival
Floats and pyrotechnics in October/November.

↑ Incredible view over the Mekong from the Nong Khai Skywalk

GREAT VIEW
Nong Khai Skywalk

In western Nong Khai province, this glass-bottomed Skywalk is set beside the mountaintop Wat Pha Tak Suea and overlooks the Laos countryside and the Mekong.

---

⑤
Wat Si Muang
วัดศรีเมือง

🏠 **Off Meechai Rd** 🕐 **Daily**

The temple buildings and *chedi* of Wat Si Muang are Lao in style. The *wat* has an ornate shrine at the main entrance, cluttered with Buddhist merit offerings. It is one of many such temples that line the main Meechai Road.

---

⑥ 🔶
Sala Kaew Ku (Wat Khaek)
ศาลาแก้วกู่

🏠 **3 miles (5 km) E of Nong Khai** 🕐 **8am–6pm daily**

By far the most unusual site of interest at Nong Khai, Sala Kaew Ku was founded in 1978 by Thai-Brahmin shaman

---

④
Wat Pho Chai
วัดโพธิ์ชัย

🏠 **Pho Chai Rd** 🕐 **Daily**

The somewhat gaudy Wat Pho Chai lies in the southwest of the city, adjacent to a street market of the same name. Its main chapel sports imposing *naga* balustrades and a pair of roaring lions at the top of the entrance stairs, protecting the highly revered Luang Pho Phra Sai Buddha image housed inside, a solid gold Buddha with a ruby-studded, flame finial molded in the ancient Lao kingdom of Lan Xang. Murals in the temple give a pictorial account of the story behind this image.

Luang Pu Bunleua Surirat. It is essentially an open-air theme park of enormous, concrete Hindu and Buddhist sculptures. Among the giant gods, saints, and demons that are depicted here are Rahu, the god of eclipses, and, tallest of all, an 82-ft (25-m) high seven-headed *naga* with a tiny Buddha seated on its coils. The atmosphere of a walk through this eccentric collection is intensified by incense and piped music.

↑ One of the impressive concrete sculptures at Sala Kaew Ku

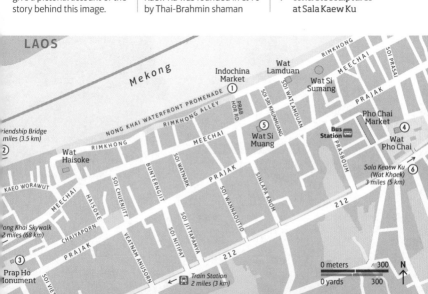

❸

VIENTIANE

เวียงจันทร์

🗺️C2 📍Vientiane province, Laos ✈️2.5 miles (4 km) W of center 🚌Off Khu Vieng Rd 🚆From Nong Khai ℹ️Corner of Setthathirat Rd and Pang Kham Rd

A day trip from Nong Khai (p270), Vientiane is the capital of Laos. In its 1,000-year history, it has come under Khmer, Vietnamese, Thai, and French colonial influence, but was destroyed by the Siamese in 1828. In 1893 the French annexed Laos and made Vientiane its capital, but 60 years later, Laos gained independence. French colonial influence can still be felt here.

THE PATHET LAO

The Lao Patriotic Front was formed after World War II and opposed French rule. The LPF's armed wing, the Pathet Lao, mounted an armed struggle against the government in the 1960s. During the Vietnam War the US repeatedly bombed Laos to stamp out Pathet Lao support for the North Vietnamese. With the withdrawal of American forces from the region in 1975, the Pathet Lao staged a bloodless coup and declared Laos the Lao People's Democratic Republic.

---

①

Haw Pha Kaew
หอพระแก้ว

📍Setthathirat Rd
🕐Daily

This temple was once home to the Emerald Buddha (p99), which was taken by the Thais in 1778. A replica was given to Laos by Thailand in 1994. The sack of 1828 left the temple in ruins. Restored in the 20th century, it is now a museum. The main door is all that remains of the original wat.

②

Chao Anouvong Riverside Park
สวนเจ้าอนุวงศ์

📍Sithane Rd 🚌5, 6, 30, 44, 49 🕐24 hrs daily

This peaceful park is centered on a statue of the eponymous Chao Anouvong, who led the Lao Rebellion (1826–28). His statue is surrounded by animal statues. By night, the park becomes a market, with food and souvenir stalls, and outdoor aerobics sessions.

③

Pha That Luang
พระธาตุหลวง

📍That Luang Rd 🕐8am–5pm daily

Perching halfway up a hill on the northeastern outskirts of the city, this is the most important monument in Laos. According to legend a chedi was built here in the 3rd century BC to house a breastbone of the Lord Buddha. The present structure was built in 1566, when

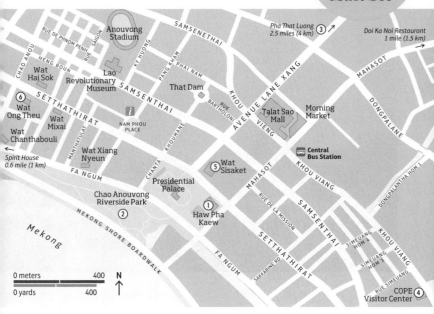

Map showing locations including Anouvong Stadium, Wat Hai Sok, Lao Revolutionary Museum, That Dam, Wat Ong Theu, Wat Mixai, Wat Chanthabouli, Wat Xiang Nyeun, Presidential Palace, Chao Anouvong Riverside Park, Haw Pha Kaew, Wat Sisaket, Talat Sao Mall, Morning Market, Central Bus Station, COPE Visitor Center, and the Mekong Shore Boardwalk

0 meters 400
0 yards 400
N

Vientiane became the capital of the Lan Xang Kingdom. It was damaged in the 18th and 19th centuries and restored, albeit badly, by the French in 1900. A better restoration of the site was undertaken in the 1930s.

④ COPE Visitor Center
ອງค์การໂคป

🏠 **Khou Vieng Rd** 🕐 **9am–6pm daily** 🌐 **copelaos.or**

Laos is the most bombed country in the world relative to its population, and there are still unexploded bombs and landmines in fields and forests across the country. This organization provides prosthetics and rehabilitation to people who have been injured by these devices. A museum exhibition is a haunting reminder of the

←

Monks leaving a monastery with the golden Pha That Luang behind

horrors of war, and includes unexploded bombs. You can help by donating or buying from the gift shop.

⑤ Wat Sisaket
ວັดສີສะเกด

🏠 **Lane Xang Rd** 🕐 **8am–noon & 1–4pm daily**

Built in 1818, this was one of the few buildings to survive the sack of 1828. It is now the oldest *wat* in Vientiane. Its most memorable feature is the 2,052 tiny Buddha images that fill the cloister walls.

⑥ Wat Ong Theu
ວັดองค์ตื้อ

🏠 **Setthathirat Rd** 🕐 **8am–5pm daily**

One of the most important *wat* complexes in Laos, Wat Ong Theu houses a large, 16th-century bronze Buddha image. The *wat* is also home to a school for monks.

EAT

Doi Ka Noi
This unpretentious restaurant is one of the best places to find traditional Lao food.

🏠 **242 Sapang Mor, Sisangvone Rd** 📞 **856-2055-898-959** 🕐 **Mon**

Ⓑ Ⓑ Ⓑ

Spirit House
Set in a traditional Laotian house overlooking the Mekong, this is an atmospheric place to spend an evening, serving a variety of Western and Lao food, as well as wine and beer.

🏠 **93/09 Fa Ngoum Rd** 📞 **856-0212-62530**

Ⓑ Ⓑ Ⓑ

4

WAT PHRA THAT PHANOM

วัดพระธาตุพนม

A E3 **🏠** Center of That Phanom, Nakhon Phanom province **📞** 0-4251-3490 **🚌** From Nakhon Phanom, Sakhon Nakhon, or Mukdahan **🕐** 6am–7pm daily

A hidden treasure in the Mekong Valley, this revered shrine is tucked away in the remote town of That Phanom. Its golden *chedi* is particularly beautiful at sunset.

Wat Phra That Phanom's *chedi* was built some 1,500 years ago, but according to legend it was constructed eight years after the death of the Buddha in 535 BC, when local dignitaries erected it as a burial place for his breastbone. The monument has been restored many times, most recently after devastating rains in 1975. Each year at the full moon of the third lunar month a week-long temple festival attracts thousands of pilgrims from Thailand and Laos. The monument is the second most sacred site to devotees from Laos, the first being Pha That Luang in Vientiane *(p272)*.

Walk around the *wat* slowly, taking in the peaceful and tranquil atmosphere as the locals do. As you move behind the cloister, stop by the That Phanom Museum, which hosts an interesting collection of religious artifacts. The museum is also an excellent place to learn about the history and legend surrounding the creation of the *wat*.

↑ Motorbikes zooming past the immaculate entrance to Wat Phra That Phanom

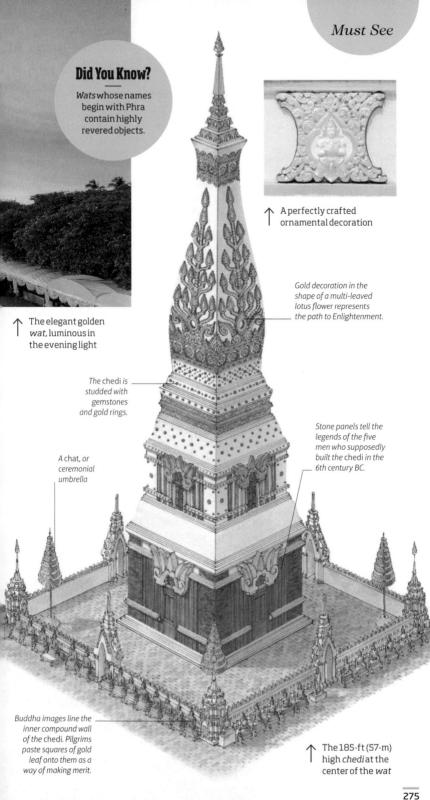

Did You Know?

Wats whose names begin with Phra contain highly revered objects.

↑ The elegant golden *wat*, luminous in the evening light

A perfectly crafted ornamental decoration

Gold decoration in the shape of a multi-leaved lotus flower represents the path to Enlightenment.

The chedi *is studded with gemstones and gold rings.*

A chat, or ceremonial umbrella

Stone panels tell the legends of the five men who supposedly built the chedi *in the 6th century BC.*

Buddha images line the inner compound wall of the chedi. *Pilgrims paste squares of gold leaf onto them as a way of making merit.*

↑ The 185-ft (57-m) high *chedi* at the center of the *wat*

EXPERIENCE MORE

5

Phu Hin Rong Kla National Park

อุทยานแห่งชาติภูหินร่องกล้า

🅐 C3 **ⓘ** Phitsanulok province; Park HQ off Hwy 2331, 19 miles (31 km) SE of Nakhon Thai; 081-596-5977 🚌 From Loei or Phitsanulok to Nakhon Thai, then *songthaew*

Covering an area of 120 sq miles (307 sq km), Phu Hin Rong Kla National Park has a wide variety of flora and fauna and an unusual open-air museum with exhibits of the Communist camp based here in the 1960s and '70s. The spread of Communism in Southeast Asia from the 1950s alarmed the Thai goverment, and hostilities between the Communist Party of Thailand (CPT) and the military commenced in 1964. Soon after, the open forests of the Phu Hin Rong Kla mountain range became a CPT stronghold. An average elevation of 3,300 ft (1,000 m), proximity to Laos – run by the Communist Pathet Lao from 1975 – and the access this facilitated to headquarters at Kunming in China, all made it an ideal site. The CPT was active after 1976, when thousands of students fled here after a coup in Bangkok. By 1979, disillusioned with Communism, many began to take advantage of an amnesty from the Thai government. Dwindling support and government attacks on Phu Hin Rong Kla in the early 1980s led the site to fall to the authorities in 1982.

Two years later it opened as a stunning national park. Its highest peak, Phu Man Khao, rises to a height of 5,300 ft (1,620 m).

At the visitors' center, some of the insurgents' buildings still stand, and a small museum tells the story of the conflict, but the real attraction today is the natural beauty of this huge park. A 3-mile (5-km.) trail from the visitors' center leads to two spectacular waterfalls, Rom Klao and Paradon. Viewpoints near the visitors' center include Lan Hin Pum, where the insurgents raised their red flag each morning, and Lan Hin Taek.

↓ Boulders dotting the Phu Hin Rong Kla National Park landscape

> For the traveler with time to explore the 47 sq miles (121 sq km) of Phu Ruea National Park, a number of marked trails lead through a beautiful landscape of meadows.

Phu Ruea National Park
อุทยานแห่งชาติภูเรือ

🗺C3 📍Loei province Park HQ off Hwy 203, 37 miles (60 km) W of Loei ☎088-509-5299 🚌From Loei to Phu Ruea village, then *songthaew*

Phu Ruea or "boat mountain" gets its name from its peak, which is shaped like a junk. It stands some 4,500 ft (1,365 m) above sea level and offers spectacular views of the town of Loei to the south and toward Laos. A modern Buddha image sits looking out over the plains in contemplation of their beauty. It is possible to drive to the summit of Phu Ruea, passing several bizarre rock formations on the way.

For the traveler with time to explore the 47 sq miles (121 sq km) of Phu Ruea National Park, a number of marked trails lead through a beautiful landscape of meadows, rock gardens, and pine and evergreen forests. Views across the surrounding lowlands can be seen from Phu Kut and the cliffs of Pha Lon Noi, Pha Dong Tham San, Pha Yat, and Pha Sap Thong. There are also several waterfalls around the park, namely Huai Phai, Huai Ta Wat, and Lan Hin Taek.

📷 PICTURE PERFECT
Tortoise Rock

Among the unusual rock formations found in Phu Ruea National Park, this huge stack of boulders, resembling a giant mushroom, is the best for photos, since it can be shot from many different angles.

Animals at Phu Ruea National Park include barking deer, wild pigs, and a wide variety of birds, including the rare *tao puru*, or Siamese big-headed turtle. Phu Ruea is also famed for being one of the coolest areas of Thailand, with a record low temperature of 25° F (-4° C) having been recorded here in 1981. This climate is perfect for a vineyard, and you can taste or buy some wine at the Chateau de Loei winery here.

Loei
เลย

🗺C3 📍Loei province ✈🚌 ℹ️Loei; 0-4281 1405

In Thai, the word *loei* means "beyond" or "to the farthest extreme," a fitting name for a town and province that lie in the northernmost part of northeast Thailand, straddling the edge of the Khorat Plateau. Though the province is administrated as part of Isan (the northeast), its climate and landscape are more similar to those of northern Thailand. In winter it is cold and foggy, in summer searingly hot. In the past, bureaucrats who had fallen out of favor with the Siamese government, based in Bangkok, were posted here as punishment for their inefficiency. One fortunate aspect of Loei's isolation is that it retains its traditional flavor.

Lying along the west bank of the Loei River, Loei has a few sights of interest. There is a lively market by the bridge across the river, and next to the bridge is the Lak Muang or "city pillar." The town also has an old Chinese shrine, Chao Pho Kut Pong, a popular place of worship. The surrounding

PHI TA KHON FESTIVAL

A less lively version of this festival is held in the provincial capital of Loei in July, but its real home is in the town of Dan Sai, 50 miles (80 km) west. Here Phi Ta Khon takes place in June. Its purpose is to make Buddhist merit and call for rain. The young men of Dan Sai dress up as spirits *(phi ta khon)*, draped in robes of patchwork rags and sporting painted masks. During the festival, they make playful jibes at onlookers as they parade a sacred Buddha image around the town. On the third day, the "spirits" bring the festival to a close by circumambulating the main building of the local *wat* three times, before casting their masks into the river.

---

valley is rich in minerals and also produces some of the finest cotton in Thailand. Examples of this can be bought in Loei, in shops along Charoenraj Road. Loei also has a reasonable amount of cheap accommodations.

An easy cruise west of Loei brings you to Huai Krathing Reservoir. Created for irrigation purposes, the lake is now a recreation area.

Did You Know?

In Chiang Khan, locals and Thai tourists wake up at dawn to give alms *(p41)* to Buddhist monks.

8

Chiang Khan
เชียงคาน

 C2 ⌂ Loei province
🚌 From Loei or Nong Khai
ℹ Loei; 0-4281-1405

Chiang Khan consists of two 1-mile (1.5-km) long parallel streets running along the south bank of the Mekong River and lined with run-down teakwood shop-houses, restaurants, and temples. Those temples most worth a visit are Wat Santi, Wat Pa Klang, built over 100 years ago by Lao immigrants, Wat Si Khun Muang, Wat Tha Kok, and Wat Mahathat. The latter is the oldest temple in Chiang Khan, its *bot* having been built

in 1654. Like Wat Tha Kok, it has French colonial influence in its colonnades and shutters.

Chiang Khan has become a popular weekend jaunt for young Bangkokians, and is now quite hip, with a good selection of boutique hotels, craft beer bars, and chic eateries.

Located 1 mile (1.5 km) east from Wat Tha Kok along the Mekong River is Wat Tha Khaek. Neglected for years, this temple is now undergoing reconstruction in a mixture of traditional and modern styles. A further 1 mile (1.5 km) downriver are the scenic Kaeng Kut Khu rapids.

9

Phu Phrabat Historical Park
อุทยานประวัติศาสตร์ภูพระบาท

🅰 C2 ⌂ Off Hwy 2021, 6 miles (10 km) W of Ban Pheu, Udon Thani province
🚌 From Nong Khai or Udon Thani to Ban Phu, then *songthaew* ⌚ Daily ℹ Udon Thani; 0-4232-5406

The distinctive sandstone formations that are the central

→ The mushroom-shaped Ho Nang Ussa in Phu Phrabat Historical Park

Hanging out among the teakwood buildings on a street in Chiang Khan

⑩ Mukdahan
มุกดาหาร

🅰E3 🏛 Mukdahan province
🚌 ℹ Nakhon Phanom;
0-4322-7714-5

Mukdahan is the capital of one of Thailand's newest provinces, created in 1980. The most interesting street is Samran Chai Khong Road, along the Mekong River front. It faces the second-largest city in Laos, Suwannakhet, on the opposite bank. In 2007, a second Thai–Lao Friendship Bridge opened across the river, linking Mukdahan with Suwannakhet. Visitors can obtain a visa on arrival to enter Laos. Mukdahan is a busy trading center, and both Lao and Thai boats can be seen at the pier, loading and unloading their goods.

A market runs most of the length of the riverside, from Wat Si Mongkol Tai and Wat Yot Kaew Siwichai. Expect an excess of plastic ephemera, though the market is worth a visit for the local sweetmeats and its colorful atmosphere.

Wat Si Mongkhol Thai was built in 1956 by Vietnamese immigrants in the town and is distinguished by statues of mythical creatures at the entrance to its main chapel. The gaudier Wat Yot Kaew Siwichai houses an enormous, seated, golden Buddha image. The figure sits in an open-fronted *wihan* with paneled glass on two of its sides. Near Wat Yot Kaew Siwichai, on Song Nang Sathit Road, is the Chinese Chao Fa Mung Muang shrine, home to Mukdahan's guardian spirit.

GREAT VIEW
Phu Manorom

Excellent views of the provincial capital can be seen from the 1,650-ft (500-m) peak of Phu Manorom, 3 miles (5 km) south of Mukdahan. A pavilion at the top shelters a replica of the Buddha's Footprint.

⑪ Renu Nakhon
เรณูนคร

🅰E3 🏛 Nakhon Phanom province 🚌 From Nakhon Phanom ℹ Nakhon Phanom; 0-4322-7714-5

Renu Nakhon is a village known for its weaving and embroidery. At the Wednesday market, colorful cottons and silks are sold by the *phun*, a measure 2 ft (75 cm) long. Ready-made garments and furnishings from all over the northeast and Laos are also sold. There is a more permanent gathering of textile stalls around Phra That Renu. This was built in 1918 and modeled loosely on the nearby *chedi* at That Phanom.

→ Buddha statue with the Phra That Renu temple behind, Renu Nakhon

attraction of this historical park cannot fail to leave their imprint on the imagination. The local population has shrouded the site in many fantastic myths and legends. According to one of these, Princess Ussa was sent to Phu Phrabat by her father to study. However, she fell in love with Prince Barot. Outraged, her father challenged the prince to a temple-building duel, but lost. A huge sandstone slab in the park, known as Kok Ma Thao Barot, is supposedly Prince Barot's stable. The mushroom-shaped Ho Nang Ussa apparently represents Princess Ussa's residence, where she pined away many long years in exile.

The 6,000-year-old human history of this site is testified to by cave paintings found on the underside of two natural rock shelters, known locally as Tham Wua and Tham Khon. At the entrance to the historical park stands a crude replica of Wat Phra That Phanom *(p274)*; the Wat Phraphutthabat Bua Bok houses the Bua Bok Buddha Footprint and is an important pilgrimage site for local Thais.

EAT

The Outside Inn

Burgers, enchiladas, and Thai classics are on the menu at this eatery in a wooden-beamed house.

E4 11 Suriyat Rd, Ubon Ratchathani
theoutsideinn ubon.com

ⓑⒷⓑ

Viewkong

At the Viewkong Hotel, overlooking the Mekong, this restaurant serves Thai, Chinese, and Western cuisine.

E3 527 Sunthorn Wichit Rd, Nakhon Phanom ⓒ0-4251-3564

ⓑⒷⓑ

Mukdahan Night Market

This bustling evening market is a great place to try classic Issan dishes.

E3 Song Nang Sathit Rd, Mukdahan

ⓑⒷⓑ

Sakhon Nakhon
สกลนคร

D3 Sakhon Nakhon province ▸▨ 𝒊Nakhon Phanom; 0-4322-7714-5

There are two *wats* of interest in the friendly town of Sakhon Nakhon. Wat Phra That Choeng Chum is a beautiful temple complex with a large *bot* and *wihan*, a 10th-century Khmer *prang*, and a whitewashed, 80-ft (24-m) Lao-style *chedi* built during the Ayutthaya period.

The old *prang* is reached through a door in the *wihan*. Etched into the *prang's* base is an ancient Khmer inscription, and around it are Lao and Khmer images of the Buddha. Also in the compound is an interesting display of *luk nimit*, which are Brahmin foundation markers that somewhat resemble giant cannon balls.

The 11th-century Khmer *prang* of Wat Phra That Narai Cheng Weng was built as a Hindu monument. The name Cheng Weng is taken from the princess responsible for its construction; Narai is a Thai

and Khmer name for Vishnu. The most important lintel – over the only entrance, to the east – shows Shiva dancing to the destruction of the universe, as he tramples the head of a lion.

Nong Han Lake, adjacent to the provincial capital, is large and filled with many small islets, notably Don Sawan, which has interesting Buddhist statuary. The lake is a popular weekend fishing, dining, and drinking spot for the locals.

Nakhon Phanom
นครพนม

E3 Nakhon Phanom province ▸▨ 𝒊1841 Soontornvijit Rd, Nakhon Phanom; 0-4322-7714-5

Nakhon Phanom ("city of hills") is a good town in which to spend a few relaxing days by the Mekong. In the dry season a beach by the river, Hat Sai Tai Muang, becomes exposed, and it is possible to walk out almost as far as Laos. However, this town cannot be used as a place

to procure a visa for, or as an entry point into, Laos.

To celebrate the end of the rains, during the night of the full moon in the 11th lunar month, there is a resplendent procession of illuminated boats on the river here. Measuring some 33 ft (10 m) in length, the boats are traditionally crafted from bamboo or banana trees.

 14

Pha Taem
ผาแต้ม

 E4 **11 miles (18 km) N of Khong Chiam, Ubon Ratchathani province** **From Ubon Ratchathani to Khong Chiam, then tuk-tuk** **Ubon Ratchathani; 0-4524-3770** **Daily**

The route, 11 miles (18 km) from Khong Chiam up to Pha Taem or "painted cliff," is a circuitous one, really accessible only by rental car or tuk-tuk. Along the way, a few miles before you arrive at the cliff top, an unusual, sandstone rock formation can be seen at the side of the road. Known as Sao Chaliang, it is reminiscent of the Ho Nang Ussa at Phu Phrabat Historical Park (p278).

At the end of the journey, an unmarked trail leads from the parking lot to the cliff face. This is decorated with huge figures and geometrical designs. Painted in an indelible red pigment derived from soil, tree gum, and fat, the paintings are thought to date back some 4,000 years. Covering 560 ft (170 m) along the cliff face, they include depictions of fish traps, wild animals, giant cockroach-like fish, angular human beings, and a 98-ft (30-m) stretch of handprints. The artists who created these decorations are

↑ The beautiful Khong Chiam landscape, where the Mun and Mekong rivers meet

thought to be related to the early inhabitants of Ban Chiang (p258) and were rice cultivators rather than cave dwellers.

15

Khong Chiam
โขงเจียม

 E4 **Ubon Ratchathani province** **Ubon Ratchathani; 0-4524-3770**

Khong Chiam is near the confluence of the muddy red Mekong and the indigo-blue Mun rivers, which creates the phenomenon of the *maenam song si* or "two-colored river." The differing colors of the rivers derive from the amounts of sand and clay suspended in their waters. Scenic views are offered from the bank at Wat Khong Chiam, and boat trips out to the confluence point itself allow a full appreciation of the blend of colored waters, which is clearest in April. It is

> PICTURE PERFECT
> **Pha Taem at Sunset**
>
> Pha Taem is particularly beautiful at sunset, when there are tremendous views across the Mekong and of the wild Lao jungle beyond.

also possible to cross from Khong Chiam to the Lao town on the opposite side of the river, but this cannot be used by travelers as an official crossing point into Laos.

You can also observe traditional conical fish traps being made out of wicker by locals in Khong Chiam.

16

Sangkhom
สังคม

C2 **Nong Khai province** **From Loei or Nong Khai** **Udon Thani; 0-4232-5406**

The main attractions of this lovely town are its peace and quiet and its location in a particularly lush part of the Mekong River Valley. Ranged along the bank of the river are some quaint wooden buildings. Sangkhom is also a good base for excursions into the surrounding countryside.

The fantastic Than Thip falls are a major highlight of this area. Outside Sangkhom, 2 miles (3 km) off the main highway, they are hidden in the jungle and banana groves. The two main, and most accessible, levels of this waterfall have pools at their bases, making them ideal for a refreshing swim.

 ←

Intricate details of Wat Phra That Choeng Chum, in the old town of Sakhon Nakhon

PRASAT KHAO PHRA WIHAN

This magnificent group of Khmer temples is perched on a promontory in Thailand's Sisaket Province overlooking the Cambodian plains below. It was built in the 11th century, when the Khmer Empire included much of what is today Thailand. The site has been a source of conflict between the two countries for over 100 years. Geographically Thai, culturally Cambodian, it was legally ruled to be on Cambodian territory by the International Court of Justice in 2011 and can be visited only from Cambodia.

 Chong Mek
ช่องเม็ก

△E4 ◘ Ubon Ratchathani province ▧ **From Ubon Ratchathani** 🚹 **Ubon Ratchathani; 0-4524-3770**

Situated on the border between Thailand and Laos, Chong Mek is one of the few places at which tourists can cross into Laos. Visitors can obtain a visa on arrival, valid for one month, for a fee of US$35 and two recent passport photographs.

Since the border crossing opened at Chong Mek, a vibrant market and shopping area has sprung up, attracting busloads of Thai tourists who also cross into Laos to visit the nearby town of Pakse.

For those who do not have a visa, it is possible, even without a passport, to walk some 660 ft (200 m) over the border to browse around the open-air market and duty-free shops that are set up there.

In the market, there may be groups of old women selling rare plants and flowers. However, many of the plants are, sadly, taken from the Lao jungle. Visitors to the market are advised not to buy these.

 Sirindhorn Dam
เขื่อนสิรินธร

△E4 ◘ Ubon Ratchathani province ▧ **From Ubon Ratchathani to Chong Mek, then** *songthaew* 🚹 **Ubon Ratchathani; 0-4524-3770**

Named after the second daughter of the late King Bhumibol, the Sirindhorn Dam was built in 1971. The reservoir it created is 27 miles (43 km) from north to south; the turbines produce 24,000 kilowatts of electricity.

There is a park at the dam HQ, and a restaurant and bungalows. It is possible to walk out over the dam and to take a boat on the reservoir.

 Prasat Prang Ku
ปราสาทปรางค์กู่

△D4 ◘ Off Hwy 2234, 43 miles (70 km) SW of Sisaket, Sisaket province ▧ **From Ubon or Sisaket to Kantharalak, then** *songthaew* ◷ **Daily** 🚹 **Ubon Ratchathani; 0-4524-3770**

This 11th-century Khmer monument comprises three brick *prangs* on a single platform. The most remarkable feature is a well-preserved lintel, divided horizontally into two sections by the tails of two long *nagas*. In the center stands Vishnu on his mount, a *garuda*. On either side of the *garuda* are two lions with garlands of flowers in their open mouths. The top half of the lintel is decorated with dancing deities.

> Following the rapid growth of Ubon during the Vietnam War, when it played host to a nearby US air base, the city is now one of the largest in Thailand.

 20

Ubon Ratchathani
อุบลราชธานี

◭E4 ◲Ubon Ratchathani province ✉☎▥ ℹ264/1 Khuan Thani Rd, Ubon Ratchathani; www.tatubon.org

The provincial capital, the city of Ubon Ratchathani was founded by Lao immigrants on the northern bank of the Mun River at the end of the 18th century, and Lao influence can be seen in the architectural features of some of the city's religious buildings. Following the rapid growth of Ubon during the Vietnam War, when it played host to a nearby US air base, the city is now one of the largest in Thailand. The **Ubon National Museum** is one of the best in the northeast, and some fascinating temples are dotted around the city. The museum is housed in the former country residence of King Vajiravudh (1910–25) and contains displays of Khmer, Hindu, and Lao Buddhist iconography. One of the rarest and most impressive exhibits is a giant bronze drum, dating back as far as the 4th century AD, that was used originally for ceremonial purposes.

The most interesting of Ubon's temples is Wat Thung Si Muang, on account of its teakwood library. Founded by King Rama III (1824–51), the *wat* houses 150-year-old murals showing some of the *jatakas*. The complex also includes a *mondop* with a Buddha Footprint.

In 1853 King Mongkut (1851–68) gave his support to build Wat Supattanaram Worawihan as the first temple in the northeast dedicated to the Thammayut sect (a branch of Theravada Buddhism) of which the king was also a member. It consists of a highly eclectic blend of architectural styles, having been built by Vietnamese craftsmen who were under instruction to incorporate an unusual mixture of Khmer, Thai, and European architectural influences.

Ubon also has several other interesting temples: Wat Cheng, with its elegant Lao-style wooden carvings; Wat Si Ubon Rattanaram, built in 1855 and housing a topaz Buddha image, originating from Chiang Saen; and Wat Sirindhorn Wanaram, with painted patterns around the grounds that glow after dark.

Ubon National Museum
◲Khuan Thani Rd ◷9am–4pm Wed–Sun ▥thailandmuseum.com

 INSIDER TIP
Buddhist Life

Wat Pah Nanachat (watpahnanachat.org), near Ubon, is not a beginner's course in meditation, but offers an experience of life in a Buddhist forest temple, with chanting and no digital devices.

↑ The lavish, highly decorative Wat Sirindhorn Wanaram, near Ubon Ratchathani

EASTERN SEABOARD

The Eastern Seaboard was a frontier between the Khmer and Sukhothai empires in the early 15th century. As Khmer power waned, large numbers of ethnic Tais settled here and discovered gem-rich deposits in the lush countryside. Chanthaburi became a center for gem trading and in the 18th and 19th centuries had to expel first Burmese then French occupying forces. Numerous Vietnamese refugees have since settled in the town.

Though still a forested region with orchards, gem-mining, and fishing communities, the Eastern Seaboard has seen dramatic changes in the late 20th century as the oil and tourist industries have grown dramatically. However, some seaside towns have retained their charm, and in Si Racha excellent seafood can be sampled in open-air restaurants overlooking the bay. In contrast to this are the neon lights of Pattaya, an infamous destination for US marines on R&R during the Vietnam War. Despite its seedy image, it is now an excellent center for water sports.

EASTERN SEABOARD

Must Sees
1 Ko Samet
2 Chanthaburi
3 Ko Chang

Experience More
4 Ko Sichang
5 Si Racha
6 Rayong
7 Khlong Yai
8 Pattaya

9 Namtok Phlio National Park
10 Khao Chamao-Khao
    Wong National Park
11 Bo Rai
12 Wat Khao Sukim
13 Khao Kitchakut
    National Park
14 Trat

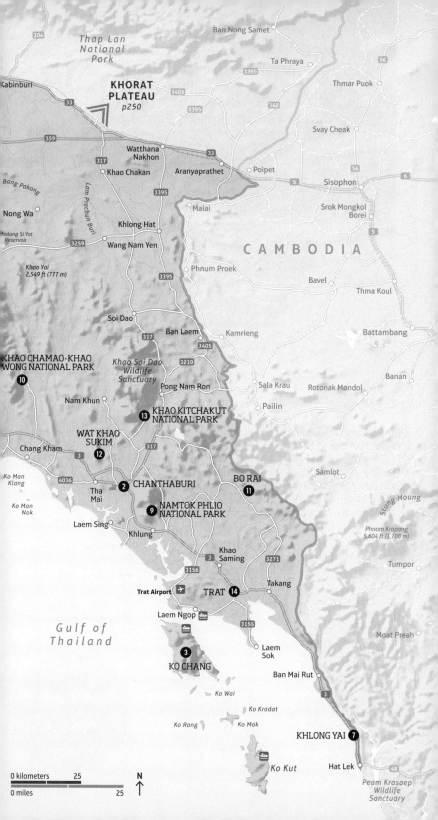

KO SAMET

เกาะเสม็ด

🗺️ C6 📍 Rayong province 🚤 From Ban Phe (Rayong) to Ao Wong Duan and Ao Phrao ℹ️ Rayong; 0-3865-5420

The closest major island to Bangkok, Ko Samet, blessed with clear blue waters and crystalline sand, is popular with foreigners and Thai weekenders. Because it is only 4 miles (6 km) long and 2 miles (3 km) wide, most of the island is accessible on foot. The western side is less crowded, while the interior's dense jungle, home to the usual geckos and hornbills, is riddled with trails.

①

Na Dan
หน้าด่าน

📍 4 miles (6 km) S of Ban Phe

A small but fairly busy pier in the northeastern part of the island, Na Dan is the entry point into Ko Samet and is used by commercial as well as privately owned speedboats and ferries. A nondescript fishing settlement, it offers basic accommodations, but very few travelers actually stay here. Communal taxis leave from Na Dan's pier to Ko Samet's many beaches.

②

Hat Sai Kaeo
หาดทรายแก้ว

📍 0.5 miles (1 km) SE of Na Dan

With its clear shallow waters, Hat Sai Kaeo ("glass sand beach") is the longest and liveliest beach. The 2-mile (3-km) stretch is lined with bungalows, bars, restaurants, and shops. Boat trips around Ko Samet and snorkeling day trips to nearby islands leave from here. Although the sea still looks pristine, the beach has lost some of its charm due to overcrowding.

③

Ao Phai
อ่าวไผ่

📍 0.5 miles (1 km) SW of Hat Sai Kaeo

This famous party zone attracts partygoers from all over the island. Full moon celebrations (p305) here tend to go over the top. Nearby is a statue of the prince and the mermaid in Phra Aphai Mani, a poem by Sunthorn Phu, Thailand's most famous poet.

④

Ao Phrao
อ่าวพร้าว

📍 1 mile (2 km) SW of Na Dan

Due to its isolation, Ao Phrao ("coconut bay") doesn't receive as many overnight visitors as beaches on the

Did You Know?

Ao Phrao is the only developed beach in the largely accessible west coast.

↑ Colored umbrellas and deck chairs on a quiet beach on Ko Samet

east coast. The narrow white beach is interspersed with trees and a lush mountainous background. Apart from a few guesthouses, Ao Phrao also has two luxury resorts with swimming pools and spas. There is a PADI center for those interested in diving. However, this is the extent of facilities on this rather peaceful beach.

⑤

Ao Nuan
อ่าวนวล

🏠 **2 miles (3 km) SW of Hat Sai Kaeo**

Just south of the commercial beaches are a couple of small secluded coves for those who want to get away from the madding crowds. Ao Nuan is a little rocky for swimming, but the stretch of sand is set amid unspoiled nature. The beach hut accommodations are very basic, but you can enjoy the

DRINK

Naga Bar
One of the most trendy spots on the island, Naga is popular with backpackers, but manages to retain a laid-back, friendly atmosphere that appeals to many people.

🏠 **Hat Sai Kaeo**
📞 **0-3864-4035**

Jump at Sea
If you're seeking an escape from the backpacker bar scene, this peaceful cafe is open into the evening and serves beers and cocktails.

🏠 **95/1 Moo 4, Hat Sai Kaeo** 📞 **0-3864-4232**

excellent restaurant or spend evenings under a beautiful canopy of stars unhindered by other lights.

⑥

Ao Wai
อ่าวหวาย

🏠 **3 miles (5 km) SW of Hat Sai Kaeo**

Heading farther south along the east coast, the beaches become quieter and less commercial. Ao Wai is a good option for mid-range accommodations, intimate dining, and a less raucous nightlife. The soft sandy beach is partially shaded and has a few shops. The beach is also close to the southern coves of Ao Kiu Na Nai and Ao Khut. Located offshore, the secluded mini island of Ko Chan has an interesting underwater landscape.

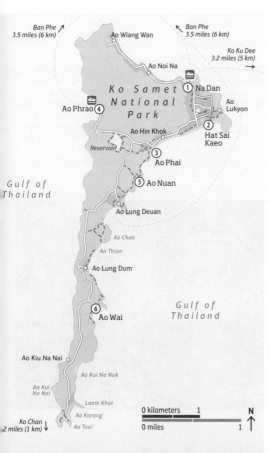

Ban Phe ↗
3.5 miles (6 km)

Ao Wiang Wan

Ban Phe ↖
3.5 miles (6 km)

Ko Ku Dee
3.2 miles (5 km) →

Ao Noi Na

K o   S a m e t
N a t i o n a l
P a r k

① Na Dan

Ao Phrao ④

Ao Lukyon

Ao Hin Khok

②
Hat Sai Kaeo

Reservoir

③
Ao Phai

Gulf of
Thailand

⑤ Ao Nuan

Ao Lung Deuan

Ao Chao

Ao Thian

Ao Lung Dum

Gulf of
Thailand

⑥
Ao Wai

Ao Kiu Na Nai

Ao Kui Na Nok

Ao Kui
Na Nai

Laem Khut

Ko Chan
2 miles (1 km) ↓

Ao Karang

Ao Toei

0 kilometers   1

0 miles   1

N ↑

2

CHANTHABURI
จันทบุรี

🗺C6 🏛Chanthaburi province ℹ️Rayong; 0-3865-5420

Surrounded by verdant chili and rubber plantations, this prosperous and friendly town is arguably Thailand's most charming settlement, packed with fading colonial houses and Vietnamese restaurants. Known as a center for gem trading since the 15th century, Chanthaburi has attracted a wide ethnic mix. The monarch most revered here today is King Taksin, who expelled the Burmese in the 18th century.

EXPERIENCE Eastern Seaboard

Did You Know?

Over 70 percent of the world's rubies have come from Thailand – a large majority found in Chanthaburi.

① Cathedral of the Immaculate Conception
โบสถ์วัดแม่พระปฏิสนธินิรมล

🏛Chanthanimit Rd
📞0-3931-1578

On the lovely bank of the Chanthaburi River is a French-style Catholic cathedral built on the site of an 18th-century missionary chapel. Also known as Chanthanburi Cathedral, it is the largest cathedral in Thailand and a legacy of French occupation. Designed in the French provincial style and built by Christian missionaries, it has been renovated numerous times, especially due to the large influx of Vietnamese Christians in Chanthanburi. Some of the stained-glass windows in the church date from before its 19th-century restoration.

Interior of the Cathedral of the Immaculate Conception and its facade *(inset)*

↓

② Gem Market
ตลาดพลอย

🏛Sri Chan Rd and Soi Kra Chang ⏰9am–6pm Fri–Sun

The Gem Quarter (*talat phloi*) attracts gem traders from all over the world. Known for its natural wealth of sapphires and rubies, Chanthaburi continues to be an important center of this trade despite the exhaustion of its natural resources. On weekends a rainbow array of precious and semi-precious gemstones from Myanmar, Cambodia, and the rich mines of Chanthaburi province are traded at street stalls, and bought and sold for jewelry production. The market is famous for the workmanship of its gem cutters, and visitors can go to the market to see dealers and prospectors doing business. The best gem stores are located along Trok Kachang and Sri Chan Road.

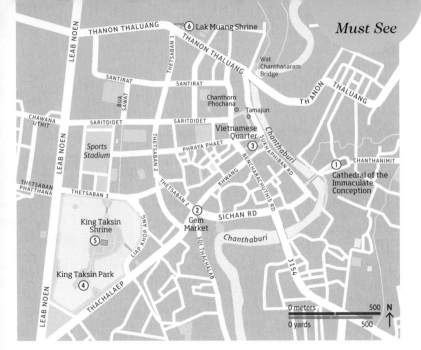

THANON THALUANG
LEAB NOEN
THETSABAN 1
THANON THALUANG
⑥ Lak Muang Shrine
SANTIRAT
BUA SAWAT
SANTIRAT
Wat Chanthanaram Bridge
Chanthorn Phochana
THANON THALUANG
Tamajun
CHAWANA UTHIT
SARITDIDET
SARITDIDET
Vietnamese Quarter
Chanthaburi
THANON THALUANG
LEAB NOEN
PHRAYA PHAET
③
SUKHAPHIBAN RD
CHANTHANIMIT
①
Cathedral of the Immaculate Conception
Sports Stadium
THETSABAN 2
BENCHARACHUTHIS RD
KHWANG
THETSABAN PHATTHANA
THETSABAN 3
KING TAKSIN SHRINE
⑤
LIAP KHOP ANG
THETSABAN 2
②
Gem Market
SICHAN RD
Chanthaburi
3154
King Taksin Park
④
THACHALAEP
SOI THACHALAB
LEAB NOEN

0 meters 500
0 yards 500
N

③
Vietnamese Quarter
ตลาดเวียดนาม

🏠 Rim Nam Rd

Extending along the west bank of Chanthaburi River, the Vietnamese Quarter is the most interesting part of the town. The Vietnamese have migrated to Thailand for over a century, initially to avoid persecution and later as political refugees. This quarter has a distinct flavor: the houses are lovely structures made out of bamboo or wood and stand on stilts, and the nearby market offers delicious Vietnamese snacks.

④
King Taksin Park
สวนสมเด็จพระเจ้าตากสิน

🏠 Leap Noen Rd

The main park area of this lush, open space is divided by two lakes filled with a variety of fish. The park is dominated by a great bronze statue of King Taksin in a heroic pose on the battlefield. Visitors can also sample tropical fruits for which Chanthaburi is famous.

⑤
King Taksin Shrine
ศาลสมเด็จพระเจ้าตากสิน

🏠 Tha Luang Rd

A nonagonal structure with a helmet-shaped roof, this shrine, constructed in 1920, houses a statue of the king that is revered by locals. Every year on December 28, a ceremony commemorates his accession to the throne.

⑥
Lak Muang Shrine
ศาลหลักเมือง

🏠 Tha Luang Rd

Most Thai cities have a *lak muang* – a city pillar – housed within a shrine, believed to house the city's protective deity. This neat building resembling a small *wat* was gifted by King Nangklao in the 19th century.

EAT

Chanthorn Phochana
A local favorite, this is a great place to savor Chanthaburi's unique blend of Thai and Chinese cuisine. The local specialty is *moo cha muang,* a spicy and sour pork curry.

🏠 102/5-8, Benchamanuthit Rd
📞 0-3930-2350

Ⓑ Ⓑ Ⓑ

Tamajun
An atmospheric place to take in views over the river – either from the waterfront terrace or the cozy interior – Tamajun offers superb regional food alongside live music.

🏠 Sukhaphiban Rd
📞 0-3931-1977

Ⓑ Ⓑ Ⓑ

③

KO CHANG
เกาะช้าง

🅰 C6 🏠 Trat province ✈ Trat 🚌 From Bangkok airport
🚤 From Laem Ngop ℹ Trat; 0-3959-7259-60

Mountainous Ko Chang is the largest of the 50 or so islands that form the extensive Ko Chang National Marine Park, which covers an area of 250 sq miles (650 sq km), two-thirds of which is ocean. Mangroves, cliffs, and clear waters make this one of Thailand's most scenic islands and the ideal place for a varied holiday, with no shortage of resorts and spas.

① 🍴

Hat Khlong Phrao
หาดคลองพร้าว

🏠 **3 miles (5 km) S of Hat Sai Khao**

A small fishing port with one of the most popular family beaches on Ko Chang, the attractive Hat Khlong Phrao is best suited for visitors seeking mid-range accommodations. The beach is divided into the northern and southern parts, each with its own peaceful stretch of beautiful sand. The southern end is screened off from the main road by a thick cluster of coconut trees.

② 🍴 🛍

Hat Sai Khao
หาดทรายขาว

🏠 **7 miles (11 km) W of Tha Dan Kao**

The longest, most popular beach on the island, Hat Sai Khao, or "White Sand Beach," is easily accessible from Tha Dan Kao, one of the many piers where ferries heading to Ko Chang arrive. The narrow 1-mile (2-km) stretch of beach is crowded with hotels, resorts, and beach bars, all competing for a glimpse of the sea. An information center on the beach arranges boat trips, fishing, and snorkeling. The road parallel to the beach is lined with shops, seafood shacks, and shopping malls.

③ 🚣

Than Mayom Waterfall
น้ำตกธารมะยม

🏠 **4 miles (6 km) S of Tha Dan Kao**

The east coast of Ko Chang is lined with mangroves and has few facilities. However, a 1-mile (2-km) walk south of the Than Mayom Port leads to a stunning waterfall on a steep hill toward the interior. This

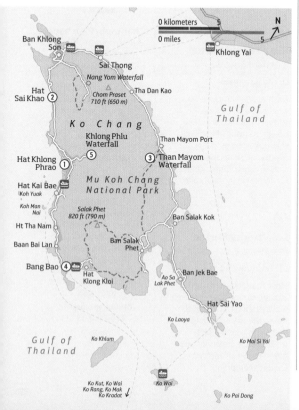

Ban Khlong Son

Sai Thong

Nang Yom Waterfall

Hat Sai Khao ②

Chom Praset 710 ft (650 m)   ○ Tha Dan Kao

Gulf of Thailand

Khlong Yai

K o C h a n g

Khlong Phlu Waterfall

Than Mayom Port

Hat Khlong Phrao ① ⑤

③ Than Mayom Waterfall

Hat Kai Bae

Koh Yuak

Koh Man Nai

Mu Koh Chang National Park

Salak Phet 820 ft (790 m)

Ban Salak Kok

Ht Tha Nam

Baan Bai Lan

Ban Salak Phet

Bang Bao ④

Hat Klong Kloi

Ao Sa Lak Phet

Ban Jek Bae

Hat Sai Yao

Ko Laoya

Gulf of Thailand

Ko Khlum

Ko Mai Si Yai

Ko Wai

Ko Kut, Ko Wai Ko Rang, Ko Mak Ko Kradat ↓

Ko Pai Dong

0 kilometers   5
0 miles   5

N

↑ Swimming in the idyllic, clear waters at Hat Sai Khao

natural cascade is surrounded by lush vegetation and offers spectacular views over the coastline. Successive kings of Thailand have visited the falls, as the inscriptions on the rocks indicate.

Bang Bao
บางเบ้า

🏠 12 miles (19 km) S of Hat Sai Khao 📧

A unique experience awaits visitors to the beautiful Bang Bao – it is a village built entirely on stilts, overlooking the bay. The lovely wooden houses, as well as shops, guesthouses, and restaurants, are connected by narrow bridges, creating a miniature colony over the sea. Several shacks have been converted into seafood restaurants, famed locally for their giant crabs and prawns. Keen anglers can go fishing; snorkeling, diving, and swimming are other options. Dolphins and sea turtles often swim off the southern coast, and tracking them can prove to be a rewarding experience, as long as you hire a tour guide.

During the day, Bang Bao receives a steady flow of camera-happy visitors, but the evenings are blissfully peaceful, after the crowds have dispersed. A hilly trail, which is marked out between Bang Bao and Ao Bai Lan, 3 miles (5 km) to the north, is excellent for hiking.

A short distance south from the village is the small and picturesque Hat Sai Noi beach. Some 330-ft (101-m) long, it has a small restaurant, a few fresh fruit bars, and some scattered chairs, with women offering traditional Thai massages.

You can also visit Ko Kut, the second largest island within the group, by taking a boat from Bang Bao. At 21 miles (34 km) south of Ko Chang, it falls outside of park boundaries and makes for a great day trip. It has some excellent beaches and waterfalls, as well as fantastic seafood restaurants.

HIDDEN GEM
Hat Wai Chek

One of Thailand's last untouched slices of paradise, the isolated cove of Hat Wai Chek, 3 miles (5 km) east of Bang Bao, is almost off the tourist map. To get here, take a boat from Bang Bao.

TOP 4 **WELLNESS CENTERS**

Santhiya Tree
🏠 8/15 Moo 4, Hat Khlong Phrao 🌐 santhiya.com/santhiyatree
The Ayurvana Beach Massage menu blends Thai and Western treatments.

Blue Lagoon Yoga
🏠 30/5 Moo 4, Hat Khlong Phrao 📞 0-8951-54617
Relaxing yoga sessions on a picturesque terrace.

Hatta Thai Massage
🏠 Emerald Cove Hotel, 11/24 Moo 4 📞 0-3955-7109
Aromatherapy and hot stone massages.

Spa Cenvaree
🏠 26/3 Moo 4, Hat Khlong Phrao 🌐 spacenvaree.com
Massages and body scrubs in a beautiful garden with a pond.

Khlong Phlu Waterfall
น้ำตกคลองพลู

🏠 1 mile (2 km) NE of Hat Khlong Phrao

Ko Chang's highest waterfall, the three-tiered Khlong Phlu, locally known as Nam Tok Khlong Phlu, cascades down 65 ft (20 m) into a small pool of clear water surrounded by smooth rocks. Located almost in the middle of the island, it flows down to Hat Khlong Phrao, forming an estuary. You can follow the 2-mile (3-km) walk upstream by taking the road inland between Ko Chang Plaza and Chang Chutiman Tours to reach it. The waterfall is very popular and gets quite crowded, except in the early morning. It's a great spot for picnics, swimming, and treks in the nearby dense rainforest.

EXPERIENCE MORE

4 Ko Sichang

เกาะสีชัง

C5 **Chon Buri province**
From Si Racha
**Pattaya; 0-3842-7667
or 0-3842-8750**

A former haunt of King Chulalongkorn (Rama V), this small island, with a rugged coastline, once functioned as the customs checkpoint for Bangkok-bound ships. Now it is a relatively quiet place with some architectural ruins and a handful of lovely guesthouses catering to visitors who want to avoid the bustle and commercialism of the resorts.

There is only one ramshackle fishing village, Tha Bon, on the eastern side of the island. Just north of it is a Chinese Temple, with colorfully decorated shrine caves. On the west coast of the island are the beaches of Hat Tham Pang and Hat Tham.

On the southern side, sprawling over a hillside, are the overgrown ruins of Rama V's Summer Palace. The palace was built in the 1890s but abandoned after a fleeting occupation by the French in 1893. One part of the palace complex that remains intact is the circular Wat Atsadang at the top of the hill. Crowned by a crumbling *chedi*, this was once a meditation chamber used by King Chulalongkorn. The island also has a temple, Wat Tham Yai Prik. Its gardens provide crops for the locals, and it has large underground rainwater tanks to meet the islanders' needs.

---

5 Si Racha

ศรีราชา

C5 **Chon Buri province**
Pattaya; 0-3842-7667

This small seaside town is the launching point for trips to Ko Sichang. Running off busy Jermjompol Road, Si Racha's main waterfront street, are several tentacle-like piers. At the end of the piers are breezy, open-air restaurants ideal for sampling the local delicacies: oysters *(hoi nang rom)* or mussels *(hoi thot)* dipped in Si Racha sauce. On a rocky promontory, which is also an occasional ferry pier, is Ko Loi, a Thai-Chinese Buddhist temple.

The streets of Si Racha (and Ko Sichang) resonate to the sound of spluttering motor-cycle taxis. They are unique to the area – their sidecars are positioned at the rear.

---

6 Rayong

ระยอง

C6 **Rayong province**
**153/4 Sukhumvit
Rd, Mu 12, Rayong; 0-3865-5420**

Rayong is a prosperous fishing town known as a starting point for trips to the nearby island of Ko Samet *(p288)*.

> **The streets of Si Racha (and Ko Sichang) resonate to the sound of spluttering motor-cycle taxis. They are unique to the area – their sidecars are positioned at the rear.**

↑ Twinkling lights around the bay at bustling Pattaya beach at night

The main attractions lie outside the town. For good beaches, head 16 miles (25 km) southeast to Ban Phe. A 12-mile (20-km) coast road winds along from here to Laem Mae Phim. From Ban Phe there are boats to Ko Samet. Ferries also run to nearby Ko Saket, Ko Man Nok and Ko Man Klang – the latter two islands are part of the Laem Ya-Mu Ko Samet National Park. The park authorities have restricted excessive development here, although jet-skiing is gradually eroding the coral reef.

Three miles (5 km) past Ban Phe is the beach park of Suan Son ("pine park"). This has crystal-white sand beaches and is a popular picnic area. It offers seafood snacks and homegrown water sports such as wave riding on inner tubes.

Rayong province is widely known for its succulent fruit, particularly the pineapple and durian (p43), and its nam pla (fish sauce) and nam phrik kapi (shrimp paste).

 7

Khlong Yai
คลองใหญ่

🅐 D6 🏙 Trat province
ℹ️ Trat; 0-3959-7259-60

This pretty seaside town near the Cambodian border sports a handful of bustling markets and stalls selling delicious noodles with seafood.

 ←

Colorful homes on the coast of peaceful Ko Sichang island

The road from Khlong Yai to the border checkpoint of Hat Lek passes through spectacular scenery, with mountains on one side and the sea on the other. Tourists can enter Cambodia at Hat Lek. A visa on arrival is available with a valid passport, recent photo, and US$30. However, border guards often demand higher fees, so it is wise to apply for a visa in advance at Bangkok's Cambodian Embassy.

 8

Pattaya
พัทยา

🅐 C5 🏙 Chon Buri province
🚌🚐 🚢 ℹ️ 609 Mu 10 Phra Tamnak Rd, Pattaya;
0-3842-7667

Pattaya's faded beauty is now difficult to discern. The once-idyllic beaches attracted visitors as early as the 1950s and later became a destination for US troops on R&R during the Vietnam War. Now dubbed "Patpong by the Sea," the town has become one of Thailand's infamous red-light districts, with a menagerie of go-go bars and glitzy transvestite shows.

Despite its seedy image, Pattaya still attracts many families, who come for the good, cheap accommodations, extensive beaches (though the sea is often polluted), excellent restaurants, and the best water sports facilities in Thailand.

Pattaya consists of three bays. At its center is the 2-mile (3-km) long Pattaya beach. Pattaya Beach Road is packed with fast-food restaurants and souvenir shops. There is the traditional ferry trip to Ko Larn from Pattaya Harbour, which can also be reached by speedboat. Ko Larn has clean beaches and is good for a day out away from Pattaya. The ferry journey is 40 minutes.

Many visitors prefer the more family-oriented 9-mile (14-km) long Jomtien beach, around the southern headland of Pattaya. Quieter Naklua bay, to the north of Pattaya beach, has a fishing village that has kept its charm.

A *chedi* in the rainforest opposite Phlio waterfall, Namtok Phlio National Park

9

Namtok Phlio National Park
อุทยานแห่งชาติน้ำตกพลิ้ว

C6 **Chanthaburi province; Park HQ off Hwy 3, 9 miles (14 km) SE of Chanthaburi** **Chanthaburi, then *songthaew*** **Rayong, 0-3865-5420**

This 52-sq-mile (135-sq-km) park contains some of Thailand's richest rainforest. It is a haven for wildlife, with over 156 species of birds and 32 of mammals, including the Asiatic black bear, leopard, tiger, barking deer, and macaque. The park's other attractions are its spectacular waterfalls – the most impressive being Phlio waterfall. Facing this are two *chedis*: the Alongkon *chedi* and a 10-ft (3-m) high pyramid-shaped *chedi*, built by King

Chulalongkorn in honor of one of his queens, Sunantha, who drowned at Bang Pa-in (*p176*) in 1876. The region was much loved by Chulalongkorn.

10

Khao Chamao-Khao Wong National Park
อุทยานแห่งชาติเขาชะเมา-เขาวง

C5 **Rayong province; Park HQ 11 miles (17 km) N of Hwy 3 at Klaeng** **Rayong, 0-3865-5420**

The two mountains in this national park, Khao Wong and Khao Chamao, loom above the farming lowlands of the Eastern Seaboard. There is no public transportation to the park, with hotels in Pattaya, Rayong, and Chanthaburi arranging transportation. Elephants, gaur, and gibbons, and Asiatic black bears find refuge in the park's tropical evergreen forests.

Park highlights include the pools of the Khao Chamao waterfall and the 80 or so Khao Wong caves – Tham Pet ("diamond cave") and Tham Lakhon ("theater cave"), situated 2 miles (4 km) southeast of the park headquarters, are the most notable. The park's most impressive waterfall is Klong Pla-Gang, a 3-mile (5-km) trek from the park headquarters.

 PICTURE PERFECT
Phlio Waterfall

The star attraction of the Namtok Phlio National Park is this photogenic waterfall, which cascades gently into carp-filled pools where you can swim and take a social media-worthy photograph.

11

Bo Rai
บ่อไร่

D6 **Trat province** **Trat; 0-3959-7259-60**

This small town used to be the thriving center of the Eastern Seaboard's gem trade. The surrounding mines, once renowned for the quality of their rubies (*tab tim*), have almost dried up. Only one morning market of any significance, the Khlong Yaw market, remains. The market has a reverse system of buying and selling – buyers sit at tables and vendors stroll around displaying their wares.

12

Wat Khao Sukim
วัดเขาสุกิม

C5 **Khao Bai Si, Tha-Mai district, 13 miles (20 km) N of Chanthaburi, off route 3322** **Chanthaburi, then *songthaew*** **Rayong; 0-3865-5420**

This huge, pale-orange *wat* is perched on the side of Sukim mountain. The temple, the home of Luang Pho Somchai, one of Thailand's most popular meditation masters, is reached via a cable car or the *naga*-lined staircase. Inside are a number of tables inlaid with mother-of-pearl, and exhibits housed in a museum include a display of jewelry and a collection of Bencharong, Khmer, and Ban Chiang pottery. They show the surprising wealth that a revered monk can accumulate from donations by merit-makers.

→

Rock formations on Phrabat mountain, Khao Khitchakut National Park

Khao Kitchakut National Park
อุทยานแห่งชาติเขาคิชฌกูฏ

C5 **Chanthaburi, then** *songthaew* **Chanthaburi province; Park HQ off Hwy 3249, 15 miles (24 km) NE of Chanthaburi; 0-3945-2074**

At just 23 sq miles (59 sq km), this is one of Thailand's smallest national parks, including Khao Kitchakut, a granite mountain over 3,300 ft (1,000 m) high. The park's best known site, the 13-tier Krathin waterfall, is near the park headquarters. From here a trail can be taken to the top. Ambitious hikers and many pilgrims make the hard four-hour climb to the summit of the Phrabat mountain to see an image of the Buddha's Footprint, which is etched here in granite.

Khao Kitchakut is near the much larger, but less visited, **Khao Soi Dao Wildlife Sanctuary** (290 sq miles, 745 sq km). Both protected areas enclose some of the last surviving tracts of a once-great lowland forest. They are vital to the economy of the region as their slopes collect water for orchards. They also provide protection for many endangered species, including sun bears and elephants. The upland forests of Khao Soi Dao provide a habitat for the tree-dwelling pileated gibbon.

> ### MAYTIME FRUIT FESTIVALS
> Held in three neighboring provinces – Chanthaburi, Rayong, and Trat – this annual fruit festival, lasting for a few days in either May or June (whenever the harvest is ripe), is a colorful, celebratory affair. These provinces are known for their flavorsome rambutan, durian, and mangosteen, and stalls selling the produce are set up on the main streets of each town. Parades of floral-and-fruit floats are held along with gaudy beauty pageants. Contests for the ripest durian or most beautifully shaped fruit, among other titles, are a highlight of the year for local farmers and a great spectacle for tourists.

Khao Soi Dao Wildlife Sanctuary
Off Hwy 317, 16 miles (25 km) NW of Chanthaburi **Chanthaburi, then** *songthaew* **TAT, Rayong; 0-3865-5420**

Trat
ตราด

C/D6 **Trat province** **Trat; 0-3959-7259-60**

This provincial capital is a small but busy commercial town. Most tourists pass through Trat only en route to Ko Chang but the busy town has several attractions, including its markets, most of which are centered around Tait Mai and Sukhumvit roads. The covered market on Sukhumvit Road has a good selection of food and drink stalls. Also of interest are the gem-mining villages around Trat, such as Bo Rai, where rubies are mined. Local guesthouses can arrange trips.

Southwest of Trat is Wat Bupharam ("flower temple"), set in pleasant grounds with large, shady trees. Some of the original buildings within the temple complex, including the *wihan*, the bell tower, and the monks' residences, or *kutis*, date from the late Ayutthaya period.

WESTERN SEABOARD

Miles of remote sandy beaches dominate long stretches of the Western Seaboard, which unites the Buddhist heartland of the nation with the maritime, Muslim-influenced south. Its major attraction is the islands that make up the Ko Samui archipelago, a backpackers' haven in the 1970s. The area is also home to Hua Hin, Thailand's first beach resort, settled by a group of farmers in the 19th century. Temples reflecting pre-Thai influences, simple fishing villages, verdant fruit orchards, and sand-rimmed resorts have long characterized this region.

The Tenasserim Mountains, rising to 4,350 ft (1,329 m), form a spine down the peninsula. They absorb much of the rain that falls during the southwest monsoon, keeping the coastal strip dry. However, this coastal region is still a fertile growing area, famed for its pineapples, corn, sugarcane, "lady-finger" bananas, and mangosteens.

Among the most interesting of the towns here is Phetchaburi, with its crumbling architectural remnants of the Khmer, Mon, Ayutthaya, and Rattanakosin epochs. Farther to the south, Chaiya still contains archeological remains that reveal its important role in the Srivijaya Empire (p318).

WESTERN
SEABOARD

Mali Kyur

Kabuzya Kyun

Tanintharyi Kyun

Mainngy Island

Linn Lune Kyun

Dome Kyun

East Sular Island

West Sular Island

Pyin Sa Bu Kyun

Pan Daung Kyun

Andaman Sea

Kyun Me Gyi

Kyun Tann Shey-Lampi Kyun

Kyun Phi Lar

Jar Lann Kyun

Zardet Kyee Kyu

Tharn Kyun

WESTERN SEABOARD

Must Sees

① Ko Pha Ngan
② Ko Tao
③ Ko Samui

Experience More

④ Cha-am
⑤ Kaeng Krachan National Park
⑥ Phetchaburi
⑦ Mareukathayawan Palace
⑧ Hua Hin
⑨ Prachuap Khiri Khan
⑩ Khao Sam Roi Yot National Park
⑪ Chumphon
⑫ Surat Thani
⑬ Chaiya
⑭ Angthong National Marine Park

KoRa

Ko Pha Thong

Ko Kho Khao

Khaya

Thai Mueang

The sun setting over the thick forest interior of Ko Pha Ngan

 1

KO PHA NGAN
เกาะพะงัน

B7 **Surat Thani province** **From Nathon on Ko Samui to Thong Sala** **Surat Thani; 0-7728-8818**

About two-thirds the size of Ko Samui *(p310)*, Ko Pha Ngan has the same tropical combination of powdery beaches, accessible coral reefs, and rugged, forested interior. The cheap accommodations, full moon parties, and bohemian atmosphere make the island attractive to budget travelers. Large parts of Ko Pha Ngan are undeveloped, and much of it is accessible only by sea or along rutted tracks by pickup truck.

 GREAT VIEW
Domsila Viewpoint

A short scramble up the hill from the Nam Tok Phaeng waterfall rewards you with the stunning Domsila Viewpoint, where you can rest on a rock and look out over the jungle.

 ①

Thong Sala
ท้องศาลา

The largest settlement and de facto capital of Ko Pha Ngan, Thong Sala is the most important town on the island. This town is the entrance port to Ko Pha Ngan, and, like Nathon on Ko Samui, acts as a service town with many banks, a post office, supermarkets, travel agents, restaurants, a food market, and weekly tourist market. There are a fair number of restaurants, budget hotels,

and bars. It is also famous for its Thai massage, which locals claim is the best on the island. Next to the pier, an armada of *songthaews* waits to take visitors around the island.

 ②

Nam Tok Phaeng National Park
อุทยานแห่งชาติน้ำตกแพง

4 miles (6 km) SW of Thong Sala

Centered on the waterfall of the same name, Nam Tok Phaeng National Park

occupies a swath of jungle in the middle of Ko Pha Ngan and offers the perfect escape from the beaches and backpacker bars. The falls themselves are beautiful and make for a fantastic photo opportunity. The park is also teeming with animals, and a trek through the jungle is the best way to spot wild boar and macaque.

 ③

Ao Si Thanu
อ่าวศรีธนู

5 miles (8 km) N of Thong Sala

Located just a short distance beyond the Laem Si Thanu headland, Ao Si Thanu has a small beach considered to be among the most beautiful in Ko Pha Ngan. There are some adequate bungalow accommodations here as well as two small and attractive hotels near the top of the cape. The main appeal of this bay, apart from the lovely sunset views, is the accessible offshore coral reef.

---

④ 🍴 🛍️

Hat Yao
หาดยาว

🏠 **7 miles (11 km) N of Thong Sala**

The main beach resort on Ko Pha Ngan, Hat Yao is a lovely curved stretch of white sand. Although it is getting busier by the year, the beach is wide enough to accommodate the upcoming resorts, restaurants, and bars, and other facilities without seeming crowded. Visitors can explore the surrounding waters on sea kayaks or travel inland on motorcycles and jeeps, which are available for hire. The surrounding waters are good for diving and snorkeling.

⑤ 🍴 🛍️

Ao Mae Hat
อ่าวแม่หาด

🏠 **9 miles (14 km) N of Thong Sala**

An isolated and beautiful cove with crisp white sand, Ao Mae Hat is located on the coast just beyond Mae Hat village in the northwestern part of the island. The eastern end of the beach is mostly used by the fishermen who go out looking for the crabs that populate this area. The western end is far more beautiful; however, Mae Hat's stunning natural beauty has led to the development of resort-style accommodations to keep pace with the tourist influx. Apart from being a good spot for swimming and snorkeling, the beach is also linked to the tiny island of Ko Ma by a beautiful sandy causeway that gets exposed at low tide and is shallow enough to cross by wading through the water. The reefs off Ko Ma are among the best snorkeling spots in Ko Pha Ngan.

DRINK

ThreeSixtyBar
Savor one of the island's best viewpoints, beer in hand, at this chilled-out hilltop bar overlooking Hat Mae Haad. Come here at sunset for the best views.

🏠 **85/2 Moo 7, Ao Mae Hat**
📞 **0-8256-19874**

Amsterdam Bar
With rugs and cushions spread out around a swimming pool on a west-facing hilltop terrace, this is one of the best places to have a cold drink while taking in Pha Ngan's dreamy sunsets.

🏠 **Wok Tum**
📞 **0-8281-8504**

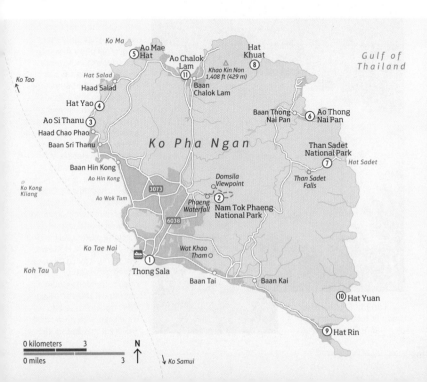

⑥ 🍴 🛍️

Ao Thong Nai Pan
อ่าวท้องนายปาน

🚗 11 miles (18 km) NE of Thong Sala 🚌 From Thong Sala

Ko Pha Ngan's coastline curves to the southeast and opens into Ao Thong Nai Pain, a lovely and deeply indented bay backed by forested hills and facing east across the Gulf of Thailand. A tall rocky outcrop divides the bay into two coves – Ao Thong Nai Pan Noi to the north and Ao Thong Nai Pan Yai to the south. The latter is perhaps the least accessible bay on the island, and as a result is relatively less crowded. However, the bay arguably offers some of the most attractive scenery on Ko Pha Ngan. Both sides of the beach are equally appealing, with shallow, warm waters that are ideal for swimming or snorkeling. The eastern end

Ko Pha Ngan's coastline curves to the southeast and opens into Ao Thong Nai Pan, a lovely and deeply indented bay backed by forested hills.

of Ao Thong Nai Pan Yai has an array of rock formations which are good for climbing. The twin bays can be reached by pickup truck or taxi from Thong Sala or, between January and September, by small ferry from Maenam on Ko Samui.

---

⑦ 🍴 🛍️

Than Sadet National Park
อุทยานแห่งชาติน้ำตกธารเสด็จ

🚗 10 miles (16 km) NE of Thong Sala 🚌 From Thong Sala

Established in 1983, Than Sadet National Park was originally much smaller before

being enlarged to its present size of 25 sq miles (65 sq km) in 1999. The word *sadet* in Thai means a "stream visited by royalty"; the name was given after Rama V's (r.1868–1910) visit to the spot in 1889. The largest waterfall on the island – Than Sadet Falls – is at the end of a popular hiking trail and has become a favored destination for those interested in an alternative to beach activities.

---

⑧ 🍴 🛍️

Hat Khuat
หาดขวด

🚗 10 miles (16 km) NE of Thong Sala 🚌 From Ban Chalok Lam

An idyllic spot, Hat Khuat, or Bottle Beach, is one of those glorious unspoiled beaches that draw millions of visitors to Thailand's coast. It is accessible by a dirt track from Hat Khom, but this entails a tough trek through heavy undergrowth. More easily reached by long-tail boats, this beach has now become a mid-range destination that is popular with the younger crowd. A delightful expanse of sand, looking out over pristine waters in different shades of aquamarine, Hat Khuat is sheltered inland by the wooded flanks of the 1,408-ft (429-m) high Khao Kin Non. Those seeking affordable bungalow accommodations in a beautiful setting away from the noisy parties will find this beach appealing. However, visitors must avoid this beach during bad weather, as they can be stranded without a way back. A short stroll along a dirt track leads to Ban Fai Mai village, with a few small grocery stores and snack bars.

Long-tail boats on the idyllic turquoise waters at Ao Thong Nai Pan ↑

FULL MOON PARTY

These famous parties are held at Hat Rin every month during full moon, and numbers can reach anything between 10,000 and 20,000 a month. The event features a mix of international and Thai DJs playing every kind of music. Visitors paint themselves with ultraviolet colors and also carry lights and other props that glow. Alcohol flows freely and is usually sold as cocktail buckets. A festive ambience is created with lamps, makeshift bars, fire shows, and food and drink stalls.

Hat Rin
หาดริ้น

7 miles (11 km) SE of Thong Sala

The most commercial town on the island, the bustling beach of Hat Rin and the adjoining village of Ban Hat Rin are the most developed places on the island as well as its party paradise. Set astride a narrow, sandy peninsula, Hat Rin is divided into two beaches – the lively Hat Rin Nok, or Sunrise Beach, to the east and the quieter Hat Rin Nai, or Sunset Beach, to the west. It is a popular destination with backpackers and party animals who come to Ko Pha Ngan for its full moon parties. Although the parties are concentrated around the southern end of Hat Rin, especially at Hat Rin Nok, the crowds often overflow to other parts of the beach. Its accommodations are often fully booked for a week either side of the monthly full moon party, which starts after dark and goes on beyond sunrise.

Hat Rin has a constantly expanding group of hotels, guesthouses, restaurants, bars, and Internet cafes. In the past, most visitors to Hat Rin were drawn to the clean, wide expanse of sand, but the tourist influx has reduced some of this charm. Today, the beach is often noisy and littered with flotsam, and should certainly be avoided by those seeking isolation.

Hat Yuan
หาดยวน

8 miles (13 km) E of Thong Sala

This small beach, strewn with rocks at either end, has a family atmosphere and there are cafes offering oven-fresh food and fruity yogurts alongside more traditional Thai dishes. This is a good and safe spot for swimming and snorkeling, although visitors should be careful during stormy weather. Although Hat Yuan is just a short distance away from noisy Hat Rin, it is laid-back, quiet, and far removed from the party scene. Visitors to this beach can indulge in regular beach activities such as swimming, sunbathing, and snorkeling.

Ao Chalok Lam
อ่าวโฉลกหล้า

6 miles (10 km) NE of Thong Sala

A strong smell of dried, salted fish emanates from Chalok Lam's storefronts. Visitors often stop here to buy fish after visiting the revered Chao Mae Koan Im shrine in the center of the island. Ban Chalok Lam offers an insight into the typical rural life on the island. Piles of squid drying on the beach are a common sight, and the smell of the freshly caught fish is part of the overall experience. Fishing-related activities such as mending nets and gutting fish coexist here with shop-houses selling pizza and other snacks. The beaches near the town tend to be rather dirty but improve farther to the east, especially as far out of town as Khom beach. There is also a Buddhist temple near Ban Chalok Lam.

TOP 3 QUIET BEACHES

Ao Wok Tum
3 miles (5 km) N of Thong Sala
Undeveloped beach with sandy stretches, good for sunbathing or strolls.

Hat Sadet
10 miles (16 km) NE of Thong Sala
This untouched and fairly inaccessible spot is a replica of the romantic and deserted beaches shown in films.

Hat Salad
8 miles (13 km) N of Thong Sala
Read, laze, or enjoy a nap in the hammocks on this small bay.

The lush interior and clear, turquoise waters of Ko Nang Yuan ↑

2

KO TAO
เกาะเต่า

B7 **Surat Thani province** **From Chumphon or Ko Samui** **Surat Thani; 0-7728-8818**

Located 25 miles (40 km) north of Ko Pha Ngan, Ko Tao is the smallest and prettiest of the islands in the Samui archipelago that offer visitors accommodations. Ko Tao's major attraction is its superb offshore diving. The island itself is rugged, with dense forest inland, quiet coves along the east coast, and a fine sweep of sandy beach on the west side.

①

Ban Mae Hat
บ้านแม่หาด

The unofficial capital of Ko Tao, Ban Mae Hat is a small, pleasant fishing village that is now being transformed into a tourist town. It is large enough to offer a reasonable selection of accommodations, the best dining facilities on the island, as well as a few Irish pubs, pool tables, and video and sports bars with wide-screen televisions. Motorcycles are available for hire for those who wish to explore the island for a day or two.

②

Hat Sai Ri
หาดทรายรี

1 mile (2 km) N of Ban Mae Hat

An idyllic beach, perfect for admiring spectacular sunsets over the Gulf of Thailand, Hat Sai Ri is the longest stretch of sandy beach on Ko Tao. It is framed to the east by swaying coconut palms, with a number of small restaurants, bars, and simple bungalow accommodations. The beach is paralleled by a narrow surfaced path and, slightly further inland, by a small

paved road leading to the settlement of Ban Hat Sai Ri. Once a tiny fishing village, it now serves as a center for the local tourism industry with dive centers, travel agents, and supermarkets.

③

Ao Hinwong
อ่าวหินวง

4 miles (6 km) NE of Ban Mae Hat

Located away from the bustle of Ban Mae Hat, Ao Hinwong is a delightful isolated cove surrounded by charming coconut groves and large boulders. Despite its isolation, its appeal lies in its peace, and the clear, and sheltered waters of the beautiful bay – an ideal spot for snorkeling and diving.

 GREAT VIEW
Nang Yuan Viewpoint

An easy 15-minute hike from Ko Nang Yuan takes you to this famous, spectacular viewpoint, overlooking the three islets. It's a popular spot, so head there early.

shallow offshore reef which usually draws snorkelers on day trips from Ban Mae Hat. There is a small beach here, as well as comfortable bungalow accommodations, restaurants, and bars. Getting here is not so easy: visitors can either take a boat or follow the narrow, unpaved track that leads east across the hump of the island from Ban Hat Sai Ri, forking to the north toward the beach. It is a great place to relax and unwind.

Hat Ao Mae
หาดอ่าวแม

Located in a shallow bay, a short distance north of the Ban Mae Hat ferry pier, and perhaps too close to the village for visitors seeking a tranquil holiday, Hat Ao Mae is a small beach. Nevertheless, it is well equipped with a comfortable resort, offering convenient access to Ban Mae Hat and Hat Sai Ri.

Ko Nang Yuan
เกาะนางยวน

🏠 2 miles (3 km) N of Ban Mae Hat 🚢 From Ban Mae Hat

Perhaps the most beautiful natural formation off Ko Tao, Ko Nang Yuan is a group of three islets linked by a narrow causeway of white sand. The smallest among them is also known as Japanese Garden. This spectacular location makes a popular sunbathing and swimming day trip. Strict regulations are in force to protect the environment and no cans, plastic bags, or bottles are permitted. Visitors have to pay a nominal fee to land, although full-day all-inclusive tours, with a picnic lunch and snorkeling or diving, can be arranged at the travel agencies in Ban Mae Hat.

Ao Mamuang
อ่าวมะม่วง

🏠 3 miles (5 km) NE of Ban Mae Hat 🚢

Ao Mamuang, or Mango Bay, is a long, lovely, cove backed with lush greenery. It has a

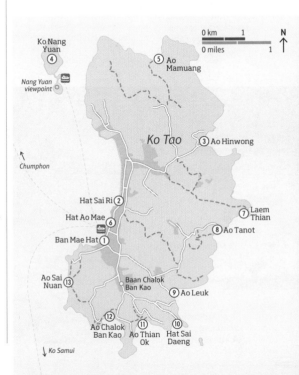

⑦

Laem Thian
แหลมเทียน

🏠 **4 miles (6 km) E of Ban Mae Hat** 🚌

An isolated cape located almost midway down the deserted east coast of Ko Tao, Laem Thian is a tiny waterbody with a white, sandy beach. Sheltered in the southern lee of a rocky headland, it is best reached by boat, although there is a treacherous dirt track that crosses the center of the island. The northern branch of this track leads to Ao Mamuang and Ao Hinwong, and the southern branch to Laem Thian. Among the more popular sites for snorkeling enthusiasts on Ko Tao, Laem Thian is well-known for its underwater tunnels and

Did You Know?

Ko Tao translates as "turtle island", and is a significant breeding ground for hawksbill and green turtles.

swim-through passages. Made of limestone, they are easy to navigate. The area is also known for frequent sightings of the exotic unicorn fish. Comfortable bungalows and other basic facilities are available on the beach here.

---

⑧

Ao Tanot
อ่าวโตนด

🏠 **4 miles (6 km) E of Ban Mae Hat** 🚌

Well-known for its vistas of fine sunrises, Ao Tanot is a small, horseshoe-shaped bay facing east across the Gulf of Thailand. Just south of Laem Thian, and clearly visible across Ao Tanot, is the isolated and beautiful beach Hat Ao Tanot. As with the other beaches on the east coast of Ko Tao, its appeal lies in its relative inaccessibility. Large boulders lie scattered across Hat Ao Tanot, as do a wide variety of seashells. The

> **A small, horseshoe-shaped bay facing east across the Gulf of Thailand, Ao Tanot is a beautiful setting, well-known for its vistas of fine sunrises.**

primary activity here is snorkeling, and enthusiasts can hire equipment from the dive shops nearby. There are several good resorts and some simple bungalow accommodations, as well as a dive school, and small, attractive terrace bars set against colorful groves of bougainvillea. Ao Tanot can also be reached by a southern track leading inland and over the mountainous spine of Ko Tao from the Ban Mae Hat-Ao Chalok surfaced road.

---

⑨

Ao Leuk
อ่าวลึก

🏠 **3 miles (5 km) SE of Ban Mae Hat**

Ao Luek, located close to Ko Tao's southeasternmost point, has among the most beautiful beaches and offers a variety of outdoor activities. Visitors can go sea-kayaking, water-skiing, and windsurfing, all of

→ Sunbathing and swimming at one of Ao Leuk's beautiful beaches

which can be easily arranged through any one of the several resorts on the beach. There are beautiful coral reefs offshore, and snorkeling in the clear waters is another delightful pastime. Despite its reputation, the waters off the bay are quite safe, with the only shark sighted being the inoffensive blacktip. Accommodations options and dining facilities are good, as are the few bars.

Hat Sai Daeng
หาดทรายแดง

◨ **3 miles (5 km) SE of Ban Mae Hat** 🚌

An attractive and unspoiled white-sand beach, backed by a narrow peninsula jutting into the warm waters of the Gulf of Thailand, Hat Sai Daeng is located along the busier and more accessible southern coast. The beach, also known as Red Sands Beach, points directly at the popular diving and snorkeling site around tiny, unpopulated Shark Island, which is also known as Ko Chalam. Hat Sai Daeng offers good views across the sea, and the beach has adequate bungalow accommodations, restaurants, and bars. It is approached by a narrow, seldom-used track running east from the main Mae Hat-Ao Chalok road, which is usable the year round. However, be careful to avoid using the smaller tracks, which are quite dangerous during heavy rains.

Ao Thian Ok
อ่าวเทียนออก

◨ **2 miles (3 km) SE of Ban Mae Hat**

The splendid Ao Thian Ok is the southernmost bay on the island has one of the prettiest beaches in Ko Tao. The waters

off Ao Thian Ok are very popular with divers, and are frequented by reef sharks. The beach offers luxurious spa accommodations as well as a few reasonably priced bungalows, a series of bars with spectacular ocean views, and some of the best restaurants on the island. Visitors can also take courses in Thai massage, yoga, and *chi gong* (a component of Chinese martial arts) as well as enjoying the usual maritime activities – swimming, snorkeling, and diving in the surrounding waters.

Ao Chalok Ban Kao
อ่าวโฉลกบ้านเก่า

◨ **1 mile (2 km) S of Ban Mae Hat**

The largest, most developed, and best-appointed beach resort on Ko Tao, Ao Chalok Ban Kao is sheltered by Laem Tato on the east and Laem Jeda Gang on the west. Easily accessible by a good, if narrow, road from Ban Mae Hat, this beautiful bay is protected by forest-clad hills during both the northeast and southwest monsoons. The bay is home to three

separate but closely linked beaches – Freedom Beach to the southeast, Hat Chalok in the center, and smaller Hat San Jao to the west. Ao Chalok Ban Kao is among the biggest dive centers on Ko Tao, and the beach is equipped with several dive shops, guesthouses, restaurants, and bars. In the center of Laem Tato, Jon Suwan Mountain Viewpoint offers fine views across the deeply indented bay and the wooded hills.

Ao Sai Nuan
อ่าวสายนวล

Sandy coves fringed by tall palms and warm, azure waters come together to form this attractive spot. Ao Sai Nuan, a short distance southwest of Ban Mae Hat, is really a southern extension of the village and is characterized by a string of bungalows and upscale resorts. Backed by a densely wooded high mountain, the bay offers stunning vistas of sunsets. The ease of accessibility makes Ao Sai Nuan a popular spot. It can be approached on foot or motorcycle from Ban Mae Hat.

Boats on the serene waters of Ko Samui against the orange sky

3

KO SAMUI

🅰F5 🏠 Surat Thani province ℹ️ Nathon; 0-7742-0504 or Surat Thani; 0-7728-8818 ✈️ 14 miles (23 km) from Nathon 🚢 From Surat Thani, Tha Thong, and Don Sak

Situated 400 miles (700 km) south of Bangkok, Ko Samui is Thailand's third-largest island, after Phuket and Ko Chang. The buzzing nightlife of Chaweng and Lamai on Samui's east coast draws tourists from all over the world, while the quieter beaches on the south and west coasts remain relatively unspoiled.

Ko Samui was originally settled by mariners from China who began cultivating coconuts on the island. A backpackers' haven in the 1970s, Samui has now seen tourism become its main income earner. With rapid development, the arrival of major hotel chains, and promotion by tourist offices, Samui has become one of the most popular islands in Southeast Asia. It also attracts foreign investors building luxury homes for wealthy business people from Hong Kong, Singapore, and Taiwan, and has a thriving luxury villa rental market serving European holidaymakers.

① 🍴 🛍️

Nathon
หน้าทอน

The island was first settled in the 1850s by Chinese merchants who had come in search of trade in cotton and coconuts. Nathon, Samui's capital and main ferry port, was founded around 1905, when it was chosen as the island's administrative center. Few visitors stay here, except in order to take an early morning boat to Surat Thani on the mainland. The island's main transportation route is the 31-mile (50-km) circular road, which passes through

Nathon. *Songthaews* from Nathon travel either northward toward Chaweng beach, or southward toward Lamai.

② 🍴 🛍️

Lamai
ละไม

🏠 12 miles (19 km) SE of Nathon

Samui's second-largest beach (after Chaweng) is also very developed, with big chain and luxury hotels along the waterfront. The main focus is at the center of the 2-mile (4-km) long beach. Behind the beach are bars, nightclubs, and restaurants.

Lamai village is at the quieter, northern end of the beach, away from the crowds.

It still has many old teak houses with thatched roofs. The village's main sight is Wat Lamai Cultural Hall, built in 1826, which has a small folk museum dedicated to arts and crafts found on Samui. On the southern promontory of Lamai beach are the Hin Ta and Hin Yai rock formations, that are famous for their similarity in shape to male and female sexual organs. The tiny, picturesque Coral Cove Beach lies between Lamai and Chaweng and is also worth a visit. It's an excellent area for swimming.

③

Bophut
บ่อผุด

📍 **11 miles (18 km) NE of Nathon**

Fisherman's Village, located to the east of the beach, is the center of Bophut. This bustling village includes many bungalows, hotels and boutique resorts, banks, bars, fine restaurants, and offers a wide range of water sports. The 1-mile (2-km) long beach is popular with families and backpackers.

④

Bangrak
บางรัก

📍 **13 miles (21 km) NE of Nathon**

Bangrak is also known as "Big Buddha" beach. The sea is not very clear here, but it does offer plenty of budget

Did You Know?

Bangrak is known as the "Village of Love," and is a popular place to tie the knot on Valentine's Day.

---

accommodations. A causeway links the eastern end of Bangrak beach to the tiny island of Ko Faan, home to the large, gold-covered Big Buddha. The imposing statue is popular with islanders and Asian tourists, who come here to make merit (p40). A gaudy bazaar of souvenir stalls and cafes has sprung up at the foot of the *naga* staircase leading to the Buddha image. From the pier at Bangrak there is a ferry service to Hat Rin (p305), home of the famous full moon parties.

---

⑤

Maenam
แม่น้ำ

📍 **7 miles (11 km) NE of Nathon**

This 2-mile (3-km) long beach is the most westerly stretch of sand on the north coast. It has extensive views of Ko Pha Ngan (p302). Visitors flock here for the excellent windsurfing opportunities, which are aided by the strong directional breezes that blow on-shore during the northeasterly monsoon December through February.

STAY

Coral Cove Chalet
Attractive chalets on a palm-covered hill with a private sand cove.

📍 **210 Moo 4, Hat Thong Ta Khian** 📞 **0-7744-8500**

Ⓑ Ⓑ ⓑ

Six Senses
Collection of opulent villas boasting an unrivaled setting.

📍 **9/10 Moo 5, Baan Plai Laem, Bophut**
🌐 **sixsenses.com**

Ⓑ Ⓑ Ⓑ

Code
Suites or villas with modern design and a superb hillside location.

📍 **13/55 Moo 6, Bang Por Soi 4, Maenam**
🌐 **samuicode.com**

Ⓑ Ⓑ ⓑ

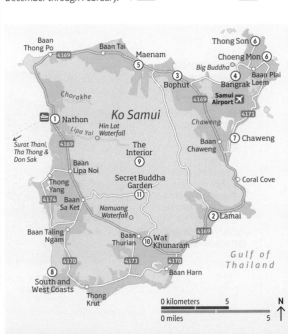

Thong Son and Choeng Mon
ท้องสนและเชิงมน

📍 15 miles (24 km) NE of Nathon

On Samui's northeastern cape there is a series of secluded rocky coves. Hat Thong Son is a peaceful inlet with views across to Ko Pha Ngan. Most of the accommodations on the headland are concentrated at Ao Choeng Mon, an attractive bay.

DRINK

Cha Cha Moon Beach Club
Elegant beach club built into the palm trees of the popular Chaweng Beach.

📍 61, Moo 2, Chaweng Beach 📞 0-8965-12777

Ark Bar
Long-standing Chaweng institution, with DJs and fire shows.

📍 159/89, Moo 2, Chaweng Beach
🌐 ark-bar.com

On Street Bar
Old favorite decorated with an ever-changing showcase of the owner's artwork.

📍 12/7 Moo 2, Chaweng Beach
🌐 onstreetbar.com

Beer Masons
Samui's finest purveyors of Thai craft beers, with ten rotating taps.

📍 39/7 Moo 3 Bophut
🌐 thebeermasons.com

Chaweng
เฉวง

📍 14 miles (22 km) E of Nathon

Chaweng is by far the longest, busiest, and most beautiful beach on the island, stretching 3 miles (5 km) down the east coast. Its warm waters and white sands have been a key attraction for budget travelers for many years. Today, though, Chaweng is also a mecca for package tourists and is lined with a variety of hotels and bars.

At the northern end is a tranquil 3-ft (1-m) deep lagoon, ideal for children and novice windsurfers. The long, inviting sweep of the middle and southern end of the beach is bordered by coconut palms. Chaweng is at its most scenic along its southern section where large boulders alternate with discreet sandy coves. The beach has a wide range of sports including windsurfing, canoeing, paragliding, scuba diving, tennis, and volleyball.

Chaweng is known for having the most developed tourist infrastructure on Samui with travel agencies, banks, supermarkets, and car and bike rental among the facilities available. The main street in Chaweng is a hub for nightlife and shopping on Ko Samui: bars, clubs, and restaurants rub shoulders with souvenir shops and upscale boutiques.

South and West Coasts
There are many quiet beaches with simple huts along the south and west coasts, such as around Thong Krut. Thong Yang – although only 1 mile (2 km) south of the pier where the vehicle ferries from Don Sak dock – is perfect for those seeking seclusion.

The Interior
For visitors tiring of the beach, the interior of Samui offers an adventurous alternative. The mix of dense tropical forest and large coconut plantations seems impenetrable, but there are rough trails – which can be negotiated by a 4WD vehicle or by motorcycle – and two roads leading to Samui's stunning waterfalls. Namuang, an impressive 98-ft (30-m) high waterfall, is a popular destination for picnics and swimming. It is situated 6 miles (10 km) from Nathon

↑ Palm trees bordering one of Chaweng's beachfront restaurants

Admiring the rushing stream of the high Namuang waterfall ↑

and 3 miles (5 km) from the circular coast road. Hin Lat, 2 miles (3 km) from Nathon, is smaller than Namuang and less interesting. Both falls are at their most spectacular in December or January at the end of the rainy season, when they swell with rainwater.

⑩ Wat Khunaram
วัดคุณาราม

🚗 8 miles (13 km) SE of Nathon

Located near Ban Thurian just south of Route 4169, Wat Khunaram is one of Ko Samui's more unusual spiritual attractions. While the *wat* is architecturally appealing, it has no historical significance. What draws visitors to it are the mummified remains of a famous Buddhist monk, Phra Khru Sammathakittikhun, who died here in 1973. The mummy of the monk, sitting in an upright position in a glass casing, is on display in a separate building within the complex. The place is highly venerated by the locals who come here to put flowers and incense on the remains of this former abbot of the *wat*. In surprisingly good condition,

the remains are said to be here in accordance with the wishes of Phra Khru himself.

⑪ Secret Buddha Garden
สวนพระ

** 7 miles (11 km) SE of Nathon**

Tucked away in the heavily forested interior of Ko Samui, the Secret Buddha Garden, also known as Magic Garden, was founded by a 76-year-old fruit farmer, Nim Thongsuk, in 1977. Surrounded by lush tropical forest and rocky hillsides, the garden is studded with beautiful statuary. Made of concrete, the stunning statues represent various deities, mythical beasts, and human beings in different postures. A waterfall continues as a stream through the length of the garden. Set in the highest part of the island, the garden offers spectacular views across the tall coconut-palm-covered lowlands. However, it is accessible only sometimes, via a dirt track using a 4WD from Lamai.

COCONUT MONKEYS

Coconut harvesting was once the main source of income for the people of Ko Samui. Much of the island's interior is covered with coconut palms and, even today, coconuts remain a significant economic crop. Palm trees can grow up to 160 ft (50 m) high and harvesting coconuts is a difficult, dangerous, and time-consuming process. To make it easier, locals train macaques to pluck the rich harvest for them.

EXPERIENCE MORE

❹ Cha-am
ชะอำ

🅰B5 🄰Phetchaburi province 🚌🚐 ℹ500/51 Phetkasem Rd, Cha-am; 0-3247-1005/6

Since the mid-1980s Cha-am has experienced a dramatic surge in popularity. It has been developed from a quiet fishing and market village into a lively playground for Bangkok weekenders. Tall condominiums and huge resort hotels have sprung up beside the long, sandy beach. During the week, however, it can be remarkably quiet.

The resort caters primarily to Thais, who focus their attentions on eating and drinking rather than swimming. At umbrella-shaded tables strung along the beach like a high tide mark, visitors feast on delicious grilled fish, squid, shrimp, and mussels. Spicy dips and cold beer complete the culinary adventure. Those who prefer more formal eating will find restaurants serving the same succulent fare at the northern end of the beach.

❺ Kaeng Krachan National Park
อุทยานแห่งชาติแก่งกระจาน

🅰B5 🚌🚐Phetchaburi then *songthaew* ℹPhetchaburi province Park HQ off Hwy 3175, 37 miles (60 km) S of Phetchaburi; 0-3247-1005/6

Thailand's largest national park is home to at least 40 species of large mammal, such as tiger, leopard, elephant, gibbon, two types of Asiatic bear, and two types of leaf-monkey (langur). Established in 1981, this 1,150-sq-mile (2,920-sq-km)

↑ A gibbon climbing a tree in Kaeng Krachan National Park

preserve covers nearly half of Phetchaburi province and contains some of Thailand's most pristine tracts of tropical evergreen forest. The park, relatively unknown to tourists, offers excellent hiking.

Its western flank is marked out by the Thai-Burmese

Huge stalactites hanging over Buddha images inside Tham Khao Luang cave ↓

border and the Tenasserim mountain range. Streams and rivers are the water source for the 17-sq-mile (45-sq-km) Kaeng Krachan reservoir, which can be explored by boat. Thousands of migratory birds coming from as far afield as China and Siberia rest, feed, and breed in the salt marshes.

 6

Phetchaburi
เพชรบุรี

AB5 **G**Phetchaburi province **G**Rot Fai Rd, 1 mile (1.5 km) NW of town **G**Chisa-in Rd, near Chomrut Bridge **i**Cha-am; 0-3247-1005/6

Settled since at least the 11th century, Phetchaburi (often spelled Phetburi) is one of Thailand's oldest towns. It has long been an important trading and cultural center, and Mon, Khmer, and Ayutthayan influences can be seen in its 30 temples. During the 19th century it became a favorite royal retreat, and King Mongkut built a summer house here on a hill, Khao Wang, west of the center. This is now part of the Phra Nakhon Khiri Historical Park, which is magnificently landscaped and offers extensive views of Phetchaburi. Other major sights are the 17th-century Wat Yai Suwannaram, the five Khmer *prangs* of Wat Kamphaeng Laeng, and an old quarter that has retained much of its original charm. Despite such attractions, accommodations are scant. Most visitors come on short breaks from Bangkok, 76 miles (123 km) away.

Phetchaburi is divided by the Phet River, which weaves its way past this provincial capital's 30 historic temples. Many are excellently preserved, especially the Ayutthayan wats, their pinnacles dominating the skyline. In the distance, to the west, three large hills loom imperiously over the city.

Phra Nakhon Khiri, locally referred to as Khao Wang, translates as the "celestial city of the mountain." This palace complex, perched on top of 302-ft (92-m) Maha Samana hill, was commissioned by King Mongkut (Rama IV) as a summer house in the 1850s. Extravagant use of European, Chinese, and Japanese architectural styles make this a bold study in Thai and foreign architecture. Set among natural caverns, woods, and rocks, it also offers vistas of Phetchaburi town and panoramic views of the province.

The complex extends over three peaks. The Royal Palace and the Ho Chatchawan Wiangchai, an observatory tower (Rama IV was an accomplished amateur astronomer), are both perched on the west rise; the Phra That Chomphet, a white *chedi* erected by Rama V, stands on the central rise; and Wat Maha Samanaram, containing some fine murals, takes up the east rise. In 1988 the complex was made a Historical Park. A cable car takes visitors up the steep ascent to the palace buildings.

A short distance north of town is **Tham Khao Luang**, an impressive cave containing stalactites, *chedis*, and Buddha images. To the right of the cave's mouth lies Wat Bun Thawi, notable for its intricately carved wooden door panels.

Phra Nakhon Khiri
⊛ **G**Khao Wang, Phetchaburi **C**0-3242-5600 **O**Daily

Tham Khao Luang
⊛ **G**Hwy 3173, 2 miles (3 km) N of Phetchaburi **O**Daily

7
Mareukathayawan Palace
พระราชวังมฤคทายวัน

◭B5 ◮Off Hwy 4, 5 miles (9 km) S of Cha-am ▭From Cha-am ◷8:30am–4:30pm daily ◨Cha-am; 0-3247-1005/6

Mareukathayawan Palace ("the palace of love and hope") was the summer residence of Rama VI. This grand golden teak building was designed by an Italian architect and constructed in just 16 days in 1923. It was abandoned when Rama VI died two years later and stood neglected for decades. The palace has undergone restoration since the 1970s and is now close to its original state. The building is cool and airy; its wooden halls, verandas, and royal chambers are decorated simply and painted in pastel shades.

8
Hua Hin
หัวหิน

◭B6 ◮Prachuap Khiri Khan province ▭▭▭ ◨Municipality Tourist Office, 114 Phetkasem Rd, Hua Hin; 0-3247-1005

Hua Hin was Thailand's first beach resort. Its rail connection to Bangkok, completed in 1911, was key to its success, making the 118-mile (190-km) journey from Bangkok a manageable excursion.

Following the trend for recuperative spa resorts at the time, Hua Hin became a popular retreat for minor Thai royalty, Bangkok's high society, and affluent foreigners. Prince Chulachakrabongse built a summer palace in the town which he called Klai Klangwon (meaning "far from worries") in 1926. It is still used by the royal family and is not open to the public. Hua Hin's fortunes declined after World War II, but it has become popular again with a new generation of Bangkokians and

Galleried walkway in the grounds of Mareukathayawan Palace, and the royal chamber inside *(inset)*

international retirees, who are catered for by holiday homes and condominiums. There has also been a rise in boutique spas, resorts, and restaurants.

For an insight into the Hua Hin of the 1920s, visit the Railway Hotel, now called the Sofitel Centara Grand Resort & Villas. By the 1960s it had

↑ The incredible landscape of Khao Sam Roi Yot National Park

fallen into disrepair, but a sensitive restoration of the elegant 1920s decor, museum tearoom, and topiaries won it an Outstanding Conservation Award in 1993. The hotel was used in the making of the film *The Killing Fields*, where it stood in for the Phnom Penh Hotel.

9

Prachuap Khiri Khan
ประจวบคีรีขันธ์

⚠B6 ⬛Prachuap Khiri Khan province 🚌🚆
ℹ Cha-am; 0-3247-1005/6

Prachuap Khiri Khan means "town among the mountain chain." And it is certainly true that its coastal sugar-loaf limestone outcrops at either end of a sandy bay give it a "little Rio" appearance. Freshly caught seafood can be purchased from a number of good restaurants and stalls along the promenade. This peaceful town has pleasant swimming beaches to the north and south of its main bay. The top of the delightful Wat Chong Kra Chok, perched on one of the surrounding hills, offers the best view of the area. About 200 macaques live on the hill, and every evening they climb to the top to feed from the lovely frangipani trees.

Khao Sam Roi Yot National Park
อุทยานแห่งชาติเขาสามร้อยยอด

⚠B6 ⬛Prachuap Khiri Khan province; Visitors' Center off Hwy 4, 23 miles (37 km) S of Pranburi 🚆Pranburi, then *songthaew* ℹCha-am, 0-3247-1005/6

This small coastal park sits in the narrowest part of the Thai peninsula, overlooking the Gulf of Thailand. Covering 38 sq miles (98 sq km), it is a region of contrasts: sea, sand, and marsh backed by caves and mountains. The park is best known for its distinctive limestone pinnacles (*Khao Sam Roi Yot* means "mountain of 300 peaks") that rise vertically from the marshland to a height of 2,150 ft (650 m). Millions of migratory birds flying from Siberia to Sumatra

Did You Know?

Khao Sam Roi Yot National Park is Thailand's largest area of wetlands.

and Australia rest, feed, and breed here between August and April. It is home to many other animals, such as the rare dusky langur, the nocturnal slow loris, and the crab-eating macaque.

11

Chumphon
ชุมพร

⚠B7 ⬛Chumphon province ✈🚌🚆🚆 ℹChumphon; 0-7750-1831

Chumphon is regarded by some as the point of cultural transition between the heartland of the Buddhist Tai peoples and the peninsular south of the country, where Muslim culture is strong. The town was the home of Prince Chumphon, the Father of the Royal Thai Navy, who died in 1923. Nearby, the 225-ft (68-m) long HMS *Chumphon* torpedo boat, decommissioned in 1975, has been preserved.

The reefs around the islands off Chumphon's coast are popular with divers. Tour companies in town will arrange diving day trips to such islands as Samet, Mattra, Ngam Yai, and Ngam Noi. Chumphon is also the most convenient place from which to get a ferry to Ko Tao (*p306*).

12

Surat Thani
สุราษฎร์ธานี

E5 **Surat Thani province** Phun Phin, 9 miles (14 km) W of Surat Thani, then bus Ban Don (in town); Thong, 4 miles (6 km) E of town **5 Talat Mai Rd, Surat Thani; 0-7728-8818**

Surat Thani, a business center and port dealing in rubber and coconuts, first grew to prominence in the Srivijaya period, since it was strategically located at the mouth of the Tapi and Phum Duang rivers. The riverside is still intriguing today with its numerous small boats ferrying people to the city's busy waterfront markets, which sell fresh products and flowers. But Surat Thani is best known as a transportation gateway to the beaches of Ko Samui and Ko Pha Ngan.

CHAIYA'S ROLE IN THE SRIVIJAYA EMPIRE

The Mahayana Buddhist Empire of Srivijaya dominated the whole Malaysian peninsula and parts of Indonesia between the 7th and 13th centuries AD. Although most scholars now believe that Palembang in Sumatra was the Srivijayan capital, discoveries of temple remains and some exquisite stone and bronze statues (many now in the National Museum in Bangkok) in Chaiya provide evidence of Chaiya's importance. Its strategic geographical position, as a then coastal port, meant the town played an important role in the east-west trade between India, the peninsula, and China.

↑ Bengali-stye Buddhas outside Phra Boromathat Chaiya, one of the few remaining Srivijayan temples

13

Chaiya
ไชยา

E5 **Surat Thani province** **Surat Thani; 0-7728-8818**

Despite the dreary look of the small railroad town of Chaiya, the settlement is one of the oldest and most historically significant in southern Thailand. Examples of sculpture dating from the Srivijaya period (7th–13th centuries) have been found here.

Many of the sculptures show clear Mon and Indian influences, depicting figures such as Bengali-style Buddha images and multi-armed Hindu deities. These, and a variety of votive tablets, can be seen at the **Chaiya National Museum**. It also holds examples of Ayutthayan art. The museum is 1 mile (1.6 km) west of Chaiya and a 10-minute walk from the train station.

Beside the museum is Phra Boromathat Chaiya, an important Srivijayan temple. Within the main compound is the central *chedi*, which has been painstakingly restored. Square in plan, it has four porches that ascend in tiers and are

→ Tranquil turquoise waters surrounding the islands of Angthong National Marine Park

topped with small towers. The 8th-century *chedi* is built of brick and vegetable mortar. Although the site is old, it is the memory of Phra Chaiya Wiwat, a locally venerated monk who died in 1949, that attracts the majority of worshippers today.

The International Dhamma Hermitage at Wat Suan Mok, southwest of Chaiya, is a popular retreat for Buddhists from all over the world. Ten-day residential meditation retreats are held here, starting on the first day of each month.

Chaiya National Museum

⊛ ⌂ Phra Boromathat Chaiya ☎ 0-7743-1066 🕓 Wed–Sun

Wat Suan Mok

⌂ 4 miles (7 km) S of Chaiya off Hwy 41 ☎ 0-7743-1552 🕓 Daily

🔍 GREAT VIEW
Ko Wua Talab

A steep 1,300-ft (400-m) climb from Ko Wua Talab leads to a vista offering wonderful panoramas of the whole archipelago and beyond to Ko Pha Ngan, Ko Samui, and the mainland. The best view is at sunrise and sunset.

⓮
Angthong National Marine Park

อุทยานแห่งชาติทางทะเลอ่างทอง

🅰 E5 🚢 From Ko Samui 🕓 Nov–Dec 🛈 Surat Thani province; Park HQ on Ko Wua Talab; 0-7728-0222

The 40 virtually uninhabited islands of the Angthong National Marine Park display a rugged beauty distinct from palm-fringed Ko Samui (*p310*) 19 miles (31 km) away to the southeast. The Angthong ("golden basin") islands, covering an area of 39 sq miles (102 sq km), are the submerged peaks of a flooded range of limestone mountains that, farther south in Nakhon Si Thammarat province, rise to 6,000 ft (1,835 m).

Angthong's pristine beauty owes much to being the preserve of the Royal Thai Navy, and therefore off-limits until 1980 when it was declared a National Marine Park. Now naval boats have been replaced by tourist ferries. Most visitors come on day trips from Ko Samui to relax on the mica-white sands, explore the lush forests, sea canoe around the islands' jagged coastlines, and snorkel among the colorful fan corals.

> The 40 virtually uninhabited islands of the Angthong National Marine Park display a rugged beauty.

Another attraction is the abundant wildlife, both on land and in the sea. Leopard cats, squirrels, long-tailed macaques, sea otters, and pythons may be glimpsed, and a lack of natural predators has made the endearingly friendly dusky langur easy to spot. Among the 40 bird species found in the archipelago are the black baza, the edible-nest swiftlet, the brahminy kite, and the Eurasian woodcock.

Divers taking advantage of the excellent coral off Ko Sam Sao will probably see short-bodied mackerel (*pla thu*), a staple of the Thai diet. The sea around the islands is favored by the fish as a breeding ground. It is also possible to spot dolphins. The park headquarters, and the islands' only tourist accommodations and facilities, are located on the largest island, Ko Wua Talab ("sleeping cow island").

On Ko Mae Ko there is a swimming beach as well as Thale Noi, a wide turquoise lake bordered by sheer cliffs. This is the "golden basin" that gives the islands their name.

UPPER ANDAMAN COAST

The abiding image of Thailand's Andaman Coast is of long sandy beaches backed by swaying palms, a verdant hinterland of rainforest, and superlative corals and aquatic life. This region suffered the most from the 2004 tsunami, in particular Ranong, and the Surin, Similan, and Phi Phi islands, where thousands of people were killed in one of the most horrific natural disasters in history. Nonetheless, rebuilding and environmental restoration work were swift.

The Andaman Coast around Phuket has long been a magnet for Thais and foreigners. Merchants were drawn by its strategic position on the spice routes between East and West, and prospectors came for the rich tin deposits. The ancient Srivijaya port at Takua Pa, and the architecture of the Chinese shop-houses and the Sino-Portuguese mansions of Phuket Town, reflect these historical connections. Toward the end of the 20th century, many traditional sea gypsy and Muslim fishing villages on Phuket and around Krabi were transformed into lush vacation resorts.

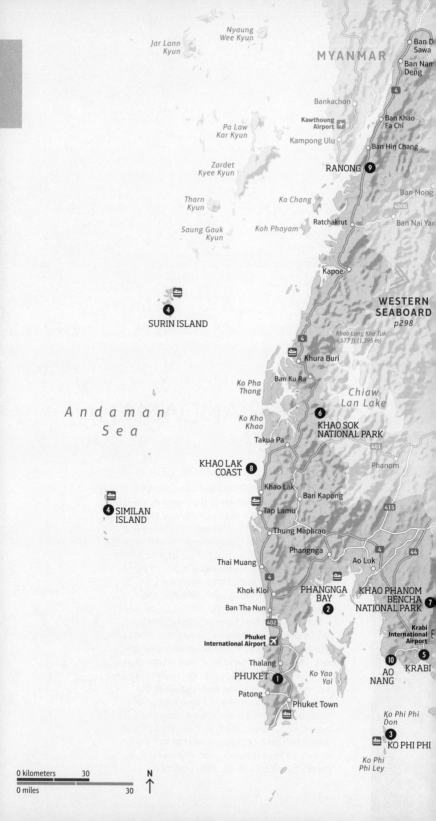

Nyaung Wee Kyun

Jar Lann Kyun

MYANMAR

Ban D Sawa

Ban Nam Deng

4

Bankachon

Kawthoung Airport ✈

Ban Khao Fa Chi

Pa Law Kar Kyun

Kampong Ulu

Ban Hin Chang

Zardet Kyee Kyun

RANONG **9**

Ban Mong

Tharn Kyun

Ko Chang

4006

Ban Nai Yar

Saung Gauk Kyun

Koh Phayam

Ratchakrut

4
SURIN ISLAND

Kapoe

WESTERN SEABOARD
p298

Khao Lang Kha Tuk 4,577 ft (1,395 m)

4

Khura Buri

Ko Pha Thong

Ban Ku Ra

Chiaw Lan Lake

A n d a m a n
S e a

Ko Kho Khao

6
KHAO SOK NATIONAL PARK

Takua Pa

401

Phanom

KHAO LAK COAST **8**

Khao Lak

Ban Kapong

4
SIMILAN ISLAND

Tap Lamu

415

Thung Maphrao

Phangnga

Ao Luk

Thai Muang

4

44

Khok Kloi

PHANGNGA BAY

KHAO PHANOM BENCHA NATIONAL PARK **7**

Ban Tha Nun

2

Krabi International Airport ✈

402

Phuket International Airport ✈

Thalang

Ko Yao Yai

5

PHUKET **1**

10
AO NANG

KRABI

Patong

Phuket Town

Ko Phi Phi Don

3
KO PHI PHI

Ko Phi Phi Ley

0 kilometers   30

0 miles   30

N ↑

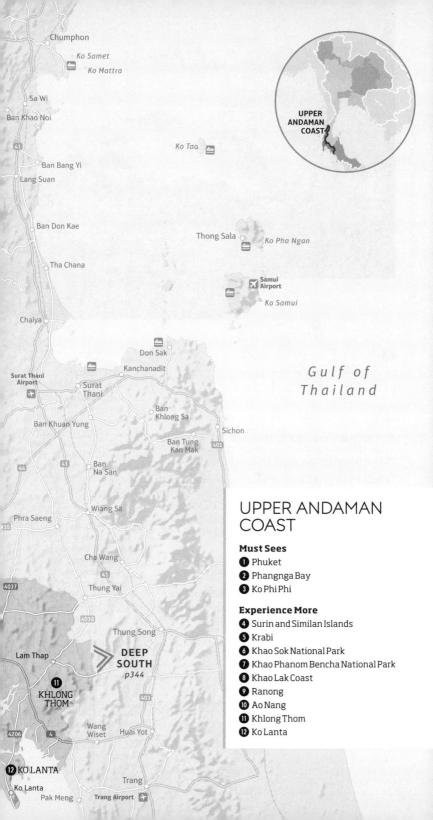

Chumphon

Ko Samet
Ko Mattra

Sa Wi

Ban Khao Noi

41

Ban Bang Yi

Lang Suan

Ko Tao

Ban Don Kae

Thong Sala
Ko Pha Ngan

Tha Chana

Samui
Airport

Chaiya
Ko Samui

Don Sak

Kanchanadit

Surat Thani
Airport
Surat
Thani

*Gulf of
Thailand*

Ban
Khlong Sa

Ban Khuan Yung

Sichon

Ban Tung
Kan Mak

401

44
41
Ban
Na San

Wiang Sa

35
Phra Saeng

Cha Wang

41

4037
Thung Yai

4038

Thung Song

Lam Thap

**DEEP
SOUTH**
p344

11
KHLONG
THOM

403

4206
Wang
Wiset Huai Yot

4

12 KO LANTA

Ko Lanta

Trang

Pak Meng Trang Airport

UPPER ANDAMAN COAST

Must Sees
❶ Phuket
❷ Phangnga Bay
❸ Ko Phi Phi

Experience More
❹ Surin and Similan Islands
❺ Krabi
❻ Khao Sok National Park
❼ Khao Phanom Bencha National Park
❽ Khao Lak Coast
❾ Ranong
❿ Ao Nang
⓫ Khlong Thom
⓬ Ko Lanta

**UPPER
ANDAMAN
COAST**

Enjoying the sun set over the tropical Patong beach ↑

PHUKET

ภูเก็ต

🅰 E6 🏠 Phuket province ✈ 18 miles (29 km) N of Phuket Town 🚌 Phangnga Rd, Phuket town ⛴ From Ko Phi Phi to Phuket Deep Sea Port ℹ 191 Thalang Rd; 0-7621-1036

Thailand's largest island, Phuket became prosperous thanks to tin production, but tourism is now the major earner. Southeast Asia's most popular vacation destination attracts visitors from all over with its stunning beaches, crystal-clear waters, and vibrant nightlife.

Phuket was called Junkceylon by early European traders, but its modern name may derive from the Malay word *bukit*, meaning hill. On arrival, many visitors head straight for a beach resort and do not leave it for the duration of their vacation – the best of the island's beaches are strung out along the west coast. However, there are several historical and cultural sights to complement the beachside attractions, and the lush, hilly interior is also worth exploring. Phuket also has many chic resorts and spas.

Western Beaches

Phuket owes its fame to the beauty, warmth, and safety of its beaches, nearly all of which are situated on the island's western, Andaman Coast, which runs from Hat Nai Harn in the south to Hat Sai Kaeo in the north. The beaches around Patong – around 40 minutes' drive from the airport – are among the best known. All of Phuket's west coast offers a fine choice of accommodations, dining, and water sports, as well as

GREAT VIEW
Karon Viewpoint

Also known as Three Beaches Hill, this spectacular spot, 2 miles (3 km) from Hat Kata Noi, takes in Hat Karon and Hat Kata Yai. You'll probably spot the image on postcards in town.

mesmerizing views, especially toward dusk, when the sun sets across the idyllic waters of the Andaman Sea.

Phuket's most developed beach is the 2-mile (3-km) long **Hat Patong**. Once a quiet banana plantation, it is now almost a city by the sea. The area has a lively nightlife, with a vibrant mix of hotels, restaurants, discos, and bars. During the day there are many water activities, such as parasailing, water-skiing, diving, and deep-sea fishing. Although Patong continues to expand, the beaches along the southern headland of Patong bay are far quieter.

South of Patong, and almost as popular, are the beaches of **Hat Karon** and

number of good restaurants on the headland between Karon and Kata.

North of Patong lies the smaller palm-covered beach of **Hat Kamala**. This beach is relatively undeveloped, with some Muslim fishermen's houses and a few restaurants.

Farther north from Hat Kamala, **Ao Bang Tao** offers a quiet, enchanting retreat, popular with families. Fronted by exclusive hotels, the beach is good for water sports.

Hat Patong
📍 🏖 🏢 10 miles (16 km) W of Phuket Town

Hat Karon
📍 🏖 🏢 12 miles (19 km) SW of Phuket Town

Hat Kata
📍 🏖 🏢 10 miles (16 km) SW of Phuket Town

Hat Kamala
📍 🏖 🏢 16 miles (26 km) W of Phuket Town

Ao Bang Tao
📍 🏖 🏢 13 miles (21 km) W of Phuket Town

Hat Kata. Karon has one long stretch of sand lined with accommodations, and a second beach at tiny Karon Noi. Kata's beaches, along the bays of Kata Yai and Kata Noi, are smaller and prettier, sheltered by rocky promontories. There are also a

STAY

Keemala
Magical resort with luxurious villas resembling huge wicker baskets, which seem to hang on the edge of the rainforest. The superb bar and restaurant have stunning beach views.

🏠 10/88 Moo 6, Nakasud Road, Hat Kamala
🌐 keemala.com

Casa Brazil
Quirky decor and friendly staff characterize this homestay and gallery, set around a garden and a nice central courtyard.

🏠 9 Moo 3 Soi Luang Por Chuan 1, Hat Karon
🌐 phukethomestay.com

ⒷⒷⒷ

Casa Blanca Boutique Hotel
Housed in a Chinese-Portuguese mansion in the heart of the Old Town, this wonderful hotel is full of beautiful art and also has a pool.

🏠 26 Phuket Rd, Phuket Town 🌐 casablanca phuket.com

Banyan Tree
One of Phuket's original and best luxury resorts. Lavish pool villas sit on a tranquil lagoon, and there are six superb restaurants and a spa.

🏠 33/37 Moo 4, Sri Soonthorn Rd, Cherng Thalae 🌐 banyan tree.com

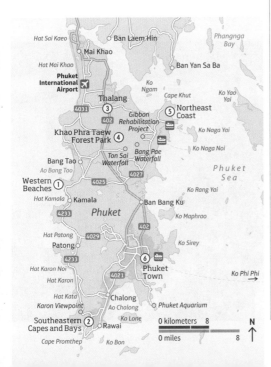

Hat Sai Kaeo · Ban Laem Hin
Mai Khao
Hat Mai Khao · *Phangnga Bay*
Phuket International Airport ✈
Ko Ngam · Ban Yan Sa Ba
Thalang ③
4031
402
Gibbon Rehabilitation Project · Cape Khut · Ko Yao Yai
Ko Yao Yai
⑤ Northeast Coast
Khao Phra Taew Forest Park ④
Ton Sai Waterfall · Bang Pae Waterfall · Ko Naga Yai
Bang Tao · Ko Naga Noi
Ao Bang Tao · 4027
Western Beaches ① · *Phuket Sea*
4025 · Ko Rang Yai
Hat Kamala · Kamala
4233
Phuket · Ban Bang Ku
Ko Maphrao
Hat Patong · 402
Patong · Ko Sirey
4233
4029
Hat Karon Noi · 4021
Hat Karon · ⑥ · Ko Phi Phi →
Phuket Town
Hat Kata · Phuket Aquarium
Karon Viewpoint · Chalong
② · Ao Chalong · Ko Lone
Southeastern Capes and Bays · Rawai
Cape Promthep · Ko Bon

0 kilometers   8
0 miles   8

N ↑

② Southeastern Capes and Bays

A bay near the southern tip of Phuket, **Hat Nai Harn** is the home of the exclusive Phuket Yacht Club. The beach (open to all) is one of the most beautiful on the island.

North of Promthep, on the east side of the island, are **Hat Rawai**, and farther along, **Ao Chalong**. The sands around this bay are not as white as those on the west coast, but there are many excellent seafood shacks here. Ao Chalong acts as an anchorage for international yachts, and is also a departure point for boat excursions to the charming islands of Lone and Bon.

Farther up the coast at Cape Phanwa is the interesting and much-visited Phuket Aquarium, which forms part of the **Marine Biological Research Center**.

Hat Nai Harn
Ⓨ Ⓐ Ⓐ 11 miles (18 km) SW of Phuket Town

Hat Rawai
Ⓨ Ⓐ Ⓐ 10 miles (16 km) from Phuket Town

SEA GYPSIES OF THE ANDAMAN SEA

Sea gypsies, known as *chao ley* in Thai, may originate from the Andaman or Nicobar islands, across the Andaman Sea. Phuket's sea gypsy population settled around 200 years ago, following routes from the Mergui archipelago, west of the Burmese mainland, and still populate the area today. They speak their own language and have animistic beliefs. Once a year they hold a spiritual cleansing ceremony to get rid of bad spirits.

Ao Chalong
Ⓨ Ⓐ Ⓐ 6 miles (10 km) SE of Phuket Town

Marine Biological Research Center
Ⓐ Ⓐ Ⓨ Ⓐ Ⓐ Tip of Cape Phanwa 🄲 0-7639-1126 🄲 Aquarium: 8:30am–4:30pm daily; Marine Biological Research Center: 8:30am–4:30pm Mon–Fri

③ Thalang
กลาง

Ⓐ 11 miles (18 km) N of Phuket Town

This town in central Phuket was the site of a famous battle in 1785 against the Burmese, which is commemorated by the Heroines' Monument 5 miles (8 km) to the south. A short walk east of the monument is the **Thalang National Museum**, which outlines the rich heritage of Phuket. Among the exhibits are 5th-century religious icons, Chinese porcelain, and information on sea gypsies.

In Thalang itself there is a good market, and every Sunday afternoon, a street food market, which continues into the night. Nearby, Wat Phra Tong has a gold-covered Buddha image, half buried in the ground. Legend has it that disaster will come to anyone who tries to move the image.

Thalang National Museum
Ⓐ Ⓐ Off Hwy 402, opposite Heroines' Monument 🄲 0-7631-1025, 0-7631-1426 🄲 Daily

Bustling street food market in Thalang in the evening

↑ Serene flora and gushing waters at Khao Phra Taew Forest Park

beach that makes a fine halt for swimming and relaxing. It is easily reached by boat from Ao Por Pier.

On the Cape Khut headland, at Phuket's northeasternmost point, there are sweeping views of the monoliths of the stunning Phangnga Bay *(p330)*. The placid waters of the narrow channel between Phuket and Phangnga province are exploited by Muslim fishermen, who farm sea bass here.

Ko Naga Noi

⌂ 3 km (5 miles) from Ao Por Pier

Khao Phra Taew Forest Park

อุทยานเขาพระแทว

⌂ 2.5 miles (4 km) E of Thalang 📞 0-7631-1998 🕐 Dawn-dusk daily

The last of Phuket's once ubiquitous rainforest is preserved at the spectacular Khao Phra Taew Forest Park. Within the park are two fine waterfalls. The prettiest, Ton Sai waterfall, is smaller but easier to reach, and is at its best June through December. It's also a good spot for bird-watching; racket-tailed drongos and red-billed malkohas are among the wonderfully named and brightly colored birds you can spot here. On the eastern fringe of the preserve is the Bang Pae waterfall. At around 33 ft (10 m), Bang Pae is far

from massive, but it's the biggest waterfall on Phuket and is a lovely spot for a dip, with rocks on either side creating a narrow pool.

Near Bang Pae is the **Gibbon Rehabilitation Project**. This volunteer-run program aims to reintroduce domesticated gibbons into the forest by encouraging them to fend for themselves. Visitors' donations buy food for the gibbons.

Gibbon Rehabilitation Project

⌂ Near Bang Pae falls 🕐 9am–4pm daily 🌐 gibbonproject.org

Northeast Coast

Off Phuket's northeast coast, **Ko Naga Noi** is the place to be. It has a tranquil, sandy

EAT

Kan Eang Seafood II

A seafood institution since the 1980s, Kan Eang started as a street-side stand, but is now a lovely beachside restaurant with a garden. There's also a play area for children on the adjacent sandy beach.

⌂ 9/3 Chofa Rd, Ao Chalong 📞 0-7638-1323

Natural Restaurant

A favorite for years, this garden restaurant is full of hidden nooks and crannies, and even little waterfalls. There is a selection of world cuisines, from Japanese to German, as well as classic Thai dishes.

⌂ 66/5 Soi Phuthon, Bangkok Rd, Phuket Town 🌐 natural restaurantphuket.com

> **The last of Phuket's once ubiquitous rainforest is preserved at the spectacular Khao Phra Taew Forest Park. Within the park are two fine waterfalls.**

↑ Driving past a row of beautiful traditional Chinese shop-houses

DRINK

Quip

This trendy rooftop bar is a great place to sit with a beer and admire Phuket's wide range of architecture.

🅐 54 Phuket Rd, Phuket Town 🆆 quipphuket.com

Pepper's Sports Bar

Phuket's favorite sports bar shows games on six screens, from rugby and soccer to boxing and cricket. There are also regular quiz nights.

🅐 16-18 Lagoon Rd, Cherngtalay, Thalang 🆆 phuketsportsbar.com

Catch Beach Club

The original beach club in Phuket is a stylish spot to see and be seen, with an infinity pool, dance floor, and exquisite cocktails.

🅐 202/88 Moo 2, Cherngtalay, Thalang 🆆 catchbeachclub.com

Phuket Town
ตัวเมืองภูเก็ต

🅐 Phuket province 🚌 Southern Bus Terminal, near Phangnga Rd 🛈 191 Thalang Rd; 0-7621-1036/2213

The bustling Phuket Town grew to prominence around the beginning of the 19th century, when the island's tin resources attracted Chinese migrants. Many merchants made fortunes from tin, built splendid residences, and sent their children to British Penang to be educated. Hokkien-speaking tin-mining families soon intermarried with the indigenous Thai population. Today, the downtown area retains some of its earlier charm, though, unlike most of the island, it is geared toward residents rather than tourists. The Chinese heritage is preserved in the Sino-Portuguese shop-houses, temples, the local cuisine, and the Vegetarian Festival.

The heart of Phuket Town is the old Sino-Portuguese quarter with its spacious, now rather run-down, colonial-style **Chinese Mansions** set in large grounds. Most date from the reigns of Rama IV and Rama V (1851–1910). Among the best examples are those

used today as offices by the Standard Chartered Bank and Thai Airways on Ranong Road. Unfortunately, no one has yet seen fit to convert any of the old mansions into a museum, and none can be visited. Many of the Chinese shop-houses are also dilapidated.

The **Thavorn Hotel Lobby Exhibition** in the center of town has a collection of Phuket artifacts and pictures displayed in the lobby and adjacent function rooms. Among the exhibits are models of tin mines, pictures of the town center in the 19th century, Chinese treasure chests, and weavers' tables. A 1-minute walk to the west lies the daily **Fresh Produce Market**, a treat that assaults the senses. The market and adjacent lanes are full of colorful characters hawking condiments, dried herbs and spices, pungent pickled kapi fish, squirming eels, and succulent durians.

Phuket Town is also home to a variety of symbolic temples. **Bang Niew Temple**, southeast of the city center, is where *naga* devotees climb knife ladders during the Vegetarian Festival. The inner

compound is devoted to Chinese mythological gods, the most prominent being Siew, Hok, and Lok, who represent longevity, power, and happiness. **Wat Mongkol Nimit** is a large, Rattanakosin-style temple with finely carved doors. It acts as a community center where monks play *takraw* with the laity. The Chinese **Chui Tui Temple** attracts a steady flow of people who come to shake numbered sticks from a canister dedicated to vegetarian god Kiu Wong In. Each number corresponds to a pre-printed fate that, according to belief, the person will inherit.

Northwest of the center stands **Rang Hill**, which overlooks the town. On the top of this hill stands a statue of Khaw Sim Bee Na-Ranong (1857–1913), governor of Phuket for 12 years from 1901. He enjoyed autonomy from Bangkok but is credited with bringing the island firmly under central rule, and also with importing the first rubber tree into Thailand.

Further from the center of town lies the island of **Ko Sirey**, linked to Phuket by a short bridge just beyond the commercial fishing port area. On this small but hilly island, rubber and coconut plantations vie with the natural fauna, and quiet beaches offer excellent seafood at low prices. Atop a hill in the center of the island, the temple of Wat Ko Sirey has great views and a massive image of a reclining Buddha.

Chinese Mansions

📍 Thalang, Yaowarat, Dibuk, Krabi, Ranong, and Phangnga roads

Thavorn Hotel Lobby Exhibition

♿ 📍 74 Rasada Rd ☎ 0-7621-1334 🕐 24 hrs daily

Fresh Produce Market

📍 Ranong Rd 🕐 2am–10pm daily

Bang Niew Temple

📍 Phuket Rd 🕐 8:30am–10pm daily

Wat Mongkol Nimit

📍 Yaowarat Rd 🕐 7am–5:30pm daily

Chui Tui Temple

📍 Ranong Rd 🕐 8am–8:30pm daily

Rang Hill

📍 1.5 miles (2.5 km) NW of Wat Mongkol Nimit

Ko Sirey

 📍 3 miles (4.5 km) E of town center

> 💬 INSIDER TIP
> ### Vegetarian Festival
>
> It's worth visiting Phuket Town at the start of the ninth Chinese lunar month when it hosts a nine-day Vegetarian Festival. Expect gruesome rites, a parade of *nagas* (spirit mediums), and firework displays.

↑ Parading a shrine through Phuket Town, marking the start of Phuket's Vegetarian Festival

②

PHANGNGA BAY

อ่าวพังงา

⚑E6 ⌂Phangnga province 🚌From Phuket or Krabi to Phangnga town, then long-tail or ferry tour 🛈Krabi; 0-7562-2163

With its weird and wonderful limestone stacks that rise dramatically from the bay, towering above its aquamarine water, Phangnga Bay is one of southern Thailand's most iconic natural beauty spots.

No one area epitomizes the splendor of the south's landscape as succinctly as 155-sq-mile (400-sq-km) Phangnga Bay. Its scenic grandeur derives from towering limestone stacks rising sheer from calm, shallow waters up to 1,150 ft (350 m) high. Inside many of the 40-odd stacks are narrow tunnels and sea caves. The island of Ko Hong, off the coast of Krabi, is known for its vast network of lagoons, chasms, and tunnels that run beneath it, as well as idyllic white-sand beaches and mangrove forest. Another highlight is Tham Lot, a 165-ft (50-m) long sea tunnel through limestone with stalactites hanging from its roof. It is possible to explore the area independently in a small boat at high tide, though skillful piloting is required.

Inland, too, this coastal area boasts majestic, scrub-clad pinnacles. Phangnga is, in fact, the most spectacular remnant of the once mighty Tenasserim Mountains, which still form a spine through Thailand to China. Boat tours of the bay once took in the best-known sights, such as "James Bond Island", as well as a number of fascinating caves. Some of the eerie caverns contain prehistoric paintings and Buddhist shrines. Because of massive erosion, however, partly due to overtourism, and partly due to the nature of the rocks themselves, big tourist boats are currently banned from large areas of Phangnga Bay.

> ## JAMES BOND AND THE ISLAND HIDEOUT
>
> In the movie *The Man With the Golden Gun* (1974), the ninth in the James Bond series, the fictional MI6 agent, played by Roger Moore, ventures to Southeast Asia in search of the villainous Francisco Scaramanga (Christopher Lee). Bond is eventually taken to Scaramanga's secret hideout, an island just off the coast of China. In fact, the island is Ko Khao Phing Kan in Phangnga Bay; the sheer limestone karst nearby, which is the location of Scaramanga's secret weapon, is Ko Tapu.

Mangrove forests thrive in the bay's saltwater estuaries ↑

Did You Know?

Mangrove species are the only trees to have adapted to the muddy intertidal zones here.

Six Senses Yao Noi
Palm-thatched villas with private pools, a spa and four exquisite restaurants.

🏠 56 Mu 5, Koh Yao Noi
🌐 sixsenses.com

Ⓑ Ⓑ Ⓑ

Yao Yai Beach Resort
On the beach with superb sunset views, each bungalow has a private garden. Diving trips are available.

🏠 Moo 7, Baan Lo Preh, Pru Nai, Ko Yao Yai
🌐 yaoyairesort.com

Ⓑ Ⓑ Ⓑ

↑ Heading toward the iconic limestone karst on "James Bond Island"

Samet Nagashe viewpoint offers a dramatic vista of Phangnga Bay

Limestone Stacks

The limestone landscape at Phangnga Bay is known by geologists as drowned karstland. Karst is characterized by its internal drainage system, whereby water finds its way into the interior of the limestone through fissures, then erodes the rock from within. A riddle of tunnels is typical; chasms and vast sea chambers (hongs) are also common at Phangnga. The karst scenery with its majestic pinnacles continues inland from the bay to the east, where cliffs soar high above hidden valleys with cascading rivers and waterfalls that carve their way through the lush landscape. A protected site, the bay is home to diverse ecosystems and a variety of wildlife.

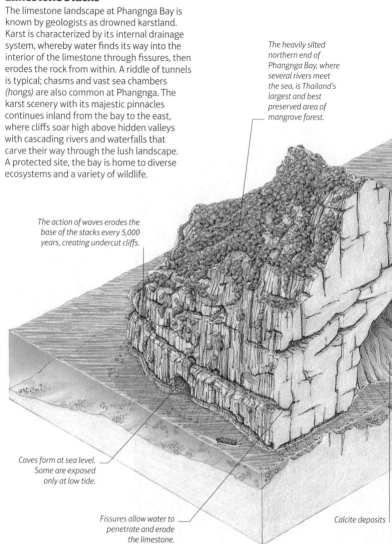

The heavily silted northern end of Phangnga Bay, where several rivers meet the sea, is Thailand's largest and best preserved area of mangrove forest.

The action of waves erodes the base of the stacks every 5,000 years, creating undercut cliffs.

Caves form at sea level. Some are exposed only at low tide.

Fissures allow water to penetrate and erode the limestone.

Calcite deposits

GREAT VIEW
Samet Nagashe Viewpoint

The karst cliffs and islets of Phangnga Bay stretch out before your eyes at this stunning viewpoint about an hour's drive northeast from Phuket.

Forest scrub clings to cracks in the limestone.

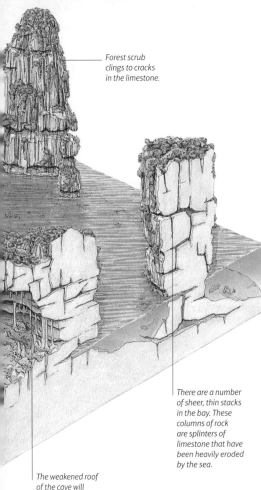

There are a number of sheer, thin stacks in the bay. These columns of rock are splinters of limestone that have been heavily eroded by the sea.

The weakened roof of the cave will eventually collapse.

↑ Cross section of typical limestone stacks and karstland in Phangnga Bay

130 million years ago

▲ The area was under water and part of a vast coral reef. Calcite deposits from dead coral built up in thick layers.

75 million years ago

▲ Plate movements pushed these deposits, which had turned to limestone, out of the ocean. The rigid rock ruptured.

20,000 years ago

▲ At the end of the last Ice Age, the sea level rose, flooding Phangnga. Wave and tide action accelerated the erosion process.

8,000 years ago

▲ The sea reached its highest level, about 13 ft (4 m) above its present height, sculpting a shelf, visible on most of the stacks.

Snorkeling in the pristine waters of Ko Phi Phi Leh ↑

3

KO PHI PHI

เกาะพีพี

△ E6 **⌂ Krabi province** **⛴ From Phuket or Krabi** **ⓘ Phuket; 0-7621-2213**

Spectacular Ko Phi Phi, pronounced "PP," 25 miles (40 km) south of Krabi Town, is in fact two separate islands: Phi Phi Don and Phi Phi Leh. The islands are famed for their spectacular landscapes. Rock climbers are attracted by the breathtaking cliffs, with tall walls of limestone rising to 1,030 ft (314 m) on Phi Phi Don, and 1,230 ft (374 m) on Phi Phi Leh. Nature lovers will find a haven in the coral beds, teeming with sea life.

①

Ban Ton Sai

บ้านต้นไทร

The two sections of Phi Phi Don, the larger of the two islands, are linked by a 1,100-yard (1,000 m) isthmus of sand. Here stands the island's original Muslim fishing village, Ban Ton Sai. This area was badly damaged by the 2004 tsunami but the village has bounced back and is busier than ever. Ban Ton Sai is the the commercial hub of the island, as well as the only ferry port with links to the mainland. It is a crowded hive of small streets packed with foreign visitors as well as Thais from the mainland. Many choose to stay here for its facilities, including hotels, restaurants, and bars. This is an ideal place for visitors to set up base to explore the rest of Ko Phi Phi.

②

Ko Phi Phi Leh

เกาะพีพีเล

⛴ From Ban Ton Sai

Only a quarter of the size of Ko Phi Phi Don and much less accessible, Ko Phi Phi Leh is completely uninhabited. With

---

DANNY BOYLE'S THE BEACH

Hollywood director Danny Boyle decided upon Ao Maya in Ko Phi Phi Leh as the perfect location for filming Alex Garland's *The Beach* (2000). The movie is about young people living on a secret island and their hedonistic lifestyle. The film ran into trouble when 20th Century Fox and their local agents were sued by Thai courts for alleged damage to the bay. Nonetheless, the movie was instrumental in bringing Ao Maya into the limelight.

pristine coves and bays and rich offshore coral reefs, the island's main attraction is its startling beauty and isolation. However, everything changed when Danny Boyle put the island on the world map with his movie *The Beach* (2000), starring Leonardo DiCaprio. Since then thousands of visitors have come here to experience this tropical paradise, and the island's greatest attraction, Ao Maya, has been closed due to damage caused by heavy tourist traffic.

Ao Lo Dalum
อ่าวโล๊ะดาลัม

Immediately north of Ban Ton Sai, Ao Lo Dalum is a gorgeous bay fringed by a fine beach with lush green coconut palms. This beach is busy, and while it is picturesque at high tide, it is somewhat less appealing at low tide, when the mudflats stretch out endlessly. A steep trail at the eastern end of the bay follows a path across the island's spine and leads up to the island's famous viewpoint, which offers a vista spanning the isthmus and its twin bays.

Hat Yao
หาดยาว

A pleasant one-hour coastal walk from Ban Ton Sai leads to Hat Yao ("long beach"), with tantalizing white sands,

vibrant offshore marine life, and unhindered views of the soaring flanks of Phi Phi Leh. This beach is a place of exquisite beauty. However, it is generally quite crowded.

Ao Lo Bakao
อ่าวโล๊ะบาเภา

This bay, which is about half a mile (1 km) north of Hat Ranti, is separated from Ban Ton Sai and the rest of the island by a rocky spine. Ao Lo Bakao is only reached on foot via a single narrow trail. Yet its beach has developed as an upscale spot, characterized by expensive, well-appointed resort accommodations. The beautiful white-sand beach is well served by restaurants and bars. This rather exclusive bay attracts upper-class Thais, and is also a popular honeymoon spot.

Hat Ranti
หาดรันตี

One of three linked beaches on the east coast of Ko Phi Phi Don, Hat Ranti can be reached by a 45-minute walk on the trail across the spine of the main island, or by long-tail boats. It is well suited for the budget traveler, and is perfect for a picnic or a day trip.

Hat Laem Thong
หาดแหลมทอง

A lovely strip of sand on Ko Phi Phi Don's northernmost tip, this area is also among the best diving spots in the archipelago. Visitors can go deep-sea fishing or even take cookery courses.

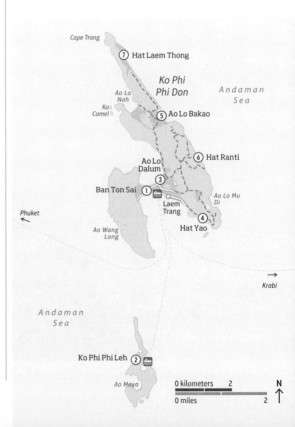

Cape Trong

⑦ Hat Laem Thong

Ko Phi Phi Don

Andaman Sea

Ao La Nah

Ko Camel

⑤ Ao Lo Bakao

Ao Lo Dalum

③

⑥ Hat Ranti

Ban Ton Sai ①

Laem Trang

Ao Lo Mu Di

Phuket

④

Ao Wang Long

Hat Yao

→ *Krabi*

Andaman Sea

Ko Phi Phi Leh ②

Ao Maya

0 kilometers   2

0 miles   2

N ↑

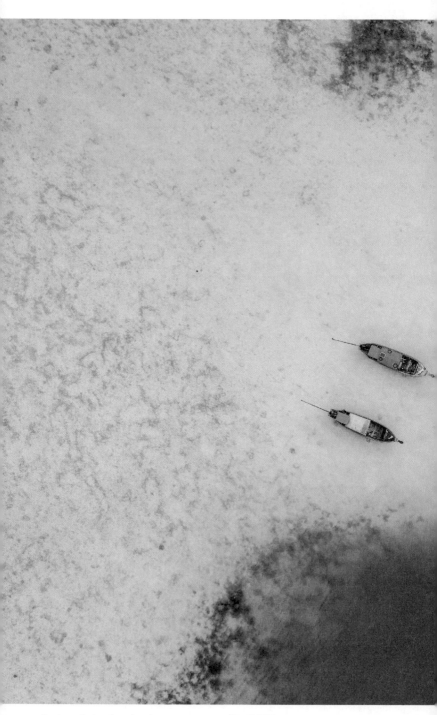

Boats exploring the calm, picturesque waters of Ko Phi Phi

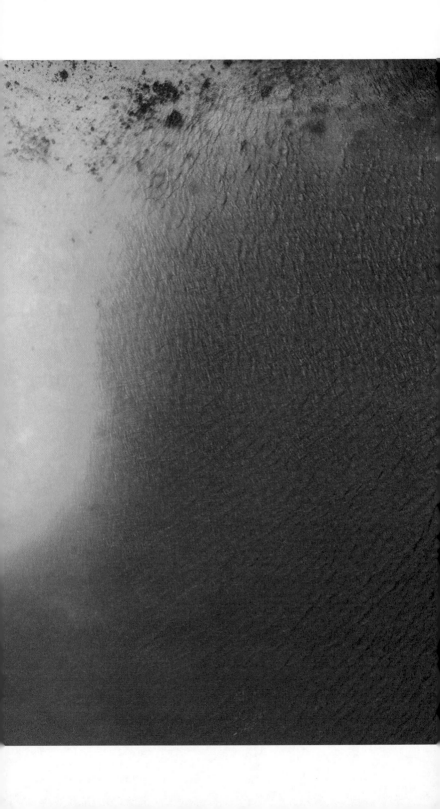

EXPERIENCE MORE

4

Surin and Similan Islands
เกาะสุรินทร์และเกาะสิมิลัน

🅐D5/6 🏛Phangnga province 🚢Surin: from Khuraburi Pier, 1 mile (1.5 km) off Hwy 4; Similan: from Tap Lamu, off Hwy 4, 24 miles (39 km) S of Takua Pa; or by diving trips from Khao Lak Coast or Ko Phuket 🕒Mid-May-mid-Nov 🛈Phuket; 0-7621-1036

Ko Surin and Ko Similan, 37 miles (60 km) off the west coast and 62 miles (100 km) apart, are the most remote islands in Thailand. Because of the southwesterly monsoon, from May to November, they are virtually inaccessible. In season, however, the two archipelagos offer some of the best diving sites in the world and some of the most spectacular wildlife and scenery in Thailand.

The five Surin Islands are virtually uninhabited, home only to a few sea gypsies and national park officials. There is a park dormitory on Ko Surin Nua, but most people camp on the islands.

The two largest islands, Ko Surin Nua and Ko Surin Tai, are heavily forested with tall hardwood trees. Sea eagles, turtles, and crab-eating macaques are common sights. The surrounding sea offers an outstanding array of soft corals and frequent sightings of shovel-nose rays, bow-mouthed guitar fish, and whale sharks. However, overfishing has unfortunately led to the depletion of the marine life of Ko Surin, and many divers maintain that the greatest sightings of sea life are to be found around the Similans instead.

Of the nine Similan Islands 4, 7, 8, and 9 were damaged by the 2004 tsunami but are still open to tourists and divers. The name Similan is thought to derive from the Malaysian word *sembilan*, meaning nine, and the islands are numbered Ko 1 through to Ko 9. Ko 4 (Ko Miang) has the park HQ, a restaurant, bungalows, and campsite (with a supply of two-person tents). Also important is Ko 9, where the ranger sub-station can be found. The interiors of these islands consist of crystal-white sand and lush rain-forest, while the headlands are made up of distinctive, giant granite boulders the size of houses. Beneath these rocks are underwater grottoes and swim-through tunnels, which appeal to divers and snorkelers.

The seabed is decorated with staghorn, star, and branching corals, and a range of fish, including manta rays, and giant sea turtles. Other, more threatening, fish include giant groupers, and poisonous stonefish, and lionfish. Sharks around the islands include black and white tips, leopard sharks, hammerheads, bull sharks, and whale sharks.

Diving in the amazing clear waters, perfect for spotting turtles *(inset)* and other sea life, around the Surin Islands

↑ Opulent Wat Tham Sua in Krabi, surrounded by lush forest

5

Krabi

กระบี่

E6 Krabi province
Maharat Rd, Krabi; www.tourismthailand.org/krabi

This small fishing town, the capital of beautiful Krabi province, has an important role as the ferry embarkation point for islands such as Ko Lanta to the south, Ko Phi Phi to the southwest, and the beaches around Ao Nang to the west. Set on the banks of the Krabi Estuary, the town takes its name from a sword, or *krabi*, allegedly discovered nearby. It is surrounded by towering limestone outcrops, similar to those in Phangnga Bay *(p330)*, which have become the symbol of Krabi province. Among the most notable are Kanap Nam twin limestone peaks, which stand like sentinels at each side of the river. To the east, the town is flanked by mangrove-lined shorelines. These outcrops and mangroves can be toured by renting a long-tail boat from the Chao Fa pier in the center of town.

Located 5 miles (8 km) north of town is Wat Tham Sua ("tiger cave temple"), named after a rock formation that resembles a tiger paw. It is one of the most renowned forest *wats* in southern Thailand, with the main hall, where meditation is practiced, built inside a cave. A circular path in the nearby forest hollow offers a pleasant walk among towering, buttressed trees and *kutis*, simple huts inhabited by monks and nuns. A 985-ft (300-m) high staircase leads to a large Buddha image and Buddha Footprint on top of the cliff. From here there are panoramic views of the province.

CLIMBING KRABI'S STACKS

Krabi and Ko Phi Phi are the only places in Thailand where organized rock-climbing takes place. Honeycombed limestone stacks around the Phra Nang headland, near Krabi, and Ko Phi Phi are challenging and attract climbers from around the world. Only the south of France is said to offer such arduous climbs. They vary in difficulty from an easy "4" according to the French system, to a very difficult "8b."

DRINK

Chuapa Beer Cafe

It might not look much, but this hole in the wall serves a superb range of craft beers and national and international labels.

E6 9/7 Chao Fa Rd, Krabi Town 0-8504-88800

Bar 79 & Grill

One of the liveliest spots in Krabi Town, this bar has generous happy hours and plenty of fun bar games to get involved in.

E6 Soi Maharaj 8, Krabi Town 0-9622-39685

Ole Bar

At this laid-back bar hours can melt away with board games, cushions set around low tables, and decent cocktails.

E6 91 Utarakit Rd, Krabi Town 0-8919-58575

STAY

A Day Inn

Lovely budget hotel with spotless high-ceilinged rooms and stylish communal areas. Dorms also available

 E5 **204 Ruengrat Rd, Ranong** 0-6378-98711

ⓑⓑⓑ

JW Marriott Khao Lak Resort & Spa

Beautiful resort on the beach, with pavilion-style buildings and Mediterranean restaurants.

E6 **41/12 Moo 3, Khuk Khak, Khao Lak** marrriott.com

ⓑⓑⓑ

Rock and Treehouse Resort

On the fringes of Khao Sok National Park, this resort combines jungle immersion with supreme comfort.

 E5 **400 Moo 6 Klong Sok, Khao Sok** rockandtree-houseresort.com

ⓑⓑⓑ

Boating on the stunning Cheow Lan Lake in Khao Sok National Park ↑

Khao Sok National Park
อุทยานแห่งชาติเขาสก

 E5 **Surat Thani province; Park HQ off Hwy 401, 25 miles (40 km) E of Takua Pa** From Surat Thani or Takua Pa Surat Thani; 0-7728-8818

Together with a range of nearby preserves, Khao Sok National Park forms the largest and most dramatic tract of virgin forest in south Thailand. The 285-sq-mile (738-sq-km) park rises to a height of 3,150 ft (960 m) and includes 100 spectacular islands, formed when the Rachabrapha Dam was built in 1982. One of the most stunning spots is Cheow Lan Lake, an artificial lake where the water is an emerald color.

Elephants, tigers, bears, boars, and monkeys live in the park, along with at least 188 species of birds. The area is popular with tourists eager to bird-watch and trek.

Khao Phanom Bencha National Park
อุทยานแห่งชาติพนมเบญจา

E6 **Krabi province; Park HQ off Hwy 4, 12.5 miles (20 km) N of Krabi** Krabi, then local bus TAT, Krabi; tel: 0-7562-2163

This 193-sq-mile (500-sq-km) national park of mostly tropical monsoon forest is named for the five-shouldered peak of Khao Phanom Bencha, rising to a height of 4,580 ft (1,397 m).

Despite illegal logging and poaching, the park's rainforest still holds at least 156 species of bird, including the white-crowned hornbill and the striped wren-babbler. Among the 32 mammal species catalogued are the Asiatic black bear, Malaysian sun bear, clouded leopard, wild boar, binturong, and serow.

The thundering Huay To waterfall and Huay Sadeh waterfall are less than 2 miles (3 km) from the park headquarters, from where treks to the summit can be arranged.

⑧ Khao Lak Coast
หาดเขาหลัก

E6 **Phangnga province** From Takua Pa or Phuket Phuket; 0-7621-1036

The coastline south of Takua Pa consists of long stretches of rocky and sandy beaches.

→

Steam rising from one of Ranong's geothermal hot springs

CAVE PAINTINGS OF THE ANDAMAN ISLANDS

There are many prehistoric paintings in Phangnga (p330) and Krabi (p339) provinces, especially in caves on the Andaman Islands. Most are stylized red and black outlines depicting human forms, hands, fish, and, in some cases, broken line patterns that are thought to have had symbolic value. Such paintings may have been drawn as part of magical-religious rituals to bring good fortune for hunting, fishing, food gathering, and tribal battles. Many paintings can be reliably dated to Neolithic times.

Khao Lak, halfway between Takua Pa and Thai Muang, has a fine beach and is a good base from which to explore the area. The nearby **Khao Lak (Lam Ru) National Park** features steep ridges of monsoon forest extending to the winding coast. Barking deer and small bears are among the wildlife living in the forest but, sadly, the park is plagued by encroachment and poaching.

The Similan Islands are only 4 hours away by boat, and visitors come here to book their dive trips. Between November and April, Tap Lamu fishing port and Hat Khao Lak operate as ferry points for Ko Similan.

Khao Lak (Lam Ru) National Park

⊗ 🏠 HQ 16 miles (25 km) S of Takua Pa 🛈 0-7648-5243

9

Ranong

ระนอง

🅰E5 🏠 Ranong province ✈🚌🚉 🛈 Chumphon; 0-7750-1831

Ranong was originally settled in the late 18th century by Hokkien Chinese who were hired to work as laborers in the region's tin mines. The area grew rich, and Ranong is now a major border town. From here Thai nationals may travel to Victoria Point in Myanmar (Burma) on a half- or full-day boat trip. Referred to as Kaw Thaung by the Burmese, the town is well known for bargain duty-free goods and handicrafts. Officially, foreigners may not go to Victoria Point without a visa, but this is not always enforced.

In Ranong, the natural hot springs are the main attraction. They rise beside the Khlong Hat Sompen River at Wat Tapotaram, 1,100 yds (1 km) east of the town center, and are channeled into three concrete tubs called Mother, Father, and Child. At an average temperature of 150° F (65° C), the water is unfortunately too hot for bathing. A short walk down the river, the Jansom Thara Spa Resort Hotel has tapped and cooled the water to 110° F (42° C). Those not staying at the hotel can use the spa for a nominal fee.

The coastline around Ranong is covered in thick mangrove forests, which are essential for the area's ecosystem. Guided tours will lead you through the forest, pointing out the varied wildlife en route; just be wary of the boisterous monkeys.

↑ A colorful long-tail boat pulled up on the pristine Phra Nang beach

 10

Ao Nang
อ่าวนาง

🗺 E6 **🚗 11 miles (18 km) W of Krabi Town, Krabi province** **🚌 Krabi, then songthaew** **🛈 Krabi; 0-7562-2163**

Until the early 1980s, fishing and coconut and rubber plantations were the mainstay for the villagers at Ao Nang. Today the 1-mile (1.6-km) sandy beach sports a growing number of hotels, seafood restaurants, scuba diving outlets, and canoe tour companies. Visitors can rent a sea canoe to paddle in the turquoise waters in the shadow of the 330-ft

Did You Know?

Ao Nang Krabi Thai Stadium claims to have the biggest *muay thai* boxing ring in southern Thailand.

(100-m) rocky eastern end of the bay. Nearby is uncrowded Pai Plong beach. In season, Ao Nang is a good base for day trips by long-tail boat to the striking Railay-Phra Nang headland, 2 miles (3 km) to the southeast. Its sheer limestone cliffs, pure white sand, and emerald sea attract many visitors.

Hat Phra Nang, west of the Phra Nang headland, is the most attractive beach in the area. Rising above it is a high limestone cliff into which Tham Phra Nang Nok ("outer princess cave") is carved. Inside is a shrine to the lost spirit of a princess, Phra Nang, whose ship allegedly sank near the beach in the 4th century BC. Inside the cliff is Sa Phra Nang, a lagoon reached by a steep path.

Flanking Phra Nang are the white sand beaches of East and West Railay. There are boats from West Railay and Phra Nang beaches to Ko Poda where striped tiger fish can be fed by hand from the shallow shore, and Ko Hua Khwan, or Chicken Island, farther south.

On Ko Hong, 16 miles (25 km) northwest of Ao Nang, the prized nests of the edible-nest swiftlet are collected from the island's network of caves.

The headquarters of the **Phi Phi-Hat Nopparat Thara National Marine Park**, to the west of Ao Nang, overlook stunning beaches. The park covers 150 sq miles (390 sq km) and takes in Ko Phi Phi (*p334*), Ko Mai Phai, and Ko Yung (also known as Ko Mosquito).

Phi Phi-Hat Nopparat Thara National Marine Park

🗺 Park HQ 2 miles (3 km) W of Ao Nang **🚌 Krabi, then songthaew** **🛈 Krabi office; 0-7562-2163**

 11

Khlong Thom
คลองท่อม

🗺 E6 **🚗 Krabi province** **🚌** **🛈 Krabi; 0-7562-2163**

Some 25 miles (40 km) south of Krabi Town, Khlong Thom is known locally for the small museum within Wat Khlong Thom. The temple's abbot has assembled archeological icons and weapons from the area. The most interesting exhibit is a collection of distinctive beads called *lukbat*.

A maritime port, Kuan Lukbat was once located on the site of Khlong Thom. From the 5th century AD onward, the port was used by foreign merchants and emissaries crossing the peninsula to Nakhon Si Thammarat and Surat Thani *(p318)*. Few traders wanted to sail through the treacherous, pirate-infested Straits of Malacca, so they traveled overland instead.

A bumpy 7.5-mile (12-km) ride inland from Khlong Thom leads to a natural hot spring in the forest – ideal for swimming. About 5 miles (8 km) farther on is the Tung Tieo forest trail in Khao No Chuchi lowland forest. The well-marked paths lead through this protected area, skirting emerald pools. The surrounding woodland is the only known area in the world where the colorful ground-dwelling Gurney's pitta survives. Previously, this bird was thought to be extinct.

12 Ko Lanta
เกาะลันตา

🅰 E6 🅺 Krabi province
🚌 From Krabi or Bo Muang
ℹ Krabi; 0-7562-2163

In the southeast corner of Krabi province, Ko Lanta is a group of 52 islands, 15 of which belong to the Ko Lanta National Marine Park. The ramshackle wooden port of Ban Sala Dan is the gateway to Ko Lanta Yai, a predominantly Muslim fishing island. This is the main island in the archipelago, and it is covered with undulating forested hills sweeping down to numerous west-facing sandy bays. The natural beauty of the island has attracted many resorts, and Ko Lanta Yai is now popular with tourists – particularly the beautiful Long Beach that snakes down the west coast – although there are still some lovely unspoiled beaches, not to mention some of the finest diving in Thailand. The Laem Kaw Kwang headland in the northwest of the island has views across to Ko Phi Phi. At the southern tip, a 2-mile (3-km) coastal trail leads to a solar-powered lighthouse on a promontory beside the park headquarters. Sea gypsies inhabit the nearby village, Ban Sangka-u. They are renowned for their colorful rituals, such as the *loi rua* ceremony. As part of the festivities, a 6-ft (2-m) replica boat is sent out to sea to banish the ill fate built up throughout the past year.

↑ Lanterns glowing on the beach after dark on Ko Lanta Yai

DEEP SOUTH

The Deep South of Thailand has more in common with Malaysia than with the distant Thai heartland to the north. The influence of Indian, Chinese, and Malaysian culture can be seen in the region's architecture and ethnic makeup. The population speaks an unusually intonated dialect of Thai, and Yawi, a language related to Malay and Indonesian. *Nang talung (p355)*, a popular style of shadow puppetry in this region, also has similarities with arts in Malaysia and Indonesia.

South of Songkhla, especially near the coasts, most people are Muslim. Indeed, Pattani, an important Malay kingdom in the 17th century, is still a center of Islamic scholarship. Also, numerous Hindu shrines and customs, not least the Hindu-inspired *manohra* dance, are evidence of Nakhon's role as a major religious center on the ocean trade routes between India and China.

Tourism in the area remains low-key due to spiraling separatist violence perpetrated by Muslim extremists seeking local autonomy. This southern Thailand insurgency originated in the mid-20th century, but became a lot more violent in 2004, resulting in hundreds of deaths. In the troubled southern provinces of Songkhla, Pattani, Yala, and Narathiwat, hostilities are ongoing.

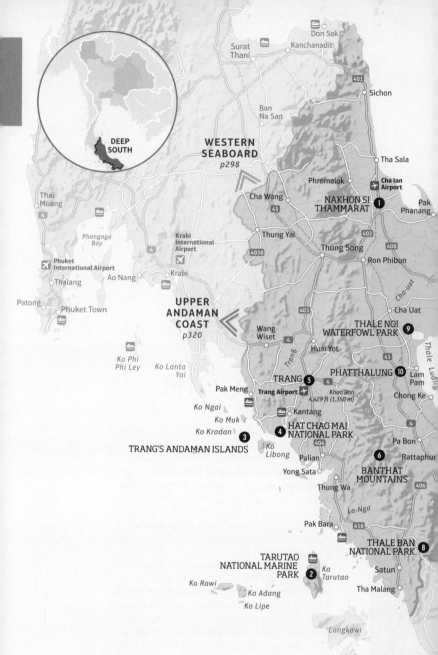

DEEP
SOUTH

WESTERN
SEABOARD
p298

Don Sak
Kanchanadit

Surat
Thani

401

Sichon

Tha Sala

Ban
Na San

Phromalok

Cha Ian
Airport

Cha Wang

41

NAKHON SI
THAMMARAT ①

Pak
Phanang

Thung Yai

403

408

Thai
Muang

4

Krabi
International
Airport

4038

Thung Song

Thung Song

Ron Phibun

Phangnga
Bay

Krabi

Phuket
International Airport

Thalang

Ao Nang

UPPER
ANDAMAN
COAST
p320

Wang
Wiset

4

403

Cha-uat

Cha Uat

THALE NOI
WATERFOWL PARK ⑨

Patong

Phuket Town

Huai Yot

Trang

PHATTHALUNG

41

Lam
Pam

⑩

Ko Phi
Phi Ley

Ko Lanta
Yai

TRANG ⑤

Trang Airport

Khao Ron
4,429 ft (1,350 m)

Chong Ke

Pak Meng

Ko Ngai

Kantang

HAT CHAO MAI
NATIONAL PARK ④

Pa Bon

Ko Muk

Ko Kradan ③

Ko
Libong

404

⑥

Rattaphur

TRANG'S ANDAMAN ISLANDS

Palian

Yong Sata

BANTHAT
MOUNTAINS

406

Thung Wa

La-Ngu

Pak Bara

416

THALE BAN
NATIONAL PARK ⑧

TARUTAO
NATIONAL MARINE
PARK

②

Ko
Tarutao

Satun

Tha Malang

Ko Rawi

Ko Adang

Ko Lipe

Langkawi

Andaman Sea

0 kilometers   40

0 miles   40

N
↑

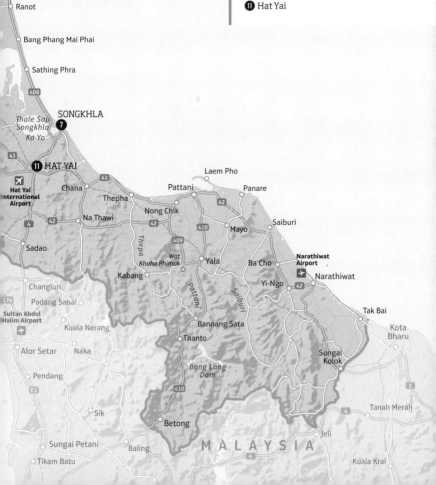

DEEP SOUTH

Must Sees
1. Nakhon Si Thammarat
2. Tarutao National Marine Park

Experience More
3. Trang's Andaman Islands
4. Hat Chao Mai National Park
5. Trang
6. Banthat Mountains
7. Songkhla
8. Thale Ban National Park
9. Thale Noi Waterfowl Park
10. Phatthalung
11. Hat Yai

Gulf of Thailand

Ranot

Bang Phang Mai Phai

Sathing Phra

408

Thale Sap Songkhla Ko Yo

SONGKHLA
7

43

11 HAT YAI

Hat Yai International Airport

Chana

43

Thepha

Laem Pho

Pattani

Panare

42

Nong Chik

42

4 42

Na Thawi

409

410

Mayo

Saiburi

Sadao

Thepa

Wat Khuha Phimuk

Yala

Ba Cho

Narathiwat Airport

Yi-Ngo

42

Narathiwat

Changlun

Kabang

Pattani

Saiburi

176

Padang Sanai

Sultan Abdul Halim Airport

Kuala Nerang

Bannang Sata

Thanto

Tak Bai

Kota Bharu

Alor Setar

Naka

Bang Lang Dam

Sungai Kolok

E1

Pendang

410

Sik

Betong

Jeli

Tanah Merah

4

Sungai Petani

Baling

M A L A Y S I A

3

Tikam Batu

Kuala Krai

❶

NAKHON SI THAMMARAT

นครศรีธรรมราช

🅰 E/F6 🏛 Nakhon Si Thammarat Province ✈ 9 miles (15 km) N of Nakhon 🚍 Yommarat Rd 🚌 Off Karom Rd 🛈 Sanam Na Muang, Rachadamnoen Rd; 0-7534-6516

From the 7th to 13th centuries Nakhon Si Thammarat was an important city of the Srivijaya Empire *(p69)*, when it became a religious center. Although Nakhon – as it is popularly known – is featured on few tourist itineraries, the most historic town in the south is a lively center with several attractions.

①

Tha Chang Road
ถนนท่าช้าง

The tradition of gold and silver shops along this road dates from 1804, when migrants from Saiburi district moved to Nakhon. Only skilled gold- and silversmiths were allowed to settle here, to the west of Sanam Na Muang parade ground. Shops selling woven fabric and local products can also be found here.

②

Wat Phra Mahathat
วัดพระมหาธาตุ

🏛 Rachadamnoen Rd, 1 mile (2 km) S of train station
🕐 Daily

Wat Phra Mahathat is one of Thailand's most sacred temples. Although its age is disputed, the *wat* is thought to be at least 1,500 years old. The Wihan Luang chapel has an intricately painted 18th-century ceiling, and the Wihan Phra Ma hall features an elaborate, emerald-inlay door from the Sukhothai period. A small museum displays an evocative but unlabeled selection of archeological finds, jewelry, and sculptures.

③

Ho Phra I-suan (Shiva)
หอพระอิศวร

🏛 Rachadamnoen Rd
🕐 Daily

In the hall of this shrine is a 3-ft (1-m) *shivalinga*, a phallic image of the Hindu god Shiva, that may date back to the 6th century AD. The worship of Shiva was a potent force in the peninsular city-states of the first millennium AD.

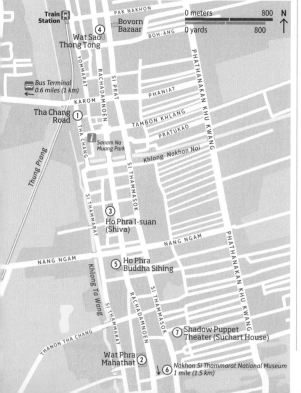

Train Station

PAK NAKHON

Bovorn Bazaar

BOH-ANG

0 meters 800
0 yards 800
N

④ Wat Sao Thong Tong

YOMMARAT

SI PRAT

RACHADAMNOEN

KAROM

PHANIAT

PHATHANAKAN KHU KWANG

Bus Terminal 0.6 miles (1 km)

Tha Chang Road ①

THA CHANG

TAMBON KHLANG

PRATUKAO

🛈 Sanam Na Muang Park

Khlong Nakhon Noi

Thung Prang

SI THAMMASOK

SI THAMMARAT

③ Ho Phra I-suan (Shiva)

NANG NGAM

⑤ Ho Phra Buddha Sihing

NANG NGAM

Khlong To Wong

SI THAMMARAT

RACHADAMNOEN

SI THAMMASOK

PHATHANAKAN KHU KWANG

⑦ Shadow Puppet Theater (Suchart House)

THANON THA CHANG

Wat Phra Mahathat ②

⑥ Nakhon Si Thammarat National Museum 1 mile (1.5 km)

← Bustling area around Wat Phra Mahathat at sunset

India. It was found in the base of a tree in Kapong district near Takua Pha in Phangnga, then a major transit point for Indians colonizing the south.

The Thai gallery displays religious art from Dvaravati and Srivijayan periods to the Rattanakosin era. Look out for Buddha images in the distinctive local Sihing style, characterized by stumpy features and animated faces.

---

 ⑦

Shadow Puppet Theater (Suchart House)
บ้านหนังตะลุงสุชาติ

🏠 10/18 Si Thammasok Soi 3 📞 0-7534-6394
🕐 Daily

The *nang talung (p355)* workshop of Suchart Subsin keeps alive a uniquely Southeast Asian form of entertainment in danger of dying out. Visitors can watch the puppets being cut from leather and buy the finished product. Sometimes impromptu shows are staged.

→ A shadow puppet used for a traditional *nang talung* show

CULTURAL CROSSROADS

For over 2,000 years, the peninsula that is now divided between Malaysia, Thailand, and Myanmar has been a major cultural crossroads. Finds from the Isthmus of Kra (especially the historic trading center of Nakhon Si Thammarat) testify to strong links with China, India, the Middle East, and even the Roman Empire. Many Indian traders settled in Nakhon.

④

Wat Sao Thong Tong
วัดเสาธงทอง

🏠 Rachadamnoen Rd
🕐 Daily

Adjoining the compound of Wang Tawan Tok temple, this ancient *wat*'s main attraction is the traditional southern Thai wooden house, started in 1888 and finished in 1901. It is actually three houses joined together and features delicately carved wooden door panels, gables, and window surrounds.

⑤

Ho Phra Buddha Sihing
หอพระพุทธสิหิงค์

🏠 Rachadamnoen Rd
🕐 8:30am-4:30pm Wed-Sun

The Phra Buddha Sihing is one of Thailand's most revered images. The replica kept in this shrine is of an original cast in Sri Lanka in AD 157 and brought to Nakhon in the 13th century. Local artisans put their stamp on the Buddha by giving it a half smile, a rounder face, and a full chest.

---

⑥

Nakhon Si Thammarat National Museum
พิพิธภัณฑ์แห่งชาตินครศรีธรรมราช

🏠 Rachadamnoen Rd, 1.5 miles (2.5 km) S of train station 📞 0-7534-1075
🕐 9am-4pm Wed-Sun

The centerpiece of this branch of the National Museum is the 9th-century statue of Vishnu in the Pala style of south

②

TARUTAO NATIONAL MARINE PARK

อุทยานแห่งชาติตะรุเตา

🗺️ E7 🏠 Satun province, 14 miles (22 km) from Pak Bara 🚢 From Pak Bara; regular crossings mid-Nov–mid-Apr only ℹ️ Park HQ: 0-7478-3485

Designated as Thailand's second marine national park in 1974, Tarutao National Marine Park comprises 51 islands. This ecologically rich area is famous for its superb diving sites, said to be among the world's best.

↑ Admiring the breathtaking view from a cliff over Ko Lipe

The islands of the Tarutao National Marine Park are the most southwesterly in Thailand, located only 5 miles (8 km) from the Malaysian island of Langkawi. The park includes spectacular, unspoiled scenery, a wide variety of wildlife, and good coral. However, these attractions are accessible to visitors mid-November through mid-April only as monsoon storms make the ferry trip from Pak Bara too risky at other times.

The archipelago, extending over 580 sq miles (1,490 sq km), is a haven for wildlife enthusiasts. Offshore sightings of sperm and minke whales,

Did You Know?

Until the 1960s, the islands had a more sinister reputation as a lair for pirates.

→ The impressive views and turquoise waters of the popular Ko Lipe

dugongs, and dolphins are common. There is also a rich concentration of fish life, with 92 species of coral fish and around 25 percent of all the world's fish species in the surrounding seas.

Island Hopping

The largest island in the group, 16-mile (26-km) long Ko Tarutao, offers the greatest scenic variety. Tropical rainforest covers most of its surface. Most accommodations and the best facilities for visitors are found near the wonderful, pristine beaches of the west coast. Ferries from Pak Bara dock at Ao Phante Malaka, which is where the park headquarters, bungalows, two restaurants, and the island's only store are located. Worthwhile excursions

> The largest island in the group, 16-mile (26-km) long Ko Tarutao, offers the greatest scenic variety.

from here include the half-hour climb to To-bo cliff with its fine views, particularly at sunset, and the 1-mile (2-km) boat trip to the impressive stalagmite-filled Crocodile Cave.

Rugged Ko Adang, 39 miles (62 km) west of the mainland, is thickly forested and has many year-round waterfalls, such as the Rattana falls on the southwest coast. Here, you can take a freshwater rock pool swim. The smaller island of Ko Lipe, 1 mile (2 km) south of Ko Adang, has pleasant footpaths through coconut plantations and the immaculate sands of Pattaya beach. Ko Yang, midway between Rawi and Adang islands, has excellent coral, and Ko Khai ("egg island"), west of Tarutao, is a major breeding ground for sea turtles, hence the island's name.

←

The endangered green sea turtle swimming among the park's colorful coral

EAT

Elephant
This trendy cafe-restaurant is a popular spot for delicious burgers, pastas, and pizzas. A great place for breakfast and coffee, too.

🏠 Walking St, Ko Lipe
🌐 elephantkolipe.com

Ⓑ Ⓑ Ⓑ

Tonkow
For traditional Thai food done well, you can't do much better than this friendly place. Try the *panang* curry.

🏠 Walking St, Ko Lipe
📞 0-8733-26375

Ⓑ Ⓑ Ⓑ

EXPERIENCE MORE

 3

Trang's Andaman Islands

หมู่เกาะตรัง

⚠ E6 ⌂ Trang province 🚌 Long-tail from Kantang to Ko Muk, Ko Kradan, and Ko Libong, and from Pak Meng to Ko Hai and Ko Muk 🛈 Trang; 0-7521-5867

Tourist development has barely touched the 50 or so small islands off the coast of Trang province. Their stunning sands, pristine corals, and rich bird and marine life remain the preserve of a handful of solitude seekers.

Forested Ko Hai, or Ko Ngai, is the island that is most easily reached from Pak Meng on the mainland and it offers a wide choice of accommodations.

There are wonderful beaches here, particularly on the east coast, and also magnificent coral offshore.

Ko Muk, 5 miles (8 km) southeast of Ko Hai, is best known for the attractive Tham Morakhot ("emerald cave") on its west coast. A long limestone tunnel leads from the sea to an inland beach surrounded by vegetation-clad cliffs. It can be entered only by boat at low tide.

Arguably the most beautiful and most remote of Trang's Andaman Islands, Ko Kradan offers white-sand beaches and good snorkeling.

Farther south and close to the mainland, Ko Libong is the largest of the islands. It is famed for its spectacular birdlife, which is at its best during March and April.

 4

Hat Chao Mai National Park

อุทยานแห่งชาติหาดเจ้าไหม

⚠ E6 ⌂ Trang province 🚌 From Trang to Kantang, then *songthaew* 🛈 Trang; 0-7521-5867

Around 31 miles (50 km) west of Trang town, the varied coastal landscape of Hat Chao Mai National Park includes mangrove creeks, coastal karsts, and hidden beaches, accessed through caves around Yao and Yongling beaches. The stunning casuarina trees lining the sandy beach at Pak Meng, in the north of the park, provide good shade and make it a popular spot for families. This is also the main departure point for boat tours around Trang's picturesque islands, nine of which are also under park control. Dugongs (*p353*) can sometimes be spotted between the mainland and the islands.

> **Arguably the most beautiful and remotest of Trang's Andaman islands, Ko Kradan offers white-sand beaches and good snorkeling.**

↑ Swimming in Ko Muk's emerald cave on Trang's Andaman Islands

GREAT VIEW
Forest Canopy Walkway

Get another perspective over Trang's Thung Khai Botanic Garden with a treetop canopy walk, with bridges up to 59 ft (18 m) off the ground, allowing you to spot birds, bats, and trees.

 6

Banthat Mountains
เขาบรรทัด

🅰E/F6 🏠Trang province
ℹ️Trang; 0-7521-5867

The Banthat Mountains, running as far as the Malaysian border, mark the eastern boundary of Trang province.

The forested higher elevations of the mountains at Khao Ron, are one of the few places in south Thailand where the Sakai tribe still maintain their hunter-gatherer existence. These ethnically unique Negrito people live in simple lean-to leaf-and-grass shelters near running water, and hunt with poison blow darts.

The mountains are home to many amphibian and reptile species, including dwarf geckos and wrinkled frogs. Rare birds include spiderhunters, hawk cuckoos, and the narcissus flycatcher. A worthwhile excursion is to the Khao Chong Nature and Wildlife Study Center, 12 miles (20 km) east of Trang, off Highway 4. It contains an impressive open zoo and two waterfalls.

The minor road south along the western flanks of the Banthat Mountains gives access to a series of spectacular waterfalls, caves, and shady picnic places. Highlights include the huge Ton Tay falls, the spray rainbow that often forms by mid-afternoon over the Sairung falls, and the stalactites and stalagmites of Tham Chang Hai ("lost elephant cave") near Muansari village in Nayong district.

 5

Trang
ตรัง

🅰E6 🏠Trang province ➡️🏠
🚌 ℹ️Trang; 0-7521-5867

Trang has been a trading center since at least the 1st century AD. It grew to prosperity between the 7th and 13th centuries during the Srivijaya period and remains an important commercial town today. Rubber, palm oil, and fishing are the mainstays of its economy.

The town has a strong Chinese character (and good Chinese restaurants) as a result of an influx of immigrant labor in the latter half of the 19th century. Trang's Vegetarian Festival, mirroring its better-known counterpart in Phuket (p326), is renowned for the intensity of its ascetic rites, which include body piercing.

A monument to Khaw Sim Bee Na-Ranong, the first governor of Trang from 1890 to 1901, stands in the Fitness Park at the eastern end of Phatthalung Road and attracts many merit-makers. The Clarion MP Hotel is notable for being partially built in the shape of an ocean liner.

The **Thung Khai Botanic Garden**, a day trip from Trang, is a relaxing way to spend an afternoon among lush and rare foliage.

Thung Khai Botanic Garden

📍135 Thung Khai, Yan Ta Khao District 📞0-7529-1456
🕐8am–6:30pm daily

DUGONGS

The once common dugong, or sea cow, was brought to the brink of extinction in Thai waters by hunting and by accidental drowning in commercial fishing nets. Today numbers are slowly increasing. The sea around Trang's Andaman Islands is one of the few places they can be seen. They feed on the seagrass around Ko Libong and the Trang Estuary. They grow up to 10 ft (3 m) long and can weigh 880 lbs (400 kg).

↑ Reflection of Masjid Central Songkhla mosque against a beautiful sunset

STAY

Club Tree Hotel
Traditional hotel with large rooms, an Old World colonial feel in the communal areas, and a lovely garden.

 F6 **165/8 Talay Luang Rd, Songkhla** **0-7431-3888**

ⒷⒷⒷ

Green House at Trang
This fun, bohemian guesthouse has basic but comfortable rooms; all have a balcony.

E6 **148/1 Rama VI Rd, Trang** **0-7521-8411**

ⒷⒷⒷ

S Hadyai
Stylish hotel with a sleek monchrome color scheme, black Chesterfield sofas, and an organic restaurant.

F6/7 **220, Prachathipat Rd, Hat Yai** Ⓦ shadyaihotel.com

ⒷⒷ

Songkhla
สงขลา

F6 **Songkhla province** **Hat Yai, 22 miles (36 km) SW of Songkhla** **Hat Yai; 0-7424-3747**

The cuisine and language of Songkhla reflect its multicultural heritage, and a subtle Portuguese influence is evident in the architecture of the houses along Nakhon Nok and Nakhon Nai roads. Today the city, built on the headland between the Gulf of Thailand and Thale Sap – the country's largest lake – is a fishing port and an administrative and educational center.

Songkhla's main beach, Hat Samila, is pleasant to walk along and it has several good seafood restaurants. Songkhla Aquarium, inland from the beach, is home to leopard sharks and catfish weighing as much as 440 lb (200 kg).

Farther south, at Khao Seng, is a Muslim fishing village where colorful *korlae* fishing boats (painted boats built and decorated by Muslim fishermen for hundreds of years) can be seen. A local myth says that if you can move the Nai Bang's Head boulder on the headland beside the village, you will inherit the gold buried underneath.

The beautiful, evocative building housing the **Songkhla National Museum** is an attraction in itself. It was built in 1878 in the Southern Thai-Chinese style as the residence of deputy Songkhla governor Phraya Suntharanuraksa. A hidden grass courtyard flanks two spiraling staircases leading to the wooden paneled second story, where most exhibits are kept. Highlights include 7th- to 9th-century Dvaravati plinths, Bencharong pottery, earthenware jars recovered from the sea around Songkhla, and Ban Chiang pottery said to date from 3000 BC.

The **Patrsee Museum** in Wat Matchimawat (sometimes called Wat Klang), south of the National Museum, is no less important. Its 14-in (35-cm) stone image of Ganesh, the elephant god, is thought to date from the late 6th century, making it the earliest such image found in the peninsula. Chinese painted enamelware from the Qwing Ching dynasty, 15th-century U Thong wares, and 18th-century European plates all indicate the importance of Songkhla's former maritime trade links.

The city's other main temple, Wat Chai Mongkhon, has a Buddha relic from Sri Lanka buried beneath it.

Songkhla is an attractive city to walk around, taking in

the topiary garden at Khao Noi and the view of Thale Sap from the peak of Khao Tung Kuan. Restaurants and live music bars can be found around Chaiya Road. Also, hidden among the old streets, is beautiful, diverse street art painted by students on the side of buildings.

Standing on the highway linking Hat Yai with Songkhla is the Masjid Central Songkhla mosque. The building is very grand and surrounding views are breathtaking. Vendors sell food underneath the building.

The Prem Tinsulanonda bridge connects Songkhla with the narrow coastal strip to the north. Once the longest bridge in Thailand, it traverses Thale Sap via the island of Ko Yo on the western side of the lake. Ko Yo is home to the excellent **Folklore Museum**, on a hilltop overlooking the lake. The museum, which aims to preserve the rich folk traditions of the south, houses displays on history, ethnology, and religion. Exhibits include fabrics and metalware.

Songkhla National Museum
⊘ ⌂ Wichianchom Rd
📞 0-7431-1728 🕒 Wed–Sun

Patrsee Museum
⊘ ⌂ Wat Matchimawat, Saiburi Rd 🕒 Wed–Sun

Folklore Museum
⊘ ⌂ Institute of Southern Thai Studies, Ko Yo, 8 miles (14 km) SW of Songkhla 🕒 Daily

---

8

Thale Ban National Park
อุทยานแห่งชาติทะเลบัน

🅰 E7 ⌂ Satun province; off Hwy 4184, 23 miles (37 km) from Satun 🚌 Satun, then *songthaew* ℹ Hat Yai; 0-7423-1055

Thale Ban is a lush expanse of dense tropical rainforest scattered with waterfalls that extends over the Banthat Mountains (p353) close to the Malaysian border. It covers only 40 sq miles (102 sq km) but contains a staggering variety of stunning wildlife, including sun bears, tigers, monkeys, gibbons, tapirs, and rare birds such as bat hawks. It's a great spot for adventurers, with a few marked trails, the pretty Yaroy waterfall, 3 miles

(5 km) north of the park headquarters, and several swimming pools. Satun is the nearest town and gateway to the park. It is within easy reach of Pak Bara, from which ferries depart for Tarutao.

NANG TALUNG
Nang talung is the Thai version of shadow puppetry, and performances are an essential part of village life in the Deep South. A single person, the *nai nag* (puppet master), creates the whole show. Sitting behind an illuminated screen, he maneuvers up to six puppets per scene. The puppets are made from leather, or *nang*, which is carved, colored, and rendered movable by joints. The changing tone of the puppeteer's voice differentiates between the characters, while a band of musicians adds tension to the plot.

↑ Wooden gazebo set among lush greenery at Thale Ban National Park

9

Thale Noi Waterfowl Park
อุทยานทะเลน้อย

◩F6 **⬚20 miles (32 km) NE of Phatthalung, Phatthalung province** **▥From Phatthalung, then hire a long-tail** **◷8:30am–4pm daily** **⒤Hat Yai; 0-7423-1055**

The largest wetland bird sanctuary in Thailand, this park serves as a resting and feeding ground for thousands of exotic birds flying to Sumatra and Australia to escape winter in Siberia and China. The best way to explore the watery preserve, covering 12 sq miles (30 sq km), is by long-tail boat, which can be hired from Phatthalung for a two-hour round trip.

Thale Noi has the appearance of a swamp, but it is predominantly a freshwater lake, with a depth of up to 5 ft

100,000

The number of birds that live in Thale Noi Waterfowl Park between January and April.

Buildings on stilts over the reserve at Thale Noi Waterfowl Park, home to purple swamp hens and lotus (inset) ↑

(1.5 m). Only in periods of high southerly winds does the lake become brackish, when saltier water from Thale Luang and Songkhla Lake to the south is pushed northward. Many of the 150 or so species of birds who visit the park arrive during January and April, swelling its population to as much as 100,000. In May the population begins to shrink, and from October to December there are only small numbers of native species left. A viewing platform in the lake is the ideal place for bird-watching. Among the birds here are the purple swamp hen, bronze-winged jaćana, whistling teal, white-throated kingfisher, the long-legged *nok i-kong*, and the white ibis.

One of the major forms of vegetation in the park is *don kok*, a reed which the *nok i-kong* use to build "platforms."

Around 100 families live along the shores of Thale Noi, mostly in raised wooden houses. They make a living from fishing and by weaving bulrush reeds into mats.

10

Phatthalung
พัทลุง

◩F6 **⬚Phatthalung province** **▣▥▤** **⒤Hat Yai; 0-7423-1055**

One of the few rice-growing areas in southern Thailand, Phatthalung province has earned a steady income from the crop throughout its history. It is better known, though, as

> 💬 **INSIDER TIP**
> **Security**
>
> At the time of writing, there are warnings against all but essential travel to areas in the Deep South, particularly Pattani, Narathiwat, Yala, and southern Songkhla province. Always check the latest travel advice before your trip (p360).

the place where *nang talung* (shadow puppetry) was first performed in Thailand (*p355*). The name *nang talung* may even derive from Phatthalung.

Phatthalung town was established in the 19th century during the reign of Rama III. Today's modern town is set out in a grid and is surrounded by limestone hills to the north and the fertile Thale Luang lake to the east.

Phatthalung lies between two peaks: Khao Ok Talu ("punctured chest mountain") to the northeast, and Khao Hua Taek ("broken head mountain") to the northwest. According to local legend, these two mountains, "the mistress" and "the wife," fought over Khao Muang (the male mountain), located to the north. It is said that they still nurse their battle scars from this confrontation. In fact, Khao Ok Talu has a naturally occurring tunnel in its peak (the punctured chest), while Khao Hua Taek has a dent

in its peak (the broken head). In the latter are the Buddhist grottoes of Wat Tham Kuha Sawan. Inside the lower cave are statues of monks and the Buddha, while the upper cave has views of Khao Ok Talu and most of Phatthalung and the surrounding area.

Ideal for relaxation while taking in stunning scenery, just outside Phattalung at the foot of Khao Chaison are the Khao Chaison Hot Springs and Cold Stream.

Hat Yai
หาดใหญ่

F6/7 **Songkhla province** **7 miles (12 km) W of Hat Yai** **1/1 Soi 2, Niphat U-thit Rd, Hat Yai; 0-7424-3747**

Hat Yai wins no prizes for beauty. It has grown affluent due to its strategic railroad junction, its cut-price products, and a constant flow of Malaysian tourists who converge on the city on weekends to enjoy its dining, shopping, and nightlife. Malay, English,

Yawi, Hokkien, Mandarin, and the clipped syllables of southern Thai dialect can be heard around the cosmopolitan downtown area. Be aware that some parlors here advertising "ancient massage" will probably offer more than a quick rubdown.

Hat Yai's cultural attractions are few, so most visitors spend daylight hours shopping in Thailand's third-largest city. Electrical goods at the Kim Yong market, durians and apples from street vendors, and Bangkok-made fashions in the department stores are a few of Hat Yai's popular buys. Hat Yai Municipal Park is a fantastic area to relax in for its fantastic scenery, especially at sunset. It features an 82-ft (25-m) tall Buddha image to marvel at, and also offers various playgrounds and food stalls.

Wat Hat Yai Nai, 1 mile (1.6 km) west of the city center, has the third-largest reclining Buddha image in the world, 115 ft (35 m) long and 49 ft (15 m) high. You can walk inside the image via a shrine room. Saunas and massages are offered in the temple grounds.

→
The enormous standing Buddha located in Hat Yai Municipal Park

NEED TO KNOW

Traveling by boat on Ko Phi Phi

BEFORE
YOU GO

Forward planning is essential to any successful trip. Be prepared for all eventualities by considering the following points before you travel.

AT A GLANCE

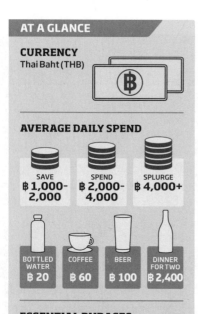

CURRENCY
Thai Baht (THB)

AVERAGE DAILY SPEND

SAVE	SPEND	SPLURGE
฿ 1,000–2,000	฿ 2,000–4,000	฿ 4,000+

BOTTLED WATER	COFFEE	BEER	DINNER FOR TWO
฿ 20	฿ 60	฿ 100	฿ 2,400

ESSENTIAL PHRASES

Note: Thai uses a politeness particle at the end of each phrase. Men should add *kap* and women should add *kha* to all the phrases below.

Hello	sawat dee
Please	chuay noi
Thank you	cop khun
I don't understand	mai cow jai

ELECTRICITY SUPPLY

Standard voltage is 220v. Power sockets fit both round and flat pins, and are of type A, B, C, F, and O.

Passports and Visas

Most travelers, including citizens of the UK, US, Australia, and the EU, can enter Thailand for up to 30 days without a pre-arranged visa. For those arriving by land borders, sometimes only 15 days are given. If you are planning to stay for more than 30 days, you will need to apply for a visa from a Thai embassy or consulate abroad. If you are planning on traveling to Vientiane *(p272)* in Laos, a visa is issued on arrival at Wattay Airport for a fee of US$35. Two passport photos are required for this. Visa requirements change regularly, however, and it's strongly advised to check the latest regulations from the **Thailand Immigration Police** or your nearest Thai embassy.

Thailand Immigration Police
🌐 immigration.go.th

Travel Safety Advice

Visitors can get up-to-date travel safety information from the **UK Foreign and Commonwealth Office**, the **US State Department**, and the **Australian Department of Foreign Affairs and Trade**.
AUS
🌐 smartraveller.gov.au
UK
🌐 gov.uk/foreign-travel-advice
US
🌐 travel.state.gov

Customs Information

There are stiff penalties for the possession of illegal drugs. Thailand also has strict regulations around the export of antiques and Buddha images without authorization. On entering the country, you'll need to fill in a customs declaration. An individual is permitted to carry the following into Thailand for personal use:
Tobacco products 200 cigarettes or 250 g of tobacco or cigars.
Alcohol 1 liter of wine or spirits.
Gifts Worth up to 10,000 Baht.
Cash US$20,000 or more must be declared.

Insurance

A general travel insurance policy is highly advisable. Make sure that, in addition to illness, injury, and theft, it covers medical evacuation in case of an emergency. Note that some policies list "hazardous activities" that are not covered, such as motorcycle riding or zip-lining.

Vaccinations

There are no legal immunization requirements unless you are traveling from a country known to be infected with yellow fever. However, it is a good idea to be immunized against polio, tetanus, typhoid, and hepatitis A. BCG (tuberculosis), hepatitis B, rabies, diphtheria, and Japanese encephalitis vaccinations are recommended for people visiting remote or rural areas, or for those who are staying for more than two to three weeks. Check the latest vaccination requirements with your doctor 4–6 weeks before traveling. Some remote areas also carry a risk of malaria and dengue fever; discuss prophylactics with your doctor before traveling.

Money

The official currency is the Thai Baht. Foreign currency may be accepted, but the rate of exchange will not be favorable. Most establishments catering to tourists accept major credit, debit, and pre-paid currency cards. Thai Baht can be withdrawn using major cards at many ATMs, although service charges can be levied. Foreign currency can be exchanged at banks for a better rate than at hotels.

Booking Accommodations

Most accommodations can be booked online, and this is especially advised during the high season in November–January and during Songkran (*p67*) and other festivals, when prices can increase. When checking into a hotel, you'll have to present your passport so that the hotel can register your presence with the local police.

Travelers with Specific Needs

While facilities for visitors with disabilities are good in Bangkok and other large cities, they are almost non-existent in small towns and rural areas. Every MRT station in Bangkok has lifts and wheelchair access, and many many high end hotels are well equipped to accommodate those with special needs. Neither trains nor buses are fully accessible, so hiring a car and driver is the best option. The following agencies make specialist arrangements:

Accessible Journeys
W disabilitytravel.com
Disability Horizons
W disabilityhorizons.com
Disability Travel Advice
W disabledtraveladvice.co.uk

Language

The official language is Thai, but basic English is widespread, although not guaranteed. Cell phone apps offering voice to voice translation can come in handy.

Closures

Public holidays Most offices and businesses close. The major national holiday is Songkran, when much of the country closes for 3–7 days.

Opening times Banks and offices usually close over the weekend.

Museums Most museums shut for public holidays, and one day a week, usually Monday.

PUBLIC HOLIDAYS	
Jan 1	New Year's Day
Feb 10	Makha Bucha Holiday
Apr 6	Chakri Day
Apr 12–14	Songkran Festival
May 6	Visakha Bucha Day
May 13	Royal Ploughing Ceremony
Jul 5	Asanha Bucha Day
Jul 6	Khao Phansa Day
Jul 28	King Vajiralongkorn's Birthday
Aug 12	Her Majesty the Queen's Birthday
Oct 13	Passing of His Majesty the Late King Bhumibol
Oct 23	Chulalongkorn Memorial Day
Dec 5	His Majesty the Late King's Birthday
Dec 10	Constitution Day
Dec 31	New Year's Eve

GETTING
AROUND

Whether you are visiting for a short city break, heading for the beaches, or trekking in the mountains, discover how best to reach your destination.

TRANSPORTATION COSTS

Typical transportation costs from Bangkok to either Chiang Mai or Phuket by:

TRAIN

฿ **1,250-1,900**

One way to Chiang Mai

"VIP" BUS

฿ **950-1,250**

One way

PLANE

฿ **1,250-2,850**

One way

SPEED LIMIT

RURAL ROADS

50 mph
(80 km/h)

URBAN AREAS

25 mph
(40 km/h)

MAJOR HIGHWAYS AND EXPRESSWAYS

70 mph
(110 km/h)

Arriving by Air

Most international travelers arrive at Bangkok's Suvarnabhumi Airport, although long haul flights also fly directly to Phuket and Chiang Mai. International flights from within the region also arrive in Ko Samui, Krabi, Don Mueang (Bangkok), U-Tapao (Pattaya), Chiang Rai and Udon Thani. Domestic flights are relatively inexpensive, with several budget carriers, such as **Air Asia** and **Nok Air**, vying for your business. For information on getting to and from the main airports, see the table opposite. There is also the Suvarnabhumi Airport Rail Link (SARL) which leaves from the basement of the airport terminal and provides transfers into the city.
Air Asia
W airasia.com
Nok Air
W nokair.com

Arriving by Land

Thailand has numerous border crossings with Laos, Myanmar (Burma), Cambodia, and Malaysia. The most heavily used crossing is that between Nong Khai and Vientiane in Laos, which is served by trains from Bangkok. It is not recommended to enter Thailand from Myanmar via any of the land routes.

Train Travel

Domestic Train Travel

Thailand has an efficient railroad system, with four major lines connecting Bangkok with the north, northeast, east, and south. Trip times are similar, sometimes even longer, than by bus, and the number of towns on the network is limited. The main station in Bangkok is Hua Lamphong, which serves all four major lines. The first line runs to Chiang Mai via the Central Plains. A second runs to Nong Khai and Ubon Ratchathani in northeast Thailand. A third connects Bangkok to the Eastern Seaboard and Cambodia, and a fourth runs to Malaysia. Thon Buri Station in Bangkok Noi is the principal departure point for trains to Kanchanaburi.

GETTING TO AND FROM THE AIRPORT

Airport	Distance to city	Taxi fare	Transportation	Journey time
Suvarnabhumi	19 miles (30 km)	400 Baht	bus	40 mins
Don Mueang	15 miles (25 km)	300 Baht	bus	40 mins
Chiang Mai	15 miles (25km)	150 Baht	bus	15 mins
Chiang Rai	6 miles (10 km)	150 Baht	bus	15 mins
Nan	3 miles (5 km)	100 Baht	none	10 mins
Mae Hong Son	1.5 miles (2 km)	100 Baht	none	5 mins
Udon Thani	4 miles (7 km)	150 Baht	bus	15 mins
Ubon	3 miles (5 km)	100 Baht	bus	10 mins
Phuket	9 miles (30 km)	500 Baht	bus	40 mins
Ko Samui	6 miles (10 km)	500 Baht	bus	20 mins
Krabi	12 miles (20 km)	300 Baht	bus	30 mins

A train timetable in English is available from Hua Lamphong Station. You can buy train tickets in advance here or from travel agents. Be aware that trains at weekends and holidays can be sold out days in advance. Fares depend on the speed of the train and the class of the carriage. First class consists of individual cabins with air-conditioning, while second-class coaches have reclining seats and a choice of fans or air-conditioning. Sleepers in second class have individual seats that are converted into curtained-off beds at night. Toilets (there should be at least one Western toilet) and washing facilities are at the end of coaches. Most people find that second class is comfortable enough for long distances and far more relaxing than a bus.

International Train Travel
The only international route from Thailand is to the south, through Malaysia. Domestic and international rail tickets can be booked from the **State Railway of Thailand**.
State Railway of Thailand
W railway.co.th

Public Transportation

Long-Distance Buses
Long-distance buses can often be faster than trains. Buses run from the eastern (Ekamai), northern (Morchit), and southern (Pin Klao) bus terminals in Bangkok. Most provincial capitals can be reached direct from Bangkok. Large cities such as Chiang Mai, Phitsanulok, Khorat, and Surat Thani also act as transit hubs, with both long-distance and local connections. All vehicles are air-conditioned, with a toilet, reclining seats, and plenty of leg room. "VIP" buses have the best facilities, including free refreshments. Overnight services can get rather chilly, but blankets should be provided on buses. Video entertainment can be loud so bring ear plugs or ear buds for your phone. It's best to book in advance at peak periods, but otherwise you can simply turn up at the coach station at least half an hour before departure.

Public Buses
BMTA runs an extensive bus network in Bangkok with very cheap fares. Most routes operate 4am–10pm, with a few providing 24-hour service. Buses can get stuck in heavy traffic, so it's best to take an air-conditioned (AC) bus. Minibuses (MB) also run in the city.
BMTA
W bmta.co.th/en/bus-lines

Bangkok's Rapid Transit Systems
Bangkok has two urban mass transit systems, the BTS Skytrain and the MRT, a subway. Between them, they cover all of the city, and are always expanding their routes. They are quite crowded during rush hour, but are a great way to beat Bangkok's notorious traffic jams. Fares are distance-based but never expensive, and you can buy stored-value or term cards.

Local Transportation

Transportation in the provinces is certainly less frenetic than in Bangkok: bicycle rickshaws (samlors) and colorful tuk-tuks run alongside services such as songthaews, and bargaining for the fare on these is part of the Thai experience. Do not climb on before agreeing a price, or you may be taken for a ride in more ways than one. The one city outside of Bangkok to run its own bus service is Chiang Mai, but the most convenient form of transportation in most towns and resorts is the ubiquitous songthaew.

Songthaews

Songthaews (literally translated as "two rows") are vans with two rows of seats in the back. They are more common than city buses outside of Bangkok and run popular routes for set fares, typically between 20 and 40 Baht, or can be chartered for negotiable rates.

Samlors and tuk-tuks

Samlors are three-wheeled vehicles that can transport one or two people up to a few kilometers. Motorized samlors are known as tuk-tuks, and riding in one is an essential part of the Thai experience. In heavy traffic or during the rainy season, tuk-tuks can be uncomfortable and unstable, but are always popular.

Taxis

Meter taxis operate in Bangkok, Chiang Mai, Chiang Rai, Hat Yai, and Pattaya and are distinguishable by the "Taxi Meter" sign on the roof. In non-meter taxis, mainly found in Ko Samui and Phuket, you need to bargain for the fare before getting in. However, be aware that taxi scams are quite common. A short journey costs about 60 Baht. Grab, an app-based taxi similar to Uber, is gaining in popularity in most Thai cities due to better fares and service. Taxis and motorbike taxis are the most convenient ways to get around the Thai islands.

Boats and Ferries

In Bangkok, the **Chao Phraya River Express** is a good way to savor some fresh breeze and get to various points along the river, or cross to the Thon Buri side. Fares are fixed and inexpensive. On the beaches, long-tail boats can transport you to yet another beach, or just for a cruise. Bargaining here is obligatory.

Chao Phraya River Express
🔲 chaophrayaexpressboat.com/en/home

Boats to the Islands

Regular services are available to Ko Samui, Ko Pha Ngan, and Ko Tao from Chumphon and Surat Thani. Ko Phi Phi is served by ferries from Phuket and Krabi. A regular daily service ferries cars and passengers between Laem Ngop and Ko Chang. Smaller islands have less regular services, sometimes just a makeshift ferry run by local fishermen. Travel agents will be able to give you rough timetables, but these will vary. Be aware that many services stop in the rainy season, June through September. Some companies offer deals on train and boat tickets combining Bangkok and the islands of Ko Samui, Ko Pha Ngan, and Ko Tao. The following ferry operators are reputable:

Lomprayah
🔲 lomprayah.com
Seatran Discovery Ferry
🔲 seatrandiscovery.com
Songserm Express Boat
🔲 songserm.com

Driving

Driving in Thailand is not for the faint-hearted. Hazards come in the form of potholed roads, confusing intersections, and dangerous driving. However, the main expressways, prefixed "AH" (Asia Highway), are excellent, with rest areas, shops, and refreshments. For those visitors who want to explore away from the usual tour routes, but are concerned about their ability to drive here, the best option may be to hire a car with a driver who is used to the roads.

Car Rental

International car rental firms operate in Bangkok and provincial capitals, and can rent either self-drive or chauffeured vehicles. Using a foreign driving license, which is valid for 60 days in Thailand, you can easily rent a car from the following services:

Avis
🔲 avisthailand.com
Hertz
🔲 hertzthailand.com
Budget
🔲 budget.co.th

Rules of the Road

Driving in Thailand is on the left. The standard international road rules apply, but are of little interest to Thais. The only consistent rule of thumb is that "size wins." The eccentric use of indicators and headlights can be unnerving. A left signal can indicate to another driver that it is fine to pass, while a right signal can indicate hazardous oncoming traffic, and a flash of the headlights means: "I'm coming through."

Horns are not used enough as Thais tend to see them as impolite, and "road rage" incidents often start with a honk. Drivers think nothing of straddling lanes and passing on curves and up hill. Yield to larger vehicles at unmarked intersections, and be careful of motorcycles that emerge from side roads without stopping. On rural roads, you should beware of animals coming out into the road. Drive slowly through army checkpoints in border areas, and be prepared to stop. Traffic fines are most commonly imposed for illegal turns, and if you get a ticket and your license is taken, go to the local police station (the address of which will be on the ticket) and pay the fine.

Motorbikes

Thailand is a famous destination for aficionados of motorcycle touring. If you possess the requisite skills and experience, the north of the country is unrivaled for this activity. Motorbikes are also a great way to get around the Thai islands. At the other end of the spectrum, the warm weather can tempt the inexperienced rider to hop on an automatic scooter and head off in sandals, often helmetless, sometimes with tragic results. Motorcycle accidents are the highest cause of injury and death of foreigners in Thailand. Quite simply put: if you are not an experienced motorcyclist, don't start here.

Note that many travel insurance policies exclude motorcycle accidents from coverage as "high risk activities." If you choose to rent a motorcycle in Thailand, note that you will be renting from small entrepreneurs whose service standards vary. Insurance is optional, and any damage to the bike will be charged to you.

Few tourists who rent small motorbikes have motorcycle licenses, making them a sure target for traffic police checkpoints.

Cycling

A pleasant way to explore Thailand is on a bicycle. One of the most popular routes follows the flow of the Mekong River from Chiang Khan to Nong Khai, or even right round to Ubon. Not only is cycling environmentally sound, it offers the chance of meaningful encounters with local people along the way. Guesthouses and small agencies often have bicycles for rent. **SpiceRoads** offers guided cycling tours across the country, and **Smiling Albino** offers deluxe tours in and around Bangkok.

Though traffic on main roads can be dangerous to negotiate, it is possible to put a bike on a bus or train and head for quieter rural areas. Use a mountain bike with fat tires and explore the unpaved roads which are traffic-free. The best time to cycle in Thailand is November through February, when temperatures are cooler, particularly in the north, although cycling in the rainy season is worth considering, since there is frequently cloud cover, tropical storms tend to pass over quickly, and the landscapes are at their most lush at this time.

Spice Roads
w spiceroads.com
Smiling Albino
w smilingalbino.com

ROAD JOURNEY PLANNER

This map is a handy reference for road travel times between some of the most popular destinations in Thailand, with typical journey times below.

Bangkok to Hua Hin	2 hrs
Bangkok to Kanchanaburi	2.5 hrs
Bangkok to Trat	4 hrs
Bangkok to Phuket	12 hrs
Bangkok to Surat Thani	9 hrs
Bangkok to Chiang Mai	9 hrs
Chiang Mai to Mae Hong Son	6 hrs
Chiang Mai to Chiang Rai	3 hrs
Chiang Rai to Nan	4 hrs
Chiang Mai to Nong Khai	10 hrs
Nong Khai to Ubon	6 hrs
Ubon to Bangkok	9 hrs

PRACTICAL
INFORMATION

A little local know-how goes a long way in Thailand. Here you will find all the essential advice and information you will need during your stay.

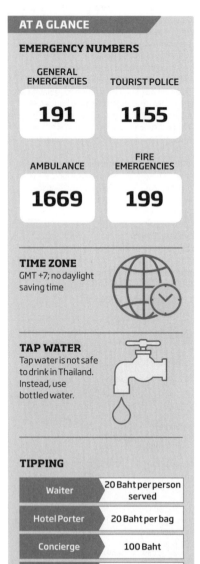

AT A GLANCE

EMERGENCY NUMBERS

GENERAL EMERGENCIES	TOURIST POLICE
191	**1155**

AMBULANCE	FIRE EMERGENCIES
1669	**199**

TIME ZONE
GMT +7; no daylight saving time

TAP WATER
Tap water is not safe to drink in Thailand. Instead, use bottled water.

TIPPING

Waiter	20 Baht per person served
Hotel Porter	20 Baht per bag
Concierge	100 Baht
Taxi Driver	Round up 10 Baht

Personal Security

Though traveling in Thailand is generally quite safe, there are some basic precautions that should be followed. Since petty crimes such as bag-snatching from passing motorcycles and pickpocketing in crowded areas do happen in larger cities, it's best to avoid carrying large sums of money or wearing much jewelry. Keep part of your cash and a copy of your passport in a hidden money belt, and leave your passport and valuables in your hotel's safe. Avoid touts and other hustlers. The area outside the Grand Palace in Bangkok is notorious for touts.

Due to the ongoing insurgency in areas around the Thai/Malay border, including Pattani, Yala, Betong, Narathiwat, and the southern Songkhla province, it is strongly advised to avoid traveling to these areas unless absolutely essential. Always check the latest travel advice before planning your trip (p360).

Health

Thailand's health-care system is fairly good, with several public and private hospitals in Bangkok, and top-notch doctors who speak good medical English. Outside the capital the best facilities are in large towns.

There are many well-stocked pharmacies in Bangkok, other big cities, and resort areas. They are all supplied with up-to-date medications and can dispense antibiotics over the counter without a prescription. Nonetheless, if you require a specific medication, bring a supply with you, with prescription labels. In small towns pharmacies have fewer supplies.

Stomach upsets caused by unfamiliarity with the food, or contaminated water, are common. Choose food stalls that are popular with locals.

Acclimatization to the sometimes oppressive humidity and heat of Thailand can often take longer than expected. It is wise to drink plenty of bottled water, rest in the shade, and avoid the midday sun for the first few days.

Sandflies and mosquitoes are a problem on the many islands, particularly Ko Chang, so take precautions and invest in insect repellent.

Smoking, Alcohol, and Drugs

Smoking is officially prohibited in most indoor public areas, including malls, restaurants, and bars. Smoking and the use of e-cigarettes is also banned on most beaches. Importation or sale of e-cigarettes is illegal. Thailand has a limit of 0.50mg/l of alcohol when driving, and fines are stiff. Possession of illegal drugs, including cannabis, risks a long prison sentence.

ID

By law you must carry photo identification at all times. A photocopy of your passport photo page and visa page is acceptable and means you can leave your passport in your hotel's safe.

Local Customs

Thais are known for their tolerance, amiability, and helpfulness. Nonetheless, there are a few local values to bear in mind. Direct confrontation and aggressive behavior are considered particularly inappropriate. The monarchy, past and present, is protected by local reverence, and the strict, draconian lèse-majesté laws, so avoid any mention of the royal family. The head is considered a sacred part of the body, so do not touch people's heads, and avoid pointing your feet (which are considered lowly) at people or religious icons when seated. Always remove your shoes when entering a home. Wearing shorts, men going shirtless in public, and women going topless on the beach, are all considered impolite.

LGBT+ Safety

Homosexuality is increasingly accepted in Thailand, particularly in Bangkok, though public displays of affection should be avoided. There are established, vibrant gay scenes in Bangkok, Phuket, and Pattaya. **Utopia Asia** is a great source of information for LGBT+ travelers.

Utopia Asia
ⓦ utopia-asia.com

Visiting Buddhist Temples

Visitors are welcome in Thai *wats*, but act and take photos respectfully, and dress modestly. Shorts and sleeveless shirts are not appropriate, and remove your shoes before entering. Greet monks with a smile and a nod. Women are not permitted to hand anything directly to a monk.

Cell Phones and Wi-Fi

Thailand uses the GSM 4G cell phone and data system, so if your cell phone is "quad band" it should work here. To be sure, check with your local service provider before departure. Alternatively, it is possible to buy a cell phone cheaply, and prepaid SIM cards can be purchased in any convenience store. Wi-Fi is available in virtually all accommodations, as well as many cafes, restaurants, and malls.

Post

Thailand has a reliable postal system, and stamps are available at all post offices and at many hotels. Letters and postcards usually take at least one week to reach Europe and North America. Packages should be sent by registered mail or via International Express Mail Service (EMS). DHL, FEDEX, and UPS are all available in large towns and cities.

Taxes and Refunds

Thailand imposes a 7 percent Value Added Tax (VAT) on goods and services. There is a VAT refund scheme for visitors who are in the country for less than 180 days. Look out for shops displaying a "VAT Refund for Tourists" sign to find out more.

WEBSITES AND APPS

tourismthailand.org
An informative website run by the government-operated Tourism Authority of Thailand (TAT), which has 35 offices throughout the country.
Amazing Thailand
An app-based version of TAT.
Google Translate
This essential app offers voice to voice and written translation.
Grab Taxi
Similar to Uber, this app will get you good rates on independent taxis.

INDEX

Page numbers in **bold** refer to main entries

Index

PHRASE BOOK

Thai is a tonal language and regarded by most linguists as head of a distinct language group, though it incorporates many Sanskrit words from ancient India, and some of modern English ones, too. There are five tones: mid, high, low, rising, and falling. The particular tone, or pitch, at which each syllable is pronounced deter-mines its meaning. For instance "mâi" (falling tone) means "not," but "ma˘i" (rising tone) is "silk." The Thai script, meanwhile, is one of the most elaborate in the world, running left to right and using over 80 letters. In the third column of this phrase book is a phonetic transliteration for English speakers, including guidance for tones in the form of accents. This differs from the system used elsewhere in the guide, which follows the Thai Royal Institute's recommended romanization of common names.

GUIDELINES FOR PRONUNCIATION

When reading the phonetics, pronounce syllables as if they form English words. For instance:

a	as in "**a**go"
e	as in "h**e**n"
i	as in "th**i**n"
o	as in "**o**n"
u	as in "g**u**n"
ah	as in "r**a**ther"
ai	as in "Th**ai**"
air	as in "p**air**"
ao	as in "M**ao** Zedong"
ay	as in "d**ay**"
er	as in "ent**er**"
ew	as in "f**ew**"
oh	as in "g**o**"
oo	as in "b**oo**t"
OO	as in "b**oo**k"
oy	as in "t**oy**"
g	as in "**g**ive"
ng	as in "si**ng**"

These sounds have no close equivalents in English:

eu	can be likened to a sound of disgust – the sound could be written as "**errgh**"
bp	a single sound between a "b" and a "p"
dt	a single sound between a "d" and a "t"

Note that when "p," "t," and "k" occur at the end of Thai words, the sound is "swallowed." Also note that many Thais use an "l" instead of an "r" sound.

THE FIVE TONES

Accents indicate the tone of each syllable.

no mark	The **mid tone** is voiced at the speaker's normal, even pitch.
á é í ó ú	The **high tone** is pitched slightly higher than the mid tone.
à è ì ò ù	The **low tone** is pitched slightly lower than the mid tone.
a˘ e˘ i˘ o˘ u˘	The **rising tone** sounds like a questioning pitch, starting low and rising.
â ê î ô û	The **falling tone** sounds similar to an English speaker stressing a one-syllable word for emphasis.

MALE AND FEMALE POLITE FORMS

In polite speech, Thai men add the particle "**krúp**" at the end of each sentence; women add "**ká**" at the end of questions and "**kâ**" at the end of statements. These particles have been omitted from all but the most essential polite terms in this phrase book, but they should be used as much as possible. The polite forms of the word "I" are, for men, "**po˘m**" and, for women, "**dee-chún**."

IN AN EMERGENCY

Help!	ช่วยด้วย	chôo-ay dôo-ay!
Fire!	ไฟไหม้	fai mâi!
Where is the nearest hospital?	แถวนี้มีโรงพยาบาล อยู่ที่ไหน	ta˘ir-o née mee rohng pa-yahbahn yòo têe nai?
Call an ambulance!	เรียกรถพยาบาลให้หน่อย	rêe-uk rót pa-yah bahn hâi nòy!
Call the police!	เรียกตำรวจให้หน่อย	rêe-uk dtum ròo-ut hâi nòy!
Call a doctor!	เรียกหมอให้หน่อย	rêe-uk mo˘r hâi nòy!

COMMUNICATION ESSENTIALS

Yes.	ใช่ or ครับ/ค่ะ	châi or krúp/kâ
No.	ไม่ใช่ or ไม่ครับ/ไม่ค่ะ	mâi châi or mâi krúp/mâi kâ
May I have ...?	ขอ......	ko˘r ...?
Please can you ...?	ช่วย.....	chôo-ay ...?
Thank you.	ขอบคุณ (ครับ/ค่ะ)	kòrp -kOOn (krúp/ka)
No, thank you.	ไม่เอา ขอบคุณ	mâi ao kòrp-kOOn
Excuse me/sorry.	ขอโทษ (ครับ/ค่ะ)	ko˘r-tôht (krúp/kâ)
Never mind	ไม่เป็นไร	mâi bpen rai
Hello.	สวัสดี (ครับ/ค่ะ)	sa-wùt dee (krúp/kâ)
Goodbye.	ลาก่อนนะ	lah gòrn ná
Here.	ที่นี่	têe-nêe
There.	ที่โน่น	têe-nûn
What?	อะไร	a-rai?
Why?	ทำไม	tum-mai?
Where?	ที่ไหน	têe na˘i?
How?	ยังไง	yung ngai?

USEFUL PHRASES

How are you?	คุณสบายดีหรือ(ครับ/ค่ะ)	kOOn sa-bai dee reu (krúp/kâ)?
Very well, thank you – and you?	สบายดี(ครับ/ค่ะ) -แล้วคุณล่ะ	sa-bai dee (krúp/kâ) - láir-o kOOn lâ?
What is your name?	คุณชื่ออะไร(ครับ/ค่ะ)	kOOn chêu a-rai (krúp/kâ)?
My name is ...	(ผม/ดิฉัน)ชื่อ......	(po˘m/dee-chún) chêu...
Where is/are ...?	...อยู่ที่ไหน	...yòo têe-na˘i?
How do I get to...?	ไป...ยังไง?	Bpai...yung- ngai?
Do you speak English?	คุณพูดภาษาอังกฤษ เป็นมั๊ย	kOOn pôot pah-sa˘h ung-grit bpen mái?
I understand.	เข้าใจ	kâo-jai
I don't understand.	ไม่เข้าใจ	mâi kâo-jai
Could you speak slowly?	ช่วยพูดช้าช้าหน่อย ได้มั๊ย	chôo-ay pôot cháhcháh nòy dâi mái?
I can't speak Thai.	พูดภาษาไทยไม่เป็น	pôot pah-sa˘h tai mâi bpen
I don't know.	ไม่ทราบ or ไม่รู้	mâi sâhp or mâi ròo

USEFUL WORDS

woman/women	ผู้หญิง	pôo-y˘ing
man/men	ผู้ชาย	pôo-chai
child/children	เด็ก	dèk

big	ใหญ่	*yài*
small	เล็ก	*lék*
hot	ร้อน	*rórn*
cold	หนาว	*yen or nǎ·o*
good	ดี	*dee*
bad	ไม่ดี	*mâi dee*
enough	พอ	*por*
open	เปิด	*bpèrt*
closed	ปิด	*bpit*
left	ซ้าย	*sái*
right	ขวา	*kwǎ·h*
straight ahead	อยู่ตรงหน้า	*yòo dtrong nâh*
between	ระหว่าง	*ra-wàhng*
on the corner of	ตรงหัวมุม	*dtrong hǒo·a mOOm*
near	ใกล้	*glâi*
far	ไกล	*glai*
up	ขึ้น	*kêun*
down	ลง	*long*
early	เช้า	*cháo*
late	ช้า or สาย	*cháh or sǎ·i*
entrance	ทางเข้า	*tahng kâo*
exit	ทางออก	*tahng òrk*
toilet	ห้องน้ำ	*hôrng nâhm*
free/no charge	ฟรี	*free*

TELEPHONING

I'd like to buy a SIM card for this phone.	(ผม/ดิฉัน) อยากซื้อ ซิมสำหรับมือถือ เมืองนี้	*(pǒm/dee-chún) yàk séu sim samrap meu tĕu ní*
Can you install it please?	ช่วยใส่ซิมได้มั้ย?	*chôo·ay sài sim dâi mái?*
Can I connect to the internet with this SIM card?	ซิมนี้ใช้ต่อเน็ตได้มั้ย?	*sim ní chai toh net dâi mái?*
Can I use it to call abroad?	ใช้โทรไป ต่างประเทศได้มั้ย?	*chai toh bpai dtàhng bpra-têt dâi mái?*
I want to add money to the SIM card in my phone.	(ผม/ดิฉัน) อยากเติมเงินในซิม ในมือถือ	*(pǒm/dee-chún) yàk teum ngern nai sim ní.*
I would like to speak to...	ขอพูดกับคุณ... หน่อย(ครับ/ค่ะ)	*kǒ·r pôot gùp khun... nòy (krúp/kâ)*
I'll call back later.	เดี๋ยวจะโทรมาใหม่	*děe·o ja toh mah mai*
Hold on.	รอสักครู่	*ror sùk krôo*

SHOPPING

How much does this cost?	ราคาเท่าไหร่	*nêe rah-kah tâo-rài?*
I would like ...	ต้องการ...	*dtôrng-gahn ...*
Do you have ...?	มี...มั้ย?	*mee ... mái?*
I am just looking.	ขอดูเฉยๆ	*chom doo tâo-nún*
What time do you open/close?	เปิด/ปิดกี่โมง?	*bpèrt/bpit gèe mohng?*
Does it come in other colors?	มีสีอื่น/อีกมั้ย?	*mee sěe èun èek mái?*
hill-tribe handicrafts	หัตถกรรม/ชาวเขา	*hùt-ta-gum chao kǎ·o*
silver	เงิน	*ngern*
Thai silk	ผ้าไหมไทย	*pâh-mǎ·i tai*
department store	ห้าง	*hâhng*
market	ตลาด	*dta-làht*
pharmacy	ร้านขายยา	*ráhn kǎ·i yah*
supermarket	ซุปเปอร์มาร์เก็ต	*sOOp-bpêr-mah-gèt*

SIGHTSEEING

travel agent	บริษัทนำเที่ยว	*bor-ri-sùt num têe·o*
tourist office	สำนักงานการท่องเที่ยว	*su·m-núk ngahn gahn tôrng têe·o*
tourist police	ตำรวจท่องเที่ยว	*dtum-ròo·ut tôrng têe·o*
beach	หาด or ชายหาด	*hàht or chai-hàht*
cave	ถ้ำ	*thûm*
cliff	หน้าผา	*nâh pa·h*
festival	งานออกร้าน	*ngahn òrk ráhn*
hill/mountain	เขา	*ka·o*

hill-tribe village	หมู่บ้านชาวเขา	*mòo bâhn chao ka·o*
historical park	อุทยาน ประวัติศาสตร์	*Ôo-ta-yahn bprawùt sàht*
island (ko)	เกาะ	*gòr*
lake	ทะเลสาบ	*ta-lay sàhp*
temple (wat)	วัด	*wút*
museum	พิพิธภัณฑ์	*pí-pít-ta-pun*
national park	อุทยานแห่งชาติ	*Ôo-ta-yahn hàirng chaht*
old town	เมืองเก่า	*meu-ung gòw*
palace	วัง	*wang*
park/garden	สวน	*so·o-un*
river	แม่น้ำ	*mâir náhm*
ruins	โบราณสถาน	*boh-rahn sa-ta·hn*
Thai massage	นวด	*nôo-ut*
trekking	การเดินป่า	*gahn dern bpàa*
waterfall	น้ำตก	*náhm dtòk*

TRANSPORTATION

When does the train for ... leave?	รถไฟไป...ออกเมื่อไหร่	*rót fai bpai ... òrk meu-rài?*
How long does it take to get to ...?	ใช้เวลานานเท่าไหร่ ไปถึงที่...	*chái way-lah nahn tâo-rài bpai tĕung tê ...?*
A ticket to ... please	ขอตั๋วไป.../ หน่อย(ครับ/ค่ะ)	*ko·r dto·o-a bpai ... nòy (krúp/kâ)*
Do I have to change?	ต้องเปลี่ยนรถกม/ รึเปล่า?	*dtôrng bplèe-un rót réu bplào?*
I'd like to reserve a seat, please.	ขอจองที่นั่ง	*ko·r jorng têe nûng*
Which platform for the ... train?	รถไฟไป... อยู่ชานชลาไหน?	*rót fai bpai ... yòo chahn cha-lah na·i?*
Which station is this?	ที่สถานีอะไร?	*tê nêe sa-ta·hn-nee a-rai?*
Where is the bus stop?	ป้ายรถเมล์/อยู่ที่ไหน?	*bpâi rót may yòo têe-na·i?*
Which buses go to ...?	รถเมล์สายไหน/ไป...?	*rót may sa·i na·i bpai ...?*
What time does the bus for ... leave?	รถเมล์ไป.../ออกกี่โมง?	*rót may bpai ... òrk gèe mohng?*
Would you tell me when we get to ...?	ถึง...แล้ว ช่วยบอกด้วย	*tĕung ... láir-o chôo-ay bòrk dôo-ay?*
Is it far?	ไกลมั้ย?	*glai mái?*
Turn left.	เลี้ยวซ้าย	*lée-o sái*
Turn right.	เลี้ยวขวา	*lée-o kwa·h*
Go straight.	เลยไปอีก	*ler-ee bpai èek*
arrivals	ถึง	*tĕung*
booking office	ที่จองตั๋ว	*tê jorng dto·o-a*
departures	ออก	*òrk*
tour bus	รถทัวร์	*rót too-a*
ticket	ตั๋ว	*dto·o-a*
ferry	เรือข้ามฟาก	*reu-a kâhm fâhk*
train	รถไฟ	*rót fai*
railroad station	สถานีรถไฟ	*sa-ta·hn-nee rót fai*
moped	รถมอเตอร์ไซค์	*rót mor-dter-sai*
bicycle	รถจักรยาน	*rót jùk-gra-yahn*
taxi	แท็กซี่	*táirk-sêe*
airport	สนามบิน	*sa-na·hm bin*

BARGAINING

How much is this?	ราคาเท่าไหร่	*nêe rah-kah tâo-rai?*
How much to go to ...?	ไป...เท่าไหร่?	*bpai ... tâo-rài?*
That's a little expensive	แพงไปหน่อย	*pairng bpai nòy*
Could you lower the price a bit?	ลดราคาหน่อย ได้มั้ย?	*lót rah-kah nòy dâi mái?*
How about ... baht?	...บาทได้มั้ย?	*... bàht dâi mái?*
Will you go for ... baht?	...บาทไปมั้ย?	*... bàht bpai mái?*
I'll settle for ... baht	...บาทก็แล้วกัน	*... bàht gôr láir-o gun*

STAYING IN A HOTEL

Do you have a vacant room?	มีห้องว่างมั้ย	*mee hôrng wâhng mái?*
double/twin room	ห้องคู่	*hôrng kôo*
single room	ห้องเดี่ยว	*hôrng dèe-o*
I have a reservation	จองห้องไว้แล้ว	*jorng hôrng wái láir-o*

one night/ three nights	พักอยู่คืนหนึ่ง/สามคืน	púk yòo keun nèung / sa˘hm keun
What is the charge per night?	ค่าห้องวันละเท่าไหร่?	kâh hôrng wun la tâo-ròi?
air conditioner	เครื่องปรับอากาศ	krêu-ung bprúp ah-gàht
bill	บิล	bin
hotel	โรงแรม	rohng-rairm
key	กุญแจ	gOOn-jair
manager	ผู้จัดการ	pôo-jùt-gahn
mosquito screen	มุ้งลวด	mÓOng lôo-ut
shower	ฝักบัว	fùk boo-a
toilet/bathroom	ห้องน้ำ	hôrng náhm

EATING OUT

A table for two please.	ขอโต๊ะสำหรับ/สองที่	ko˘r dtó su˘m-rùp / so˘rng kon
May I see the menu?	ขอดูเมนูหน่อย	ko˘r doo may-noo nòy
Do you have ...?	มี...บ้ัย?	mee ... mái?
I'd like ...	ขอ...	ko˘r ...
Not too spicy, ok?	ไม่เอาเผ็ดมากนะ	mâi ao pèt mâhk na
Is it spicy?	เผ็ดบ้ัย?	pèt mái?
I am a vegetarian.	(ผม/ดิฉัน)ทานมังสวิรัติ	(po˘m/dee-chún) thaan màng-sà wí-rát
May I have a glass of water, please.	ขอน้ำแข็งเปล่า/แก้วหนึ่ง	ko˘r núm ka˘irng bplào gâir-o nèung
I didn't order this.	นี่ไม่ได้สั่ง/(ครับ/ค่ะ)	nêe mâi dâi sùng (krúp/kâ)
That was an excellent meal.	อร่อยมาก(ครับ/ค่ะ)	a-ròy mâhk (krúp/kâ)
The check, please.	ขอบิลหน่อย(ครับ/ค่ะ)	ko˘r bin nòy (krúp/kâ)
beef	เนื้อวัว	néu-a woo-a
beer	เบียร์	bee-a
chicken	ไก่	gài
chili	พริก	prík
chopsticks	ตะเกียบ	dta-gèe-up
coffee	กาแฟ	gah-fair
deep fried	ทอด	tôrt
drink(s)	เครื่องดื่ม	krêu-ung dèum
duck	เป็ด	bpèt
durian	ทุเรียน	tÓO-ree-un
egg	ไข่	kài
fish	ปลา	bplah
fish sauce	น้ำปลา	núm bplah
fork	ส้อม	sôrm
fruit	ผลไม้	po˘n-la-mái
noodles	ก๋วยเตี๋ยว	gÕo-ay dtĕe-o
pork	เนื้อหมู	néu-a mo˘o
restaurant	ร้านอาหาร	ráhn ah-ha˘hn
rice	ข้าว	kâo
soy sauce	ซีอิ๊ว	see éw
spoon	ช้อน	chórn
stir-fried	ผัด	pùt
tea	ชา	núm chah
vegetables	ผัก	pùk
waiter	คนเสิร์ฟ	kon sèrp
waitress	คนเสิร์ฟหญิง	kon sèrp yı˘ng
water	น้ำ	náhm
wine	ไวน์	wai

HEALTH

I do not feel well	รู้สึกไม่สบาย	róo-sèuk mâi sa-bai
I have a pain in ...	เจ็บที่...	jèp têe ...
It hurts here.	เจ็บตรงนี้	jèp dtrong née
It hurts all the time.	เจ็บ ตลอดเวลา	jèp dta-lòrt way-lah
It hurts only now and then.	เจ็บเป็นบางครั้ง/บางคราว	jèp bpen bahng krúng bahng krao
I have a fever.	ตัวร้อนเป็นไข้	dtoo-a rórn bpen kâi
I'm allergic to ...	(ผม/ดิฉัน)แพ้...	po˘m/dee-chún) páir ...
How many tablets do I take?	ต้องกินยากี่เม็ด/ต่อครั้ง?	dtôrng gin yah gèe mét dtòr krúng?
acupuncture	ฝังเข็ม	fu˘ng kĕm
aspirin	แอสไพริน	air-sa-bprin
asthma	โรคหืด	rôhk hèut
bite (by dog)	หมากัด	ma˘h gùt

bite (by insect)	แมลงกัด	ma-lairng gùt
blood	เลือด	lêu-ut
burn	ไหม้	mâi
cough	ไอ	ai
dentist	หมอฟัน	mo˘r fun
diabetes	โรคเบาหวาน	rôhk bao wa˘hn
diarrhea	ท้องเสีย	tórng sĕe-a
dizzy	เวียนหัว	wee-un ho˘o-a
doctor	หมอ	mo˘r
fever	ตัวร้อน	dtoo-ah rórn
hayfever	ไข้จาม	kâi jahm
headache	ปวดหัว	bpòo-ut ho˘o-a
heart attack	หัวใจวาย	ho˘o-a jai wai
hepatitis	ตับอักเสบ	dtùp ùk-sàyp
hospital	โรงพยาบาล	rohng pa-yah-bahn
injection	ฉีดยา	chèet yah
medicine	ยา	yah
penicillin	เพนิซิลิน	yah pen-ní-seen-lin
prescription	ใบสั่งยา	bai sùng yah
traditional medicine	ยาแผน/โบราณ	yah pa˘irn boh-rahn
temperature	ตัวร้อน	dtoo-ah rórn
vomit	อาเจียน	ah-jee-un

NUMBERS

0	ศูนย์	so˘on
1	หนึ่ง	nèung
2	สอง	so˘rng
3	สาม	sa˘hm
4	สี่	sèe
5	ห้า	hâh
6	หก	hòk
7	เจ็ด	jèt
8	แปด	bpàirt
9	เก้า	gâo
10	สิบ	sìp
11	สิบเอ็ด	sìp-èt
12	สิบสอง	sìp-so˘rng
13	สิบสาม	sìp-sa˘hm
14	สิบสี่	sìp-sèe
15	สิบห้า	sìp-hâh
16	สิบหก	sìp-hòk
17	สิบเจ็ด	sìp-jèt
18	สิบแปด	sìp-bpàirt
19	สิบเก้า	sìp-gâo
20	ยี่สิบ	yêe-sìp
30	สามสิบ	sa˘hm-sìp
40	สี่สิบ	sèe-sìp
50	ห้าสิบ	hâh-sìp
60	หกสิบ	hòk-sìp
70	เจ็ดสิบ	jèt-sìp
80	แปดสิบ	bpàirt-sìp
90	เก้าสิบ	gâo-sìp
100	หนึ่งร้อย	nèung róy
1,000	หนึ่งพัน	nèung pun
1,001	หนึ่งพันหนึ่ง	nèung pun nèung
10,000	หนึ่งหมื่น	nèung mèun
100,000	หนึ่งแสน	nèung sa˘irn

TIMES AND SEASONS

one minute	หนึ่งนาที	nèung nah-tee
one hour	หนึ่งชั่วโมง	nèung chôo-a mohng
half an hour	ครึ่งชั่วโมง	krêung chôo-a mohng
monday	วันจันทร์	wun jun
tuesday	วันอังคาร	wun ung-kahn
wednesday	วันพุธ	wun pÓOt
thursday	วันพฤหัสบดี	wun pa-réu-hùt
friday	วันศุกร์	wun sÒOk
saturday	วันเสาร์	wun sa˘o
sunday	วันอาทิตย์	wun ah-tít
public holiday	วันหยุดประจำปี	wun yÒOt bprajum-bpee
Christmas	คริสต์มาส	krít-sa-maht
New Year	ปีใหม่	bpee mài
Thai New Year	สงกรานต์	so˘ng-grahn
Chinese New Year	ตรุษจีน	dtrÒOt jeen

ACKNOWLEDGMENTS

The publisher would like to thank the following for their kind permission to reproduce their photographs:

Key: a-above; b-below/bottom; c-centre; f-far; l-left; r-right; t-top

123RF.com: Chonlapoom Banharn 38bl; Bloodua 28bl, 30tl; Boonsom 70cla; Kwanchai Chai-udom 69cb; Nudda Chollamark 173tl; Coward_Lion 192bl; Ionut David 207tl; Suriya Desatit 193clb; Kobchai Matasurawit 235tr, 235cr; Nirut123rf 59br, 172-3b; Prin Pattaworo 206cl; Sean Pavone 97tl; Weera prongsiri 256cb, 257t; Rat Puanrak 66cr; puthithon 221bl; Joshua Resnick 42tl; Prasit Rodphan 41cra; Surasak Saneha 24cr; Pongthorn Sathaporn 193crb; Wanlop Sonngam 275ca; Meenamal Supaphon 247br; Wirojsid 255cra; Noppasin Wongchum 214-5b.

Alamy Stock Photo: AGE Fotostock 138bl; amnat 260t; amnat99 32clb, 258bl; Konstantin Andreev 204br; Frédéric Araujo 101tr, 205cb; Around the World in a Viewfinder / Jean-Philippe Soule 41crb; Paul Ashby 213tr; Avalon / Photoshot License 177tr; Krzysztof Bargiel 30-1ca; Lucy Brown (loca4motion) 45cl; Paul Brown 106crb; Neil Calbrade 175cra; Cavan 94cra, 308b; David Cherepuschak 111br; Chronicle 72tl; Coward_Lion 108-9b, 182bl, 193t, 193cb; Crystite licenced 193fcrb; Crystite RF 215cra; Michael Cullen 49cr; CulturalEyes - AusGS2 111tl; DPK-Photo 158-9b; Oscar Espinosa 107br, 246cl; Ray Evans 48cla; Eye Ubiquitous 117cr; F1online digitale Bildagentur GmbH 98bl; Ana Flašker 356t; Viktor Gladkov 318-9b; Goldquest 277tr; Larry Goodman 89tr; Chris Hellier 70br, 129cr, 166fcrb; Kevin Hellon 226cl; hemis.fr / Bertrand Gardel 212bl, / Franck Guiziou 53bl, 120bl, 129tr, 196-7b, 350cla, / Ludovic Maisant 137tr; 139tl; Shaun Higson / Thailand - Bangkok 82bl; Imagebroker 47tr, 48bl, 61crb, 99tc, 235cb; imageBROKER / Dirk Bleyer 119tr, / Mara Brandl 135br; INSADCO Photography 256br; INTERFOTO 349br; Ivoha 43cl; Lukasz Janyst 99tr; JeffG 297cra; Jon Bower Thailand 331br; Thanayu Jongwattanasilkul 220-1t; Martin Karius 28t; Witthaya Khampanant 281tr; Andrey Khrobostov 238b; Rainer Krack 107tl, 147tl; Lena Kuhnt 103tr; Buree Lalitathada 69br; Kevin Landwer-Johan 65cl, 67tl, 239t, 243tl; Look 82t, 211tl, / Kay Maeritz 282tl; Marco Pompeo Photography 313t; Barry Mason 28cra; Mauritius Images Gmbh 312br; Mayday 31tr; Miguel Sobreira 327tl; Tuul and Bruno Morandi 255tl; Sawassakorn Muttapraprut 262clb; Nalidsa 339t; Jatesada Natayo 243br; National Geographic Image Collection 235br; Jim Newberry 210bl; Duy Phuong Nguyen 153tr; Suntorn Niamwhan 68cb; Narong Niemhom 241bl; Ozimages 64cr; Pacific Press / Vichan Poti 101br; Panther Media GmbH 183tl, 274-5t, / AMNAT 278br; Sanga Park 105tl; David Parker 171cra; Peter Adams Photography Ltd 222tl; Panuwat Phengkhumphu 279br; Janusz Pieńkowski 71cb; Marina Pissarova 106b; Igor Prahin 128-9t, 356cra, 357br; Suwin Puengsamrong 282-3b; Quality Stock 223b, 224-5b; Sergi Reboredo 82cr, 343b; Jeerawut Rityakul 237tr; Robertharding 61tr, 71tr, 87crb, 102bl, 168bl, 313br, 328tl, / Luca Tettoni 355tl; Prasit Rodphan 180bl; Rolf_52 64cra; RSMultimedia 101crb; Schmerbeck 13br; Leonid Serebrennikov 166crb; Neil Setchfield 131br; Mike Sivyer 65tl; Michael Snell 145tr; Lee Snider 166cb; M. Sobreira 99cla; Chatchai Somwat 48-9t; Anucha Songsap 198-9t; Dave Stamboulis 32br, 215ca, 263tr; Constantin Stanciu 54-5b; Stockinasia 295tr; StoryLife 63c; Sermsak Sukwajikhlong 259t; Thananit Suntiviriyanon 225tr; Thailand Wildlife 244tr, 314tr; Thaiways 179b; Travel Images 52t; Travelstock44 53tr; Jorgen Udvang 62bl; Lucas Vallecillos 146bl, 159tl, 168tc, 168-9t, 207cr; Colin Waters 96bl; Westend61 GmbH 61cl; Edd Westmacott 129crb; Nik Wheeler 129clb; Leslie Wilk 223clb; Noppakun Wiropart 261bl; Jan Wlodarczyk 96bc, 324-5t; World History Archive 72crb, 72bl; ZUMA Press; Inc. 51b, 62tl.

AWL Images: Jon Arnold 16, 74-5; Matteo Colombo 188br; Michele Falzone 6-7; Guiziou Franck 189tl; Jason Langle 96clb; Travel Pix Collection 37cla; Andrew Watson 66crb.

Bangkok Art and Culture Centre: 136b.

Bridgeman Images: © Bonhams, London, UK 68t; Pictures from History 70-1t; Luca Tettoni 237tl.

Depositphotos Inc: Cakeio 173ca; Deerphoto 234-5b; Foto76 89t; OlezzoSimon 302t; thawats 245cr.

Dreamstime.com: Anekoho 306-7t; Assoonas 269ca; Stéphane Bidouze 47cl, 86-7t; Jaromír Chalabala 85cr; Denis Costille 326b; Cowardlion 170tl, 192br; Devy 4; Dorinmarius 334t; Edwardroom501 37tr; Eermakova 208t; Empire331 175br; Ericsch 57cl; Viktor Gladkov 10c; Bradley Hay 175t; Idmanjoe 305cla; Alexandra Insinga 46tr; Wasana Jaigunta 262-3b; Thanayu Jongwattanasilkul 176-7b, 350-1b; Jaume Juncadella 272b; Kajornyot 34cr; Kampwit 71br, 207tr, 271cr; Pradeep Raja Kannaiah 67clb; Katyenka 60tr;

Chadchawal Kedkoedklao 332-3t; Keerati 121br; Krajinar 34bl; Manit Larpluechai 66cl; Loopphoto 205fcrb; Maicyber 254cra; Karin De Mamiel 235ca; Manjik 13cr; Jakub Michankow 26-7ca; Monticello 52b; Ran Mor 46-7b; Tanes Ngamsom 244-5b; Narong Niemhom 26cla; Nitinut380 316clb; Nokhook 67cr; Matee Nuserm 268-9b; Chinnasorn Pangcharoen 256bl; Phanuwatn 190-1t; Photosimo 171b; Pakpoom Phummee 232t; Janusz Pieńkowski 96crb; Pramote Polyamate 160-1; Tawatchai Prakobkit 44-5b; Presse750 204t; Psstockfoto 23bl, 344-5; Siam Pukkato 269cra; Pzaxe 166clb; Redlunar 69tl; Rsinghjoo 68br; Itsanan Sampuntarat 53cr; Nipa Sawangsri 290clb; Yali Shi 66clb; Jan Skwara 26-7t; Skynetphoto 328-9b; Nataliia Sokolovska 100-1b, 292-3t; Pramote Soongkitboon 149tr; Thanakorn Suppamethasawat 101tl; Pavarid Tarapan 58tl; Tesimsamer 270-1t; Sarayut Thaneerat 348-9t; Suthin Thesdee 194-5t; Tiwakorn07 34crb; Toa555 66cla; Tofumax 122-3t; Tortoon 236cra; Mr.Nopparat Wannasuk 274br; Weerapat Wattanapichayakul 276br; Wuttichok 39ca; Yongkiet 32t.

Getty Images: AFP / Adek Berry 49crb; The Asahi Shimbun 73br; Corbis Documentary / Sylvain Sonnet 134t; Cultura / Alex Eggermont 59cl; DEA / Biblioteca Ambrosiana / De Agostini 70tl; DigitalVision / Linka A Odom 219tr; EyeEm / Cristian Mihai Vela 8clb, / Junjira Konsang 43tl; Gargolas 152b; Getty Images News 72-3t, / David Silverman 73tr; Hulton Archive / Alex Bowie 73bc; LightRocket / Leisa Tyler 56-7b, / Peter Charlesworth 84bl; Moment / Abraham 24bl, / Marco Bottigelli 352-3t, / Supoj Buranaprapapong 19cb, 228-9, / Virojt Changyencham 10-1b, / [Genesis] - Korawee Ratchapakdee 19tl, 200-1, / Jung Getty 215tr, / Kiyoshi Hijiki 317t, / IronHeart 10clb, / Peerakit JIrachetthakun 156-7b, Siripong Kaewla-iad 191cra, / Kritsada Kata 67crb, / Somnuk Krobkum 55tr, Peerapas Mahamongkolsawas 11t, / Thanapol Marattana 39crb; / Mekdet 166-7t, / Woothisak Nirongboot 8cla, / Kampee Patisena 34t, Vichien Petchmai 188-9, / Michael Rheault - madfire@gmail.com 11crb, / Arun Roisri 175crb, / Chaiyut Samsuk 8-9b, 354t, / Sangkhom Simma 12-3b, / Thianchai Sitthikongsak 13t, / Pakin Songmor 144t, 340tr, / Sam Spicer 338b, / Std 63t, / Suttipong Sutiratanachai 117b, / Dulyanut Swdp 88crb, / Carlina Teteris 84ca, / Kriangkrai Thitimakorn 269tr, / Thatree Thitivongvaroon 2-3, 45tr, 73crb, / Chakarin Wattanamongkol 67tr, Wiratgasem 216-7; Moment Open / ARZTSAMUI 310t, / Weerakarn Satitniramai 174br, / kitchakron sonnoy 195tr, / Chakarin Wattanamongkol 297b; Moment Unreleased / Nathan Hutchinson 36-7b, / Sunphol Sorakul 78c,

90-1; Igor Prahin 104-5b; Room / Sangkhomhungkhunthod 20cb, 264-5; simonlong 342t; Tuayai 318tr; Valentin Wolf 304bl.

iStockphoto.com: 4FR 45br; 501room 12t, 40-1b; 9Air 120-1t; 9george 218b; abcphotosystem 338cl; Ake1150sb 41cr; aluxum 65cla, 84-5t, 108tl, 118tl, 133t; anan796 278-9t; Anyaberkut 21, 284-5, 288-9t; artpritsadee 240t; banjongseal324 26tl, 178-9t; BirdHunter591 175cr; David Bokuchava 57br; Boyloso 242b; Bpbomb 290b; Joel Carillet 54tr; Chayathonwong 22, 298-9; Coward_Lion 70cr; Digitalvision Vectors / Duncan1890 97cb; E+ / Deimagine 18, 184-5, / Primeimages 80c,124-5, / Oleh_Slobodeniuk 358-9, / T-lorien 81bl, 150, / Urilux 65clb; Flukyfluky 40cra; Foto_iM 58-9b; Gwengoat 191br; Hans Harms 205crb; Hikaru1222 70cb; Holgs 55clb; iphotothailand 116t; Jakkree7727 280b; justhavealook 134cr; Keanu2 50bl; KeongDaGreat 55b; khamlaksana 314-5b; Angkana Kittayachaweng 296tl; Blade_Kostas 63br; Krithnarong 249br; Magnus Larsson 351cl; Laughingmango 191c; Lechatnoir 42b, 53cla; Luamduan 64-5; Martinhosmart 69cra, 248bl; Mikeinlondon 31cla; miroslav_1 157tr; MongkolChuewong 206-7b; Mumemories 180-1t; Nattanan726 227br; NicoElNino 60bl; Nikada 24t; MC_Noppadol 43br, 85bl; R.M. Nunes 38-9t; nuttapong 316b; NuttKomo 341b; Oneclearvision 79c, 112-3; Preto_Perola 44tl; Photogrape 223tr; Pigphoto 50-1t, 51cl; PixHound 95; Pong6400 67cla; primeimages 132bl; Kuntalee Rangnoi 17, 162-3; saiko3p 118-9bc; SanerG 81t, 140-1, 148-9b; Skynesher 12clb; Slava296 30-1t; Oleh_Slobodeniuk 330-1, 336-7; Strmko 23t, 320-1; Tarzan9280 57tr; Themorningglory 27tr, 309cra; Tobiasjo 24crb; Tortoon 32cl; Preecha Wannalert 197cl; wanrung 294b; waranan 355b; Yupiyan 8cl, 41tr.

Maggie Choo's: 87cl.

Mandarin Oriental Hotel Group: 130-1t.

Pattaya Bungy Jump: 59tr.

Picfair.com: Alizee 82crb; Stéphane Bidouze 56tl; Christopher PB 97bl; David Sutton 47crb; Urf, Switzerland 20tl, 250-1.

Robert Harding Picture Library: Art Wolfe 154-5; Gavin Hellier 11br; Kay Maeritz 101ca; Chris Mouyiaris 30cla, 66cra.

Sing Sing Theater: 86bl.

SuperStock: AGF photo / Charles Mahaux 205clb; Imagebroker / Bernd Biedero 26cra.

Suranat Leather Studio: 36tl.

Front flap:
Alamy Stock Photo: Lucy Brown (loca4motion) cb; anucha songsap tc; **Depositphotos Inc:** thawats cra; **iStockphoto.com:** Blade_Kostas cla; Primeimages bl; saiko3p br.

Cover images:
Front and spine: **Dreamstime.com:** Apixmaker.
Back: **Dreamstime.com:** Apixmaker b; Cowardlion cla; Pramote Polyamate tr; **Getty Images:** Pakin Songmor c.

For further information see:
www.dkimages.com

Transliteration of Thai words in this book mostly follows the General System recommended by the Thai Royal Institute, but visitors will encounter many variant spellings in Thailand.

DK Penguin Random House

Main Contributers Daniel Stables, Peter Holmshaw, Philip Cornwel-Smith, Andrew Forbes, Tim Forsyth, Rachel Harrison, David Henley, John Hoskin, Gavin Pattison, Jonathan Rigg, Sarah Rooney, Ken Scott

Senior Editor Alison McGill

Senior Designer Laura O'Brien

Project Editor Zoë Rutland

Designers Bharti Karakoti, Jaileen Kaur, Van Anh Le, Nidhi Mehra, Ian Midson, Sarah Snelling, Vinita Venugopal, Nehal Verma

Factchecker Neil Ray

Editors Lucy Sara-Kelly, Jackie Staddon, Danielle Watt

Proofreader Kathryn Glendenning

Indexer Hilary Bird

Thai Language Consultant Malee Holmshaw

Senior Picture Researcher Ellen Root

Picture Research Nimesh Agrawal, Sumita Khatwani, Phoebe Lowndes, Surya Sankash Sarangi

Illustrators Stephen Conlin, Gary Cross, Richard Draper, Roger Hutchins, Chris Orr & Assocs, John Woodcock

Cartographic Editor James Macdonald

Cartography Subhashree Bharati, Uma Bhattacharya, Schchida Nand Pradhan

Jacket Designers Maxine Pedliham, Van Anh Le

Jacket Picture Research Susie Watters

Senior DTP Designer Jason Little

Producer Samantha Cross

Managing Editor Rachel Fox

Art Director Maxine Pedliham

Publishing Director Georgina Dee

First edition 1997

Published in Great Britain by Dorling Kindersley Limited, 80 Strand, London, WC2R 0RL

Published in the United States by DK Publishing, 1450 Broadway, Suite 801, New York, NY 10018

Copyright © 1997, 2019 Dorling Kindersley Limited
A Penguin Random House Company
19 20 21 22 10 9 8 7 6 5 4 3 2 1

A CIP catalog record for this book is available from the British Library.

A catalog record for this book is available from the Library of Congress.

ISSN: 1542 1554
ISBN: 978 0 2413 6887 9

Printed and bound in Malaysia.

www.dk.com

MIX
Paper from responsible sources
FSC™ C018179
www.fsc.org

The information in this DK Eyewitness Travel Guide is checked regularly.
Every effort has been made to ensure that this book is as up-to-date as possible at the time of going to press. Some details, however, such as telephone numbers, opening hours, prices, gallery hanging arrangements and travel information, are liable to change. The publishers cannot accept responsibility for any consequences arising from the use of this book, nor for any material on third party websites, and cannot guarantee that any website address in this book will be a suitable source of travel information. We value the views and suggestions of our readers very highly. Please write to: Publisher, DK Eyewitness Travel Guides, Dorling Kindersley, 80 Strand, London, WC2R 0RL, UK, or email: travelguides@dk.com